1,000,000 Books

are available to read at

www.ForgottenBooks.com

Read online
Download PDF
Purchase in print

ISBN 978-1-333-86794-2
PIBN 10596108

This book is a reproduction of an important historical work. Forgotten Books uses state-of-the-art technology to digitally reconstruct the work, preserving the original format whilst repairing imperfections present in the aged copy. In rare cases, an imperfection in the original, such as a blemish or missing page, may be replicated in our edition. We do, however, repair the vast majority of imperfections successfully; any imperfections that remain are intentionally left to preserve the state of such historical works.

Forgotten Books is a registered trademark of FB &c Ltd.
Copyright © 2018 FB &c Ltd.
FB &c Ltd, Dalton House, 60 Windsor Avenue, London, SW19 2RR.
Company number 08720141. Registered in England and Wales.

For support please visit www.forgottenbooks.com

1 MONTH OF FREE READING

at
www.ForgottenBooks.com

By purchasing this book you are eligible for one month membership to ForgottenBooks.com, giving you unlimited access to our entire collection of over 1,000,000 titles via our web site and mobile apps.

To claim your free month visit:
www.forgottenbooks.com/free596108

* Offer is valid for 45 days from date of purchase. Terms and conditions apply.

English
Français
Deutsche
Italiano
Español
Português

www.forgottenbooks.com

Mythology Photography **Fiction** Fishing Christianity **Art** Cooking Essays Buddhism Freemasonry Medicine **Biology** Music **Ancient Egypt** Evolution Carpentry Physics Dance Geology **Mathematics** Fitness Shakespeare **Folklore** Yoga Marketing **Confidence** Immortality Biographies Poetry **Psychology** Witchcraft Electronics Chemistry History **Law** Accounting **Philosophy** Anthropology Alchemy Drama Quantum Mechanics Atheism Sexual Health **Ancient History Entrepreneurship** Languages Sport Paleontology Needlework Islam **Metaphysics** Investment Archaeology Parenting Statistics Criminology **Motivational**

THE
WOMEN OF TURKEY
AND THEIR FOLK-LORE

BY

LUCY M. J. GARNETT

With an Ethnographical Map

AND INTRODUCTORY CHAPTERS
ON THE ETHNOGRAPHY OF TURKEY; AND
FOLK-CONCEPTIONS OF NATURE

BY

JOHN S. STUART-GLENNIE, M.A.
OF THE MIDDLE TEMPLE, BARRISTER-AT-LAW

THE CHRISTIAN WOMEN

LONDON
DAVID NUTT, 270–271 STRAND, W.C.
1890

Αἱ Γυναῖκες .... μάλιστα τὴν ἀρχαίαν φωνὴν σώζουσι.
PLATO, Κρατ. 74.

Facilius enim Mulieres incorruptam antiquitatem conservant.
CICERO, *De Orat.* iii. 12.

GENERAL TABLE OF CONTENTS.

                                                                             PAGE

PREFACE TO INTRODUCTION xv

INTRODUCTORY CHAPTER I.

    THE ETHNOGRAPHY OF TURKEY xvii

NOTE ON THE ETHNOGRAPHICAL MAP lii

MAP . . . . *facing* liv

INTRODUCTORY CHAPTER II.

    FOLK-CONCEPTIONS OF NATURE lv

PREFACE lxxvi

DEDICATION lxxix

CHAP. I.—VLACH WOMEN: THEIR SOCIAL STATUS AND ACTIVITIES—FAMILY CEREMONIES—BELIEFS AND SUPERSTITIONS—AND FOLK-POESY 3

  „ II.—GREEK WOMEN: THEIR SOCIAL STATUS AND ACTIVITIES 30

  „ III.—GREEK WOMEN: THEIR FAMILY CEREMONIES . . 69

  „ IV.—GREEK WOMEN: THEIR BELIEFS AND SUPERSTITIONS . 103

  „ V.—GREEK WOMEN: THEIR FOLK-POESY 154

        NOTE ON THE IDENTIFICATION OF ST. GEORGE WITH HORUS AND KHIDHR 191

GENERAL TABLE OF CONTENTS.

	PAGE
CHAP. VI.—ARMENIAN WOMEN: THEIR SOCIAL STATUS AND ACTIVITIES	194
" VII.—ARMENIAN WOMEN: THEIR FAMILY CEREMONIES	222
" VIII.—ARMENIAN WOMEN: THEIR BELIEFS AND SUPERSTITIONS	249
" IX.—ARMENIAN WOMEN: THEIR FOLK-POESY	270
" X.—BULGARIAN WOMEN: THEIR SOCIAL STATUS AND ACTIVITIES	297
" XI.—BULGARIAN WOMEN: THEIR FAMILY CEREMONIES	315
" XII.—BULGARIAN WOMEN: THEIR BELIEFS AND SUPERSTITIONS	327
" XIII.—BULGARIAN WOMEN: THEIR FOLK-POESY	342
" XIV.—FRANK WOMEN: THEIR SOCIAL STATUS AND ACTIVITIES—FAMILY CEREMONIES—BELIEFS AND SUPERSTITIONS—AND FOLK-POESY	366

ANALYTICAL TABLE OF CONTENTS.

PREFACE TO INTRODUCTION, xv.

INTRODUCTORY CHAPTER I.

THE ETHNOGRAPHY OF TURKEY.

The Ethnological Theory of the Origin of Civilisation, xvii.
  1. The Race-relations of the Kurds, xxi.
  2. The Race-relations of the Cirassians, xxiii.
  3. The Race-relations of the Albanians, xxv.
  4. The Race-relations of the Vlachs, xxvii.
  5. The Race-relations of the Greeks, xxix.
  6. The Race-relations of the Armenians, xxxii.
  7. The Race-relations of the Jews, xxxv.
  8. The Race-relations of the Bulgarians, xxxvi.
  9. The Race-relations of the Franks, xxxix.
  10. The Race-relations of the Gipsies, xl.
  11. The Race-relations of the Ottomans, xliii.

The Deduced Theory of the Origin of the Aryans, xlvi.

NOTE ON THE ETHNOGRAPHICAL MAP, lii.

INTRODUCTORY CHAPTER II.

FOLK-CONCEPTIONS OF NATURE.

The Deduced Theory of the Origin of Mythology, lv.
  1. The Primitive Theory of Mutual Influence, lix.
  2. Dr. Tylor's Self-contradictory Theory of "Animism," lx.
  3. Mr. Spencer's Paradoxical Theory of "Stages," lxi.
  4. The Term "Zoönism" instead of "Fetichism," lxii.
  5. The Zoönist and Spiritist Conceptions of Nature, lxiii.
  6. Criticism of the Ghost Theory of Messrs. Spencer and Tylor, lxv.
  7. Zoönism and Spiritism possibly both Primordial, lxvii.
  8. The Essential Similarity of Zoönism and Kosmism, lxviii.
  9. Mr. Spencer's and the New Conception of Matter, lxix.
  10. The Historical Relation between Zoönism and Kosmism, lxx.
  11. The Essential Similarity of Theism and Spiritism, lxxii.

The Deduced Theory of the Method of Folklore-study, lxxiii.

CHAPTER I.

VLACH WOMEN: THEIR SOCIAL STATUS AND ACTIVITIES—FAMILY CEREMONIES—BELIEFS AND SUPERSTITIONS—AND FOLK-POESY.

Vlach Nomads, 3; An Encampment, 4; Mountain Homes, 5; Vlach Centres, 6; A Vlach Household, 7; Social Status and Morality, 9; Industries, 10; Appearance, 10; Attachment to Homes, 11; Education, 11; The Roumanian Propaganda, 12; Birth Customs, 13; Evil Spirits, 13; Baptism, 13; Wedding Customs, 13; The Preliminaries, 14; Announcing the Betrothal, 14; The *Flamboro*, 14; The Bridegroom's Toilet, 15; Wedding by Capture, 15; Scrambling for the Cake, 15; The Procession, 16; Bringing Home the Bride, 16; Anointing the Door, 16; Kissing Hands, 16; Death Customs, 17; The Feast of the Dead, 17; The *Rosalia*, 17; Religious Observances, 18; New Year's Day, 18; The "Feast of the Kings," 18; *Vikliemi*, 18; *Stea*, 19; The *Filipi*, 19; The "Fairy of Tuesday Even," 20; The Procession for Rain, 20; The *Klithona*, 20; Christmas Customs, 21; The House Serpent, 21; A Preventive of Hydrophobia, 21; Folk-poesy, 22; Supernatural Beings, 22; The *Doinas*, or Ballads, 23; "The Ring and the Veil," 23; "The Cuckoo and the Turtle-dove," 25; "The Sun and the Moon," 27.

CHAPTER II.

GREEK WOMEN: THEIR SOCIAL STATUS AND ACTIVITIES.

Appearance, 31; *Romeots*, 32; Social Status, 32; Introduction of Divorce, 32; Respect for Parents, 33; Greek Heroines, 33; A Company of Amazons, 34; The Women of Missolonghi, 35; A Greek Authoress, 36; A Heroine's Funeral, 37; Marighitza, 38; A Brigand Chieftainess, 38; Haidée, 39; Peasant Women, 39; Habitations, 40; Field and Farm Work, 40; The Shepherdess, 41; Industries, 42; Spinning and Weaving, 43; Silkworm-rearing, 43; Cretan Women, 43; The Olive Harvest, 44; Cypriote Needlework, 44; Holidays, 44; Dress, 44; The Dance on the Green, 45; Dancing Songs, 46; Pantomimic Dancing, 47; The Swing, 48; A Swing Song, 48; The Harvest Home, 48; Married Life, 49; Rigidity of Morals, 49; A Terrible Expiation, 49; Domestic Virtues, 50; The Absent Husband, 51; Domestic Service, 51; Cooks and Nurses, 52; Thrifty Habits, 52; Slovenliness, 53; "Soul-Children," 53; Honesty and Sobriety, 53; Relations with Turks, 54; "Demos and the Turkish Maid," 54; A Perversion at Salonica, 55; Terrible Tragedy, 56; "A Turk I'll not Wed," 57; Greek Townswomen, 58; Dress, 58; Occupations, 58; Love of Display, 59; Family Ties, 60; Songs of Exile, 61; Education, 62; Increase of

ANALYTICAL TABLE OF CONTENTS. ix

Girls' Schools, 62; Subjects, 63; Training Colleges and High Schools, 64; Munificent Ladies, 64; A Greek *Mnemosynon*, 65; Phanariote Women, 67; Their Culture, 67; Philanthropic Work, 68; Proposed Educational Changes, 68.

CHAPTER III.

GREEK WOMEN : THEIR FAMILY CEREMONIES.

Pagan Customs, 69; Salting the Baby, 69; Precautions against the Nereids, 70; Changelings, 70; The Libation, 71; Propitiating the Fates, 71; The Christening, 71; Godfathers and Godmothers, 71; Conventional Relationships, 72; The Procession, 72; Trine Immersion, 73; Infant Confirmation and Communion, 73; Dedication of Hair, 73; Bonbons and Crosses, 73; Wedding Customs, 74; Prohibited Degrees, 74; Gobetweens, 75; The Betrothal, 75; The Trousseau, 76; Marriage Portions, 76; Broken Engagements, 77; Observances at Vodhena, 78; The Week's Festivities, 78; Making the Wedding Cake, 78; The Exchange of Presents, 79; The Bride's Toilette, 80; Wedding Songs, 80; Shaving the Bridegroom, 81; Lucky and Unlucky Days, 82; The Bridegroom's Procession, 82; The Libation, 82; The Second Betrothal, 83; Girding the Bridegroom, 84; The Wedding Dress, 84; "Bride, hast thou the Shoes?" 84; The Religious Ceremony, 84; Emblems of Plenty, 85; The Bride's Farewell, 86; The Dance on the Green, 87; Taking Home the Bride, 88; Propitiating the Water Deities, 89; Final Festivities, 89; Death Customs, 90; Laying out the Corpse, 90; Dirges, 91; Lament for a Father, 93; For a House-mistress, 93; For a Daughter, 94; For a Son, 94, 96; The Fee for Charon, 97; The Procession to the Grave, 97; The Religious Rite, 98; The Funeral Feast, 98; Sweeping the House, 98; Mourning, 98; The *Kólyva*, 99; Gifts to the Poor, 100; Exhumation of the Body, 100; The *Saïa*, 101; Pranks of the Turkish *gamin*, 102.

CHAPTER IV.

GREEK WOMEN : BELIEFS AND SUPERSTITIONS.

The Orthodox Greek Church, 103; Dogmas, 103; Clergy, 103; Importance attached to Ritual, 104; Reform Impossible, 105; The Wives of the Clergy, 105; Greek Churches, 106; Convents and Nuns, 107; An Epirote Nunnery, 107; An Island Convent, 109; Morality of the Nuns, 109; The Ecclesiastical Year, 109; Fasting, 109; Church Festivals, 111; St. Basil, 111; Epiphany, 112; The Feast of the Lights, 112; The Carnival, 112; Lent, 113; The Feast of St. Lazarus, 114; Palm

ANALYTICAL TABLE OF CONTENTS.

Sunday, 114; Red Eggs, 115; Good Friday Superstitions, 116; The Solemnity in the Church, 116; Turkish Guards, 117; The Resurrection, 117; Easter Greetings, 118; The Feast of the Annunciation, 119; Nature Worship, 119; The Swallows' Greeting, 120; May Day, 120; St. John's Eve in Thessaly, 120; In Macedonia, 121; In Cappadocia, 122; The *Fishoti*, 123; The Procession for Rain, 123; Pagan Gods and Christian Saints, 124; Their Annual Festivals, 125; Votive Offerings, 125; Family Festivals, 126; Charity, 127; Sacred Fountains, 127; Their Festivals, 128; Classic Nymphs replaced by the Virgin, 128; The Genius, or *Stoicheion*, 128; The Widow's Sons and the Stoicheion, 129; The Battle of the Stoicheia, 130; The Stoicheia of St. Paul, 130; The Drakos, 131; Nereids, Lamias, and Sirens, 131; Precautions taken against them, 132; Their Connection with Storms, 133; The Lamia and Yanni, 134; The Lamia as a Housewife, 135; The Fates, 135; The Vampire, 136; Not of Slav Origin, 136; Causes of Vampirism, 136; "Laying" a Vampire, 137; A Cretan Vampire Story, 139; A Vampire Panic at Adrianople, 141; Witches, 142; Spells and Curses, 142; Fortune-telling, 143; Corpse Candles, 144; Antidotes for the Evil Eye, 145; "The Envy of the Gods," 146; Passing a Child through the Fire, 147; Antipathy to Grey Eyes, 148; Divinations, 149; Owls Heralds of Death, 150; Omens, 150; Things Lucky and Things Unlucky, 151; Exorcising Vermin, 152; Oriental Gestures, 152; Contemptuous Epithets, 153.

CHAPTER V.

GREEK WOMEN: THEIR FOLK-POESY.

Religious Legends, 154; Histories of Saints, 154; St. George of Cappadocia, 155; His Martyrdom, 155; His Amenability to Bribery, 156; The Vow to St. George, 156; The Fox and St. George, 157; The Story of Kosma and Damianus, 159; The Head of St. John the Baptist, 161; The Peddler and the Serpent, 163; The Three Wonderful Dresses, 165; The Prince and the Foal, 178; The Just One, 185.

NOTE ON THE IDENTIFICATION OF ST. GEORGE WITH HORUS AND KHIDHR, 191.

CHAPTER VI.

ARMENIAN WOMEN; THEIR SOCIAL STATUS AND ACTIVITIES.

The Armenians in History, 194; The Last Armenian King, 195; Legendary Origin of the Armenians, 195; The Armenian Quarter, 196; Ancient Houses, 196; Modern Dwellings, 197; Middle-class Homes,

ANALYTICAL TABLE OF CONTENTS. xi

197; Armenian Mansions, 198; Houses at Erzeroum, 199; The Ox Stable. 200; Erzeroum in Winter, 201; Dwellings of the Armenian Peasantry, 201; Social Status of Women in Armenia, 202; Patriarchal Customs, 202; The "Subjection of the Daughter-in-law," 203; Status in Smyrna and Constantinople, 205; An Armenian Ball, 206; The Travelled Armenian Lady, 206; Domestic Virtues, 207; "Pure" and "Coarse" Armenians, 208; Armenian Beauties, 208; "The Seventh Heaven of Mohammed," 209; Use of Cosmetics, 209; Home-made Rose-water, 210; Dress, 211; Fondness for Bright Colours, 211; Dishabille, 212; Native Costumes, 212; The Cone-fruit Pattern, 213; Costumes at Kaisariyeh and Sivas, 213; Domestic Service, 214; Lacemaking, 214; A School of Art Needlework, 214; Home Industries, 215; Fondness for Animals, 216; Cats with Dyed Tails, 216; Armenian Salutations, 217; Education, 217; Training Colleges, 218; Mission Schools, 218; Loss of Language, 219; Schools at Smyrna and Constantinople, 219; Literary Women, 220; Armenian Actresses, 220; Armenian Literature, 220; More Imitation than Creation, 220; Literary Revival, 221; Armenian Patriotism, 221.

CHAPTER VII.

ARMENIAN WOMEN: THEIR FAMILY CEREMONIES.

Armenian Birth Customs, 222; Keeping away the Demons, 222; The Mother's Reception, 222; Irregular Training, 223; The Christening, 223; The Holy Chrism, 226; The Baby's Confirmation, 228; Its First Communion, 229; The Bath Feast, 229; The Forty Days' Ceremony, 229; Superstitions connected with the Forty Days, 230; Precautions against the *Djins*, 231; Wedding Observances, 232; The Betrothal, 232; Courtship, 233; The *Hars'nik*, 233; Preliminary Festivities, 234; The Wedding Dress, 235; A Shower of Coins, 235; The Bridegroom's Toilet, 235; The Barber's Benefit, 236; The Second Betrothal, 236; The Procession to Church, 237; The Religious Ceremony, 238; The Sacrifice, 239; Subsequent Festivities, 239; "Wearing the Crowns," 240; The Husband's Gift, 240; The "Veil of Silence," 241; The Ceremony at the Well, 241; Precautions against the *Djins*, 241; Blessing the Wedding Garments, 242; Propitious Days, 242; Mixing the Brides, 243; Funeral Customs, 243; Laying out the Corpse, 244; The Religious Ceremony, 244; Funeral Cakes, 246; Ancient Tombstones, 246; "Passage Money," 247; Journey of the Soul to Jerusalem, 248; Appropriating the Lost Life of the Dead, 248.

CHAPTER VIII.

ARMENIAN WOMEN: THEIR BELIEFS AND SUPERSTITIONS.

The Gregorian Church, 249; Its Three Periods, 249; Legendary Correspondence between Jesus and Abgar, 250; St. Gregory, "the Illuminator," 251; His Tortures, 252; The Story of Ripsimeh and Gaianeh, 252; Conversion of Tiridates, 253; Doctrines, 254; Fasts and Feasts, 254; May Day at Smyrna, 255; Holy Pictures, 256; Attendance at Church, 257; Wives of the Clergy, 257; Blessing the House, 258; Pilgrimages, 259; Armenian Churches, 259; The Monastery and Church of Etchmiadzin, 260; Its Legends, 261; Mount Ararat, or Massis, 261; The Abode of Supernatural Beings, 262; "Noah's Vineyard," 263; Erzeroum the Site of Paradise, 264; Legend of Khosref Purveez, 264; Flowers of Eden, 265; Catholic Missionaries, 266; "United Armenians," 266; Mekhitar, Theologian, Scholar, and Patriot, 267; Educational Work of the Mekhitarists, 268; The Armenian Bible, 268; Protestant Missions, 268.

CHAPTER IX.

ARMENIAN WOMEN: THEIR FOLK-POESY.

National Traditions, 270; Religious Legends, 271; The Story of the Fall. 271; Animal Stories, 276; "How the Tame Goose lost the Use of its Wings," 276; "How the Devil invented the Rudder," 277; "The King's Daughter and the Bath Boy," 278; Armenian Folk-songs, 293; The Stork's Welcome, 294; The Partridge, 295; Children's Song, 296.

CHAPTER X.

BULGARIAN WOMEN: THEIR SOCIAL STATUS AND ACTIVITIES.

Physical Features, 297; Social Status of Townswomen, 298; Evening Parties, 298; Status of Peasant Women, 299; Patriarchal Customs, 300; Dwellings, 301; Thrift, 302; National Costumes, 302; Industry, 303; Field-work, 304; Arcadian Scenes, 304; The Harvest, 304; The Vintage, 304; "French Plums," 305; Rose Culture, 305; The Rose Harvest, 305; Silk Rearing, 306; Women-labourers, 307; An Old Servant, 307; Amusements, 309; The Dance, 309; The Bear-dance, 310; Women as Brigands, 310; Morals, 311; Education, 312; Irregularities of the Language, 312; Girls' Schools, 313; A Lyceum at Philipopolis, 313; Foreign Education, 314.

ANALYTICAL TABLE OF CONTENTS.

CHAPTER XI.

BULGARIAN WOMEN: THEIR FAMILY CEREMONIES.

Birth Customs, 315; Salting the Baby, 315; A Strange Preventive of Sunstroke, 315; Precautions against the Evil Eye, 316; Against the Powers of the Air, 316; Taking the Bread Shovel to Church, 316; Wedding Observances, 316; The Trousseau, 317; Buying a Wife, 317; The Betrothal, 317; Runaway Matches, 319; Preparations for the Wedding, 319; Invitation Cakes, 320; Inspecting the Trousseau, 320; The Bride's Toilette, 321; The Wedding Dress, 321; A Wedding near Salonica, 321; The Religious Ceremony, 322; The Feast, 322; Taking Home the Bride, 323; Offering to the Water Nymphs, 324; Funeral Customs, 324; Laying out the Corpse, 325; The Religious Ceremony, 325; The Death Feast, 326; Food for the Dead, 326.

CHAPTER XII.

BULGARIAN WOMEN: THEIR BELIEFS AND SUPERSTITIONS.

The Bulgarian Church, 327; Religion a Practical Matter, 328; Pantheism, 328; Heathen Festivals and Christian Anniversaries, 329; The *Kulada*, 329; The Feast of St. Demetrius, 330; The Matrons' Day, 330; Lent, 330; "Mother March," 330; Why Fish may be Eaten on the Blagostina, 331; Legend of St. George's Day, 332; Assumption Offerings, 333; Nature Worship, 333; Supernatural Beings, 334; Precautions against the Sun, 335; The *Tellestim*, 335; The Vampire, 336; His First Stage, 336; His Second Stage, 337; Laying the Vampire, 337; The Witch, 337; Her Medical Powers, 338; Antidotes for the Evil Eye, 339; *Adets* or Customs, 339; Exorcising Vermin, 340.

CHAPTER XIII.

BULGARIAN WOMEN: THEIR FOLK-POESY.

The Bulgarian Vernacular, 342; Historical Traditions, 342; Legend of Deli Marko, 343; The Story of Yanko the Wrestler, 345; Bulgarian Folk-poetry, 348; Dancing Songs, 349; Native Collectors, 349; Character of the Songs, 349; Ballad of the Wife of Momir, 350; Fraternal Affection, 351; The *Youdas*, or Fates, 351; The Samodiva Married against her Will, 352; Casting Spells on Nature, 355; Rada carried off by a Dragon, 355; The Sun Bewitched, 357; Christ and the Samodivas, 358; Penka's Adieu to her Brigand Life, 359; "There's but Niko in the World," 361; The Idle Reapers, 362; The Toilette, or the Helpful Mother-in-Law, 363.

CHAPTER XIV.

FRANK WOMEN: THEIR SOCIAL STATUS AND ACTIVITIES—FAMILY CEREMONIES—BELIEFS AND SUPERSTITIONS—AND FOLK-POESY.

The Frank Quarters, 366; "Only Catholics." 367; Convent Schools, 367; Education, 368; Polyglots, 369; Appearance, 369; Protestant Franks, 370; Curious Manners, 371; The *Tandour*, 372; Consuls' Wives, 372; Their Influence for Good, 373; A Romantic Incident, 374; Amusements, 375; East and West, 376; *Levées* at the Windows, 376; Carnival Diversions, 377; A Conspiracy, 378; Borrowed Folk-lore, 379; The Franks in Greek Folk-poesy, 379; The *Yanneotopoula*, 380; "A Frank I'll not Marry," 380 The Siren and the Seamen, 381.

PREFACE TO INTRODUCTION.

IN perusing the proof-sheets of Miss Garnett's *Women of Turkey and their Folk-lore*, it seemed to me that such an unique collection of facts was presented as should not only be found entertaining by the general reader, but might also be found serviceable by the scientific student; and I have written the Introductory Chapters to this volume, and propose to write the Concluding Chapters of the next, in the hope, at least, that I may thus, perhaps, make this collection of facts more suggestively instructive in relation to current theories. But facts cannot but be regarded from the point of view of some hypothesis or other, either formulated or unformulated. And naturally, therefore, there will be found in these Introductory Chapters, not only the special ethnographical and other facts which it has appeared desirable to set forth, but outlines of that new ethnological theory of the Origin of Civilisation, and of the chief deductions therefrom, from the point of view of which I would myself regard the facts brought together in Miss Garnett's Chapters.

I have thus been led to express views, not only with respect to the Origin of Civilisation, but to the Origin of the Aryans, the importance of Race-relations and -intermixtures, the Origin of Mythology, and the Method of Folk-lore, which are in direct opposition to the views now generally current, and to which the works of Professor Max Müller, Mr. Herbert Spencer, and Professor Edward Tylor have given a certain orthodoxy. But it must be noted, that the characteristic views of these eminent authors were for the most part formed, and even formulated, a quarter of a century ago; and that hardly any quarter of a century can be named during which the results of scientific research have been so revolutionary in their bearing on formerly accepted theories. And if my present very narrow limits of space have obliged me, with an appearance of dogmatism which these limits made unavoidable, to express views more in accordance, as I think, with the results of later research, I trust that I shall not be deemed guilty of any sort of disrespect to authors the perusal of whose earlier works formed epochs in my life.

If, however, I must thus excuse my opposition to some scholars and thinkers, I must express my obligations to others for much encouragement and assistance, and particularly to Professor Sayce and Professor De Lacouperie. For they have seen that the main drift of my researches is to generalise that derivation of later Civilisations from Egyptian, and particularly from Chaldean Civilisation, which Professor Sayce has so admirably demonstrated in the case of Semitic, and Professor De Lacouperie in the case of Chinese Civilisation, and which I hope to be able to demonstrate in the case of the European Civilisations. And if, without implicating Professor De Lacouperie in my shortcomings, I may give myself the satisfaction of expressing my gratitude, I would especially acknowledge the quite invaluable assistance I have received from that distinguished scholar ever since I had the honour of making his acquaintance, on reading my first paper, in 1887, on the ethnological theory of the Origin of Civilisation.

J. S. S.-G.

THE SHEALING, WIMBLEDON COMMON,
June 20, 1890.

THE

WOMEN OF TURKEY.

INTRODUCTORY CHAPTER I.

THE ETHNOGRAPHY OF TURKEY.

IN the highest degree misleading is, I think, the hypothesis which dispenses with study of Ethnology as properly both an antecedent to, and a concomitant of, study of Folk-lore. This hypothesis, in the words of Professor Tylor, affirms that "it is both possible and desirable [in a scientific study of Folk-beliefs and -customs] to eliminate considerations of hereditary varieties or races of men, and to treat mankind as homogeneous in nature."[1] On this hypothesis are based all the presently popular collections of Folk-lore—collections of facts as to so-called "Primitive Culture," and the so-called "Origin of Civilisation," &c. And with this hypothesis is intimately associated another—"the thesis" which Dr. Tylor "sustains"—"that the savage state in some measure represents an early condition of mankind out of which the higher culture has gradually been developed or evolved by

[1] *Primitive Culture*, vol. i. p. 6.

processes still in regular operation as of old."[1] These "processes," however, Professor Tylor nowhere defines, and he appears to regard them as of a spontaneous, certainly, at least, not as of an ethnological character.

But, in an earlier book of Dr. Tylor's, there is a passage which the contradictory dogmatism of his later work[2] makes remarkable. "It does not seem," said Mr. Tylor, in his earlier *Researches*, "to be an unreasonable, or even an over-sanguine view that the mass of analogies in art and knowledge, mythology, and custom . . . . may already be taken to indicate that the civilisations of many races . . . . have . . . . derived common material from a common source. But that such lines of argument should ever . . . . enable the student to infer . . . . that the civilisation of the whole world has its origin in one parent stock is . . . . rather a theoretical possibility than a state of things of which even the most dim and distant view is to be obtained."[3] This bare "theoretical possibility," however, as Professor Tylor esteemed it in 1865, and appears, since then, altogether to have lost sight of, I believe that I shall be able—by a mere co-ordination of the results of research during the last

[1] *Primitive Culture*, vol. i. p. 28.

[2] I may refer particularly to Dr. Tylor's confident assertions that such "traditions" as those in which "the half-civilised races of South America traced their rise from the condition of the savage tribes around them"—(*ibid.* pp. 318 *seq.*, and compare p. 35)—are mere Sun and Moon myths. "These legends," he continues, "have been appealed to even by modern writers" (as if the supposition were quite too ridiculous) "as gratefully remembered records of real human benefactors who carried long ago to America the culture of the Old World." But I venture to think that the facts which I have brought together in my *Traditions of the Archaian White Races* (*Trans. R. Hist. Soc.* 1889), though not a tenth part of those which I have collected as bearing on the subject, give a rather different aspect to these Tylorian "Sun and Moon myths."

[3] *Early History of Mankind*, p. 368.

quarter of a century—to verify as an historical reality. It will then be shown that it is not the fact—as Professor Tylor, Mr. Spencer,[1] and Sir John Lubbock appear, in the words of the last-named, to believe—" that various races have independently raised themselves from utter barbarism."[2] On the contrary, not only will it be shown that eighty years of research have not disproved Niebuhr's assertion that no single savage race can be named which has risen independently to civilisation,[3] but it will be shown that all the facts accumulated, during the last decade particularly of these eighty years, with respect to the Primitive Civilisations of the origins of which we know anything—those of Egypt and Chaldea—go to prove that the essential condition of such origins was the action of a Higher White Race on Lower Coloured and Black Races; and that research is almost every week bringing forward new proof that all the Later Civilisations—as certainly the Semitic Civilisations of Assyria and Judea,[4] the Chinese Civilisation,[5] and probably also the Aryan Civilisations of both Asia[6] and Europe[7]—were either

[1] Compare *Principles of Sociology—The Factors of Social Phenomena*, either in the original work, or in Mr. Collins's *Epitome*.

[2] *Origin of Civilisation*, p. 479.

[3] "Kein einziges Beyspiel von einem wirklich wilden Volk aufzuweisen ist, welches frey zur Cultur übergegangen wäre"—*Römische Geschichte*, Theil i. s. 88 (1811). Comp. Whately, *Origin of Civilisation*, and *Polit. Economy*, p. 68.

[4] See, *e.g.*, Sayce, *Babylonian Religion*, and Wellhausen, *Proleg. to History of Israel*.

[5] See De Lacouperie, *The Languages of China before the Chinese*, and his articles in the *Bab. and Or. Record*, vols. i. ii. and iii., and particularly the last.

[6] See Hewitt, *Early History of Northern India*—J. R. Asiatic Soc. 1889-90.

[7] The results of research leading to this conclusion will be co-ordinated and summarised in my forthcoming work on *Ancient Hellas*. D'Arbois de

directly or indirectly derived from one or other of these Primitive Civilisations. Nothing of a supernatural character, however, is—it should be unnecessary to say—attributed to the Higher White Races, the Founders of these Primitive Civilisations, nor in fact anything more, in the way of intellectual and practical ability, than an anatomist would infer who compared an ancient Archaian, and an ancient Negroid or Mongoloid skull of the Nile, or of the Euphrates Valley, and who considered, at the same time, the conditions under which the brains in these respective brain-pans functioned. For not only is the Archaian type—and especially the earlier the skull or portrait is—as fine cerebrally as we believe our own Aryan type to be; but the Archaian Colonists knew how to exact from their Coloured and Black subjects all the produce of their labour, save so much as was required to ensure the continuance of such labour; and through the wealth thus obtained they enjoyed the fullest means of intellectual development in abundant leisure for observation and speculation.

Such is the ethnological theory of the Origin of Civilisation which I venture to oppose to the theories, not essentially differing from each other, of Mr. Spencer, Dr. Tylor, and Sir John Lubbock; and which I hope to be able, not only fully to verify, but directly to connect with the correlative physiological principles

---

Jubainville (*Premiers Habitants de l'Europe*, t. i. l. i. chaps. iv. and v.) has shown the extent of the settlements of the Pelasgians, recognised their non-Aryan character, and even connected them with the Hittites. But, as he has "laissé de côté" both prehistoric archæology and ethnology, he has missed, as I think, the solution of the problem of European, and more particularly Hellenic, Origins.

of Anabolism and Katabolism; and hence, with the ultimate principles of the General Theory of Origins, and with that, as I believe, most fundamental of scientific facts and philosophical principles : *Every Existence has a determined, and determining Co-existence.* Here, however, I need only point out that, with such a theory of the Origin of Civilisation, an Ethnographical Chapter must be considered a necessary introduction to any such comparative account of social activities, family ceremonies, beliefs, and superstitions, and folk-poesies as will be found in these volumes; and especially as the Women of Turkey belong, not only to the oldest, and most historically interesting, but to the most diverse races of that White Variety of Mankind, the conquerors and civilisers of all other peoples. And in these ethnographical notes on the dozen peoples of Turkey, I shall deal with the various races in the order of their historical antiquity.

1. Following the rule just stated, we must begin our notes with the KŪRDS. For the very name of the Kūrds, variously called by classic authors, Κάρδακες, Καρδοῦχοι, Κορδυαῖοι, Γορδυηνοί, Γορδυαῖοι, Κύρτιοι, *Gordiaei*, and even Χαλδαῖοι,[1] affords at least *primâ facie* evidence for connecting them with the ancient Chaldeans, the initiators of Civilisation in the Euphrates Valley. It would here be out of place to set forth the various facts which corroborate this inference from the very name of Kūrds.[2] Here I

---

[1] See the classical authorities as cited by Lenormant, *Origines de l'Histoire*, tom. ii. 1ʳᵉ partie, p. 4.

[2] To the "nombreuses dissertations de la part des érudits modernes," referred to by Lenormant (*op. cit.* p. 5, n. 1), as treating of the "parenté réelle ou supposée" of the Kūrds with the Chaldeans, I may add the essay

need only say that I believe that I have already verified,[1] and shall be able, in forthcoming works, still more conclusively, both from monumental and traditional evidence, to verify the following generalisations. First, that the initiators of Civilisation in the two great River Valleys of the Euphrates and the Nile, belonged to a White Race which, as pre-Semitic and pre-Aryan, and as a race, indeed, from which both Semites and Aryans were probably derived, may best, perhaps, be distinguished as the Archaian White Race; secondly, that White Races may be ethnologically defined as Races with long or short heads, high noses, unprojecting jaws, long hair and beards, and light-coloured skins; and, thirdly, that, save the mainly Aryan character now of the Kūrdish language —a fact of little ethnological significance—there are, to say the least, no facts definitely disproving, while many facts may be adduced, from the later results of research, which distinctly corroborate, that connection with the Archaian White Races which appears to be indicated by the names given to the Kūrds by Greek and Latin authors. Among such facts are, for instance, those recently set forth by M. Halévy, in his paper on *The Nation of the Mards*.[2] For it is there shown that the whole of the vast chain of the Zagros, part of which has now the name of Kūrdistan, and all the highland country between the plains

of Eberhard Schrader, *Die Abstammung der Chaldäer*, &c. in the *Zeitschr. d. deutsch. morgenl. Gesellsch.*, Bd. xxvii., though I here suggest a conclusion different to that which he maintains.

[1] *The Traditions of the Archaian White Races*, in the *Trans. of the Roy. Hist. Soc.* for 1889.

[2] See *Babylonian and Oriental Record*, March 1890; and compare *Rev. des Etudes Juives*, 1889, p. 174.

of the Euphrates and Tigris, and the ancient Aryana of Iran or Persia—in other words, Media and Susiana, Kossea and Elam—was, from the remotest historic times, inhabited by non-Semitic and non-Aryan, or, as I have ventured to distinguish them, Archaian tribes, forming the great nation of the Amardians, or Mards. And hence, to refer the Kūrds ethnologically to the Archaian Stock is but to suppose that they belong to the same Stock as that which, from the earliest historic times, and without any known break caused by extermination, has occupied the country of the Kūrds. The independent position also of the Kūrdish women, with the freedom and consideration they enjoy, is but one of the customs which might be cited in corroboration of this theory of the ethnological connection of the Kūrds with the ancient Chaldeans.[1] Nor, seeing how very much an affair of blood Religion is, is it irrelevant to note that the Kūrds have the reputation of being very bad Moslems, or, in other words, of being very little touched by the Semitic notion of Allah. And the national Kūrdish characteristic of energetic enterprise, though now chiefly manifested but in predatory raids, might also be held, if not to corroborate, at least to harmonise with, this theory of their Amardian descent and Chaldean kinship.

2. The CIRCASSIANS, with the Georgians and other White Races of the Caucasus, are now grouped under the general name of Alarodians, derived from the 'Ἀλαρόδιοι of Herodotus,[2] which again was de-

[1] See *Women of Turkey: Semitic and Moslem Women*, ch. i., and *Conclusion*.
[2] See Rawlinson, *Herod.*, vol. iv. Essay iii. pp. 250 *seq.*, "On the Alarodians of Herodotus." In accordance with the still current, though now

rived from the Semitic name *Urardu, Alarud*, or *Ararat*, given to the highlands north of Assyria, and about Lake Van and Lake Urumiyeh. And still more unquestionably than the Kūrds do the Alarodians belong to the Archaian White Stock. For while the language of the Kūrds appears, as I have just said, to be now of a distinctly Aryan character, the languages of the Georgians and Circassians are not only non-Aryan, but can—or at least the Georgian can—be clearly related to the ancient non-Aryan and non-Semitic languages of Asia Minor, still preserved in cuneiform inscriptions,[1] and even, perhaps, in certain words of unknown derivation, still current.[2] Nor certainly do the national characteristics shown by the Georgians and Circassians belie this theory as to their ethnological connection with the Archaian founders of Civilisation. The

---

somewhat discredited, "Turanian" theory, these Urardians or Alarodians are declared by Canon Rawlinson to have been "closely connected with the Scythic inhabitants of Babylonia" (p. 252). But no reason is advanced against what, I believe, we shall find to be in every way more probable, that they were such White Races as we now distinguish by the term "Alarodian."

[1] Compare Sayce, *The Monuments of the Hittites, Trans. Soc. Bibl. Arch.*, vol. vii. p. 285; and *The Decipherment of the Vannic Inscriptions; Verhandl. der 5. Orient. Congresses*, 1881, 2te Theile, where he says, "The language of the inscriptions is of the same semi-agglutinative, semi-inflexional character as that of the Georgian of to-day. In fact, the similarity between it and modern Georgian is remarkable, and I am inclined to believe will turn out to be the result of relationship" (s. 308). See also Zagarelli, *Examen de la Littérature relative à la Grammaire Georgienne*, 1873; and Smirnow, in *Rev. d'Anthropologie*, 15 Av. 1878; Von Erckhart, *Der Kaukasus und seine Völker*, 1887; and Abercromby, *The Eastern Caucasus*, 1889.

[2] See *below*, Chap. IV. p. 123. Mr. Abercromby remarks that "Early Lesgian or Albanian has characteristics in common with Medic." It would have been better to have said Proto-Medic or Medo-Scythic. For Delattre has shown that the Medes of the centuries after the 9th B.C. were Aryans (*Le Peuple et l'Empire des Mèdes*).

Georgians, who, at a very early period, appear to have come down from the Pambaki highlands in the south to the plain of the Kyros or Gurj[1]—from which they and their country (Gurjistan) are named in Persian—maintained their historic kingdom of Iberia, between the Caspian and the Euxine, for upwards of 2000 years (302 B.C.-1799 A.C.), till overthrown by the Russian Tzarate with a treachery and violence of a peculiarly unscrupulous and remorseless character. As for the Circassians, their vigour as a conquering race is witnessed to by their rule in Egypt of more than 400 years, from the foundation of the Circassian Dynasty of Memlook Sultans (1382) to the treacherous massacre in the citadel of Cairo by Mehmet Ali (1811) of the Circassian Beys, who still, after the overthrow of the Circassian Dynasty by the Ottoman Sultan, Selim I. (1517), retained power as the real lords, while the Ottoman Pachas were but the titular rulers, of Egypt. And though the heroic Schamyl was taken prisoner in 1854, not till 1864 were the Circassians at length conquered in their native land. About a century ago they were converted to Islam by the Dervish Mansūr. But, as their Folk-poesy shows, they are as little affected by the Semitic notion of Allah, as their kindred, the Kūrds.

3. The ALBANIANS—not, however, of the Albania on the Caspian, which lies beyond the Ottoman frontier, but of the Albania on the Adriatic—next claim a brief notice. For though their language

---

[1] Compare Abercromby, *Eastern Caucasus*, Conclusion.

was proved by Bopp to be Aryan, and is placed by Meyer[1] in a fifth Aryan family, of which it is the sole surviving member, its character is shown to be such as indicates a mixed race. This mixed race was not till the eleventh century called Albanians (τὸ τῶν Ἀλβανῶν ἔθνος), having previously been called Ἰλλύριοι. "Illyrian" was equated with "Pelasgian" by Von Hahn.[2] But I would regard the Pelasgians as an Archaian Race, and the Illyrians—of whom the Albanians may, perhaps, be the best representatives now in Europe—as a mixed Race of Archaian Pelasgians and Aryan Thrakians. That, however, generally, the Pelasgians were of a non-Semitic and non-Aryan White Race, ethnologically and historically connected with the founders of the civilisations of Egypt and of Chaldea; and that, particularly, the Albanians are such an Archaian-Aryan race as I have suggested, has still to be proved. But this suggestion I believe that I shall be able fully to verify in forthcoming works; though I can here only note one or two minor ethnological indications. For instance: so far as the religious characteristics of the Albanians have any ethnological significance, they point in the same direction as those of the Kūrds.

[1] *Albanesische Studien*, 1883. He also shows that, though an Aryan language, Albanian is *not* particularly closely related to Greek, while remarkable coincidences appear to connect it with North European languages. Compare Brugmann, *Grundriss der vergleichenden Grammatik der indogermanischen Sprachen*, Bd. i. s. 7; Karl Pauli, *Die Inschriften des nordetruskischen Alphabets*, ss. 120–128; and Dozon, *Langue Chkipe*.

[2] *Albanesische Studien*, "Illyrisch = Pelasgisch im weiteren sinne," s. 215. Compare Niebuhr, *Lectures on Ancient Ethnography*, &c., vol. i. p. 301; Retzen, *Ethnologische Schriften*; Virchow, in the *Berichte* of the Berlin Academy of Sciences, 1877. As to the extension of the Illyrians, see D'Arbois de Jubainville, *Premiers Habitants de l'Europe*, t. i. pp. 302–3.

Like this other presumably Archaian Race, the Albanians are notoriously bad Moslems. Almost all, indeed, belong to the Bektashí Order of Dervishes; and many a Bektashí story have I heard, on hunting and other excursions, ridiculing, with a fine Oriental irony, the very notion of Allah. Besides, it will hardly be contended that the mountaineers of Pelasgian Dodona, and of the neighbouring Tosk—or Tuscan (?)—country, are of pure Aryan race. And I can testify, from what I saw of them in three different journeys in Albania, that they are of so splendid a physical type as to prove themselves, if a mixed race, still a mixture of exclusively White Races. And, confining myself to the peoples mentioned in the following pages, I believe that, of a similar Archaian-Aryan race will be found the Zeibeck Highlanders of the Asiatic Vilayet of Aidin. For their striking features often recall those of the "Peoples of the Sea," portrayed on the Egyptian monuments, and photographed by Mr. Flinders Petrie in his *Racial Types from Egypt.*

4. Next, perhaps, on the score of historical antiquity, I may note the VLACHS, or Cis-Danubian ROUMANS. For if the Archaian Pelasgians were the first White Conquerors and Civilisers of the Coloured Races of Europe, they were, in their turn, conquered by the Aryan Thrakians—Thrace being certainly the first *known* historical home and centre of dispersion of the Western Aryans.[1] But if the Thrakians were the Western offshoot from the stock of the undivided Aryans, the Mother-tongue from which the

[1] See *below*, p. xlvi. n. 2.

Kelto-Italic languages were derived was the first offshoot from the speech of the undivided Aryans. And it would appear, not only that the Vlachs are the best representatives now to be found of the ancient Thrakians;[1] but that the name, Vlach, Wallach, and Walloon, Valais, Wälsch, and Welsh, had a common origin.[2] If this is so, however, some, at least, of the various traits—linguistic, mythological, and customary—which the Roumans have in common with the Romans, may have a far more ancient origin than the Roman occupation of Thrace. But here I must pass on to note that of the ethnographical characteristics of the Thrakians, in at least the seventh century B.C., we have very clear though curious evidence in the description of the famous Thrakian beauty, Doricha, usually called "Rosy Cheeks" ('Ροδῶπις), who infatuated with love of her the Greek merchant Kháraxos, the brother of Sappho, by whom he was greatly ridiculed for his folly in a famous song.[3] Now, to

[1] With this view Professor Freeman, among others, agrees. "They [the Vlachs] must," he says, "mainly represent the Thracian race in its widest sense": *Historical Geography*, p. 364.

[2] With reference to the question raised by Schaffarik (*Slavische Alterthümer*, Bd. i. ss. 236 *seq.*), Professor Rhys, of Oxford, has favoured me with a note from which I am kindly permitted to make the following extracts:—"No Celtist holds that the words *Vlach* and *Kelt* are in any way related. *Kelt* is a word of unknown origin. . . . . *Vlach* I should suppose of the same origin as *Welsh*, *Walloon*, &c.; and in point of origin these are now supposed to be derived by the early Teutons from the tribe name of the Gauls, called *Volcæ* Tectosages and *Volcæ* Arecomici —a Gaulish people which was widely spread at the dawn of Gaulish history. The meaning of the word Volcæ is unknown, but it has nothing to do with *Belgæ*, which is another word of obscure meaning and etymology."

[3] See Herodot. ii. 134; Athenæus, *Deipn.* xiii. 596; and Grote, *History of Greece*, vol. ii. p. 505, n.

this day, Vlach maidens frequently deserve the name of "Rosy Cheeks" as much as any Thrakian beauty of old could have done; and, as numberless folk-songs[1] testify, "Vlachopoúlas" still infatuate Greeks, both old and young, as much as ever did Thrakian Dorichas. And to a Scottish traveller who so often enjoyed their hospitality in their mountain villages, on Pindus and Olympus, it was interesting to reflect that, not only were Vlach and Kelt probably of the same Thrakian origin,[2] but that in the now mixed blood of the Vlachs there was probably a not inconsiderable strain of a distinctively Keltic character. For the long domination of the Kelts in Thrace during that Classic Period in which their kingdoms extended across all Europe, from the British Islands to Asiatic Galatia,[3] having certainly, in Thrace, left traces in Keltic[4] names, has probably also left traces in Keltic blood.

5. Whether, however, the Vlachs, or Cis-Danubian Roumans, may or may not be with probability regarded as modern representatives of the ancient

---

[1] See *Greek Folk-songs*, 145, 146, and 191.

[2] With respect to the Thrakian kinship thus claimed for the Kelts, see Bacmeister, *Allemanischen Wanderungen;* Coutzen, *Wanderungen der Kelten;* Rhys, *Celtic Britain;* Koch, *Älteste Geschichte Œsterreichs und Bayerns,* and *Celtische Alterthümer;* Robiou, *Hist. des Gaulois d'Orient;* and Perrot, *Exploration de la Galatie.* See also, Taylor, *Origin of the Aryans,* who truly remarks (p. 256, n. 2) that "the theory that the Celts extended themselves, at a comparatively recent period, from Gaul down the valley of the Danube is now very generally abandoned." But compare the authorities for the Teutonic kinship of the Thrakians cited in *Greek Folk-songs,* p. 33, n. 35.

[3] See D'Arbois de Jubainville, *L'Empire Celtique au ivme siècle avant notre ère—Revue Historique,* t. xxx.

[4] See Renan, *St. Paul,* p. 136, n.; and Heuzey, *Miss. de Macédoine,* p. 149.

Thrakians, there can apparently be little doubt that both the Ionian and Dorian GREEKS came of the Thrakian Stock.[1] Homer knew of the Dorians only in Crete.[2] And, should further investigation not disprove present suppositions, I may perhaps be able to show—from an analysis of the legend of the great Dorian hero, Herakles, and from a variety of other considerations relating chiefly to the pre-Hellenic, Pelasgian, and Asiatic Civilisation of Greece—that we may trace the formation of the Dorian Race in migrations, first, southward from Olympus to Crete; thence, westward and northward to the islands off the mainland which they called Epeiros; thence, to the Epeirote valleys; thence, across Pindus to the Thessalian plains; and finally, in that new southward migration—that invasion of the Peloponnesus and overthrow of an Asiatic and Pelasgian, rather than Hellenic, Civilisation—that invasion of the Peloponnesus, which figures in legend as the "Return of the Herakleids." Most contrastedly different were the conditions under which was formed that other race derived from the Thrakian Stock—that Race which became known in history as Ionian Greeks. Even to this day the Greeks of Chios are, in appearance, markedly different from other Greeks, and particularly in their dolichokephalic characteristics; so much so, indeed, that I have heard a lady, an acute observer, say that one could always distinguish Chiote Greeks by what she

---

[1] Compare O. Schrader, *Sprachvergleichung*, s. 449, and Fick, *Sprache der Makedonier*, ii. p. 718.
[2] *Od.* xix. 174.

called their "melon-shaped heads"—and the Turkish melon is always of an elongated shape. To what extent such differences characterised the Dorian and Ionian Greeks of the Classic Period, I do not accurately know. They were, however, certainly distinguished by other great differences, both historical and ethnological—differences, reflection on the interaction of which may enable us better to understand the unsurpassed splendour of the flower-and-fruit-time of Hellenic Civilisation. But in the modern Greeks of at least Greece Proper, the Ionian and Dorian blood to which, under favouring circumstances, the triumphs of Hellenic Civilisation were due, has been overwhelmed by the intermarriages consequent on the resistless tides of Slav immigration and of Frank conquest. And so far as the Greeks of the European mainland retain Greek characteristics, these are probably due more to community of language and of traditions, than to community of lineage and of blood, with those ancient Hellenes who made the Greek name famous. But occasionally—at least on the Asiatic mainland—the facts on which is founded this conclusion with respect to the Greeks of the European mainland are precisely reversed. For in some districts of Asia Minor we find that the Greek blood is comparatively pure, while the Greek language, till the recent Hellenic revival, had ceased to be used save in the ritual of the churches; that it was, even in the ritual, repeated rather by rote than with intelligence; and that the sermon was in Turkish, the only language understood by the people. On the European mainland, however, the name of "Hellene" now generally indicates the inheritor of a tradition rather than the descendant of a race.[1]

6. But there was another ancient offshoot from the old Thrakian Stock. Across the narrow Straits the Thrakians appear, about 1500 B.C.,[2] to have swept into Asia Minor, where we know them chiefly under the related name of Phrygians. With these Phrygians—and hence with the Western, and not Eastern, branch of the Aryans—linguistic and other considerations connect the ARMENIANS.[3] But not even by the middle of the sixth century B.C. had Aryan Armenians reached Lake Van; and we have nothing like authentic Armenian history till the time of Vahé, who fell in battle with Alexander the Great.[4] Such is the derivation of the Armenians, according to the combined conclusions of ethnological and linguistic research. A very different account of them, however, is given in the national legends put into form, if not invented, since the conversion of the Armenians

---

[1] In confirmation of this conclusion, long since arrived at, I am glad to be able to note that it is in complete accordance with that of Dr. A. Philippson, in his paper *Zur Ethnographie des Peloponnes*, in the February number of Petermann's *Mittheilungen* (1890). For Dr. Philippson's conclusion is, that Greeks in blood form but one element in a vast Hellenised conglomerate of which about 90,000 of the Albanian element still retain their native language, while the Slavs have become completely Hellenised, as also all the descendants of Romans, Goths, Vandals, French, Italians, Spaniards, Jews, Arabs, and Turks who have at various epochs settled in the country. I must, however, dissent from the opinion that Hellenised descendants of the three last-named races are to be found among the modern Greeks.

[2] D'Arbois de Jubainville, *Premiers Habitants de l'Europe*, t. i. p. 266.

[3] As to the connection of Armenian with Phrygian, see Fick, *Spracheinheit*, p. 411.

[4] See Sayce, *The Decipherment of the Vannic Inscriptions*—Congrès des Orientalistes, 1881. Compare Thomas, *Early Armenian Coins*.

to Christianity. Their descent is, in these legends, traced to Haik, the great-grandson of Noah. But national legends are a species of amber in which something of the nature of historic fact is almost always imbedded. Hence, the "Noah" of the Armenian legend may primarily represent, not the "Noah" of the Hebrew legend, but the name from which both the "Noah" of *Genesis,* and the "Nahouscha" of the *Rig-Veda* [1]—often referred to as the primæval ancestor of the Aryans—were derived. And on my suggesting this to Professor De Lacouperie, he pointed out to me that in the Chaldean Deluge-tradition, the variously read name, "Hasisadra" (Smith), "Adrahasis" (Oppert), "Xisuthros" (Haupt), is in the original, *Samas-Napisti(m).*[2] Another probably historical fact imbedded in these Christian Armenian legends is the description of Dikran (Tigran) I. as having "long fair hair, shining at the ends, and being rosy-cheeked, and honey-eyed"[3]—a description which graphically depicts a typical Aryan, and is, at the same time, in striking accordance with that of the Thrakian beauty above referred to.[4] And as further confirming the probable derivation both of Armenians and of Vlachs from the same Thrako-Phrygian Stock, it may be worth while

---

[1] See Windischmann, *Ursagen der Arischen Volker,* ss. 7-10; and Bothlingk et Roth, *Dictionnaire Sanscrit,* t. iv. p. 87.

[2] See Haupt, *Cuneiform Account of the Deluge—Johns Hopkins University Circulars,* Feb. 1889.

[3] See Dulaurier, *Chants pop. de l'Arménie—Revue des Deux Mondes,* Avril 1852. The last epithet—"yeux de miel," as it is rendered by Dulaurier—means "sweet-eyed," or "with fascinating eyes." *Bal guzlü* means exactly the same thing in Turkish. [4] P. xxix.

to note that the traditional name of the son of Haik was *Armedag*, and that my Vlach hosts at Mezzovo, in the heart of Pindus, called themselves *Armeng*. Nor may it be irrelevant[1] to recall " Eros, the son of Arminios, by descent a Pamphyllian," whom Plato makes the hero of the mythical adventure with the story of which he concludes his *Republic*.[2] But whether the traditional type of the early Armenian kings was originally general among the people or not, two very distinct types are now found among them—the one, with brown hair, fair skin, and sometimes blue eyes; and the other, with black hair and eyes, and dark complexion: the former distinguished by the Turks as *Indjé*, or " Pure;" and the latter as *Kalun*, or " Coarse." Some fancy that these types are coincident respectively with the ecclesiastical divisions of Uniate and Gregorian Armenians. But this is not really the case. For as persons of these two different types intermarry, both types may occasionally be found among members of the same family, whether Uniates or Gregorians. In Armenians of the coarse type, the features have often what may, perhaps, be called a Semitic, though not a Hebrew, cast. And it appears not at all improbable that, as Eastern Armenia has, on the south, Northern Assyria, Armenian, may, at a very early period, have mixed, in these borderlands, with Assyrian, blood.[3]

---

[1] Compare Sayce, *Academy*, 28 January 1882, and *Journal R. Asiatic Soc.*, vol. xiv., 1882.   [2] X. xiii., &c.

[3] Possibly this may be the fact at the root of the Christian Armenian legend of the descent of the Pakradunians from Abraham, and of their having come to Armenia during the captivity of their race by Nebuchad-

7. Still following the chronological order of settlement within what are now the frontiers of Turkey, the JEWS next claim some ethnological notice. For certainly a considerable time before the Christian era they had established colonies in Europe, and particularly at Salonica;[1] and this ancient city—renamed by Kassander, in honour of his wife, the half-sister of Alexander the Great, Thessaloniké—the Hebrews have now, by their preponderating numbers, made a very Jerusalem-on-Sea. With the question as to the origin of the Semites we need not here further concern ourselves than briefly to note that, as the Aryan Variety of the Archaian White Stock probably originated in the North, and, as I venture to suggest, most probably perhaps in the North Caucasian region, in part between, and in part north of, the Caspian and Euxine;[2] so, the Semitic Variety of that Primitive Stock originated, but millenniums earlier than the Aryan Variety, in the South—in Central or Northern Arabia;[3] and, as both physical features[4] and moral characteristics[5] appear to indicate,

---

nezzar. See Issaverdens, *Armenia*, p. 216. It may be noted also that the eastern part of the Armenian Taurus is called *Sim* by Moses of Khor'ni, i. 5 & 22 and ii. 7 & 81.

[1] See Renan, *St. Paul*, and Cousinéry, *Voyage dans la Macédoine*, t. i. p. 19.

[2] See *below*, pp. xlvi-xlix.

[3] See Sprenger, *Alte Geographie Arabiens*, § 427; Eberhard Schrader, *Die Abstammung der Chaldaer, und die Ursitze der Semiten*, in the *Zeitschr. d. deutsch. morgenl. Gesellsch.*, Bd. xxvii.; Sayce, *Assyrian Grammar*, pp. 3 and 13; and *The Origin of Semitic Civilisation*, in *Trans. Soc. Bibl. Arch.* vol. i. 1872.

[4] The large mouth and thick lips, and certain other characteristics.

[5] Particularly the prodigious boastfulness of the Jews. As to their intellectual character, the historical fact is that the Jews have absolutely no place in the history of progressive philosophic speculation and scien-

through some admixture of Negro blood. But though colonies of Jews may have settled in what is now European and Asiatic Turkey antecedently to the Christian era, yet the settlement of the great majority of the Jews now in the country dates back only to the beginning of the sixteenth century, after their expulsion from Spain by Ferdinand and Isabella. Hence, the language of the Jews of Turkey is, to this day, an old and mispronounced Spanish, corrupted by Hebrew words and idioms. As this language, though mainly still Spanish, is written and printed in Hebrew characters, it may be said to be a literary language; and such is also, in a way, the still more mongrel Judæo-German of the Jews of Russia.[1] But a remarkable physical feature differentiates the Jews of Turkey descended from the Spanish immigrants from the earlier settlers in the country. These last are distinguished by the flat instep, which accords with the other features indicating an original Negroid admixture; while the former are distinguished, on the contrary, by a high instep, derived probably from intermarriage in Spain with the Moors, who, so far as they are fair Berbers, would seem to be ethnologically connected with the Archaian White Stock.

8. The sixth century of the Christian era, the

---

tific discovery, save when, like a Philo Judæus, or a Spinoza, saturated with Aryan thought, and writing in Aryan languages, or when, as in the case of many distinguished Semites of the present day, elaborating Aryan discoveries. With reference to the suggested original mixture of White with Negro blood, the excellent results of the contemporary cross between Semite and Negro in Africa are very significant. See, for instance, Thomson, *Central African Lakes*, i. pp. 91-2; and Butler, *Campaign of the Cataracts*, p. 282.

[1] See *Rep. British and Foreign Bible Soc.*, 1888, p. 535.

epoch of the origin of the Modern Nationalities of Europe, is the epoch also of the introduction of new ethnological elements into the population of ancient Thrace. The elements to which I refer are those which are now the chief constituents of the BULGARIAN nationality. Originally, the Bulgarians appear to have been a tribe of the Huns of Attila who, after their defeat, on the death of the "Scourge of God" (453 A.C.), retreated eastward towards the Great Bulgaria, which extended between the shores of the Caspian and the Euxine to the confluence of the Kama and the Volga,[1] which last river-name appears still to indicate the former occupation of its banks by the Bulgarians. Certain tribes of the Bulgarians, who had for a time been subject to the Avars, threw off their yoke in 634, and, about 670, crossing the Danube and uniting themselves with the Slavs, by whom Thrace was now in great part peopled, founded the Bulgarian kingdom between the Danube and the Hæmus, a kingdom sometimes distinguished from that on the Volga by the name of Little Bulgaria. But as the Slavs were, in Greece, Hellenised; so the Bulgarians were, in Thrace, Slavonised. It may be noted, however, that the Court language of the independent Wallacho-Bulgarian kingdom, which established itself in 1186, was not Slav, but Roumanian. Slav, however, though both the Court- and the Folk-language of the Bulgarians now is, the two ethnological elements of which the people is composed are still easily distinguishable. As markedly Slavo-Tartar are the Bulgarians—save those of

[1] The original seat, perhaps, of the undivided Aryans; see *below*, p. xlvii.

Roumelia—as are the Russians. Among Bulgarians, generally, as among Russians, one finds two distinct types—often, indeed, standing side by side in the most striking contrast—the one, the Aryan Slav, tall, fair, and well-proportioned, full-eyed, high-nosed, and low-cheekboned; and the other, the non-Aryan Tartar, or rather Tatar, short, dark, and often disproportionately broad, small-eyed, flat-nosed, and high-cheekboned. And near cousins of this latter type, or of their ancestors, are those later Tatar immigrants, now found, not only in the Dobrudja, but at Constantinople—(where their frequent employment as mounted postmen has led to all such couriers being called Tatars)—and throughout Bulgaria.[1] But I have excepted the Bulgarians of Roumelia, or of Thrace, and Macedonia, whose blood is certainly mixed with Thrakian and Greek. Hence, in the provinces south of the Balkans, we find, in some districts, persons with Bulgarian features speaking Greek; and in neighbouring districts, persons with Greek features speaking Bulgarian. And generally the mixture of blood among the Bulgarians is indicated by the number of different dialects of Bulgarian —dialects hardly reducible to fewer than three divisions[2]: (1) those of Bulgaria and Thrace; (2) of Southern Macedonia; and (3) of Northern Macedonia, and Old Servia.

[1] How very marked the non-Aryan element among the Bulgarians still is will be brought home to the reader by the following little incident. Mrs. Blunt, being at the Aquarium with Miss Garnett after the publication of their book, *The People of Turkey*, exclaimed, on seeing some Lapps who were then being exhibited with their reindeer, "Why, they are exactly like Bulgarians!"

[2] See Dozon, *Chants Populaires Bulgares*, Introduction, p. xii.

9. The chronological order followed in these brief ethnological notes brings us to what, in its origin, was the most, and, in its present reality, is the least, romantic of all the constituents of the population of Turkey—the FRANKS. They are the relics, and in some cases the direct descendants, if not of Crusading knights and their retainers, of the traders by whom they were succeeded—first, Venetian and Genoese merchant-princes and their mercenaries, and, later, merchant-adventurers and their clerks. Their language among themselves is either Italian, as generally at Salonica, or French, as generally at Smyrna and Constantinople; but all speak Greek, as that is usually the language of their servants; while Turkish is spoken according to the necessities of business, or the circumstances of locality, as, for instance, at the Capital, at Broussa, and at the Dardanelles. Not one of these languages, however, is learned by the Franks grammatically or spoken with purity, and all are frequently blended in a most singularly polyglot jargon. Corresponding to this mixture of languages is the mixture of descents, which is nowhere, within Aryan limits, so great as among the Franks. Religious creed alone restricts to some degree the intermixture, in the Levant, of descendants of every people in Europe. Hence, the descendants of Swiss, Dutch, English, and Scotch adventurers, still retaining their Protestantism, do not often intermarry with the Catholic descendants of French, Italian, and Austrian adventurers. Yet the mixture of race is very great, and particularly when, as not unfrequently happens, it is further

increased by marriage with Greeks and Armenians, the latter generally of the Uniate or Catholic sect. And of the complicated family-ties thence resulting a striking example was till lately, if it is not still, afforded by the marriage-relationships of the British Consuls in the Levant. I could reckon up a dozen different British Consular families connected with each other by marriage with Franks, or with the Armenian family of Zohrab, which again is partly Frank. But the general result of this cross-breeding is certainly a race which is physically handsome. Morally, however, little of a favourable kind can be said of the Franks. Indeed, this cosmopolitan compound of all nationalities, which is itself of no nationality, gives the most convincing proof of the lower moral tone consequent on the want of national sentiment and tradition; and, as most of the Franks are fanatical Catholics, a proof is thus also given of the utter failure of Ritual Religion to supply the want of that great natural condition of social morality—National Institutions, and the feelings of social duty which they stimulate and direct.

10. We now come to the last but one of the invaders who still constitute an element in the population of Turkey—a very small and scattered element indeed, but an element which has always attracted a singular degree of interest—the GIPSIES. In accordance with the chronological order of these notes, I mention the Gipsies here, because—impelled westwards, as supposed, by the Mongol conquests begun by Genghis Khan in the thirteenth century (1205), we find them

in the next, the fourteenth century, in the Greek Islands, and particularly in Corfu (1346), and long before the end of the century in Wallachia. As the cause of the first westward and northward migration of the Gipsies is supposed to have been the Afghan conquest of India in the eleventh century; and that of their second migration, the Mongol conquest of Persia, in the thirteenth century; the cause of a third westward and northward migration was the Ottoman conquest of South-eastern Europe, in the fifteenth century. But notwithstanding this flight before the Ottoman conquerors, nowhere else in Europe are the Gipsies still to be found in such numbers as in those south-eastern lands of European Turkey, in which they settled at the end of their supposed second migration. Nor does one find them only in tents in the woodlands, but in hovels in the towns—as, for instance, to name but two of the town-settlements where I have visited them—at Uskup, the former Skópia, the birthplace of Justinian, and at Vódhena, the former Edessa, the capital of Macedonia. This account, however, of the first appearance of the Gipsies in Europe is based on the hypothesis of their being representatives of the three inferior Panjab tribes of Djatts, Doms, and Luris, severally described as minstrels, thieves, and horsemen—occupations generally combined by the mixed tribes of European Gipsies. But I question whether this once generally accepted theory gives by any means the full solution of the problem of the origin of the Gipsies. No doubt the Romany is an Aryan dialect related to that of the Panjab tribes just named. But I venture to think that these now Aryan-speaking tribes of the Panjab, though they have the high features and long hair specially characteristic of White Races, are far less probably of Aryan blood than of the blood of those pre-Aryan White conquerors of India now represented by the purer Dravidian races.[1] And these facts may be worth considering. The calling of a tinker, or smith, still a distinctive occupation of Gipsies, has been exercised in Europe by nomad bands from time immemorial, and ages before the arrival of these, as supposed, Panjab Gipsies. Everywhere also throughout Europe, as I hope, at least, to be able to prove, the Aryan Civilisations were preceded by, and founded on, the pre-Aryan Civilisations of Archaian White Races—as we already know that the Semitic Civilisation of Assyria was. And hence the question arises whether we may not verifiably regard the Gipsies who seem to have arrived in South-eastern Europe in the fourteenth, and in North-western Europe in the fifteenth century, as but adding to the probably then very much diminished numbers of the nomadic metal-workers? verifiably regard the Scottish *Tinklers*, German *Zigeuner*, and Greek 'Ατσίγανοι, &c., as descendants of the Σίγυνναι of Herodotos?[2] and verifiably regard these metal-working nomads as remnants of the Archaian Race that carried bronze to West-

---

[1] See Caldwell, *Dravidian Grammar, Introd.* And with reference to his extraordinary contention that the Dravidians are Turanians, transformed into Caucasians by change of climate and mode of life, compare Ujfalvy on the Hungarians, in *L'Année Géographique*, 9, 10, 1872, and De Gerando, *Origine des Hongrois*.   [2] *Terpsichoré*, 9.

ern and Northern Europe; maintained their power over the European Aborigines, by the immense advantages given them by the possession of metallic weapons; and, by exclusive intermarriage, kept their knowledge to themselves, and made of metal-working not an art only, but a mystery?"[1]

11. We have now traced the descent of the various present populations of Turkey to a succession of invaders, beginning with those pre-Aryan and pre-Semitic White Conquerors ethnologically connected, as I hope to show, with the founders of the Egyptian and Chaldean Civilisations, and at the present day represented by Kŭrds and Circassians in Asia, and by Albanians in Europe—if, at least, as suggested, the Albanians have in them a Pelasgian element, and if this Pelasgian element is to be ethnologically connected with the Archaian Stock of White Races. And we come now to those last invaders of all, who have not invaded only, but have, for half a millennium, kept within the bond of a united Empire, the various peoples of these European-Asian lands, the so-called TURKS. No "Liberal" assumption, however—except that, perhaps, as to the universal "subjection of Women"—is in such utter contradiction to historical facts as the assumption that the OSMANLIS are Turks in the sense in which that term, as likewise that of Turanian, is ordinarily used—namely, to designate not

[1] Compare the works of Bataillard, *Nouvelles Recherches sur les Bohémiens*, &c.; and Leland, *The Original Gipsies and their Language* (Congrès des Orientalistes, Vienna, 1886). I would suggest not only the names of the Pictish localities, but the words of the Tinkler language of Scotland should be examined, with a view to see whether they have any Alarodian or Proto-Medic affinities.

only a non-Aryan, but a Coloured Race. For it is very doubtful whether even the small original following of the Central Asian chief, Othman, who called themselves Osmanlis (or, as we now say, OTTOMANS), were, save in their lower orders, what we commonly now mean by the term Turk, Tatar, and Turanian—doubtful whether, at least, the descendants of Othman, or "Bonebreaker," and Malkatoon, or "Treasure of a Woman" (1288), and their chief followers were not of such a White Race, non-Aryan and non-Semitic, as ethnological research has shown to be still, as from the earliest historic times it has been, widely distributed over Central Asia, and as far even as to the eastern borders of Thibet.[1] But however this may be, it is certain that the original small tribe of Osmanlis has, for more than six hundred years, increased, not only by intermarriage with,[2] but recruitment from, the best White blood both of Asia and of Europe. Nor has this recruitment from the subject Aryan populations been only forced, but also voluntary. The ranks of the Turks were for centuries recruited, not only by that profoundly statesmanlike scheme of forced conversions which created the Janissaries (1326-1675), but by what Protestants ought surely to be able to understand—a moral revolt against an idolatrous Christianity which was but a paganism with its

---

[1] I allude to Mr. Baber's remarkable discovery in this region of three millions of Lolos, whom he took, on first seeing them, for Europeans. See *R. Geog. Soc. Supplementary Papers*, 1882; and compare Gill, *River of Golden Sand*, vol. ii. p. 272.

[2] Not predecessors only, as in the case of the Tzar, but direct ancestors of the Sultan took to wife Byzantine princesses.

gods renamed. Hence it has come to pass that, in many provinces of the Ottoman Empire—Bosnia, for instance, Albania, and Crete—the majority of the so-called Turks were, and are, of the purest Aryan, or at least White blood of the country, though they happen to be descendants of men who saw good—doubtless from as mixed motives as those which influenced most Christian Protestants—to embrace the Protestantism of Islam. Aryan thus, in very great part, is the blood of the so-called Turks; and so far as, in Asia Minor, it is not Armenian or Greek, it is, and predominantly perhaps, Circassian. And the Circassians of, at least, the higher orders, with whom alone the Osmanlis intermarried, are, as we have seen,[1] with the Georgians, the purest contemporary representatives of the Archaian White Stock.[2] As I have already had occasion to say, one finds a distinctly Tatar type among the Russians. No Tatar type, however, does one find among the Osmanlis. And hence the ethnological fact is precisely the reverse of that assumed by popular ignorance, misled, for party purposes, by "Liberal" politicians.

[1] P. xxiii.
[2] With reference to such a descent, the Crescent symbol of the Osmanlis becomes very significant. For the chief deity of the Chaldeans was the Moon-Goddess, of whose widespread worship we find topographical traces from Asia Minor to Arabia. *Ai*, the Turkish word for "Moon," is, indeed, masculine, but this change of gender may be due to the linguistic influence of Arabic. Note also that a Christian Greek, quoted by Pashley (*Travels in Crete*, vol. ii. p. 36), distinguished himself as a Sun-worshipper from the Turk who was a Moon-worshipper. Ἐγὼ προσκυνῶ τον ἥλιον, καὶ ὁ τοῦρκος τὸ φεγγάρι. It is also worthy of notice that, rich as Ottoman literature is in tales, there is no tradition or trace in it connecting the Osmanlis with Tatars.

But from the new ethnological theory of the Origin of Civilisation indicated in the introductory paragraph, three conditions may be deduced which must be fulfilled by any true solution of the problems of Semitic and of Aryan origins. First, the locality must be one in which such a new race could have ethnologically—and, secondly, philologically—arisen as a Variety of the Archaian White Race; and, thirdly, it must be such as to make easily possible the historical facts of dispersion and early civilisation. Such conditions seem to be fulfilled by localising Semitic origins in Central and Northern Arabia. And as hardly any ethnological question can now be satisfactorily treated without more or less directly leading to the consideration of the problem of Aryan origins, I shall conclude these notes on the Ethnography of Turkey with a brief indication of the grounds of an hypothesis which appears to fulfil those deduced conditions of a true solution of the problem.

The first set of facts to be considered are the following:—The Aryans, on our first historical knowledge of them, are in two widely separated centres—Transoxiana[1] and Thrace[2]; to Transoxiana

---

[1] The earliest local traditions of the Aryans are probably those of the *First Fargard of the Vendıdad*. The date, however, of the *first* Aryan settlements in Transoxiana is conjectural. But there were Aryan tribes in Kwarism (the modern Khiva) in 1304 B.C. See *Central Asia* (Sir H. Rawlinson), *Q. Rev.*, Oct. 1866.

[2] The date of the first settlement of the Aryans in Thrace may be as uncertain as that of their first settlement in Transoxiana. But it is admitted not only that the Thrakians were Aryans; but that, from the Thrakian stock the Greeks were derived, as, from the related Phrygian stock, the Armenians; and this necessarily gives to the Aryan settlements in Thrace the date of, at least, 1500 or 2000 B.C. And as Teutons are

as a Secondary Centre of Dispersion, the Eastern Aryans, and to Thrace, as a Secondary Centre of Dispersion, the Western Aryans, can, with more or less clear evidence, be traced; and the mid-region north-west of Transoxiana, and north-east of Thrace —and which may be more definitely described as lying between the Caspian and the Euxine, the Ural and the Dniester (or Pruth-Danube?), and extending from the 45th to the 50th parallel of latitude—suggests itself as such a Primary Centre of Origin and Dispersion as would fulfil the above-stated conditions. For the second set of facts to be considered reveal a White Race of which, if the Aryans originated in this region, they might naturally be a Variety. Such are the facts which connect the Finns, both in their Tavastian and their Karelian branch, with that non-Semitic and non-Aryan White Stock which I have distinguished as Archaian[1]; which prove that, so late as the ninth century of the Christian era, these Finns extended south of Moscow; and further, that they were, at an earlier period, probably in contact with the Archaian Races of the Caucasus,[2] though, at a still earlier period, they may have been separated

unknown to history till eleven or sixteen hundred years later (the fourth century B.C.), there certainly appears to be a Chauvinism unworthy of men of science in German pretensions that Germans are the only real Aryans, Germany the only true Aryan cradle-land, and Indo-German the only right name for Slavs and Kelts, so far as their being Aryan at all is admitted. See O. Schrader, *Sprachvergleichung*, ss. 444–6.

[1] See Retzius, *Finiske Kranier*, and De Quatrefage's *Hommes fossiles et Hommes sauvages.*

[2] From one of these, the *Meschech* of the Hebrews, Μόσχοι of the Greeks, and *Meschag* of the Armenians, the name of Moscow, and Muscovy may perhaps be derived. See Lenormant's dissertation on this people, *Origines*, t. ii., 2me ptie., pp. 181–249.

from them by that ancient Mediterranean formed by the junction of the Caspian and the Euxine.[1] So far as to ethnological, and now as to philological conditions. In the contemporary language of the Finnic groups, Professor De Lacouperie thinks that we may detect survivals of a former language presenting affinities with the general characteristics of Aryan speech;[2] in the physical conditions of this *Punjab*—or rather, indeed, Region of *Seven* Rivers—there were the conditions necessary for the development of such tribes as not only Language but Archæology show the Aryans to have been; and in those great geological changes of, as would appear, comparatively recent date—the upheaval of the Urals, and the draining off of the Central Asian Mediterranean [3]—there would certainly have been further conditions naturally resulting in the formation of a new variety of the Archaian White Stock. A fourth set of veri-

[1] Even so late as two centuries ago there would appear to have been water communication between the two seas. And M. Elisée Reclus suggests the possibility of such a canal between the Euxine and the Caspian as would make it possible for a steamer sailing from Gibraltar to reach the Himalayan region of the Upper Oxus.—*Geog. Univ., L'Europe Scandinave et Russe.*

[2] This appears to be the form in which Prof. De Lacouperie would express at once his partial dissent from, and partial assent to, that theory of the derivation of Aryan from Finnic, which is now gaining currency among scholars.

[3] With these geological events may also have been connected the rending asunder of Asia and Europe, to form the straits of the Bosphorus and the Dardanelles, and give issue to the Euxine; and of Olympus and Ossa, to form the Vale of Tempe, and give issue to the lake formerly occupying what are now the plains of Thessaly. And in a forthcoming paper in the *Babylonian and Oriental Record* I hope to show grounds for identifying the traditional Deluge with the actual Deluge which must have been the result of the geological events thus indicated, and all connected probably with what French geologists distinguish as the *Soulèvement du Tenare.*

fying facts are such links of relationship between the various Aryan languages, as geographically spoken in historical times, such links of relationship as appear to postulate a common speech in that very area above indicated,[1] and where an ancient Aryan language still survives along with primitive Aryan Customs.[2] For such a common speech would have a different class of differentiations on the Asiatic, and on the European side, caused by the different linguistic reactions of conquered non-Aryan tribes on primitive Aryan speech, or the dialects of it already developed in those great river-partitioned plains.[3] And the fifth, and, as I venture to think, almost conclusively verifying, set of facts are those which prove that, immediately on their separation from such a Primary Centre of Dispersion as that supposed by this theory, the nomadic Aryan Shepherds would come into contact, in Thrace, with a Pelasgian, and in Transoxiana, with a Medic, or rather Proto-Medic, Archaian Civilisation derived from the Chaldean; and hence, that such a Primary Centre of Dispersion as that indicated would fulfil the third of the above deduced

---

[1] See the map and diagram of Aryan languages in the Rev. Canon Taylor's admirable *multum in parvo* on *The Origin of the Aryans*, pp. 253–269. For this map and diagram appear to me to give incomparably more support to the here-suggested localising of Aryan Origins in the plains of Southern Russia, than to that localising of the Aryan Home in the plains of Northern Europe, and particularly of Germany, contended for by Geiger (*Zur Entwickelungsgeschichte der Menschheit*, pp. 113-150, 1871) and Cuno (*Forschungen im Gebiete der alten Völkerkunde*, 1871) and supported by Friedrich Müller, and the learned Canon.

[2] See *The Customs of the Ossetes* in *Journal of the R. Asiatic Soc.*, vol. xx., summarising the results of the *Ossete Studies* of Kovalefsky and V. Miller.

[3] Compare Delbrück, *Einleitung in das Sprachstudium*, ss. 131-7.

d

conditions of a true solution of the problem of Aryan Origins.

But I cannot conclude even outlines of such a theory without mentioning the names of Latham, who, in 1851,[1] first questioned, at least, the Central Asian Theory of Aryan Origins, overbearingly maintained by Professor Max Müller; of Benfey,[2] who, after Latham's questioning had been for seventeen years ignored or ridiculed, first supported it by the suggestion of a North Euxine Cradle-land;[3] and of De Lacouperie, who, in 1888, made a similar but more definitely formulated suggestion.[4] The solution, however, of the problem of Aryan Origins above outlined was reached by me in ignorance of Benfey's, and previously to De Lacouperie's suggestion, and simply as a fulfilment of conditions of solution deduced from a far more general theory—that new ethnological theory of the Origin of Civilisation which I first published in the Spring and Autumn of 1887,[5] and which my researches since then appear

---

[1] In his *Germania*, lxvii. p. cxxxvii. Compare his *Native Races of the Russian Empire*, 1854; and *Elements of Comparative Philology*, 1862.

[2] In his *Vorwort* to Fick's *Wörterb. der Indogerm. Grundsprache*, s. ix. 1868.

[3] Thus indicated by him in the *Allg. Zeitung*, 1875, p. 3270:—"In der Gegend nordwärts des Schwartzen Meeres, von den Mündungen der Donau bis zum Kaspisee verlegt."

[4] "Should the former changes of climate and soil have permitted it some five thousand years ago, the region bordering the Caspian, north and west, may have been the seat of the Aryan formation, and therefore the Primitive Home of the Race."—*Academy*, May 5, 1888.

[5] The Papers referred to were entitled respectively, *The White Races, the Founders of the First Civilisations*, read at the Meeting of the Royal Historical Society, April 21, 1887; and *The Archaian White Races, and their Place in the History of Civilisation*, read at the Meeting of the British Association, September 1, 1887.

to have further verified. And this deduced solution of the problem of the Origin and Primary Centre of Dispersion of the Aryans, I hope to verify—to prove, or disprove—not only from ethnological, philological, and historical facts already ascertained, but from a projected personal exploration of the North Caucasian region indicated.

NOTE ON THE ETHNOGRAPHICAL MAP.

1. YET another deduction from this new ethnological theory of the Origin of Civilisation has led to the Colour-scheme of the accompanying Ethnological Map. For—if the currently granted postulate of the original homogeneity of Mankind is not granted; and if, on the contrary, our theory of the Origin of Civilisation is based on the fact of—so far as we can say—the original heterogeneity of Mankind; the fact of the extraordinary permanence, not only of the physical, but of the mental characteristics of Races; and, above all, on the fact that the foundation of the Earliest Civilisations was due to the action of a certain Higher White on Lower Coloured and Black Races, and that the Later Civilisations were either founded on Civilisations due to this same stock of White Races, or to these White Races themselves in their world-wide distribution—it will be seen to be of the highest importance, not only to gain knowledge of the Hybridism of Races, but to possess a Colour-scheme by which the results of investigation of this Hybridism may be ocularly presented. And this Map is presented as a first and faltering attempt at what, in even approximate perfection, is an achievement of the future—a scientifically based Colour-representation of the Races of Mankind as what they now chiefly are—Hybrids of various Classes.

INT.] NOTE ON THE ETHNOGRAPHICAL MAP. liii

2. The following are the general principles of this Colour-scheme. The three Primary Varieties of Mankind—or what may conveniently be provisionally assumed to be such—are represented by the three Primary Colours—Red, Green, and Blue. These Varieties may be named: (I.) The Black-skin, or Melanochroan;¹ (II.) The Coloured-skin, or Pœkilochroan;² and (III.) the White-skin, or Levkochroan.³ Following, so far, at least, the Colour-scheme of the Egyptian Ethnographers of three or four thousand years ago, I would indicate the White Races by *red* and its modifications; the Coloured Races by *green* and its modifications; and the Black Races by *blue* and its modifications. Hybrids of the Primitive Varieties I would indicate by the complementary or Secondary Colours—Sea-green (green added to blue), for the cross between Coloured and Black Races; Pink (blue added to red), for the cross between Black and White; and Yellow (red added to green), for the cross between White and Coloured Races. And for what here more particularly concerns us—the White Races and the Coloured Races without black blood—I would take the colours containing no Blue. Shades Red (Vermilion) may thus denote the Archaian White Races; shades of Yellow Red (Orange) the Eastern; and shades of Dark Red (Crimson Lake), the Western Aryans.⁴

---

¹ Μελανό-χροος, as in *Od.* xix. 246. In folk-songs, blondes and brunettes are celebrated as "ἄστραις καὶ μελάχροιναις."
² Ποικιλό-χροος, as in Arist. *ap.* Ath. 319 c.
³ Λευκό-χροος, as in Eurip. *Phœn.* 322.
⁴ See Benson, *Science of Colour.* Sections at right angles with the primary axes of Red, of Green, and of Blue, p. 27 and coloured plate.

The following are the Maps I have chiefly used :—
Language Map of the Turkish Empire (British and Foreign Bible Society), 1888; the *Future Map of the Balkan Peninsula* issued semi-officially by the Greeks, 1886; Kiepert's *Ethnographische Uebersicht der Europäischen Orients*, 1878; Lejean's *Carte ethnographique de la Turquie d'Europe, et de ses états vassaux autonomes*, 1876; *Carta d' Epiro compilata dietro gli studi fatti negli anni* 1869-75, dal R. Console De Gubernatis; *Ethnographische Karte von Russland* nach A. F. Rettich von A. Petermann. And as to my corrections from personal observations, I may say that I not only found the distribution of the Bulgarians in Macedonia far wider, and their numbers far greater, than I had been led to believe; but that, along even the coast of Thrace, I found the Greek line far thinner than it is usually represented. Fishermen's huts on the shore were occupied by Greeks; but farms, of which the fields ran down to the beach, were tilled by Bulgarians. My representation, however, of the ethnography of Bulgaria I desire to be considered as merely provisional. For even Dr. Kiepert's Map is practically worthless here, because, most erroneously identifying Race with Language, he represents Osmanlis and Tatars by the same colour. And still more provisional, unfortunately, must my representation of the ethnography of the Anatolian Peninsula be considered. For Dr. Kiepert's "Map of the Western Part of Asia Minor" is still announced as only "nearly ready for publication;" while his Map of the whole of Asia Minor he only "hopes to be able to publish in the course of next year."

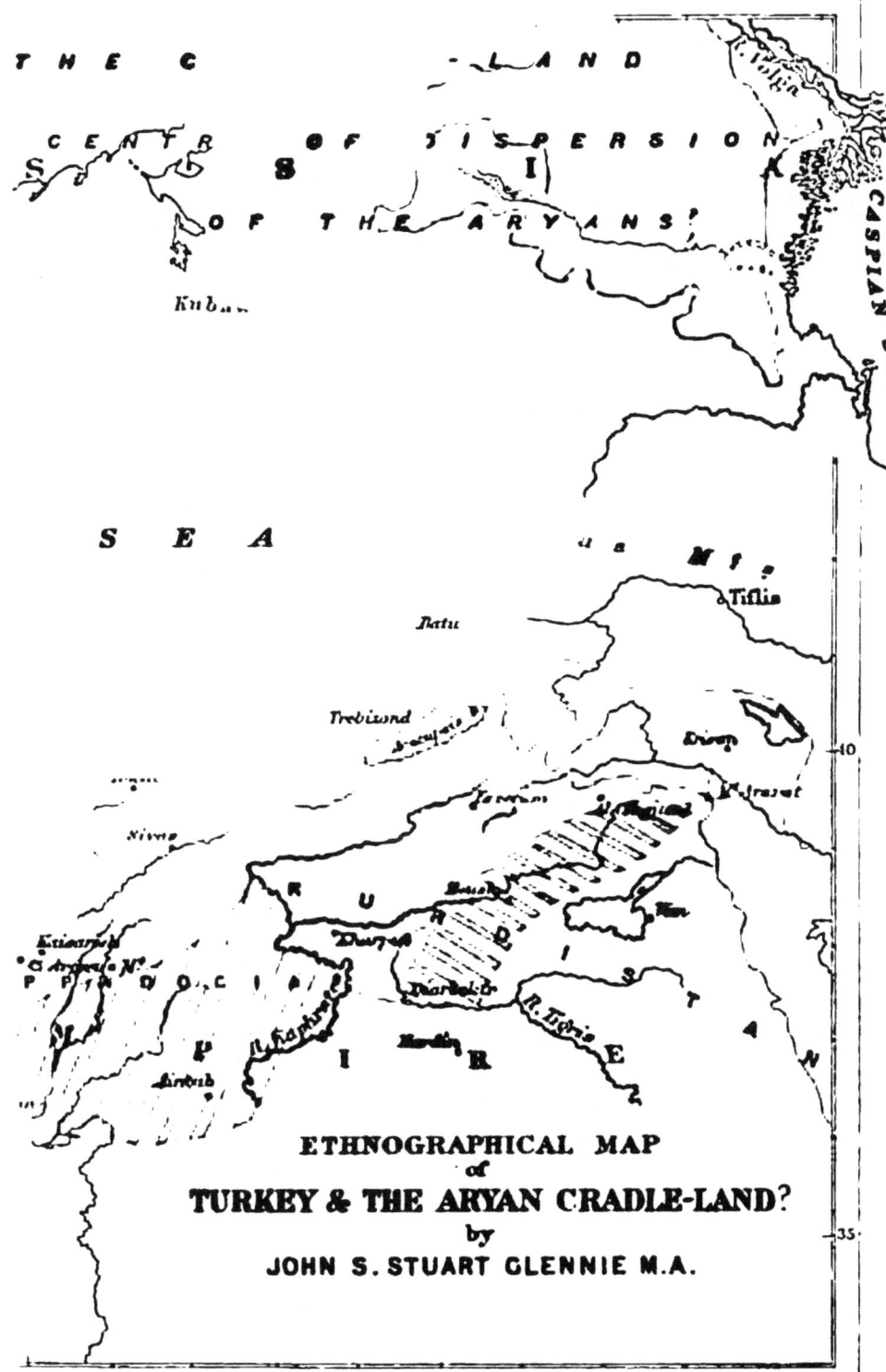

INTRODUCTORY CHAPTER II.

FOLK-CONCEPTIONS OF NATURE.

WE have seen that a new theory of the Origin of the Aryans appears to be a verifiable deduction from that new ethnological theory of the Origin of Civilisation, of which I have briefly indicated the grounds in the introductory paragraph of the foregoing chapter. An even more important, and also, as I venture to think, verifiable, deduction from that new General Theory is a new theory of the Origin of Mythology. For if Social Evolution can no more arise (as believed, however, by Mr. Spencer) from the action of "External Factors" among which a Higher Race is not included, than offspring can be born of a Female, without the inclusion of a correlated Male, among the "External Factors"; and if the fact is, that all the Civilisations, of which we know anything, originated in the action either of naturally Higher, or of—through already acquired arts of Civilisation—artificially Higher, on either naturally or artificially Lower Races—then, evidently, the development of Mythology, no less than the development of Religion and of Civilisation generally, will be regarded as originating, and being worked out, in the action and reaction of two different Ethnological Elements, or products of such Elements. In the case of Mythology, these reacting elements are Culture-lore and Folk-lore—the one, the product either of an ethnologically or economically Higher, and the other, either of an ethnologically or economically Lower Race. And in a true theory of Mythology, both these Elements will have such due weight attached to them as may be justified by the facts of Ethnology and of History.

Hitherto we have had two great schools of theorists with regard to the origin of Mythology and Religion—first, that of the Culture-lorists, and now that of the Folk-lorists—first, those who derived their facts from the records of Culture, and particularly from Vedic Hymns and Sanskrit Etymologies; and now, those who derive their facts from the records of Folk-lore, and particularly from Savage Customs and Missionary-reported Beliefs. But if Civilisation originated, as everything we know of the historical origin of Civilisation leads us to believe that it did originate, in the action of intellectually Higher on intellectually Lower Races[1]—then, it will be impossible to follow the present school of Folk-lorists in attributing to the White Founders of Civilisation myths of no higher character than those of the lowest contemporary Negroids or Mongoloids—nay, it will become a question whether,

---

[1] And considering that all the evidence points to the existence of at least more than one race at the earliest period at which we find any number of human remains (see, for instance, Hamy and De Quatrefages' *Crania Ethnica*), the persistency with which the postulate of a single sort of "Primitive Man" is maintained is certainly remarkable.

some, at least, of these contemporary Savage myths may not be mere distortions of misunderstood hieroglyphic expressions of the cosmogonic ideas of the class of wealthy and leisured speculative thinkers which we know existed among the Archaian White Rulers of subject Lower Races. Nor, when one duly considers the numerical proportion between these White Colonists and the Πολύ πλῆθος ἀνθρωπῶν, " the vast multitude of people," living ἀτάκτως," lawlessly," καὶ ὥσπερ τὰ θερία, "and after the manner of beasts,"[1] will it be supposed likely that the Otherworld myths received their systematic elaborations without deliberate intention of making political use of so potent a means of terrorising into, and maintaining in subjection. For every tyrant has been of the opinion frankly expressed by Napoleon, " Priests are the most splendid gifts which Heaven can make to a Government." And thus we get three elements through the action and reaction of which we may explain the origin and history of Mythology and Religion. First, the higher ideas of Culture— not only the astronomical generalisations[2] which led to those successive theories of the Year, which have so profoundly influenced the Rituals of all Religions; but also those ideas of the Oneness of the Universe, or, at least, Unity of God, and hence fictitiousness of the Gods of the popular Religions, which now and again partially escaped from the Colleges of Priests, and particularly, for instance, in the great Revolution of the sixth century B.C. : Secondly,

---

[1] Berossos, Χαλδαϊκα.
[2] See Epping, *Astronomisches aus Babylon.*

systematically terrorising elaborations, by Priestly Rulers, of popular superstitions, and especially with reference to the supposed Other-world; and under this head may be included the reaction on thought of the hieroglyphic forms in which ideas were expressed: And thirdly, the simpler Folk-superstitions of the Lower Races themselves, and of those of naturally higher endowment, reduced, in later times, to the intellectual level of the Lower Races by penury and oppression; but with respect to these Folk-superstitions it must be noted that they are certainly, in many cases, but fancifully expressed traditions of historical facts—such, for instance, as the former existence of Giants and Dwarfs.[1]

But just as we must distinguish Culture-conceptions and Folk-conceptions of Nature, and take account of their perpetual action and reaction from the very origin of Civilisation; so must we also distinguish at least two very different forms of Folk-conception. And seeing that three-fourths of the facts collected in these volumes with respect to the Women of Turkey are facts of Folk-lore, an Introductory Chapter dealing with the characteristics and relations of Folk-conceptions of Nature may possibly be of interest to the scientific reader. For to characterise these Folk-conceptions in relation to later Culture-conceptions will define Strata of Human Belief which will give the same sort of interest and

[1] My long cherished belief that the Northern Fairies were no mere creatures of popular fancy has been confirmed, not merely by the discovery of still existing Races of Dwarfs, but by finding that, in South-eastern Europe, where they would probably be sooner extirpated than in the North, there are apparently no traces of such beings in Folk-lore.

instructiveness to what would otherwise be isolated facts, as the theory of Geological Strata gives to a collection of the fossils which at once define Strata, and have significance given to them by the theory of the succession of Strata. And, fortunately, whatever theoretical differences there may be as to the nature of the Strata of Human Belief, and the causes of their succession, there can be none as to the general characteristics of the various Conceptions of Nature which define these Strata.

1. The first of these Strata of Belief is characterised by a conception of all the objects of Nature as themselves living; not as living because they are the abodes of Spirits; but as living because of their own proper powers, or because they are Self-powers.[1] Certain theories, which I shall presently more particularly specify, tend unfortunately to make the realisation of this conception of Nature difficult and obscure. A course, however, of the study of Folk-lore with an effort, at least, at sympathetic insight into the conceptions expressed in Folk-poesy, and given practical effect to in Folk-custom, can hardly, I think, but result in a realising understanding of this conception of Nature as living—this conception of it as made up of Will-powers, or say rather, perhaps, Self-powers—this undifferentiating conception of all things as possessed of sentiments and wills because of their own proper

---

[1] I am indebted to Professor De Lacouperie for the suggestion of this term as, perhaps, more clearly connoting what I mean by the conception of objects "as themselves Will-powers."

nature, and not because of the indwelling of a soul, *anima*, or spirit. Realise this conception of Nature, and not only will there be gained a new understanding of, and delight in, Folk-poesy, but there will flash upon one new intelligence of innumerable hitherto unintelligible customs. Consider, for instance, the superstition of the Evil Eye. We are now beginning to see that belief in the Evil Eye has, like so many other superstitions, a basis in scientifically ascertained facts—the psycho-physical facts now generally, but inadequately, qualified as "Hypnotic." But apart from this basis in ascertained facts, is not belief in the Evil Eye, and in the efficacy of counter-charms, a quite intelligible, and, indeed, necessary, result of the above-defined conception of Nature? Suppose all the objects of Nature to be conceived as living, and as related to each other in mutual sympathies, and will it not necessarily follow that a malignant wish, accompanied by a sinister look, will be believed to have evil effects? And will it not likewise follow that, in a world of which all the parts are conceived to be thus sympathetically connected, certain objects, words, and gestures will be believed to have the effect of counter-charms?

2. This Folk-conception of Nature, as itself living, is usually designated "Fetichism." Professor Tylor, however, thinks that it will "add to the clearness of our conceptions" if we "give the name of 'Animism' instead of 'Fetichism,' to the state of mind which sees in all nature the action of animated life, *and* the presence of innumerable spiritual beings." In other

words, Dr. Tylor thinks that it will "add to the clearness of our conceptions" if we give the name of "Animism" to two conceptions of Nature which are not only different, but which, according to the Professor's own contention, have two different origins—the origin of the one being a primitive tendency "quite independent of the Ghost-theory," and the origin of the other being entirely derived from the Ghost-theory. But I submit that the notion of an object "acting by its own will and force" is so distinctly different from "the action of some foreign spirit entering into its substance, or acting on it from without," that it is in the highest degree unscientific to give the same name to two notions thus utterly different. And hence I venture to think that the term "Animism," as used by Dr. Tylor, is one of the most contradictory in its different meanings, and the most inimical, therefore, to clear ideas that has ever been introduced into, and had a vogue in science.[1]

[1] As I am passing these sheets for press, I have the satisfaction of finding a similar opinion expressed by Professor Max Müller in his Gifford Lectures on *Natural Religion*, p. 158: "Animism .... has proved so misleading a name that hardly any scholar now likes to employ it. .... In itself it might not be objectionable, but unfortunately it has been used for a totally different phase of religious thought, namely, for the recognition of an active, living, or even personal element in trees, rivers, mountains, and other parts of Nature. .... Nay, Fetichism has been identified with Animism, and defined as the capability of the soul to take possession of anything whatsoever." It is, however, seventeen years now since I first entered my protest against this most disastrously confusing and obscuring term, and proposed instead, as above, the plain word *Spiritism*, and that, among other reasons, on the ground that it "explains itself at once as the doctrine of Spirits," and, therefore, as the direct antithesis of the Fetichist, or, as I now prefer to name it, Zoönist conception of Nature. See *The New Phil. of History*, p. 11, note 2.

3. The self-contradictions in which Professor Tylor involves himself while professing, on one page, a belief in Fetichism precisely as it was defined by Comte, and reducing it, on the next page, "to a mere secondary development of the doctrine of Spirits," were long ago exposed by Mr. Herbert Spencer.[1] Mr. Spencer's own theory, however, is, I submit, no less paradoxical than Dr. Tylor's is self-contradictory. Three Stages of Intelligence are distinguished by Mr. Spencer: the "cirrhiped and seafly" stage, in which there is no discrimination between animate and inanimate; a second—the general animal stage—in which there is an almost perfect discrimination between animate beings and inanimate things; and a third, or human stage, after the development of the Ghost-theory, in which there is again non-discrimination between animate and inanimate, even as in the first stage, but due now to that disastrous Ghost-theory, the consequence of speculation on dreams and shadows.[2] The essential fallacy of this paradoxical theory will, I think, be found in the assumption that what every creature was compelled "under penalties of death by starvation or destruction" to discriminate between, was "the animate" and "the inanimate." For the fact, of course, is, that every creature is compelled to discriminate simply between things, whether "animate or inanimate," that the creature may eat, and the things, whether "animate or inanimate," that the creature may be eaten by.

4. I must here, however, pass on to suggest for

[1] In *Mind*. [2] See *Principles of Sociology*, or *Epitome*. pp. 354 *seq*.

that conception of Nature in which "animate" and "inanimate" are not discriminated, a better designation, perhaps, than "Fetichism." For this conception of Nature, as may be further apparent in the sequel, is of the most general character, and has the most varied expression. But the term "Fetichism" cannot be well used in a highly generalised sense, because of the associations connected with its low origin in the Portuguese *Fetico*, and which still cling to it inseparably. Either in themselves, however, or in their English derivatives, the Greek words —Ζάω, Ζῶ, Ζωή, Ζωός, Ζῶον, κ.τ.λ.—are sufficiently familiar to make "Zoönism" immediately understood as denoting some conception or other of *life*. And hence, it may very readily denote a conception of the objects of the physical environment as Self-powers, or as themselves Will-powers, whether these objects are of the most sublime or of the meanest character: both such a higher Fetichism as that recorded by Pausanias[1] in the chant of the Peleiades Priestesses of Dodona—

Γῆ καρποὺς ἀνίει, διὸ κλῄζετε μητέρα Γαῖαν

(Earth bringeth forth fruits, Mother, therefore, call Earth!)

and such a lower Fetichism as that observed by Habakkuk[2]—"They sacrifice unto their net, and burn incense unto their drag, because by these their portion is fat, and their meat plenteous."

5. But if we must recognise a stratum of Zoönist belief—a fact which is recognised by Mr. Spencer, notwithstanding his paradoxical theory

---

[1] X. xii. 10. [2] Ch. i. 26.

of it as secondary, and by Dr. Tylor, notwithstanding his self-contradictory labelling of it as secondary—no less certainly must we recognise a stratum of what may, I think, in contradistinction to Zoönism, be most aptly, perhaps, termed Spiritism. As, by the former term, I would denote the conception of the objects of Nature as themselves Will-powers; by the latter term I would denote the conception of more or less independent Will-powers, more or less intimately associated with the objects of Nature, and of every sort of fantastic shape—anthropomorphic, theriomorphic, chimeramorphic. According to the Zoönist conception of things, there is but *one* Living World, in which every single thing is conceived as akin to every other thing, sympathetically actable on by other things, and transformable into every other thing. According, on the other hand, to the Spiritist conception of things, there are *two* worlds—the Natural World, and that quite literally Supernatural World which is the result of the exercise of the imagination in the creation of beings whose forms are the mere symbols of the Wills attributed to them in their action on Nature. But there is not only a notable intellectual difference between these two conceptions of Nature, but an even more notable, because less noted, moral difference, or difference of sentiment. In the Zoönist conception of it, Nature is almost unexceptionally regarded, not only with affection, but with touching confidence in reciprocated affection. On the other hand, in the Spiritist conception of it, Nature is regarded as but the theatre of the action of beings for the most part malignant and malevolent; beings whose favour can be gained only by atoning sacrifices, and such propitiatory flatteries as attribute to them qualities belied by the fears prompting these flatteries; beings whose favour, notwithstanding these sacrifices and flatteries, one may either lose by some treacherous caprice, or never gain because of predestination to perdition.

6. Mr. Spencer and Dr. Tylor agree in deriving this world of Spirits, whether lowest Demons, or highest Deities, from that theory of Ghosts which they believe to be a necessary result of necessary reflection on dreams, shadows, &c. It would be irrelevant here to enter on a detailed criticism of this theory of the origin of Spirits, but one or two remarks may be permitted. And first, I may say that I very much question whether Ghosts, as conceived by Messrs. Spencer and Tylor, are not a merely Christian, and Western Christian, superstition. I think I may say that, in Eastern Folklore, or, at least, in the Folk-lore of the Women of Turkey, there are no Ghosts in the usual Western sense of the word—" as the air, invulnerable."[1] The notion is rather that of "sheeted dead" who leave the "graves tenantless," like those who

> A little ere the mightiest Julius fell,
> Did squeak and gibber in the Roman streets.[2]

If, for instance, due reverence is not observed in washing a Moslem corpse, the maladroit washer will not be haunted by the boneless Ghost, but— as veraciously recorded by Evliya Effendi[3]—kicked

---

[1] *Hamlet*, act i. sc. 1.   [2] *Ibid.*   [3] *Travels*, Oriental Transl. Fund.

by the bony foot of the corpse. Again, if an old building is haunted, it is haunted, not by the *ghost* of a former occupant, but by the *djin*, or *tellestim* which came into existence on the erection of the building, and is its guardian. According to Mr. Spencer's theory, Spirits are associated with inanimate objects because of the multitude of Ghosts which are ever flitting about. According to the facts of Eastern Folk-belief, Spirits are associated with inanimate objects because the very formation of these objects implies creation of their Spirits. Again, if a dead person " re-visits the glimpses of the moon," it is not as a Ghost, but as a Vampire, with body and soul united, as formerly. Hence a Vampire is believed to be effectually "laid," not by such wordy formalities as "lay" Western Ghosts, but by such practical processes as disinterring and burning the body, or, at least, driving a stake through the heart. We now know that the Vampire superstition can be traced back to ancient Chaldea.[1] We also know that, in Ancient Egypt, bodies were preserved with such careful embalmments as appear certainly to testify to a belief that the existence of the soul was dependent on that of the body. And when, in Modern Greek superstition, we find that it was not the mere ghost, but the resuscitated body of Thanasé Vaghia that was dragged from its grave; and that this was accomplished, not by the ghosts, but by the actual hands and teeth of his massacred victims; we are led to a more careful reading of the Witch of Endor texts, and then find that it was not the mere

---

[1] See *below*, pp. 136-7.

ghost of Samuel, but Samuel himself whom the Witch called up.[1] In a word, Spirits in the East seem to be either what may be generally termed Djins, or, they are Vampires. And as most *Djins* are so indissolubly connected with some object of Nature or Art that the destruction of the one is the death of the other, so every Vampire is so indissolubly connected with its own body, that its *post-mortem* crimes can be put an end to only by the destruction of its corpse.

7. But if questionable is the actuality anywhere, save in Northern and Western Christendom, of such a primitive Ghost-theory as that which Messrs. Spencer and Tylor attribute to all races of mankind, their theory of the origin of all Gods in Ghosts must become in the highest degree doubtful. A great variety of facts, which I cannot here set forth, lead me to think it far more probable that the three chief varieties of mankind—the Black, Coloured, and White—were from the first as much distinguished mentally as physically, and that they were distinguished, therefore, by different conceptions of Nature. To reduce the chaos of things to an ordered unity, is no doubt the true aim of philosophy. But philosophers, as I venture to think, are too apt to imagine that this can be done only by deducing everything from one thing. I think, on the contrary, that all our later knowledge indicates the necessity of supposing at the origin of every scientifically conceived process of evolution correlated Co-existents, rather than a single Existent; and that no proposition in science

[1] 1 Sam. xxviii. 11–14.

will be found more fundamental than this: *Every Existence has a determined and determining Co-existence.* And, hence, with reference to the question before us, I think it far more probable (considering also the facts above referred to), that we shall find that the mixture now in all Folk-lores of both Zoönist and Spiritist conceptions of Nature is due, not, certainly, to a development of the Zoönist from the Spiritist conception; but *ultimately* to primitive racial differences. These primitive racial differences we may find to be similar, in their historical interaction, to those physiological differences to which sexual differences are now traced back.[1] And *proximate* causes of intermixture are those strategraphical elevations and subsidences, eruptions and overlappings, which give to Ethnography as great a variety as similar phenomena give to Geography.

8. But earlier developments can be understood only from the point of view of later, and later, only from the point of view of earlier developments. These Zoönist and Spiritist Folk-conceptions of Nature cannot therefore be clearly understood save from the point of view of the Culture-conceptions of Nature. Nor can the Culture-conception, which, in its highest form, may be called the Kosmist conception of Nature, be clearly understood save in relation to those Folk-conceptions which have contributed to its development. Consider, therefore, those conceptions of the inter-relations and inter-actions of all the parts of Nature—those enlarged conceptions of universal Reciprocal Action, which have not only been

[1] See, for instance, Geddes and Thomson, *The Evolution of Sex.*

enunciated by philosophers since Kant, but verified by the scientific discoverers of those quantitative relations which have established the principle of the Conservation of Energy. Duly consider this Kosmist conception of Nature, and particularly in its contrast with that Spiritist conception of Nature, which is common to all Supernatural Religions. Between the Zoönist Folk-conception, and the Kosmist Culture-conception of Nature, there will be found a prodigious difference in degree of verifiable accordance with the facts of things. But surely it will be evident that there is incomparably more essential community of conception between Kosmism and Zoönism than between Kosmism and Spiritism.

9. Mr. Spencer, indeed, in his "System of Synthetic Philosophy," presents us with a dead Nature, acted on by "Forces." But this is because his whole System is based on what are, in fact, but abstract metempirical entities. The Matter and Motion which he opposes to each other, in his definition of Evolution, as "an integration of Matter and a dissipation of Motion," have no separate existence whatever. Motion is inconceivable as a concrete reality save as Matter changing its relative place. As to Matter, all our later knowledge leads to the conception of it as, in all its parts, and down even to the ultimate constituents of the Elements, in a perpetual state of motion. And "Force" is mechanically conceivable only as a differential or equilibrate relation between pressures, while, as an entity, it is scientifically as inconceivable

as Mr. Spencer's "Infinite Energy."[1] In opposition to these fundamental entities of Mr. Spencer's system, I believe that I am justified in saying that modern physical research tends, in all its departments, to the establishment of a new basis of Science and Philosophy in a conception of Matter as simply space-occupying Energy, of which the manifestations depend on the relations between existents and co-existents, and of which there can be no true theory save one which co-ordinates the conceptions of all the three orders of Atoms—Ultimate, Elementary, and Cellular. But what will be the result of the development of such a conception of Matter, through that development of mathematical calculi which will make a mathematical chemistry possible? What will be the result of the new and mathematically verifiable conception of the Oneness of Nature, thus given? What will be the result of this but a verification of the essential truth, though formal error, of that Zoönist, as distinguished from Spiritist, conception of Nature, expressed—not only in the sublimest passages, and even in whole poems of the greatest Culture-poets as distinguished from the lesser ones, whose rhymes are but of "Spirits"—but expressed also by the Folk-poets, particularly perhaps by the Greek and Keltic Folk-poets, in passages, and whole poems innumerable, instinct with what Matthew Arnold felicitously called "natural magic"?

10. But that there is a relation between this latest

---

[1] Compare Mr. Fletcher Moulton's damaging, but, so far as I am aware, unrefuted criticism of the bases of Mr. Spencer's System in the *Brit. Quart. Rev.*, 1873; and Mr. Spencer's controversy with Professor Tait, *Nature*, 1879-80.

scientific conception of Matter and the Zoönist Folk-conception of Matter is also, I believe, historically provable. Very far indeed from being true is the current assumption that the Philosophy of the Greeks arose in a sort of spontaneous way—" out of their own heads." I trust to be elsewhere able to show that Greek Philosophy, no less than Greek Mythology, was based on far more ancient ideas; that the theories more particularly of the earlier Ionic philosophers, the Hylicists, were essentially but those old Chaldean cosmogonies in which Deities were rather Elements of Nature than Gods of Nature; and that those Greek Philosophies differed from these Chaldean Cosmogonies chiefly but in being expressed in such unmythologic language as corresponded with the new alphabetic, which had then begun to take the place of the old hieroglyphic, Writing. In the oldest Chaldean texts—and, by a strange irony, in none more clearly than in one which was, at first, hastily assumed to be the original of that Hebrew Creation-legend of which it was, in essential conception, the very antithesis—the Gods are expressly said to have been not yet in existence when the World, by its own Self-powers, formed itself from chaos.[1] And as to the Archaian systematisers of Chaldean Cosmogony, so to the Greek founders of European Philosophy, it was not imaginary "Spirits" of Nature, but the actual Elements of Nature themselves that were divine. It was from the Elements themselves, therefore, that Thales, Anaximander, and Anaximenes, Herakleitos

[1] See Oppert, *Trad. de quelques Textes Assyriens—Atti del IV. Cong. Internat. degli Oriental.*, 1880, p. 238.

and Empedokles, Levkippos and Demokritos, and even Pythagóras, Parmenides, and Anaxagóras endeavoured to explain the origin of the Universe. And though, no doubt, the expression given in the theories of the philosophers to the conception of the innate powers of Nature itself was incomparably higher and more abstract than that to be found in any Folk-expression of the Zoönist conception of Nature, I submit that it is still esscutially the same conception of Nature that is, in both cases, expressed.

11. Such are the relations, not only in essential notion, but in historical development, of Zoönism and of Kosmism—the one a merely fanciful Folk-conception, the other a more and more verified Culture-conception of the oneness and life of Nature, because of its own correlated Energies, and not because of actuating "Spirits." But as there is a lower and a higher Zoönism—Kosmism ; so there is a lower and a higher Spiritism—Theism. Of the relations, however, of Spiritism and that higher form of it called Theism, I need here say nothing. For Dr. Tylor and Mr. Spencer have already made pretty generally clear the relation between the expressions in Folk-poesy, of the Spiritist conception of Nature and the expressions in Culture-religions of essentially the same conception. In the Religions of Civilisation, "Spirits" are of greater potency and more abstract character than in the poesies of Folk-lore ; not only, however, in their essential character, but, according to Dr. Tylor and Mr. Spencer in their "Ghost-theory" origin, they are identical. No more, however, than Hume, in his *Natural History of Religion*, upwards of a century

ago, do either Dr. Tylor or Mr. Spencer advance any definite and verifiable theory of the development either of the higher from the lower Spiritism, or of the higher, or Kosmist, from the lower, or Zoönist, conception of the oneness of Nature. Nor, I believe, can a scientific theory of such development be stated save on the basis of such facts as those on which I found the ethnological theory of the Origin of Civilisation.

But if a new theory of the Origin of Mythology is a verifiable deduction from the new ethnological theory of the Origin of Civilisation, a new theory of the Method of Folklore-study must be a still further deduction. If Civilisation originated in the action of Higher on Lower Races, and if the direct result of such action was the rise of a wealthy and leisured literary class, not only with higher intellectual faculties, but with an incomparably more favourable environment for their exercise—then, evidently, there must have been, from the very beginning of Civilisation, a constant interaction between Culture-lore and Folk-lore. If so, however, then a new method must be followed in the study both of Culture-lore and of Folk-lore. Culture-lore and Folk-lore must be henceforth looked upon and studied as correlative —each having been influenced by, and hence, requiring to be studied with, the other.

But again, if so, then such a Classification of the facts of Folk-lore must be worked out as will enable us to institute scientific comparisons between the conceptions of Higher Races, or Higher Classes, as expressed in Culture-lore, and the conceptions of Lower Races, or Lower Classes, as expressed in Folk-lore; and such a Classification as will enable us to trace the reactions of these conceptions on each other. The principles of such a Scientific Classification I have elsewhere stated,[1] and with respect to it, therefore, I shall here premise but two remarks. A Scientific Classification, whether of Fossils or of Folk-lore, must be derived from the study of *constitution* and of *organology*—that is to say, from the study of interior *content*, rather than from the observation of external *form*. And in order, therefore, scientifically to classify the *expressions* of Folk-life, we must endeavour, first, scientifically to classify the *conceptions* of Folk-life.

CONCEPTIONS OF FOLK-LIFE.		EXPRESSIONS OF FOLK-LIFE.	
	I. Customs.	II. Sayings.	III. Poesies.
A. *Cosmical Ideas.*	(I)	(I)	(I)
(a) Ideas of Nature (b) ,, Supernals (c) ,, After-life	} Usages	{ 1. 2. Spells 3.	{ 1. Lays 2. and 3. Litanies	{ 1. 2. 3.
B. *Moral Notions.*	(II)	(II)	(II)
(a) Sexual (b) Domestic (c) Communal	} Ceremonies	{ 1. 2. Saw 3.	{ 1. Songs 2. and 3. Stories	{ 1. 2. 3.
C. *Historical Memories.*	(III)	(III)	(III)
(a) Memories of Seasons (b) ,, Heroes (c) ,, Rights	} Festivals	{ 1. 2. Reades 3.	{ 1. Ballads 2. and 3. Sagas	{ 1. 2. 3.

Customs, Sayings, and Poesies, in the various divisions and subdivisions indicated in this table, and

---

[1] See *Greek Folk-songs—Conclusion; The Science of Folk-lore;* my Papers in the *Folk-lore Journal*, March, July, and December 1886; and in the *Archæological Review*, May 1889.

amounting in all to *twenty-seven*, appear to furnish fit and related general headings for the numberless expressions of Folk-life. These expressions of Folk-life are expressions of Cosmical Ideas (or Ideas of the Universe), of Moral Notions, and of the Historical Memories of the People. Influenced, however, these have always been, by the corresponding conceptions of Culture; and similarly, and to a still greater extent, unfortunately, have the conceptions derived from the observations and reflections of the few, been influenced by Folk-conceptions—follies that have sprung but from emotional need, and undisciplined fancy.

One remark, in conclusion, I trust that I may be permitted to make. As these sheets have been passing through the press, I have had an occasional opportunity of looking into a book which none can take up without being impressed by the learning, literary skill, and ingenuity of the author—*The Golden Bough*. But surely, if I may say it with the high respect to which the author's great ability and attainments entitle him, this book is something like a *reductio ad absurdum* of the Method hitherto ordinarily pursued in studying Folk-lore. Zevs, Osiris, and all the other Sun-gods—Tree-spirits! Surely the time has come for such a new method in the study of Folk-lore as that which I have just indicated as a final practical deduction from the ethnological theory of the Origin of Civilisation.

PREFACE.

THE following description of the social position, domestic life, and folk-lore of the Women of Turkey is based, for the most part, on personal observations made during various sojourns in the East, amounting in all to eight years, and particularly at the great capitals of the Levant—Smyrna, Constantinople, and Salonica. In addition to the exceptional opportunities which were afforded me for studying the inner life of the native races, I was also able, when at Salonica, to acquire much valuable information from Mrs. Blunt, a lady of unrivalled Oriental experience, and especially while assisting her in writing *The People of Turkey*. And in order to complete, as far as possible, the knowledge personally acquired, I have consulted every available book on the East. My researches, however, save in the matter of folk-poesy, have had very small results. For the generality of travellers in Turkey might confess, with the Rev. Mr. Tozer, that "throughout our journey, the female sex may be said not to have existed for us at all."

I regret to say that I have not received from Greeks the assistance which a former work might have led me to expect. At the best, those to whom I applied for information referred me to some one else, who again referred me to a third person; though members of other Eastern Nationalities took some trouble themselves to procure for me the details I required. Especially to Mr. M. Sevasly, the Editor of the *Haïasdan*, and to Mr. M. Schéraz, the Editor of *L'Arménie*, are due my cordial thanks for their ever ready and valuable help in making the chapters on the Armenian Women as complete as possible. I have also to thank Mr. O'Conor, our Agent and Consul-General at Sofia, for his kind offer to obtain for me, through the Minister of Public Instruction, some further informatian on Bulgarian folk-lore and female education, though, unfortunately, it has not reached me in time for insertion. And I must likewise acknowledge my obligations to Mr. Stuart Glennie for many important suggestions, emendations, and additions.

Still, I am conscious that this work is, in many respects, far from complete. And as I desire that it should be full and accurate, as well, I hope, as entertaining, I should gratefully receive any further information with respect to the Women of Turkey, whether Christian, Semitic, or Moslem. And perhaps this may be the more readily given, if I add that it is my earnest desire that this book may contribute to the better understanding of these Eastern Nationalities, and excite more interest in their cause, whether Moslem or Christian. For no less intolerable is the present state of things felt to be by the great mass of the Moslem, than by the great mass of the Christian, population. And the ambitious despotism of the Czar would be a still more formidable foe to free national development than is the decaying despotism of the Sultan.

L. M. J. G.

SLOANE GARDENS HOUSE, CHELSEA, S.W.
June 5, 1890.

TO

JOHN E. BLUNT, Esq., C.B.

H.B.M. CONSUL-GENERAL AT SALONICA,

AND TO

MRS. BLUNT,

UNDER WHOSE HOSPITABLE ROOF
MUCH OF MY EUROPEAN EXPERIENCE OF

THE WOMEN OF TURKEY

WAS GAINED,

THIS WORK, THE FRUIT OF EIGHT YEARS'

SOJOURN IN BOTH DIVISIONS OF

THE OTTOMAN EMPIRE,

IS, WITH GRATEFUL RECOLLECTIONS,

Dedicated.

THE
CHRISTIAN WOMEN OF TURKEY

CHAPTER I.

VLACH WOMEN: THEIR SOCIAL STATUS AND ACTIVITIES—FAMILY CEREMONIES—BELIEFS AND SUPERSTITIONS—AND FOLK-POESY.

BEGINNING my account of the Women of Turkey with the women of the Christian nationalities, I shall deal with them in the order of the historic antiquity of these nationalities, as indicated in the foregoing *Introduction*. First, then, as to the Vlach Women. For the Vlachs appear, as has been pointed out, to have the best claim to be regarded as the representatives of the ancient Thrakian Stock of the Western Aryans. Now, we have every reason to believe that the Primitive Aryans of some 5000 years ago were nomad shepherds. And it is exceedingly interesting, therefore, to find that the best contemporary representatives of that ancient Thrako-Phrygian Stock from which first, perhaps, the Kelto-Italiots, and then both Greeks and Armenians, appear to have been off-shoots, are to this day characterised by their wandering habits, both as shepherds and as traders.

The Vlachs are, indeed, such an essentially pastoral race that their very name has become, among the surrounding people, a synonym for "shepherd." In this they are singularly unlike the Greeks, who are passionately attached to their native towns or villages, and to the dwellings of their fathers. The Vlachs have their homes in the mountain villages, where they pass the winter, but all the rest of the year they wander in communities, with their wives and children and their united flocks and herds, often travelling long distances in search of pasturage. When on the road, they make use of their tents of black goat's hair, and carry all their goods and chattels in capacious bags of hair-cloth. A Vlach encampment is a very picturesque sight. The place chosen for it is generally the common, or green, found on the outskirts of every town and village. I remember especially a large encampment outside the Vardar gate of Salonica, under the picturesque towers and bastions of those old mediæval, and, in their foundations, pre-Hellenic, walls, which have witnessed so many a siege. While the men pitch the tents, the women and girls milk the sheep and goats, and prepare the evening meal. Arrived at the pasturage, which they rent from the villagers, or, in the case of Crown lands, from the Forest-inspectors, they build themselves huts or shealings of branches, set up their *stánia*, or sheepfolds, into which the flocks are driven every evening at milking-time, and prepare for some months of dairy work. The passionate fondness of the pastoral Vlachs for this wild, out-of-door life has given rise to a popular belief in the country that, if a shepherd attempts to adopt a settled life by purchasing a field and building a house, he will soon fall ill, his flesh will rot, and engender worms.

Even the Vlachs of the burgher class, who are not flockmasters, are mostly engaged in pursuits which require them to lead a more or less nomadic life. The wealthier class consists of merchants, who trade in Italy, Spain, Austria, and Russia, and who are often absent for periods extending over many years—a mode of life which they seldom renounce until obliged by age to do so. The inferior class of traders do not, as a rule, leave the Ottoman Empire, but travel with goods of all kinds for sale from one town or village to another, like the peddlers in England in the Feudal Period, when, as in Turkey at the present day, shops were few in towns, and non-existent in the country. And there is also another industrial class of Vlachs who go to the towns for the greater part of the year to work as tailors, embroiderers, gold- and silver-smiths, &c.

The homes to which these nomadic shepherds and wandering traders return are now, as has been said, in the mountains. Previously to the Ottoman conquest, the Vlachs occupied the plains of Thessaly in such numbers that the province acquired the name of "Great Wallachia," while Ætolia and Acarnania were called "Little Wallachia." But with the true Aryan hatred of servitude and passion for self-government, they preferred a life of hardship, with freedom, in the mountains, to one of comfort, with subjection, in the plains; and, retiring before the Turks, took up their abode in the ranges of Olympus and Pindus. Here they founded numerous large villages or townships, the most considerable of which are Vlacholivádia, "The Meadows of the Vlachs," on the west of Olympus, and Mezzovo, "Mid-mountain,"[1] in the

---

[1] According to Aravandinos, the name of this town is an abbreviation of Mesovouno—Μέσο βουνόν: Συλλογὴ δημωδῶν ασμάτων, Πρόλογος.

heart of Pindus. The former contains some four hundred houses and five handsome churches with bells, presided over by a bishop; while, grouped around on the neighbouring hills, are four other Vlach villages, surrounded by fields and vineyards. Mezzovo is the most picturesquely situated town it is possible to imagine, clinging to both sides of a sublime ravine, and overhung by the highest crests of Pindus, which tower so perpendicularly on either hand that not till long after sunrise is the *Prosélion* (πρὸς ἥλιον), or "sunny side" of the town, out of shadow. The opposite side is appropriately called the *Anélion* (ἄν ἥλιον), or "sunless." Several Vlach villages surround Mezzovo also; and the most remarkable of them is Kalyarites. The hill on which it stands is so steep that the highest houses are five hundred feet above the lowest, and the vertical streets are mere zigzag paths formed into steps. In these elevated situations the snow lies for five months of the year. The villages are inhabited in winter almost exclusively by old men, priests, women, and children. Under these circumstances, there is little communication with the surrounding country, and it is customary for each family to lay in a store of oil, rice, flour, and other provisions, and also a stock of firewood.

Another of the Vlach centres is Voskopoli, "the shepherd town." A large number of Vlachs are to be found in Albania, between Antivari and Dulcigno, and also in the mountainous districts near El Bassan and Berat. And their villages are scattered all through Macedonia, Thessaly, and Epirus. The total number of Vlachs inhabiting Macedonia is computed to be some 500,000.[1] But there appear to be no trustworthy statistics of the total number of Vlachs in Turkey.

Yet, even in these mountain homes, the industry of the Vlach is conspicuous. Cornfields and vineyards clothe the hill-sides, and grapes, apples, and vegetables flourish in the gardens. The houses are small, but generally neat and well arranged, and in many cases also well furnished, according to native notions. Like those of Greek mountain villages, they are roofed with broad limestone slabs, which require, in addition to their other fastenings, heavy stones to keep them from being displaced by the furious winds to which these elevated regions are exposed, and which, in spite of all these precautions, frequently unroof the houses. The terraced gardens which surround every dwelling are well watered by streamlets from numerous fountains, which supply every part of the village with a pure cold water of which the inhabitants are justly proud. Hospitality is a marked characteristic of the Vlachs, who in this respect at least contrast favourably with the Greeks, the most inhospitable perhaps of all peoples. But though it is no uncommon thing to see a company of Vlach shepherds with their flocks, on the road to their summer quarters, it is rarely that an English traveller has an opportunity of seeing anything of the family life of this interesting people. Mr. Stuart Glennie, however, chanced to have such an opportunity; and I am indebted to the proof-sheets of his forthcoming work on *Ancient*

[1] Picot, *Revue d'Anthropologie*, tom. iv. p. 414.

Hellas for the following description of the household of a Vlach burgher at Mezzovo.

"Most snugly furnished, but in Eastern fashion, was the room in which I was installed by my Vlach, or, as he would have called himself, *Armeng*, host. There was neither chair nor table; but the floor was covered with thick, richly coloured rugs, the handiwork of the household; and along the wall on either side of the hearth, and under the windows, was a range of comfortable cushions. All the wall opposite the hearth was occupied by a most artistically designed and elaborately carved wardrobe, also of native workmanship; and thence the additional rugs, &c., were produced with which at night my bed was made up. . . . . While supper was being prepared, the usual Turkish service of coffee and cigarettes was preceded by the Græco-Slav service of preserves and a glass of cold water. For my evening meal, a Turkish *sofra*, or low round table, was brought in, and an excellent repast of various courses was served, of which I partook seated on my cushion on the floor, in the warmly coloured, brightly lighted chamber. Like the Vlachs generally, my hosts were handsome, pleasant, kindly people with innumerable pretty children. Among the bairns, particularly, the arrival of the stranger from the West appeared to cause great excitement and curiosity. But when their mother tried to put them out of the room, and away from the room-door, I begged that they might be allowed to remain. So, after a time, one after another they mustered up courage to approach, take my hand, kiss it, and press it to their little foreheads; and I kissed their fair little faces in return."

The frequent and protracted absence of the men of the family to which I have just referred, naturally throws great responsibility and various duties on the women, and these give them a social independence and influence which they would not otherwise enjoy. For the legal status of the Vlach, as of all other Christian women, is determined by the Christian Law of Marriage, and that, as we know, enforces an absolute subjection of the wife to the husband, as the necessary consequence of the indissolubility of marriage, while it gives no rights whatever as against men to any other woman than a legal wife. The Christian law of the indissolubility of marriage has been greatly relaxed by the facilities given to divorce among the Roumanian compatriots of the Vlachs in the Trans-Danubian Kingdom. But there is a great difference of manners in this respect between the Roumanian Trans-Danubian town-folk, and Cis-Danubian village-folk. And such a difference of manners the reader will at once see must necessarily arise from the social conditions above described. In hard-working village-communities where the men are only at home for short periods, causes of divorce are not likely to arise.

But though there is thus a legal subjection of the Vlach women, the circumstances of their lives give them at once great responsibility and independence. Far away as the men of the family may be, each cottage and homestead has its little field or vineyard and garden, which must be cultivated, its harvest reaped, and the produce converted into winter provisions. The domestic animals must be tended, the sheep shorn, and the wool prepared for the loom which occupies a corner of every dwelling. The Vlach women excel in the manufacture of the thick cloth called *skouti*, used for clothing and domestic purposes, and they also weave the carpets and rugs of which the furniture of their houses chiefly consists. The daughters are from an early age accustomed to both domestic and out-of-door labour, and in their capacity of shepherdesses—*Vlachopoúlas*—figure frequently in Greek folk-song. The *Vlachopoúla* may often be seen returning from the fountain or the riverside, bearing on her back, besides a barrel of water, the load of wet linen which she has washed, a metal basin poised on her head, and her untiring hands occupied in twisting thread with a spindle. Nor does she lack time to embroider in bright wools and silks, dyed with her own hands, her picturesque native costume, or to knit and stitch with coloured wools the socks she sells to the shepherds.

The proceeds of these sales she invests in the coarse silver jewellery which she delights to wear on Sundays and festivals. It requires a strong frame to support the weight of the gala dress when completed with belt, collar, bracelets, and headgear of this alloyed metal. But such a frame is characteristic of these hardy daughters of the mountains, who are often tall, and always above the middle height, well-knit, well-poised, and incapable of fatigue. For the Vlach women are, as a rule, exceedingly handsome, with regular features, dark hair and eyes, and small hands and feet. The women of Voskopolis and Monastir, and those living in the neighbourhood of Lake Ochrida, are considered the most elegant and refined of all the Southern Vlachs. The "Voskopoliotissas" are distinguished by the fairness of their skins and their lighter-coloured hair. Their countenances are fine and open, their gestures and movements most graceful, and their demeanour is particularly affable and obliging. Speaking of the men of this town, M. Picot says, "They make use of elegant phrases and refined language to every one, even to their wives."[1] The women, however, notwithstanding their greater refinement, are as industrious as the other women of their race, and do not disdain to work in the fields, tend the flocks, and fulfil all the other multifarious duties which fall to their share.

The Vlach women submit cheerfully to their laborious life, and the wives of the traders willingly add to their many duties that of waiting on their husbands with the most assiduous attention during the short and rare periods they spend in the bosom of their families. No stranger, however, can command their services, for they have an invincible repugnance to leaving their homes, to which they are devotedly attached.

The women belonging to the more sedentary portion of the Vlach population may be said to be equally well educated with the Greek women of the country towns and villages; but their nomadic sisters

---

[1] *Les Valaques de la Macédoine*, Revue d'Anthropologie, tom. iv.

naturally receive little or no education. Previous to the union of the Principalities, in 1861, under the name of Roumania, the Greek language was alone taught in their schools and used in the services of the Church. Close contact and every-day intercourse with the surrounding Greek population had also Hellenised the men of some villages, and caused them to a great extent to abandon the use of their mother tongue. But, Γυναῖκες αἵ περ μάλιστα τὴν ἀρχαίαν φωνὴν σώζουσι[1] ("It is the women who retain the old forms of speech"); and the Vlach women, though conversant with Greek, still clung to their nationality and continued to use their soft Roumanian tongue. Bolintineanu, who was greatly struck by this conservatism, as other travellers have also been, remarks that, "If ever this people escapes from servitude, if ever it possesses a cultivated language, a literature, a history—in a word, a name—it will owe it to the women."[2] The language spoken by the Vlachs of Southern Turkey still differs little from that used in the kingdom of Roumania, save for a certain admixture of Greek words, referring more particularly to modern civilised life. And within a year of the creation of Roumania, a propaganda was organised with the object of substituting, in the Vlach settlements south of the Danube, the Roumanian for the Greek language in the churches and schools. The leader of this movement was Mr. Apostolu Margaritu, a Macedonian Vlach educated at Bucharest, who, despite Greek opposition and intrigue, succeeded in many places in exciting a national feeling in his fellow-countrymen, and in

[1] Plato, Κράτυλος, 74 (Bekker, t. iv.).   [2] See Picot, as above.

inducing them to employ Roumanian instead of Greek teachers in their schools. This propaganda received a fresh impulse on the elevation of Roumania to a kingdom in 1877, by the appointment of a Roumanian Consul-General at Salonica, which city immediately became the head-quarters of an active rivalry between the two nationalities.

The customs of the Vlachs at the birth of a child do not differ materially from those of the Greeks. The Nereids feared by the latter on these occasions are merely replaced by the *Stringæ* (στρίγγοι), who, like them, are wicked spirits bearing ill-will especially to new-born infants. It is usual for those in attendance to cast a stone behind them with the words, "This in the mouth of the *Stringæ!*" The baptism is also performed according to the rites of the Orthodox Church, described at length in the chapter on Greek Family Ceremonies.[1]

Although the Vlach communities, in Thessaly and Macedonia especially, maintain, as I have already mentioned, various social relations with the Greeks, they do not to any great extent intermarry with them. Indeed, it is said that while the Vlach men occasionally take Greek brides, no Vlach girl ever marries out of her own community. But the customs connected with marriage among the Vlachs, with the exception, of course, of the religious rite, differ materially from those observed by the Greeks, and bear a considerable resemblance to the ceremonies of the ancient Romans. A young man,

[1] See below, Chap. III.

wishing to marry, employs no go-between, but goes in person to the father of the maiden of his choice, and asks his permission to wed his daughter. If he is considered an eligible match, the father assents, and the suitor ratifies the contract by opening his purse and placing some pieces of gold in the hand of his future father-in-law. A similar sum is also paid on the wedding-day, and recalls the *Coemptio* customary among the ancient Romans. The bride brings no dowry to her husband, only a trousseau and "plenishing," which she has herself manufactured from the raw material supplied by the flocks and fields, dyed in brilliant and lasting colours, and embellished with thick embroidery.

The preliminaries settled, the betrothal is publicly announced in the *stani,* or village sheepfold. A week before the day fixed for the commencement of the marriage festivities, the girls of the village go in a troop to the forest to cut firewood for the use of the young couple. They choose at the same time a branch having at its extremity five twigs. On one they fasten an apple, and on the other four, tufts of red wool. The apple is an emblem of love and maternity, and the wool is symbolical of the household thrift and industry which are the glory of every Vlach woman. This *flamboro,* as it is called, is carried in triumph back to the village, accompanied by shouts of "*Troé, flamboro! Troé, cokkella!*" when it is fixed on the roof of the bride's abode. The home ceremonies attendant upon a wedding occupy several days, and, as with the provincial Greeks, are made the occasion of great merry-making by the village maidens, who are invited to dress and adorn the bride for the ceremony, and to assist in the various domestic preparations for the important event.

On the Sunday of the wedding week the bridegroom goes, accompanied by his friends, to fetch home the bride to his father's house. On the morning of this day, while some of the girls are busy " busking the bride," others assemble, dressed in their holiday costumes, at the bridegroom's home, and while he is being carefully shaved for the auspicious occasion, they dance round him, singing wedding songs. The marriage which, so far, has taken rather the form of a sale, the singers now transform in fancy into something like a wedding by capture.

> He found the maiden all alone,
>   Beneath a willow-tree;
> And lightly took her 'neath his arm,
>   And with her far did flee.[1]

The bridegroom's toilet completed, he sets out on horseback, escorted by a number of friends on foot, for the abode of his betrothed. The arrival of the procession is announced by one of the party, who starts a little in advance of the rest. In return for his news the herald receives at the cottage door a large ring-shaped cake, for pieces of which a struggle ensues as soon as the other young men come up, the original possessor doing his best to retain it. The bride, bedizened in all her wedding finery, is led forth and mounted on a horse, and accompanied by her own friends in addition to those of the bridegroom,

---

[1] Heuzey, *Le Mont Olympe*, &c.

is conducted to her new home. On the arrival of the procession at its destination, a similar struggle takes place for a cake presented by the bridegroom's mother to the messenger who announces the approach of the bridal party. A singular rite of purely Latin origin is now performed by the bride. As she is lifted from her horse at the threshold, butter or honey is handed to her, with which she proceeds to anoint the door, signifying that she brings with her into the house, peace, plenty, and joy. The word *uxor*, originally *unxor*, is derived from *ungere*, " to anoint." A commentator on Terence thus describes this ceremony: "Uxor dicitur . . . . ab ungendis postibus . . . . hoc est quod, quum puellæ unberunt, maritorum postes unguebant."[1] The bride respectfully salutes her future father- and mother-in-law by kissing their hands before the assembled company, and is then conducted to a sofa corner, where she passes the night. On the following day the marriage ceremony is performed according to the rite of the Greek Church.[2] Feasting and dancing occupy the remainder of the day, and are resumed at intervals until Wednesday evening, when the wedded couple are left alone for the first time. On the following day the young wife may be already seen busily spinning or working at her loom in the open air, still dressed in her wedding costume.

As members of the Orthodox Church, the Vlachs have assimilated all the Christian, and many of the classical, observances of the Greeks relating to death. They still, however, retain among their funeral

---

[1] Heuzey, *Le Mont Olympe*.   [2] See Chap. III.

customs some which would appear to be survivals rather of Roman, than of Greek, pagan rites. The Lares, for instance, are still honoured on the anniversary of the saint under whose special protection each family is placed. On the days previous to these celebrations the house undergoes a thorough cleaning and whitewashing, the furniture is scrubbed and polished, and the mats and rugs are shaken and beaten, and everything is washed that will bear washing. The day is observed as a festival, and the poorest family will spread a table with dishes prepared specially for the occasion. While these are being partaken of, allusion is made to deceased relatives, to whom invocations are addressed by name. They are prayed to seat themselves at the table, where covers are laid for them, and to take their share of the good things prepared in their honour. This custom bears in some of its features a strong resemblance to the ceremony of the *Saïa*, hereafter described,[1] and in others to the family festivals, observed by the Greeks. Another pagan festival which the Vlachs, in common with the inhabitants of Roumania, celebrate in honour of the dead, is the *Rusalŭ* or *Rosalia*. This festival is held in summer, and every day of the six weeks during which it is prolonged, a tribute of fresh roses is laid on the graves of departed relatives and friends. Women and girls are careful not to wash anything in warm water while the feast of the *Rosalia* lasts, as this would be sure to bring them ill-luck. This may, perhaps, have some reference to the warm

[1] See Chap. III.

water with which it is customary to wash the dead.

The Christianity of the Vlachs, like that of the Greeks, consists chiefly in keeping fast and feast days, in the adoration of saints, holy pictures, and relics, and in the observance of all the legendary customs by which the events of the ecclesiastical year are honoured. These customs, though in the main similar to those of the neighbouring Greeks, differ somewhat in their details, and others are identical with the religious folk-customs of the Trans-Danubian Roumanians.

On New Year's Day the children take olive-branches and go from house to house to compliment the neighbours with their good wishes, in return for which they receive little presents. On the second day of the year, every stranger who may enter a house is required to throw on the fire small quantities of salt, which are placed in cups on the table for that purpose. He must then go to the hen-house and place an egg in the nest for the hen to sit upon. If the hen comes and does her duty, the guest is considered an auspicious person, and is fêted in that house until evening. This custom is called "The lucky foot."

"The Feast of the Kings" is celebrated at Epiphany, and even all through the Carnival, by boys and youths who stroll through the towns and villages performing a Scriptural play, something in the style of the "Miracles" of the Middle Ages. These players, called *Vikliemi*, or "Bethlehems," personate Herod and the "Three Kings," or "Wise Men," under the names of Melchior, Balthazar, and Gaspar. Bedecked with all kinds of frippery, and crowned with gilt paper, they present an absurd travesty of the poetical old legend of the Adoration of the Magi, all the original sacred character of the custom having disappeared in the ludicrous extravagance which now accompanies its observance. The following is a literal translation of one of the verses sung by Herod:

> I am the Emperor Herod,
> Who have mounted on horseback.
> I have taken my sword in my hand,
> I have entered into Bethlehem,
> I have cut to pieces thousands of children,
> And made the whole world to tremble.

Other bands, called *Stea*, or "Stars," make the round of the neighbourhood, carrying a great paper star with a rude representation of a cradle, and singing songs describing the apparition of the Star of Bethlehem.

Another custom which the Vlachs observe in common with the Roumanians of the kingdom is the *Filipi*. During the first weeks of Lent, cakes are made in every house and distributed to the neighbours and passers-by in memory of a legendary lame individual named Philip (Filipŭ celu schiopŭ), whom popular reverence has raised to the rank of a saint.

Thursday and Friday are still to a certain extent, as among the ancient Romans, sacred to Jupiter and Venus. During part of the spring of every year Thursday is observed as a holiday, in order to guard against hail and stormy weather which would damage the young crops. Tuesday and Friday are both considered unlucky days by the women. A vindictive female spirit, called the *Marz Sara*, or "Fairy of Tuesday Even," is particularly active on the former day, and must be guarded against; and on the latter day women and girls avoid, if possible, working with sharp instruments, such as scissors or needles.

The procession of the *Perperuda*, which I shall have occasion to describe more at length in a subsequent chapter,[1] is also an institution among the Vlach women. They, however, have their children drenched by proxy in the persons of gipsy girls. The third Thursday after Easter is the day chosen for this propitiation of the Water Deities. Crowned with flowers, the gipsies go from house to house, dancing and singing the invocation, and every housewife, after throwing over them a jar of water or milk, rewards their exertions with a cake, some flour, or a small coin.

The ceremony of the *Klithona*, observed by the Greeks on St. John's Eve,[2] is also performed by the Vlach youths and maidens under the same name, but with slight differences of detail. While the articles are being taken out of the jar, little snatches of song are sung by the girls, and good or bad luck is predicted according to whether the object has been withdrawn to a gay, or to a melancholy air.

The custom called the *Craciunŭ*, observed on the eve of Christmas, would seem to be, like our baking

---

[1] See Chap. IV. [2] *Ibid.*

of mince-pies, a survival of the Feast of the Winter Solstice. On the night of the 23rd or 24th of December, circular cakes with a hole in the centre are made in every house, and in the morning the children come round singing this Christian salutation:

> Good morrow, the advent of the feast !
> Good morrow, the advent of the *Craciunŭ*.

Then, changing their tune, they recall the Pagan character of the custom by adding these words:

> Give to me a ring-cake,
> For I am dying of cold !

A relic of ancient serpent-worship would seem to survive in the consideration paid by Vlachs to that reptile. If one of the harmless white snakes common in the country happens to enter a Vlach cottage, it is allowed to remain unmolested and supplied with food, its arrival being considered a good augury. When it has again gone forth, snake dainties are placed outside the door, and finding itself so well treated, it not unfrequently gets into the habit of paying a daily visit, when it receives the title of *Serpa di Casa*, or " house serpent."[1]

It is customary among the Vlachs of Thessaly, and also to a certain extent among those of Albania and Macedonia, to administer on a certain day in February a beating to all the dogs in the village in order to prevent their going mad during the ensuing summer. I have not, however, ascertained that this curious precaution, which is also observed by the Bulgarians, has the desired effect on the dogs, whose

---

[1] Todorescŭ, *Incercari Critice*, &c. See also Picot, *Les Roumains*, &c.

howls during the operation are certainly calculated to drive mad any unlucky auditor.

In the folk-poesy of the Vlachs, as in their folk-customs, the influence of long contact with Slavs and Hellenes is seen in the large admixture of Slav and Greek mythology with that which the Vlachs have in common with the ancient Romans. Under the names of *Babū* and *Stringa* we have the malevolent Nereid of the Greeks and the *Strouga* of the Bulgarians. The *Zmok* is directly borrowed from the Slav demonology, in which he appears as an elemental demon of the same character as the Greek Stoicheiòn. This spirit is also the jealous guardian of hidden treasures, and wily and daring indeed is the mortal who succeeds in outwitting him. Sometimes, as in the Bulgarian folk-songs, he appears as a winged dragon and carries off young maidens into the clouds, with which he is also identified. Some of the *doïnas*, as the Roumanian popular ballads are called, contain, like those of the Greeks and Bulgarians, an element of rugged savagery, here, however, accompanied and in a degree modified by the poetic grace which is characteristic of Roumanian folk-literature. The ballad of the "Monastery of Argis," while illustrating the widespread custom of offering a human sacrifice at the foundation of every important building, at the same time presents us with two types of men—Negru Voda, the *boyard* who founded the principality of Moldavia in the thirteenth century, the ruthless and capricious tyrant; and Manoli, the master-mason, the man of strong affections, who is yet capable of sacrificing everything in order to fulfil the task he has undertaken.

Many of the ballads are purely idyllic, and are full of the graceful personalising of Nature so often found in Greek folk-song. The Roumanian language possesses such cadence and harmony that in poetry rhyme can be, and is, dispensed with. The words ending in *e*, with which the lines so frequently terminate throughout a poem, are merely an accident of the language, and do not constitute a rhyme. For this, as in French, the preceding syllable is required. I have, consequently, in translating specimens of the *doïnas*, from Mr. Alecsandri's collection, followed his example in translating them into French; and, instead of cramping the expression by attempting to present them in metrical form, I have rendered them literally into poetical prose.

The Ring and the Veil.

There was once a prince, young and handsome as forest-pine on mountain-summit, who took for his wife a girl from the neighbouring village, a lovely Roumanian whom all adored, and who could be compared only to the flowers of the field which shine in the sun's rays.

But soon there came an order from the king his father, a written order commanding him to return to the camp. Sadly and mournfully he thus addressed his partner:

"My well-beloved! my soul! take this ring and

wear it on thy finger. When thou seest the rust gather upon it, know that I am dead."

"O! my dear one, take thou this silken veil with the border of gold broidery. When the gold shall melt, know thou that I am dead."

The prince mounted his horse, and started on a long march. Arrived in the depths of an ancient forest, he kindled a great fire near to the Fountain of the Raven. He put his hand into its bosom, and drew forth the silken veil. At the sight of it his heart broke with grief.

"My friends," he said, "my dear companions in arms, brave children of the *Zméï*,[1] halt here to dine, and rest in the shade of this forest. I will return to the village to look for my two-edged sword which I left on the green table in my house."

So said, he retraced his steps. On the road he met a warrior mounted on a little horse.

"Hail, young hero! What news is there in the country from which thou comest?"

"If thou must needs be told, my lord, know that this news might perhaps be good for another, but for thee it is fatal. Thy father has devastated the country, and drowned thy wife in a wide and deep pond."

At this news the prince shed bitter tears, and said: "Young man, take thou my horse and go to my father. If the king ask thee where I am, say that I have sought the shores of the pond, and have thrown myself into its waters to rejoin my young wife, my well-beloved!"

* * *

[1] Plural of Zmok. See p. 22.

The father assembled all the men from the country side to drain off the water from the pond; and when the pond was emptied he found the two children lying on the sand in a tender embrace; their hair shone like gold and their cheeks were rosy red. The king placed their bodies on richly covered biers, and had them interred near the church, the prince near the holy altar towards the east, and his bride near the door towards the west. And from the grave of the prince soon grew up a tall pine-tree, which bent over the church; and from the grave of his young wife sprang up a vine-stem, whose pliant shoots climbed along the walls until they met the pine's branches, with which they lovingly interlaced themselves.

The Cuckoo and the Turtle-dove.[1]

"Dear Turtle-dove, sweet bird, be my love till Sunday!"

"I would not say thee nay, but I say nay to thy mother, who is a wicked witch. She would reproach me ever for loving thee too much and caressing thee too often."

"Sweet Turtle-dove, be not mine enemy. Love me till next Sunday."

"No, dear Cuckoo, I will not listen to thee. Let me live in peace, or I will change myself into a little

---

[1] These two birds appear very often in Roumanian popular poetry. The cuckoo is regarded with a certain mysterious respect by the country people, and his note is considered a good or bad augury according to whether it is heard on the right or the left.

cake of white bread, moist with tears, and hide me among the ashes on the hearth."

"Whatever thou wilt do, and whatever thou wilt become, I will not leave thee alone; for I too will change myself into a little shovel, and though I may be consumed by the fire, yet will I seek thee among the ashes, and shield thee from burning. Then I will refresh thee with my breath, and cover thee with kisses, so that thou must perforce be my love, beloved Turtle-dove!"

"I would not say thee nay, but I say nay to thy mother, who is a wicked sorceress. She would reproach me ever for loving thee too much, and would throw evil spells upon me, so that I could no more caress thee. And rather than be the butt of her fault-finding, and rather than be bewitched, I would change me to a bending reed, and hide me in the bosom of a mere to escape thy pursuit."

"Whatever thou wilt do, and whatever thou wilt become, thou shalt not escape me. For I, too, will change myself into a shepherd, a player on the pipe, and I will seek in the mere for a slender reed of which to make me a flute. Then shall I see thee, and I will cut thy stem, and my lips shall cover thee with kisses. So that perforce thou must be my love until Sunday, dear Turtle-dove!"

"No, I will not listen to thee, dear and pretty grey-plumaged Cuckoo. I know how sweet life would be with thee. But, alas! thy mother is so wicked. Rather than live with her, I would change myself into a little *eikon*, and, hidden in the recesses of the church, think ever of thee."

"Whatever thou wilt do, and whatever thou wilt become, I will not leave thee in peace. For I, too, will transform myself into an acolyte or a deacon, and I will be so pious, so pious, that I shall come every day to church, from Monday to Sunday, to bow before the holy pictures and to kiss thee,[1] so that perforce thou must be my love, dear Turtle-dove!"

The Sun and the Moon.

Brother![2] one day the Sun took a fancy to be married. For nine years he, drawn by nine horses, rushed over sky and earth with the swiftness of an arrow or of the wind. But in vain did he fatigue his steeds. Nowhere could he find a spouse worthy of him, nowhere in all the universe did he see one who rivalled in beauty his sister Helen,[3] the beautiful Helen, with the long golden tresses. The Sun, when he met her, thus spoke to her:

"My dear little sister Helen, Helen with the long golden tresses, let us go and plight our troth together, for we resemble each other in our hair and in our features, and in our incomparable beauty. I have shining rays, and thou golden tresses. My face is resplendent, and thine is radiant."

"Oh, my brother, light of the world, thou who art free from all sin, such a thing as a brother and

---

[1] It is customary in the Eastern Churches to kiss the *eikons*, or holy pictures, after making the usual reverences before them.

[2] Roumanian ballads frequently commence with an invocation to some person or object. "Green darnel leaf" is a common introduction.

[3] Helen is the favourite heroine of all popular Roumanian stories and songs.

sister married together was never before seen, for it is a sin, a grievous sin."

At these words the Sun was darkened. He mounted to the throne of God, and bowed before the Lord and said:

"Holy God, our Father, the time has come for me to marry. But, alas! I have not found in the world a spouse worthy of me save my sister, the beautiful Helen with the golden hair."

The Lord God heard him. Then He took him by the hand and led him to Hell in order to terrify his heart, and afterwards to Paradise in order to enchant his soul, and thus He spoke to him (and while God spoke the sky shone gladly and the clouds had disappeared):

"Sun, O radiant Sun, thou who art free from all sin, thou hast visited Paradise and thou hast passed through Hell. Choose between the two."

But the Sun answered gaily: "I choose Hell while living, if so be that I dwell no longer alone, but with my sister Helen, Helen with the long golden hair."

* * * * *

The Sun descended to earth, he alighted at the house of his sister, and ordered them to make ready for the wedding. He decked the forehead of Helen with the golden bridal threads,[1] and placed on her head a royal crown. He dressed her in a diaphanous robe embroidered with fine pearls. Then they two repaired to the church. But during the wedding ceremony—woe to her! woe to him!—the lamps

[1] One of the usual wedding adornments. See Greek weddings, Chap. III.

went out, the bells fell down, the choir stalls were overturned, the tower trembled to its foundations, the priests became dumb, and their vestments fell to pieces. The unhappy Helen was terror-stricken; for suddenly—woe to her!—an invisible hand seized her, bore her aloft into space, and dropped her into the sea, where she was immediately transformed into a beautiful golden fish. The Sun, too, grew pale, and reascended into the blue vault. Then, sinking towards the west, he, too, plunged into the sea to seek his sister Helen, Helen with the long golden tresses. But the Lord God, who is blessed in heaven and in earth, took the fish in His hand, threw it again into the air, and transformed it into the Moon. And then He spake (and when He spoke the whole world shook, the waves of the sea were still, the tops of the mountains bowed themselves, and men trembled with terror):

"Thou, Helen with the long golden tresses, and thou, resplendent Sun, ye who are free from all sin, I condemn you to all eternity to gaze on each other in the sky without ever being able to meet or overtake each other in the blue vault. Follow each other then for ever across the sky, and give light to the world!"

CHAPTER II.

GREEK WOMEN: THEIR SOCIAL STATUS AND ACTIVITIES.

FOLLOWING the order the reasons of which have been indicated in the Introduction, we come next to the Greek women of Turkey. Physically, as well as mentally, the Greek women of to-day often exhibit the more characteristic traits of ancient Hellenic types, and forms of almost classical purity are to be met with, not only in free Hellas, but also in all parts of the Ottoman Empire. There still may be seen the broad, low forehead, the straight line of the profile, the dark lustrous eye and crimson lips (the lower one slightly full), the firm chin, and rounded throat. The figure is usually above the middle height, if not "divinely tall;" the carriage erect and graceful; the hands are small, and the feet often exhibit the peculiarity noticeable in ancient statues of the second toe being the same length as the first. In certain localities, and more particularly in Macedonia, the Greek type has much deteriorated from admixture with Slav and other elements. It has, however, remained almost perfect in many of the islands, and some of the finest specimens of the race are to be found in Asia Minor, not only on the sea-board, but in many towns and villages of the interior, where, at the beginning of the century, the Greeks had become so denationalised as to have lost the use of their mother tongue.

In the capital, and in European Turkey generally, every Greek considers himself as much a *Hellene* as are the dwellers in the free Kingdom. The Greeks of Asia Minor, however, still, as a rule, designate themselves *Romeots* (Romans), a term which included in Byzantime times all the subjects of the Eastern Empire. But the development of national sentiment, which has resulted from the spread of education, is causing this name to be gradually superseded by the classic designation, and it will no doubt be soon altogether abandoned.

The social position of women is, of course, chiefly determined by the law of marriage of the established religion. Hence, among the Greeks, as among all the other Christian nationalities of Turkey, the social position of women is, first of all, determined by that Christian law of marriage which abolished the old rights and privileges enjoyed by the women of the Roman Empire, and introduced the subjection of the wife to the husband in an indissoluble marriage. By the Greek Church, however, this general Christian law was modified so long ago as the eleventh century, when the Patriarch Alexius permitted the clergy to solemnise the second marriage of a divorced woman if the conduct of her first husband had occasioned the divorce. And at the present day little difficulty is experienced in dissolving an incompatible union without misconduct on either side, and whether the suit is brought by husband or wife. The case is tried by a Council of Elders, presided over by the Archbishop of the diocese, who hear all the evidence *in camera*, thus avoiding the scandal attaching to divorce cases in the West.

It must, however, be said that the privilege of divorce among the Greeks is rarely made use of without good and serious reasons, both social opinion and pecuniary considerations weighing strongly against it, and in all my long acquaintance with persons of this nation, two cases only have come to my knowledge. For though Greek matches are, to a great extent, *mariages de convenance*, marital dissensions are extremely rare, especially among the upper and middle classes. The Greek men, besides being good sons and brothers, are exemplary husbands, and the women in their turn are the most devoted of wives. There exist, too, as will appear elsewhere, considerable remains of patriarchal customs, even among the wealthy and educated classes. One of these is that the sons, on marrying, often bring their wives to the paternal home. The mother, on the death of her husband, is not banished to "the dower house," but retains the place of honour in the household, and receives every mark of attention and respect, not only from her sons, but from their wives, who consider it no indignity to kiss her hand, or that of their father-in-law, when receiving their morning greeting or evening benediction. And in these irreverent days it is very refreshing, on visiting a Greek family, to see the widowed mother at the head of the table, and remark the deference paid to her by her son and her daughter-in-law.

The degree of seclusion observed by the Christian women of Turkey has always varied according to external circumstances, and would appear to be due rather to the considerations for their safety, necessitated by their peculiar position among peoples of alien race and creed, than to any desire on the part of men for their "subjection." And that this is really the case is, I think, proved by the fact that not only have the women of Greece, since their emancipation from Turkish rule, enjoyed the same freedom as other European women, but that, in the Ottoman capital, and more especially in "Smyrna of the Giaours" (*Giaourdi Izmir*), where the Muslim element is in the minority, and where there is consequently little or nothing to fear from Turkish licence, this seclusion is now a thing of the past.

The heroism which the War of Independence called forth in the Greek men was shared by their mothers, their sisters, and their daughters. During the whole of this stirring period the women shared the trials and combats of the Hellenes as they had done the glory of the Cæsars. The struggle had really begun long before the outbreak of 1821, and bands of *Armatoles* (ἁρματολοι) had maintained their independence in the mountains of Agrapha, where they were frequently joined by refugees from Turkish injustice. The domestic history of these troubled times is recorded in the folk-songs of the suffering people, and to these spontaneous outbursts of untutored feeling we must turn to hear how the wife of the Klepht chieftain awaited with feverish impatience for news of her husband, or lamented him dead; was carried a captive to the harem of the Turkish general; or, rather than submit to such a fate, precipitated herself and her child over some precipice.

"The wives of the Klephts," says a Greek historian,[1] "are worthy to be extolled for their courage and virtues. When their husbands were setting out on a military expedition, it was they who girded them with their swords, gave them a parting kiss, and prayed for their victorious return. Often their towns and villages were besieged by the enemy, when women and girls bravely came to the aid of their fathers, husbands, and brothers. The Mainote women specially distinguished themselves by their Spartan-like heroism. On the approach of the Turkish soldiers the women and girls left their villages, and, lying in ambush in the mountain passes, and in the vicinity of the roads, kept up a constant guerilla warfare against the invaders. One of these amazons, Helen, the niece of a magnate of Kytherías, was visited by M. Pouqueville in the castle or tower of that name, where she lived surrounded by a number of the women whom she had formerly led to battle. Another leader of the insurgents, Christos, had among his forces a company of twenty amazons, including his own sister, who was wounded while fighting with the Turks. Such was the respect with which these women were treated by their fellow-combatants, that a German musician was shot dead by the captain for venturing to address an insulting remark to one of them.

---

[1] Neroulos, *Hist. Moderne de la Grèce*, partie iii. ch. i.

Two of the most renowned heroines of the time were Constance Zacharías and Modéna Mavroyennis. On the outbreak of the insurrection, the former planted the standard of the Cross on her house, and called upon all patriotic women to join her. Numbers responded to her appeal, and, after receiving the benediction of the Bishop of Helos, she led them against the Turks, who retired into the castle of Christea. The amazons then proceeded to Londari, where they tore down the crescents from the mosques, and set fire to the house of the Turkish *voivode*, who fell beneath the sword of their leader.

The father of Modéna Mavroyennis had been strangled by order of the Pasha of Eubœa, and after his death she took refuge in Mykóné. When the call to arms roused the patriotism of the Peloponnesus, Modéna incited her friends in Eubœa to revolt, promising to marry the conqueror of the Ottomans. Such was the effect of her eloquence on the Mykonians that they equipped and despatched four large war vessels as their contribution to the Hellenic fleet. And when the Algerian ships disembarked their soldiers on the shores of Mykóné, crying, " Death to the Giaours ! " it was Modéna who, with the band of patriots she had hastily collected, drove them back to their ships with the loss of their leader.

During the long siege of Missolonghi the women and girls aided the defenders by bringing materials of every description to stop the breaches made by the Turkish artillery, directed—shameful to say— by European officers. The chief women of the beleaguered town drew up and signed a petition, which they addressed to the Philhellenic ladies of Europe, entreating them to use their influence with their respective Governments to prevent this partisanship of the strong against the weak, and describing in touching terms the sufferings of the brave defenders. "Most of us," they wrote, "have seen mothers dying in the arms of their daughters, daughters expiring in the sight of their wounded fathers, children seeking nourishment from the breasts of their dead mothers; nakedness, famine, cold, and death are the least evils witnessed by our tear-dimmed eyes. Most of us have lost brothers and sisters, many are left destitute orphans. But, friends of Hellas, we assure you that none of these evils has touched our hearts so profoundly as the inhumanity manifested towards our nation by those who boast of being born in the bosom of civilised Europe." This touching appeal was, however, without avail. After a siege of eleven months, maintained by a garrison of 5700 men against an army of a hundred thousand, a sortie was attempted. Two detachments succeeded in forcing the Turkish lines, but the third, after losing three-fourths of their number, were driven back with the women and children into the town, where they still for two days bravely defended themselves. At last, rather than fall into the hands of the victors, the survivors set fire to the powder and perished together.

One of the surviving signatories of this appeal, Kyria Evanthia Kairis, subsequently wrote a tragedy embodying the events of this famous siege. During a conversation which the Greek poet, M. Soutzo, had with this lady at Syra, he relates that she observed to him, in reference to her work: "You well know what a profound impression the fall of Missolonghi made upon our minds, what a deep wound it inflicted on our hearts. I could never banish from my memory the fatal night of the 10th of April (old style). Those heroic phantoms, after struggling so long with death, gathering fresh courage, and in the dead of night striking terror into the barbaric hosts; the last farewells of mothers, the sobs of children, the heroes resolved to die with the aged and the wounded—this picture was perpetually present to my sight. I could never have unburdened my heart of the weight which oppressed it save by attempting to describe with my pen the scenes which were ever present to my memory."

One of the surviving heroines of this memorable siege, who died in Athens nine years ago, expressed on her death-bed a wish to be buried in the pallikar's dress which she had worn during the war, and had ever since treasured in secret. The poet Kostas Palamas has made this incident the subject of a long poem,[1] in which he describes how Kapitan Philio's daughter donned, at her father's command, the full white kilt, the braided vest and jacket, and the felt capote, and stood in the breach at his side, pistol in hand, while he directed his gun at the enemy. Her father slain, she had escaped in one of the sorties, with the assistance of a comrade, who afterwards became her husband.

[1] "Τα νιάτα τῆς γιαγιᾶς," in Τραγούδια τῆς πατρίδος μου.

Nor was the outbreak on Pelion, of 1878, without its heroines. The daughters and sisters of the patriots braved the whizzing rifle-bullets and the risk of capture, in order to carry food and water to their relatives in the entrenchments on the hills above Volo, now Greek territory. The name of one girl, Marighitza, of Makrinitza, was more specially mentioned for intrepidity, and when the insurrection was over she was sent for to Athens to be presented to the King and Queen, and fêted by the inhabitants.

A far more sensational story, however, is that of a woman named Peristéra, "the Pigeon," who was, it appears, an actual combatant in the rebellion, during which her brother met with his death. On the cessation of hostilities, this woman joined a band of brigands, and became their leader under the name of Vanghelli, to which her followers added the sobriquet of *Spanò*, or Beardless.[1] After pursuing the calling of klepht for some two years, Peristéra seems to have grown tired of it. So, leaving the mountains, she repaired to the British Vice-consulate at Larissa, and there gave in her submission to Her Majesty's representative. The Ottoman authorities, as is usual in such cases, granted a pardon to the penitent brigand, who, being apparently homeless and friendless, was then received into the service of the Greek Archbishop of Kodjani. A photograph taken at the time represents her in full klepht costume—swords, pistols, and yataghans at waist, and gun in hand, and round her neck is suspended the insignia of chieftainship, a broad silver disc,

---

[1] See Chap. IV., "The Beardless," in Folk-lore.

bearing in relief a representation of the patron saint, St. George,[1] in his conflict with the Dragon.[2]

Not only, however, during crises in their national history have Greek women laid aside distaff and spindle to assume the sword and *tophaiki*. To Greek, as to Bulgarian women the charms of a life in the greenwood have occasionally proved as irresistible as they were to our own Maid Marians. And various folk-songs tell us how

> For twelve long years had Haidée lived an Armatole and Klephtë,
> And no one had her secret learnt among her ten companions,

until one Easter Sunday, when, engaged with the other *pallikars* in athletic exercises, her sex was accidentally disclosed.[3]

These have, however, been rare exceptions, for, as I shall now proceed to show, the virtues of the Greek women generally are essentially domestic.

Though widely dispersed throughout the Ottoman Empire, the Greek peasants seldom occupy the same villages with those of other races. Some of the Greek villages, with the lands adjoining, are owned and tilled by peasant proprietors. These are called Κεφαλοχώρια, or "Head-villages," and Ελευθεροχώρια, or "Free-villages," and many of them are tolerably

---

[1] See Chap. V., St. George.
[2] I am indebted for the above details to a Consular despatch sent to the Foreign Office on the subject, and to some notes made by Mr. Stuart Glennie, who met the Archbishop of Kodjani, in 1881, at Servia, the fortress which defends the great pass between Macedonia and Thessaly, and received from him a photograph of the heroine.
[3] *Greek Folk-songs*, p. 247.

wealthy and prosperous. The majority of the Greek agricultural population of European Turkey are, however, tenants on the *metayer* system, and are called *yeradjis*. They receive the seed grain from the landlord, for whom they cultivate the land, and share with him the produce of the fields. They labour under great disadvantages, and are, as a class, poor, and much oppressed. Their dwellings present a pitiable aspect, being usually miserable, one-storied huts, constructed of wattle, plastered with mud inside and out, and consisting at most of two rooms, with holes for windows. A fence encloses the small farmyard, with its granary and cattle-shed. The houses of the Head or Free villages are, however, often built of stone. Sometimes they are of two stories, enclosed in a courtyard, and, when the locality is not subject to the attacks of brigands and other similar dangers, they may have shuttered glass windows. Tables, chairs, and even bedsteads, are not unknown luxuries among the more prosperous peasant farmers; a few pictures hang on their whitewashed walls, and there is usually a rude *eikon*, or picture of the Virgin and Child, before which hangs a small oil-lamp. The kitchen is furnished with well-burnished copper pans, and the *kilér*, or storeroom, contains an ample supply of native wine, oil, and winter provisions.

The Greek peasant women are not employed to any great extent in field-work. They, however, take an active part in much of the labour connected with the farm, and their household and dairy duties are many and varied. In

Roumelia and Macedonia, the girls and young women hire themselves out for the June harvest, and assist in the reaping and threshing. Agricultural machinery has found little favour in the East, being quite unsuited for the method of farming followed by the natives, and the implements of husbandry used are of the most rude and primitive description, entailing a great deal of hand-labour and involving a considerable amount of waste. Threshing is performed by the girls with the aid of an instrument which must surely have been used in Pelasgian times. It is composed of two pieces of wood joined together in something like the form of a horseshoe, and studded on the underside with a number of flints. A couple of ponies are attached to the curved end of this implement, on which a girl stands, and are driven over the grain spread out on the threshing-floor. Unscientific as this method may be, the scene presented is very picturesque, when the presiding Koré is a lithe and lissome lass. The corn is winnowed by being thrown up in the air with wooden shovels, the chaff being carried away by the breeze. In some parts of Macedonia the process of threshing is even more primitive. A team of horses or oxen is driven round and round the threshing-floor, the women and children beating out the remainder of the grain with sticks.

To the Greek peasant girl also is committed the care of her father's flock, which she must lead every day to the pasture, and fold at night. The *Voskopoúla*, or shepherdess, is one of the most prominent characters in rural folk-song, and many a charming idyll has been composed in her honour by amorous swains. But she has little time for sylvan dallying, for the sheep and goats must be milked, and the milk must be converted into cheese and *giaoúrti* (γιαούρτι), a delicious and wholesome sour curd, which is in great demand in the towns. When the sheep have been shorn, the wool must first be bleached and spun, and then knitted and woven into garments for the family, or into cloth for sale. The cotton and flax grown on the farm must also be gathered in their seasons, and prepared for use. The cotton pods are put through a small hand-machine called the *mángano* (μάγγανος), which turns two rollers different ways, and separates the fibre from the seed. The instrument next used is the *toxeuein* (τοξεύειν), a large bow made from a curved piece of wood five or more feet long, the two ends of which are connected by a stout string. The cotton is placed loosely on the string, which is made to vibrate by being struck with a stick, producing a not unmusical sound. This process detaches the particles of cotton, and it is now ready to use as wadding for the large quilts (παπλώματα), which, with a sheet tacked to the under-side, forms all the winter bed-covering used by the lower orders of natives of every race. The mattresses are also usually stuffed with cotton, and the palliasses with the husks of Indian corn.

If, however, the cotton is to be converted into yarn for weaving, it is twisted as it leaves the *toxeuein* into a loose rope, wound round the distaff, and spun. When the yarn has been dyed or bleached, according to the use that is to be made of it, the women or girls set to work at the hand-looms, which form an important part of the furniture of every cottage, and weave it into strong, durable calico, or brightly striped stuff for dresses and household purposes. A certain proportion of the cotton and wool is reserved for knitting, and it is most pleasing to watch the graceful motions and picturesque poses of the women and girls as, standing on their balconies or terraced roofs, they send the spindle whirling down into courtyard or village street while twisting the thread for this purpose. The knitting is done with five curved needles, having ends like crochet-hooks, and the stocking is always made inside out. This method produces a close, even stitch, and the work is extremely durable. The old women usually undertake this part of the household work, and with needles in hand and the "feed" of the yarn regulated by a pin fastened to their bodices, they sit in their doorways for hours together, either gossiping with each other, or telling fairy tales (παραμύθια), and crooning old songs to the little ones.

In some districts the silkworm industry keeps the women fully occupied during the spring months. The long, switch-like branches of the pollarded mulberry-trees are gathered every morning, and their fresh leaves given to the caterpillars; and all the tedious and laborious details connected with the silkworm nurseries must be carefully performed in order to keep the worms in good health, and thus secure a successful crop.

The Greek women of Crete lead for the most part

retired and sedentary, though most industrious, lives. The chief industry of the island is the cultivation of silk, which is carried on at home, each family raising its own little crop. The gayest time of the year for the Cretan women is the olive harvest, to which the girls especially look forward with pleasure, as the usual restraints are then set aside, and they enjoy, besides the open-air work, in company with others of their age, the social gatherings which are customary after the day's toil is over. Their earnings are, however, very small, and are paid in kind, being generally only two-sevenths of the yield of oil from the olives which each one has gathered, though in abundant seasons, when hands are scarce, they receive as much as a third. The work is, however, very fatiguing, and when carried on, as it often must be, in rainy weather, exceedingly trying.

Cyprus also is famous for its home industries in linen, cotton, and wool. The women of Larnaca and Nicosia still maintain the renown for cunning needlework which belonged of old to the island more especially associated with the Queen of Beauty.

But laborious as the lives of these thrifty countrywomen may appear, Sundays and Saints' Days are holidays duly observed and thoroughly enjoyed. The working dress of plain homespun is laid aside, and the picturesque gala costume donned. This consists of a skirt, woven in stripes of silk and woollen, reaching to the ankles, with a tight-fitting bodice of the same, a cloth jacket braided or embroidered round the borders in gold thread, and lined with fur, and in some districts a bright-coloured apron ornamented with needlework. The Greek maiden's carefully combed hair—brushes are unknown amongst the natives—is plaited into innumerable little tails, and surmounted with a small cap of red felt, decorated with silver and gold coins similar to those she wears as a necklace. Thus adorned, she accompanies her parents to the early Mass in the little white-washed church, summoned by the sound of the primitive *sýmandro*—a board struck with a mallet —in lieu of bell. Returning home, the simple morning meal is soon despatched, the cattle and poultry are fed, and the rest of the day is given up to well-earned repose and amusement.

In the afternoon the peasants resort *en masse* to the village green. The middle-aged and elderly men take their places in the background under the rustic vine-embowered verandah of the coffee-house; the matrons gather under the trees, with their little ones, to gossip, while their elder sons and daughters perform the *syrtò* (συρτὸς χόρος), the "long-drawn" classic dance. Each youth produces his handkerchief, which he holds by one corner, presenting the other to his partner. She, in her turn, extends her own to the dancer next to her. The line thus formed, "Romaika's dull round" is danced to the rhythm of a song chanted in dialogue form, with or without the accompaniment of pipe and viol, until the lengthening shadows of evening send the villagers home to their sunset meal. The kerchiefs of the youths are frequently love-tokens from their sweethearts, as sung by the love-sick swain in the following dancing song:

Whoever did green tree behold—
Thine eyes are black, thy hair is gold—
   That with silver leaves was set ?—
   Jet black eyes, and brows of jet—

And on whose bosom there was gold—
O eyes that so much weeping hold—
   At its foot a fountain flowing—
   Who can right from wrong be knowing ?

There I bent, the fount above,
To quench the burning flame of love;
   There I drank that I might fill me,
   That my heart I thus might cool me.

But my kerchief I let slip—
O what burning has my lip !—
   Gold embroidered for my pleasure,
   'Twas a gift to me, the treasure.

That one it was they broidered me,
While sweetly they did sing for me !
   Little maids so young and gay,
   Cherries of the month of May.

One in Yannina was born,
Robe of silk did her adorn;
   The other from Zagórie strayed,
   Rosy-cheek'd this little maid.

An eagle one embroidered me—
Come forth, my love, thee would I see !—
   T' other a robin red-breast tidy,
   Thursday—yes, and also Friday.

Should a youth my kerchief find—
Black-eyed with gold tresses twined—
   And a maiden from him bear it,
   Round her slim waist let her wear it ![1]

---

[1] *Greek Folk-songs*, p. 155.

Most of these dancing songs are sung antiphonically by two sets of voices. Sometimes, as in the above, one set begins the song and the other adds to each line in turn a kind of parenthesis extending it. In the following song, and in many others, the end of the line is repeated, or altered, by the second set of voices.

A youngster me an apple sent, he sent a braid of scarlet—
    He sent a braid of scarlet.
The apple I did eat anon, and kept the braid of scarlet—
    And kept the braid of scarlet.
I wove it in my tresses fair, and in my hair so golden—
    And in my hair so golden;
And to the sea-beach I went down, and to the shore of ocean—
    And to the shore of ocean.
And there the women dancing were, and drew me in among them—
    And drew me in among them.
The youngster's mother there I found, and there too was his sister—
    There was his elder sister;
And as I leapt and danced amain, and as I skipped and strutted—
    And as I skipped and strutted—
My cap fell off, and ev'ry one could see my braid of scarlet—
    Could see my braid of scarlet.
"I say, the braid you're wearing there was to my son belonging—
    My dearest son belonging."
"And if the braid that now I wear was to your son belonging—
    Your dearest son belonging—
He sent an apple which I ate, my hair the braid I wound through;
    And I will soon be crowned[1] too!"[2]

In some of the islands the *syrtò* has a much more pantomimic character. The leader of the dance accompanies the words of the song with appropriate

---

[1] *I.e.*, Married. See Chap. III.   [2] *Greek Folk-songs*, p. 193.

gestures and facial expression, and the words of the chorus or antistrophé are similarly represented by the dancer at the other end of the wavy line.

A favourite amusement, and opportunity for flirtation, in the islands is the swing. The girls suspend a rope across the narrow street from the wall of their own house to that of a neighbour, and every youth who wishes to pass by must pay toll in the form of a small coin, and give one of the girls a swing, while he sings the following verse :

> O swing the clove-carnation red,
>   The gold and silver shining :
> And swing the girl with golden hair,[1]
>   For love of her I'm pining.

To which the maiden replies :

> O say what youth is swinging me—
>   What do they call him, girls?
> For I a fez will broider him,
>   With fairest, whitest pearls.

The Harvest Home is also a great holiday in the country districts, and is celebrated on the 21st of August (old style). Attired in their best, and crowned with flowers, the harvesters carry small sheaves or bundles of the golden grain to the nearest town, where they dance and sing before the doors of the principal inhabitants.

The more remote the community, and the more isolated from contact with the outer world, the more rigid generally is found to be the code of social

[1] Golden hair is as much admired in the East at the present day as it appears to have been in classical times, though I could never learn that modern Greek women resorted, like their ancestresses, to artificial means of producing τρίχας ξανθάς.

morals. In the mountain villages of Crete, female misconduct is visited with the severest penalties, and even so late as the beginning of this century was punishable with death. Whenever a married woman was suspected even of faithlessness, or an unmarried one of frailty, her hours were from that moment numbered, and her end was so tragical and so shocking to all the feelings of natural affection, and even to the ordinary notions of humanity, that one can hardly believe such a practice to have been observed on the very confines of civilised Europe, and in the nineteenth century, by any Christian people. Her nearest relations were at once her accusers, her judges, and her executioners. An illustration of the ruthless severity with which such offences were punished is given by Mr. Pashley, and was related to him by an eye-witness, a cousin of the victim. A young wife was suspected of having broken her marriage vow. The charge was not proved, but, the suspicion being general, her father, a priest, consented to leave it to her near relations to decide as they thought best respecting her. Their decision was soon taken. They proceeded to the number of between thirty and forty to the home of the condemned woman, who was, as yet, totally ignorant of her impending fate, seized her, and, after tying her to a tree, made her person the mark at which all their muskets were pointed and discharged. Shocking to say that, though thirty balls had lodged in her body, she still breathed. One of her executioners immediately drew his pistol from his girdle, placed it close to her breast, and fired. The suspected partner of her guilt was not shot, for he belonged to a powerful family. But the Protopapas, the unfortunate woman's father, excommunicated him,[1] and, "in consequence of the sacerdotal ban, he not only himself perished by falling over a precipice, but all his brothers likewise came to untimely ends."[2]

The Greek peasant women are, on the whole, honest and industrious, affectionate mothers, and devoted and virtuous wives. A striking proof of their morality is afforded by the long absences from home which their husbands are often compelled to make in the pursuit of their avocations—absences often extending over many years. During this time the care and education of the children and the local interests of the family are left entirely in the hands of the wife, who generally proves herself equal to the occasion, and worthy of the trust reposed in her. There are many touching folk-songs describing the return of the husband after long years of absence, so changed that his faithful wife refused to receive him into her house until he had satisfied her by his knowledge of a mole, or other slight personal mark, that he was indeed her husband.

"Tell me the signs my body bears, and then I may believe thee!"
"Thou hast a mole upon thy chest, another in thine armpit;
There lies between thy two soft breasts, a grain, 'tis white and pearl-like."[3]

Many, too, are the songs which describe the wife's grief and loneliness during her husband's absence.

[1] "Τὸν ἀφόρισεν ὁ Πρωτόπαπας."
[2] *Travels in Crete*, ii. 257. See also below, Chap. IV., for excommunication.
[3] *Greek Folk-songs*, p. 165.

The woman of Malakassi curses the foreign lands which "take the husbands when they're young, and sends them back when aged;" and the complaint of the Greek woman of Zagórie married to a Vlach husband is most pathetic.

> Why didst thou, *mána*, marry me, and give me a Vlach husband;
> Twelve long years in Wallachia, and at his home three evenings.
> On Tuesday night, a bitter night, two hours before the dawning,
> My hand I did outstretch to him, but did not find my husband.
> Then to the stable-door I ran; no horse fed at the manger.
> I sped me to the chamber back; I could not find his weapons.
> I threw me on my lonely couch, to make my sad complaining;
> "O pillow, lone and desolate! O couch of mine, forsaken!
> Where is thy lord who yesternight did lay him down upon thee?"
> "Our lord has left us here behind, and gone upon a journey—
> Gone back to wild Wallachia, to famous Bucharesti."[1]

As girls of the peasant class can usually find plenty of occupation at home, they seldom go out to service, except when there happen to be more girls in a family than the father can afford to portion. There is also a general prejudice against allowing girls to leave the paternal roof until they are married, and a reproach is implied in the expression, "So-and-so has gone to strangers."

There are, however, districts which form an exception to this rule, and some of the islands are famous

---

[1] *Greek Folk-songs*, p. 176.

for their women cooks, who can always command good wages in the towns of Greece and Turkey. From the islands, too, come the good old nurses, bringing with them their antiquated costumes and charming lullabies and folk-lore. The girls who enter domestic service save their wages carefully for a marriage dowry, and, in the country towns, wear the coins strung together round their necks, a fashion formerly common to all classes, when φλουριὰ, or Venetian sequins, were in great demand for this purpose. As the folk-song says,

> I'll a lady to thee bring,
> Who has sequins by the string! [1]

The amount of a girl's dowry is thus easily ascertained by *pallikars* on the look-out for a "well tochered" bride. In the maritime cities, however, the national costume has, unfortunately, been quite discarded by the women, and the collar of coins has also been laid aside. As there are no savings-banks, or other convenient methods of safely investing small sums, servants often allow their wages to accumulate in their masters' hands until they marry or return to their homes. A laundry-maid in the house of one of my friends had upwards of £100 to receive when she left after a long period of service.

The costume now worn by women of this class is merely an ordinary stuff or cotton skirt, with a short jacket of cloth for winter, and of calico in summer. The hair is plaited into two tails, either left hanging down the back, or twisted round the *chimbéri*, or

---

[1] *Greek Folk-songs*, p. 187.

muslin kerchief often worn on the head. Out of doors it is the same, for hats and bonnets have not yet been adopted by the lower orders of Christians.

Greek servants are, generally speaking, hopelessly untidy and slatternly. Indeed, it is only in the houses of foreigners that a tidy maid is ever seen, and even there they often present themselves with stockingless feet, shoes down at heel, and unkempt hair. It is customary in the East to provide servants annually with a stipulated quantity of clothing in addition to their wages. Not a penny of the latter will they spend on dress; and, consequently, the European lady, who has generally more regard for appearances than the native lady, finds it her best policy to offer small wages, and a large allowance of garments and shoes.

Many girls, and especially orphans, are taken when still quite young into wealthy families, and adopted as φυχόπαιδα, or "soul children." They attend the public schools until the age of thirteen or fourteen, are clothed by the family, and assist in the lighter household duties. No wages are given, but they receive presents at the New Year and other festivals; and, when they reach the age of twenty-five or so, a trousseau and small dowry are provided, and a husband found for them, generally a small shopkeeper or artisan.

Greek domestics are, on the whole, honest and respectable; and, considering that cases of petty theft are punished only by dismissal and loss of character— for few employers would have the heart to subject a woman to the horrors of a Turkish prison—

these offences are exceedingly rare; drunkenness is unknown, and graver misdeeds I have never heard of.

There is, as a rule, no social intercourse between the Greek and the Turkish peasantry, although they live amicably enough together as neighbours when fanatical feeling is not excited by war or other circumstances. The prejudice against mixed marriages is naturally very great, and no alliance of the kind can take place without perversion on one side or the other. The perversion, however, must be on the side of the Christian, for apostasy is a crime in Islam. The laws, too, regulating the sexual relations of Christians and Moslems are exceedingly severe, and the probable fate of a *Giaour* hardy enough to fall in love with a fair Moslem is illustrated in the folk-song of

DEMOS AND THE TURKISH MAIDEN.

O list to me, and I will tell what has this week befallen:
Our Demos fell in love, he loved a charming Turkish maiden.
On Friday did he pay his court, on Saturday the whole day;
And early on the Sunday morn at last did leave his lady.
They caught him, and they bound his arms, and to be hung they led him,
A thousand went in front of him, five hundred walked behind him;
And Demos in the midst of them walked bound, with mournful aspect,
Like rose that from the parent tree two days ago was severed.
The Turkish maiden hears the news, and hastens to her window;
"Demos," she cries, "be not afraid, be not o'ercome with terror,
For coin I'll in my apron take, and sequins in my pocket;

And if the gold will not suffice, the rings from off my fingers;
If these will not thy ransom buy, I'll sell my every chattel.
O thou *Kadi*, O thou *Krité*,[1] who knowest human nature,
Hast ever branchless vineyard seen, or youth without a sweetheart!"[2]

Though one seldom hears of a Christian man embracing Islam for the sake of a Moslem love, it is by no means a rare occurrence that a Christian peasant girl, prompted by vanity or ambition, renounces the faith of her fathers in order that she may marry a Turk who has flattered her by his attentions. She is not, however, allowed to do this hurriedly, or without due consideration. The usual mode of procedure is for the girl to run away from home and take refuge in a harem. She then appears before the Medjliss, or Town Council, and announces her desire to be received into the ranks of the True Believers. Her parents and friends, supported by the Greek bishop, use their influence to prevent her taking this final step, and painful and sometimes tumultuous scenes ensue. If the girl persists in her determination, she is permitted to make a formal declaration of belief in the tenets of Islam, and becomes to all intents and purposes a Moslem, endowed with all the privileges enjoyed by a woman of that creed.

The opposition displayed by a Christian community to the perversion of one of its members, from such a motive, generally produces great ill feeling between them and their Moslem neighbours, and sometimes leads to fatal results. Such was the case

---

[1] The Judge is here addressed under his Turkish and Greek titles.
[2] Aravandinos, &c., Συλλογή, No. 275.

in 1876, when the apostasy of a village girl of doubtful reputation resulted in an outbreak of fanaticism at Salonica, during which the French and German Consuls were cruelly massacred. The girl had been brought by rail from the interior, and her mother, who had accompanied her, prevailed upon some Greek gentleman, who happened to be at the station on the arrival of the train, to carry off the convert, and secrete her in the Greek quarter. The news of the abduction spread quickly among the Moslem population, and on the afternoon of the following day the streets were suddenly filled with armed Albanians and Turks, who demanded that the girl should be given up by the Greeks. Apparently ignorant of the excited state of public feeling, the French and German Consuls, the latter at once a British subject of the name of Abbott and an Orthodox Greek, were proceeding home from a visit, when they were confronted by the angry and fanatical crowd. In vain they took refuge in the courtyard of a mosque. The furious mob followed them to an upper room of the Hodja's apartments, tore down the iron bars which defended the windows, and literally slashed them to death with daggers and knives. What further excesses might have been committed it is impossible to say, had not the Albanian Cavass attached to the British Consulate, in obedience to the Consul's instructions, succeeded in finding the unworthy cause of the tumult, and in delivering her over to the Turkish authorities.[1] German and French ships of war shortly

[1] The presence of mind and sense of duty displayed by the Cavass, Husein, on this occasion were rewarded by Her Majesty's Government with a donation of £60, and by the Sultan with a decoration and the rank of *Aga*, or Colonel. His eldest daughter, however, never recovered from the fright of

afterwards arrived, and it was now the turn of the Moslems to be in a panic, for it was threatened, or reported to be threatened, that the upper or Turkish quarter would be bombarded as a reprisal for the insult offered to the foreign flags. But another such catastrophe, arising from a similar love affair, was narrowly escaped at Larissa in 1880 during Mr. Stuart Glennie's stay there.

If, however, folk-song is any authority, it is sometimes mothers who persuade unwilling daughters to marry Turks. Of the two songs in Aravandino's collection illustrating this, one is from Zagórie, and the other from Prevesa, but one appears to be only a variant of the other. The following is a transla- of the Zagórie version of

A TURK I'LL NOT WED.[1]

(Τοῦρκον δὲν παίρνω.)

Over in Sálona, in Saloníki
Come forth the fair ones all proudly walking.
One dark-skinned maiden has the good fortune
Loved by a Turk to be, asked too in marriage.
"*Mána*, I'll kill myself, Turk I'll not marry!"
"Maiden, e'en kill thyself, Turk thou wilt marry!"
"Partridge small I'll become, to hillside wander!"
"Hunter will I become, and I will catch thee."
"*Mána*, I'll kill myself, Turk I'll not marry,
Blade of grass I'll become, in the earth plant me."
"Lambkin will I become, and I will eat thee."
"*Mána*, I'll kill myself, Turk I'll not marry,
Tiny grape I'll become, from vine branch hanging."
"Harvester I'll become, and there I'll find thee."
"*Mána*, I'll kill myself, Turk I'll not marry!"

the anticipated bombardment; and a subsequent panic at Adrianople, to which town Husein *Aga's* duties had obliged him to remove with his family during the war, put an end to her frail young life.

[1] Aravandinos, Συλλογή, &c., No. 402.

The Greek women of the towns have few occupations outside their own homes. Their lives are passed for the most part in a dull routine of household duties, varied only by gossip at their doors in warm weather, occasional attendance at church, and a walk on the public promenade on some great holiday. Some of the girls and young women earn their living by doing needlework and embroidery, or by lace-making; but even girls of this class cannot with propriety go out unattended either by a relative or some elderly woman, so strict is national prejudice on this point. I remember on one occasion a seamstress, having finished her day's work, could not return home because her brother had failed to fetch her, as promised. She was offered the services of the Albanian Cavass, or guard, who usually escorted us on our walks abroad, but scouted with indignation the proposal that *she* should traverse the streets with an *Arnaout*. Dress is a passion with girls of this class. On the rare occasions on which they are seen in public, their toilettes are wonderful—though, as I have said, they go hatless, and often gloveless—the great object of their ambition being to rival their wealthier neighbours, whose dresses, in large cities like Constantinople and Smyrna, are sure to be copied by the carpenters', shoemakers', and boatmen's daughters. And proud, too, is the maiden who also wears in her hair a clove carnation, the gift of some devoted admirer.

In some districts where the culture of silk is carried on on a large scale, Greek girls and women find employment in the silk factories. This is especially the case at Broussa, where they work side by side with Armenian and Turkish women.

The women of the middle classes present a curious medley of homeliness and pretension. They are good wives and devoted mothers, and often, though their education is but slight, are not without great good sense and intelligence. The majority, however, while retaining the customs they dare not throw aside without scandalising the *Mahallá*, seem possessed with a frantic desire to be considered in other respects *Franks*, or foreigners, as distinguished from *Rayahs*, or subject Christians. To this end, instead of being content, as formerly, to furnish her reception-room with a Turkish divan and a few chairs, and to dress herself on Sundays and holidays in her substantial but old-fashioned wedding dress—shawl, fez, and kerchief—as her mother did, many a Greek matron stints her household and sacrifices the real comforts of life in order to furnish her *salóne* with gaudy Austrian furniture, and to display an ill-assorted French bonnet and trashy over-trimmed dress to her admiring and, it may be, envious neighbours. To such an extent is this emulation sometimes carried, that I have heard of ladies sending out their servants on fête days to make note of the toilettes of their rivals, in order to be able to eclipse them when they themselves appeared on the promenade.

But, notwithstanding these feminine weaknesses of petty vanity and love of display, the Greek women, besides being, as before mentioned, faithful and affectionate wives, are also the most tender—if not always the most judicious—mothers to be found in any country. And their devotion is well repaid by the dutiful and affectionate regard of their sons and daughters. Indeed, it would be difficult to find a people in whom family affection is more strongly developed, or with whom the ties of kindred are held more sacred. The young men who leave their native towns or villages to seek fortune in a distant town or foreign land, generally return home to marry the wives chosen for them by their parents, and, when they retire from commercial or professional pursuits, endeavour to spend the rest of their days in the midst of their kindred. When a youth is leaving for the first time the bosom of his family, it is customary for his relatives and friends to accompany him some distance on the road. Before taking her final leave of her son, the mother laments his departure in song, to which the youth responds, bewailing the hard fate which drives him forth from his home. These Songs of Exile are sometimes extempore effusions called forth by the circumstances which induce or compel the youth to leave his home. Others, more conventional, describe the condition of the stranger in a foreign land, without mother, wife, or sister to minister to his wants, or cheer him in sickness and sorrow. In one, which is entitled "The Last Farewell," is depicted the evil augury of excessive sorrow at a son's departure:

> "Mother, arise, and knead for me, with whitest flour, some biscuits;
> With yearning put the water in, and knead it with affection,
> That speedily from foreign lands thy son may be returning."

With tears she poured the water in, with tears, too, did she
    knead it;
With weeping did she roll it out, and with sad lamentation.
O sad was Tuesday, Wednesday too, and Thursday was most
    bitter,
When mounted his good horse the youth, but ne'er was return-
    ing.[1]

In the following, it is either his wife or his sweetheart that the exile is addressing:

" Now's the hour of my departure, yearns and fails my heart
    o'erflowing;
Shall I e'er return—who knoweth? To a stranger land I'm
    going.
Hill and valley must I traverse, rocky wilds and deserts dreary,
Where the timid game his haunt has, where the wild bird builds
    his eyrie.
Now has come the hour despairful, hour which tears me from
    my home;
Now has come the sentence fateful, which abroad doth bid me
    roam.
Lassie, like the gladsome dawning, gentle lassie, kind and true,
Burns my heart with bitter anguish, now I'm bidding thee
    'Adieu!'"[2]

An exile song from Zagórie has a pathetic little history attached to it. The youngest of three sons had, for some cause or other, always been treated by his mother with coldness. Having decided upon expatriating himself, he was escorted, as usual, to some distance by his relatives, and, on taking leave of his mother, sang a farewell which so touched her heart that, falling on his neck, she begged his forgiveness

---

[1] Passow, *Popularia Carmina Græciæ Recenteoris*, No. cccxxx.
[2] *Ibid.*

for her past neglect, and promised to atone for it in the future.[1]

The Greeks of Turkey, though foremost in point of education and general enlightenment among the nationalities, are yet in this respect, as in many others, far behind their brethren in free Hellas, who rank very high, educationally, among the nations of Europe. While instruction is, in the little kingdom, enforced by law, no authority exists in Turkey to compel the Greek communities to follow the lead of the free Hellenes, and any initiative they may take in the matter is prompted by the lively patriotism and love of learning usually evinced by the race. But though ready to make sacrifices for the education of their sons, the Greeks of the old school had many prejudices to overcome before they would consent to give equal advantages to their daughters. "What do girls want with τὰ γραμματικὰ (letters)?" they would ask of those who proposed this innovation. "Let them learn housewifely duties, sewing and spinning, cooking and baking; if we have them taught to read and write, they will be for ever writing love-letters and reading romances, and we shall have to watch their conduct more vigilantly than ever!" Little by little, however, these prejudices are dying out, and, though the proportion of girls' to boys' schools in the Turkish provinces is as yet only about one to five, the numbers are gradually increasing, and fathers begin to take a pride in the scholastic attainments of their daughters.

---

[1] Compare also Passow, as above, "'Ηκακὴ μάνα,'" Nos. cccxliii to cccxlix. inclusive.

With the few exceptions, however, which I shall presently particularise, the instruction given in the majority of these schools is merely elementary, but comprises the following various branches :—

1. Scripture History and Catechism.
2. Reading and writing Modern Greek.
3. Arithmetic, including Weights and Measures, and the relative value of the Coinages current in the country.
4. Practical definitions of the principal Geometrical Forms.
5. Elementary Geography, Physical and Political, and particularly of Greece and the Hellenic provinces, and Cosmography.
6. Elementary History, and in particular that of Greece.
7. Elementary Zoology, Mineralogy, and Botany.
8. Elementary Anthropology.
9. Elementary Physics.
10. Freehand Drawing.
11. Vocal Music.
12. Gymnastics.

The principal centres of Greek education in Turkey are Constantinople, Smyrna, Salonica, Serres, Adrianople, Philipopolis, and Ioannina. In these towns and cities the primary and intermediate system of instruction provided for girls is the same as that followed in Independent Greece, and is for the most part sufficient to meet the social and intellectual needs of society. Intercourse with Europeans has, however, latterly become so much more general, that it has been found necessary to make the study of the

French tongue compulsory in the schools. The new ideas introduced by the French and German teachers, and by the works of foreign authors studied under their direction, naturally resulted in creating a desire for higher education, which, fortunately, had not to wait long for its fulfilment.

In 1874 the "Pallas" Training College was founded; and in the following year, thanks to the munificence of M. Zappas, and to the exertions of the "Ladies' Syllogos,"[1] a second High School or College was organised, and called, in honour of its benefactor, the "Zappíon." In both of these institutions the curriculum resembles in all essential particulars that of similar colleges in the West, and their Greek graduates may consequently consider themselves the equals of the educated women of England, France, or Germany. Training colleges with equally advanced methods have also been established in several provincial towns and cities, in order to provide teachers for the elementary village schools, which were formerly supplied exclusively from the Athenian colleges.

The Greek schools at Salonica are by no means institutions of modern foundation. The benefits of education have never been undervalued by the Greeks, even in the darkest period of their enslavement, and it is to the public-spirited munificence of a lady of the sixteenth century that these schools chiefly owe their existence. This was the Kyria Kastrissio, a native of Ioannina, the widow of a Greek of Salonica, who, at her death, bequeathed the

[1] A society of Athenian ladies formed for the furtherance of various educational and philanthropic objects.

whole of her large fortune to the schools of those two cities. The memory of this munificent lady,[1] together with that of a later benefactor, Demetrius Roggoti, is annually honoured with a Mnemósynon (Μνημόσυνον), or Commemoration, by the Greek community of Salonica, when the chief families of the city, together with all the officials, both Turkish and foreign, are invited to the examination held on the occasion. It was always an interesting ceremony, and I never failed to avail myself of the kind invitation of the "Ephors," or Managers. As we passed through the narrow lanes leading upwards from the main street, a part of the ancient *Via Egnatia*, still spanned by the triumphal arch of Constantine—lanes bordered by a picturesque perspective of projecting latticed windows and overhanging acacia and mulberry trees—we found ourselves in a throng of Greeks, all going in the direction of the "Gymnasium." The girls' school occupies the upper story of a large *konak*, or mansion, built in the style so common throughout the East—a large central hall or corridor, extending from one end to the other, and having on one side the class-rooms, and on the other a range of windows looking on the courtyard, with doors opening into the wings at each end. This room was densely crowded. At the upper end sat a number of schoolgirls on a raised gallery, on the wall at the back of which hung portraits of the before-mentioned benefactors. The centre of the

[1] In the basilica of St. Demetrios at Salonica, converted into a Turkish mosque in 1397, is still to be seen a mural tablet with an inscription in Greek, extolling the charity and munificence of a Greek lady of that city, named Kyria Spandoni.

E

hall was reserved for the invited guests, who included the Governor-General, the Greek Archbishop, and the foreign Consuls and their families, the ladies on one side and the men on the other, in true Oriental fashion. The ceremony began with the bringing in of the *Kólyva*, or Funeral Dish, of boiled wheat, decorated on the top with designs in coloured sugar, almonds and raisins, and other dried fruits, of crosses, coffins, leaves and flowers, monograms and inscriptions. A hymn was sung by the pupils, followed by a song, " Rejoice in Life " (Τὸν βίον χαρῆτε), which, though its words were translated from German, was in spirit truly classic ; and then came an " Ode to the Fatherland " (Εἰς τὴν Πατρίδα).

> Long as the universe shall last,
> Long as the sphere shall circling roll,
> Thy glory, O my Fatherland,
> And name thy sons shall still extol.

The Director of the school now advanced to the rostrum, and delivered an eloquent discourse on the great Macedonian philosopher, Aristotle. This was followed by more singing, including an " Ode to the Sultan," which, to judge from the expression one could detect on the faces of the elder girls, was by no means given *con amore*. Questions were then put on a variety of subjects, and answered with great intelligence and readiness by the Macedonian maidens, who also read passages from Homer and Æschylos, with the soft, musical pronunciation which only Hellenes know how to give to the ancient language. From one of the class-rooms there emerged a number of little ones belonging to the Infant School, who, under the direction of a young assistant-mistress, performed, with great spirit and accuracy, a variety of Kindergarten exercises. In the meantime a paper was being handed round among the visitors—the usual lottery list for the distribution of the plain and fancy needle-work on view in another room. The latter could hardly be described as artistic, but the plain sewing and white embroidery left nothing to be desired, so microscopic were the stitches; and the work bestowed on an elaborately embroidered linen jacket which fell to my share has often excited the wonder of feminine critics in this country. The *liras* paid for these lottery tickets are applied to the maintenance of the schools, which are unfortunately often in debt owing to the deterioration in value of the property in which the endowments are invested.[1]

The women belonging to the remarkable little aristocratic community known by the name of Phanariotes are worthy of special mention. These survivors of the noble Greek families of Byzantium take their distinctive name from the locality, called the Fanar, or Beacon, allotted to them by Sultan Mohammed II. at the conquest of Constantinople. At the present day they are represented among others by the well-known names of Ypsilante, Karatheodory, Mavrocordatos, Mavroyenni, and Karadjas. The daughters of these ancient houses have long been as distinguished for the elegance of their appearance and manners, and their conversational ability, as for their culture and accomplishments. One gifted

---

[1] Compare Stuart Glennie: *A Greek Mnemósynon, Social Notes*, 1881.

Phanariote lady has translated Byron's *Giaour* into Greek verse, and to many the language of Homer, Pindar, and the tragic poets is as familiar as the vernacular. Some of these able women, organised in societies, also devote much of their time to the management of schools, and to the supervision of hospitals and asylums. Under their auspices an industrial establishment has been opened at Constantinople, on the lines of one already founded in Athens, for training, and providing with employment, poor women and girls who would otherwise have been obliged to have recourse to charity.

A Bill is now, I am informed, before the Greek Chamber of Deputies, which, should it become law, will cause several important modifications in the present school system. Among these are the conversion of a number of the existing gymnasia into *Real Schule* on the German model, and the establishment in all the capitals of departments (νομοί) of High Schools for Girls. These measures would also affect the Greek schools in Turkey, the committees of which naturally follow the lead taken in Athens; and we may expect to see, in the course of a few years, Girls' High Schools established in all the chief cities of the Ottoman Empire.

CHAPTER III.

GREEK WOMEN: THEIR FAMILY CEREMONIES.

As will be pointed out at greater length in the chapter dealing more particularly with superstitions, survivals of pagan beliefs still hold sway over the minds of the Greek populace, and are connected with every detail of domestic life. These remnants of an ancient civilisation linger especially, with other old-world customs, round the important events of birth, marriage, and death; varying somewhat, perhaps, according to locality and contact with other nationalities, but remaining the same in their general features. In South Macedonia the arrival of the little stranger is awaited in solemn silence by the *mammé*, and a group of elderly relatives, whose presence and prayers keep away "all things harmful." The baby gains its first experience of the miseries of life by being pickled in salt and water; after which it is bundled up in innumerable garments of mysterious form and fashion, and left to sleep, if it can. The glad news has meanwhile been circulated through the household, who flock into the room to offer their felicitations. These are generally couched in the conventional phrases, "May it live for you!" (Νὰ σὲ ζήσῃ), and "Long life to it!" (Νὰ πολυχρονήση), the latter salutation being also addressed to the unconscious infant. But mother and child must be carefully watched over, and never left alone, as the Nereids of the fountains and springs are sure to be hovering near a house in which a birth has recently taken place, on the look out for an opportunity to exchange one of their own fractious offspring for a mortal babe. For the manners and customs of these imaginary beings strongly resemble those of Northern fairies, thus poetically described by Ben Jonson:

> When larks 'gin sing,
> Away we fling,
> And babes new-born steal as we go;
> An elf in bed
> We leave instead,
> And wind out laughing, Ho! Ho! Ho![1]

In Rhodes, no stranger save the *mammé* is on any account allowed to enter the house until the baby has been blessed by the priest. For forty days the house-door is shut at sunset and not opened until sunrise, for fear of the Nereids. These mythic folk, it would appear, imitate some of the ceremonials of mortals. For Mrs. Edmonds relates that, when travelling in Greece a few years ago, she asked a countrywoman of whom she was purchasing some embroidery why her work was always so stained and soiled; and the woman replied quite seriously that "it was the doing of the Nereids, who often borrowed these articles for their christenings"![2]

The mother rises on the third day, and walks

---

[1] Halliwell, *Fairy Mythology*, p. 169. See also Shakespeare, *Henry IV.*, Pt. I. act i. sc. 1; Brand's *Popular Antiquities*, ii. p. 484.

[2] *Greek Lays and Legends.*

round her bed in a stream of water, which the *mammié* pours from a jar as she proceeds. The meaning of this custom is not very clear. Taken in connection, however, with the other superstitious rites, and also with the similar custom observed on the wedding-day, it would appear rather to be either a libation to the earth, or a tribute to the water deities. On the fifth day the Fates (Μοῖραι) must be propitiated, in order to induce them to confer upon the infant favours which will influence its future career. If the new-born babe is a boy, coins of gold and silver, a sword, and a cake of bread are placed beneath its pillow to remind the " Dealers out of Destinies "[1] that fortune, valour, and abundance are the best gifts; if it is a girl, a distaff or spindle is substituted for the sword, intimating the value attached to female industry.

The christening generally takes place before the infant is a week old, and is made the occasion of much display. For it is remarkable that the more secluded the domestic life of a people, the greater is the publicity given to religious ceremonies connected with family events. The groomsman and first bridesmaid who have officiated at the wedding of the parents become sponsors for the children under the names of *Nono* (Νονὸς) and *Nona* (Νονὰ), and *synteknoi* (Σύντεχνοι) to their father and mother. For, among members of the Greek Church, the terms "godfather" and "godmother" are by no means the empty titles into which they have degenerated with us. The responsibilities undertaken by bap-

[1] Αἱ Μοῖραι τῶν Μοιρῶν.

tismal sponsors are religiously fulfilled, and they are treated by their godchildren with an affectionate respect little less than that shown to their parents according to the flesh. The children of both families are considered brothers and sisters, and a relationship is supposed which forms as complete a bar to intermarriage as the closest consanguinity. A man could not wed a widow if he had stood sponsor to her children at the baptismal font, and a Greek would as soon think of marrying his own sister as the daughter of his *Nono*. In some of the islands it has become difficult for the young people of the better classes to find spouses, so closely are they already connected by intermarriages and baptisms.

The expenses of the christening are borne by the *Nono*, who pays the priest's fees, buys the baptismal robe, and furnishes the bonbons, liqueurs, and other customary refreshments. The lowest estimate of the cost is some three hundred piastres (£2 10s.), which, though a considerable outlay for a poor godfather, is never known to be dispensed with. The Greek Church prides itself, and probably with reason, on keeping up primitive forms more strictly than the Roman Catholic, or any other Christian sect. Baptism is, therefore, performed, not by a conventional sprinkling, but by trine immersion. The baby is carried to church by the *mammé*, followed by a long irregular procession of sponsors, relatives, and friends. At the church-door they are met by the officiating priest. The *Nono* takes the infant from the nurse's arms, and retains it while the *papas* reads the preliminary prayers, to which he makes the customary responses. He then delivers the baby to the priest, who, turning to the east, makes with its body the sign of the cross in the air. While the preparations for its immersion are going forward, the infant is laid before an *eikon* of Christ or the Virgin, according to its sex. It is then undressed by the *mammé* and given to the priest, who dips it three times in the font, to the water of which has been added a small quantity of consecrated oil. Three tiny locks of hair, if these can be found, are then cut from the baby's head and thrown into the font, "in the name of the Father, Son, and Holy Ghost." This dedication of hair was no doubt originally a sacrifice to the elementary spirits; for the water from the font is emptied into a pit or well under the floor of the church.[1]

Then follows the "confirmation" of the baby, which consists in anointing the head and some parts of the body with consecrated oil. It is then dressed, and after being carried by the godmother three times round the font, while prayers are intoned, the infant is taken to the Holy Gates, where it receives the Communion in both kinds, administered, as it always is in the Eastern Church, in a spoon. The party then return to the house to congratulate the mother and partake of the before-mentioned refreshments. The bonbons are handed round on trays and taken in

---

[1] When visiting the fine basilica of St. Demetrios at Salonica, formerly the metropolitan church, but converted into a mosque by Sultan Bajazid in 1397, the Mevlevi Dervish, who acts as sexton, offered us a cup of water from the church well. In spite, however, of his eulogiums of its miraculous properties, we refrained from partaking of the precious fluid, much to his disappointment.

handfuls; and, on leaving, a tiny gilt cross, fastened to a white rosette, is pinned on the breast of each guest as a souvenir of the event.

Although the Greeks of the large seaport cities, and the upper classes generally, have abandoned some of the old customs formerly observed in connection with marriage, many curious and interesting usages are still to be found in the towns and villages of the interior, and in the islands of the Ægean. These ancient folk-customs vary somewhat in their minor details according to locality; but in their leading features they are everywhere identical. There are the same ceremonies of betrothal, and songs for each successive stage of the week's festivities, whether they take place in Macedonia, Epirus, Thessaly, Thrace, on the coasts of Asia Minor, or in the Islands.

The prohibited degrees of relationship, both natural and conventional, are even more rigorously observed in the Greek, than in the Latin Church, no powers of granting dispensations in special cases being vested in the Patriarchal Office. I have heard of rare instances of marriage between second cousins being celebrated by priests belonging to the inferior grades under the influence of bribes. These unions have, however, always been subsequently annulled as unlawful, and the unfortunate parties, whose mutual attachment had caused them thus to violate the canonical law, were compelled for ever to renounce each other's society under pain of excommunication.

National etiquette requires that the principals should ostensibly take no part in the preliminary arrangements, which are carried out by the parents of the contracting parties with the help of a professional match-maker, known as the *proxenetes* (προξενητὴς) or *proxenetra* (προξενήτρα). This agent is commissioned by the parents of a marriageable girl to find a suitable husband for her; or, it may be, to open negotiations with the parents of a young man whom they have themselves selected among the eligible *partis* of their acquaintance. When all the preliminaries are settled, the cinnamon eaten by the mother and the *proxenetes*, and the amount of dowry the maiden will bring has been agreed upon in the presence of witnesses, the first betrothal (ἀῤῥαβὸν) is concluded. As soon as it is made public, the *arravoniasticòs*, accompanied by his relatives, pays a visit to the family of his future wife. They are received with great formality, the *arravoniastiké* standing in a posture of affected humility and modesty, with hands crossed on her breast and eyes cast down, to receive the felicitations of the visitors, a custom which has given rise to the Greek saying, "Affected as a bride" (Καμαρώνει σὰ νύμφη). When all the customary compliments have been interchanged, the inevitable *glico* is handed round, followed by coffee and cigarettes, and the party then take their leave. The betrothed maiden accompanies them to the head of the staircase, and kisses the hands of her future spouse and his relatives, who present her in return with gold coins and sweet basil (βασιλικός).

Marriage being thus looked forward to as a matter of course, the preparation of a girl's trousseau is often, especially among the working and peasant classes, begun by the careful mother while her daughter is still a child. The parents purchase by degrees the materials necessary, according to their means, and the maiden herself performs a great part of the task of converting them into wearing apparel and articles for domestic use. The daughter of a well-to-do peasant will receive as her portion a sum ranging from £30 to £100, a good stock of house-linen and home-made carpets and rugs, several articles of furniture, and two or three suits of clothes, including a gala costume for Sundays and holidays. This varies according to locality. In Lower Macedonia a full skirt and short-waisted bodice are worn over a sort of nightdress (ὑποκάμισον) of native linen crêpe—a costume somewhat resembling that of the Italian *contadina*. In some districts this costume is not complete without a bright-coloured apron, thickly embroidered on the lower edge, and a belt or girdle. For out-of-door wear a jacket is added, fitting tightly to the figure, and reaching below the knees. This is usually of fine cloth, and worked round the borders and sleeves with gold thread or coloured silks, and is invariably lined with fur. Among the middle classes of the towns from £300 to £500 is the average dowry, and the trousseau is more or less of European fashion and materials.

It is very difficult indeed to find a husband for a portionless girl. A father will, consequently, make it his first duty to save a *dot* for his daughters; and brothers, in a father's place, consider it incumbent on them to see their sisters satisfactorily settled in life before taking wives themselves. Social opinion is very strong on this point among the Greeks, with whom fraternal affection apparently covers a multitude of sins. I was at one time in the habit of meeting occasionally in Greek society an *avocat*, whom I was advised to avoid, as he was "not very nice." I naturally asked why, if he were objectionable, he was invited to private parties. The reply was: "To exclude him from society would injure him professionally, and so he is countenanced because he is good to his orphan sisters. He has worked hard to portion and marry the eldest, and he is now amassing a dowry for the second."

The interval between the first *arravón* and the wedding varies, but seldom extends over many months. One rarely hears of an engagement being broken off in the meantime, and when this does happen it is the result of no disagreement between the principals, who are usually comparative strangers to each other, but of some impeding circumstance. I knew, for instance, a girl who had been betrothed to a doctor in a distant town. When the time fixed for the wedding drew near, this gentleman informed the parents of his *fiancée* that it was impossible for him to leave his practice for a whole week in order to be married at Salonica, and he begged that they would bring the bride to Adrianople, and have the ceremony performed there. This was, however, contrary to their ideas of propriety, and, although the girl and her mother were terribly distressed at the event, the match was broken off.

Some of the most interesting old customs in connection with the marriage ceremony may be found still lingering in Southern Macedonia, and especially at, and in the neighbourhood of, its ancient capital, Edessa, now called by the Slav name of Vodhena, "the Waters," from its magnificent cascades. A week or more is devoted to the preparatory nuptial observances and festivities. On the Sunday, a copy of the marriage contract is formally delivered at the house of the bridegroom, who sends in return a present to the bride, consisting of sugar-plums, henna, rouge, soap, &c., and a large jar of wine for her parents. On Monday, the maiden friends of the bride arrive to assist her in sifting and otherwise preparing the grain, which they subsequently carry to the mill. On the morning of Wednesday, they again assemble to fetch home the flour, and in the evening a number of female relatives and friends come in to help in the making of the wedding-cakes. The long wooden trough is brought in and filled with the yellow flour. A boy, armed with a sword, seats himself at one extremity, and at the other is placed a little girl, who, as she pretends to mix the dough with her tiny hands, hides in it the wedding-ring and some coins. Bright and joyful must the lives of these little ones have been, and unclouded by any family bereavement. The boy with his weapon signifies that the husband is the natural guardian of his home, and the kneading girl that domestic duties are woman's sphere. The bread-making is then performed in earnest by experienced hands amid songs and laughter—for these occasions are red-letter days in the monotonous lives of the Greek women of the interior—and then left till the morrow to "rise." On Thursday the kneaders again assemble and divide the dough into portions, each girl and woman searching in her portion for the ring and coins. The bridegroom must redeem the ring with a present from the one who has been lucky enough to find it. The dough is then returned to the kneading-trough, and made into a variety of cakes, among them a large one, called the *propkasto*. On the afternoon of Thursday, the bridegroom arrives with his friends; the *propkasto* is placed over a bowl of water, and round it the assembled youths and maidens dance three times, singing the "Song of the Wedding Cake."[1]

The cake is then broken into small pieces, which are showered over the heads of the young couple, interspersed with figs and other fruits, and while the children scramble for these, a great quilt is thrown over them, as a further emblem of fruitfulness and plenty.

On Friday the bride and bridegroom exchange presents. The bearers of the bridegroom's gifts set out, preceded by music, for the abode of the bride, who awaits their arrival with eager expectation. The envoys, after having been warmly welcomed, thanked, and refreshed on special nuptial viands and a glass of wine, are in turn entrusted with the

---

[1] I have not, unfortunately, been able to procure the words of this song in time for insertion.

bride's presents to her betrothed, carefully wrapped in embroidered *boktchás,* or bundle wraps, tied up with bunches of *blíra* (μπλίρα), a kind of tinsel thread. If the bridegroom's home is in the same neighbourhood as that of the bride, parties of the near relatives of the couple go from house to house, bearing invitations to all the guests who are to take part in the festivities of that evening and the following day, a ceremony also extended to the happy pair, who invite one another. The *koumbáros* and *koumbára,* groomsman and head bridesmaid, are the last called upon, and, accompanied by the band, proceed to the house of rejoicing. Music, dancing, and feasting occupy the time until the evening, when the maidens carry off the bride to perform part of her toilette for the morrow. After washing, perfuming, and perhaps dyeing her long hair, they plait it in a multitude of long braids, amid jokes and merry laughter, one after another bursting into songs suited to the occasion, and of a highly complimentary character, such as the following:

> Dress thee, and busk thee, winsome one,
>   Dress thee, and busk thee, maiden,
> So to the bridegroom thou appear
>   As flowery field and garden.
> The nightingales all envy thee,
>   They fly in troops before thee;
> Singing and saying in their song,
>   "Joy we all in thy beauty!
> So brightly shine the golden locks
>   Rippling upon thy shoulders;
> Angels have surely combed them out,
>   Combed them with combs of silver!"[1]

[1] Aravandinos, Συλλογὴ δημωδῶν Ἠπειρωτικῶν ἀσμάτων, No. 283.

Or,

> Thou didst but sit upon the chair,
>   When, lo! its wood, all lifeless,
> Thy beauty quickened into leaf,
>   And flushed all o'er with blossom.
> The very deer made holiday
>   The day thy mother bore thee.
> For dowry the Apostles twelve
>   Bestowed on thee thy beauty.
> Of all the stars of heaven so bright,
>   One only thee resembles,
> The star that shines at early dawn
>   When sweet the morn is breaking.
> From out of heaven the Angels came
>   The Saviour's orders bearing;
> The brightest radiance of the sun
>   They brought thee on descending.
> Thou hast the hair of Absalom,
>   The comeliness of Joseph;[1]
> He'll lucky be and prosperous,
>   The youth who thee shall marry.
> Joy to the bridegroom's *mána* be,
>   Joy to the bride's new mother!
> Who such a noble son has borne,
>   Fit mate for such a maiden!
> What *proxenétra* made the match,
>   Who cinnamon has eaten,
> When such a partridge was betrothed,
>   And pledged to such an eagle![2]

The bridegroom has, in the meantime, been conducted by his friends to another room, where the local barber proceeds to shave him carefully, a con-

---

[1] Joseph is extolled by Ottoman poets, and Eastern writers generally, as the type of ideal beauty. The story runs that when Zulaikha introduced him into the presence of her lady friends, who were eating oranges, they were so bewildered by his comeliness that they cut their fingers instead of the fruit.

[2] Aravandinos, Συλλογὴ, &c., No. 286; and *Greek Folk-songs*, p. 157.

siderable time being devoted to the operation, as is usual in the East. The ceremony is enlivened with music and complimentary songs:

> Down upon the shore,
> Down upon the sea-coast,
> Now they busk a bride
> And adorn a bridegroom.
> Handsome the bridegroom,
> Handsome he, and youthful;
> Fair as gold his hair,
> Broad and dark his eyebrows;
> Like an eagle he,
> He is like a red-breast.[1]

Or such absurd nonsense as:

> Shave, O silver razor,
> Deftly and with care,
> From the bridegroom's lovelocks
> Sever not a hair![2]

As there are "lucky" and "unlucky" days for every incident of domestic life, Sunday is considered the most propitious for the termination of a wedding. On the morning of this day, accordingly, friends and relatives assemble at the house of the bridegroom, embrace and congratulate him on the auspicious event, and escort him to the home of the bride. As they leave the house, his mother, in accordance with ancient custom, pours a libation of water before him at the gate, and lays across his path a girdle, over which he steps. If the parties are well-to-do, or the distance is long, he may ride to the ceremony; but most frequently the procession takes its way on

---

[1] Aravandinos, Συλλογή, &c., No. 291.
[2] Compare Aravandinos as above, Nos. 289 and 290.

foot, calling *en route* for the *koumbáros* and *koumbára*, and singing as they go :

> My own beloved has bidden me to come to the betrothal,
> Before the Danube shall come down and water fill the torrents.
> But I would at her bidding go through heavy rain and snow-fall ;
> Or if the Danube should come down, and overflow the rivers,
> Upon my ring I then would stand, and steer me safely over.[1]

> Set out, my tree, start gaily,
> Set out, set out, my cypress,
> Set out to seek the poplar,
> With long and slender branches.
> Beside thee thou shalt plant it,
> And tenderly bedew it ;
> And when the breezes bend thee,
> Thou'lt stoop, and kiss it sweetly.[2]

Arrived at the house of the bride, the ceremony commences with the exchange of the documents containing the marriage contracts, which are presented by the priest to the respective parents of the bride and bridegroom. The amount of the dowry is then paid in cash to the bridegroom, some of whose friends convey it to his residence. The second ἀρραβών, a ceremony similar to that observed in classical times, now takes place. The father of the bride, or, failing him, her nearest male relative, offers to the corresponding relative of the bridegroom some sweet basil on a plate, thrice repeating the words, "Accept the betrothal of my daughter to your son." The same ceremony is also performed by the bridegroom's nearest of kin. A male relative of the bride then

---

[1] Aravandinos, Συλλογή, &c., No. 292.   [2] *Ibid.* No. 294.

presents, on her part, to her future spouse a glass of wine, a *kouloúra* (κουλούρα), or ring-shaped cake, and a spoon. After drinking the wine, he drops some coins into the glass for the bride, eats half the cake, and gives the remainder, with the spoon, into the keeping of the *koumbáros*. Another envoy from the bride comes up to gird the bridegroom, and while doing this he essays to lift him from the ground, the happy man resisting to the best of his ability. These preliminaries are concluded by the best man, in a rather prosaic fashion, for it is now his duty and privilege to put on the bride's feet the shoes which have been provided by the bridegroom. Bedizened in all her bridal finery, her rouged and spangled cheeks partly hidden by a gauze veil, over which hangs a long tassel of *blíras*, the maiden walks forth into the street, stepping through a libation of water poured by her mother. The musicians play a wedding march, and hymeneal songs are chanted as the procession paces slowly to the church. At the door the bridegroom's mother accosts her future daughter with the question, "Νύμφη, ἔχεις τὰ παπούτσια;" (Bride, hast thou the shoes?) The procession then enters the church. The bridal pair, carrying tapers decorated with flowers and knots of white ribbon, take their places before the Ἁγία Τράπεζα (holy table), the bride standing to the left of the bridegroom. The third ἀῤῥαβὸν is now performed by the priest, who, after reading part of the ritual, makes the sign of the cross three times with the rings over the heads of the couple, and then places them on their respective hands, saying, "Give thy troth, servant of God (adding the man's name), to the servant of God (adding the woman's name), in the name of the Father, the Son, and the Holy Ghost." The priest then takes the wedding wreaths—constructions of white artificial flowers and ribbons—from the hand of the *koumbáros*—and places them on the heads of the bride and bridegroom, with the words, "Crown thyself, servant of God," &c., as above. The groomsman, standing behind the couple, changes the wreaths three times, while the priest repeats these words. The bridegroom, bride, and *koumbáros* then drink a glass of wine, which has been blessed by the priest; and the pair, holding each other's hands, are led three times round the holy table, the best man following, with his hands on the "crowns." The remainder of the liturgy chanted—with nasal intonation, and many repetitions of Κύριε ἐλείσον—the priest removes the wreath of the bridegroom, and then that of the bride, pronouncing at the same time a blessing upon them in scriptural language.

The κουμπάρος having set the example by kissing the bride and bridegroom, the assembled friends crowd round to offer their felicitations. On the return of the procession to the bride's home, her mother places a loaf on the heads of the newly wedded pair, while comfits are showered over them by the rest of the company. The bridal feast follows, and is prolonged until it is time for the bride's departure. After drinking healths the glasses are thrown away over the shoulder, and if they do not break it is considered a bad omen. And then comes the farewell to the paternal home, which is expressed in many touching folk-songs, sung while the bride is weeping in her mother's arms.

> Fare thee well, father dear, farewell!
> Good-bye, my sweet kind mother,
> Fare ye well, loving brothers all!
> And you, my friends and kinsfolk!
> For to my mother-in-law's I go,
> To my new home I'm going;
> And letters there I'm going to learn,
> To write down all my treasures.
> Farewell! adieu! my neighbours all,
> And you my neighbours' daughters,
> For to my mother-in-law's I go, &c.[1]

> Down among the meadows,
> 'Mong the little meadows,
> Come the mules a-grazing,
> Cool, and quiet gazing,
> One is not a-grazing,
> Cool and quiet gazing.
> "Mule, why art not grazing,
> Cool and quiet gazing?"
> What enjoyment can I have?
> Or what grazing can I crave?
> I am going from my father,
> And am wan and withered;
> I am going from my mother,
> And am wan and withered;
> I am going from my brother,
> And am wan and withered.[2]

As the bride leaves the house, a loaf is divided, one-half of which she takes with her to her new home. The guests now escort the pair to the village

---

[1] Aravandinos, Συλλογὴ, &c., No. 296.
[2] *Ibid.* No. 299; and *Greek Folk-songs*, p. 158.

green, where the bride and bridegroom will open the dance. As they go, they sing :

> To-day the heavens are decked in white,
>   This is a day right gladsome;
> To-day we have in marriage joined
>   An eagle and a partridge;
> A little spotted partridge here
>   Has come to us a stranger;
> Her little claws are coloured red,
>   And finely marked her feathers.
> She in her claws has water ta'en,
>   And oil upon her feathers,
> That she may wash her ladyship,
>   That she may preen her beauty.
> To-day it is a worthy day,
>   With sequins in its pocket;
> For we two birds have wedded now,
>   And we a pair have made them.[1]

Fierce shone the sun, and down swooped an eagle,
  Seized he a birdling, far off with her flew;
White-skinned and lovely was she, yea, and black-eyed,
  Tiny as partridge that crouches in dew.[2]

The *syrto* danced, the procession re-forms, and the happy pair are conducted with songs and music to the paternal roof of the bridegroom. Some of the songs sung on this occasion are in dialogue form, and, like the foregoing, express the bride's regret at leaving the home of her youth :

> " Wand'ring nightingale, and exiled birdie,
>   Where wert thou yestreen, where wilt be this even ?"
> " Yesternight I slept safely with my parents,
>   Now my father-in-law's, husband's roof must shield me.

---

[1] Sung at Ioannina. Aravandinos, Συλλογή, &c., No. 315
[2] *Ibid.* No. 297.

'Neath my husband's roof must I bide this evening."
" Wand'ring nightingale, and exiled swallow,
What sad thoughts are thine ? Why should'st thou be
    pensive ?
See the bridegroom gay ! How he on thee gazes !
See him how he leaps, and archly looks toward thee ! "[1]

Red and white cherry on a branch, in newly planted orchard,
She hangs like tassel on the horse, like saddle rayed with sunshine.
Happy he'll be whose 'tis to kiss the winter and the summer;
To kiss the summer rosy red, to kiss the winter snow-white.[2]

When the party approach their destination, the bridegroom's mother is thus addressed :

> Dame and mother-in-law, forth come,
> Welcome now the partridge home !
> Take the bird to your abode,
> Lightly trips she o'er the road.
>   Receive her now,
>   Receive her now.
> Ye sun and moon, command her now !
> O see her as she walks along,
> She's like an angel 'mid the throng !
> O rise, go forth and thou shalt see
> Both sun and moon appear to thee !
> Dame and mother-in-law, forth come,
> Welcome now the partridge home !
> Within the cage thou her must bring,
> Like little bird she'll sweetly sing ![3]

Crossed knives are often placed over the door of a house to which a bride has been brought, in order to keep off evil spirits, who are generally believed to be specially alert on the occasion of any family event.

On the following morning, friends assemble before the house to greet the young couple with songs and

---

[1] Aravandinos, Συλλογή, No. 303.   [2] *Ibid.* No. 307.   [3] *Ibid.* No. 311.

music. The *koumbáros* arrives to breakfast, bringing with him the half-cake and the spoon confided to his care on the preceding day.[1] The bride uses the spoon in commencing her meal, and eats the cake. The meal concluded, she proceeds, accompanied by the women and girls who have serenaded her, to the well from which her husband's family draw their supply of water, in order to perform the ceremony, observed from time immemorial, of propitiating the "Naiad of the spring" with the gift of a coin dropped into it from her lips. She then draws a pail of water and pours it into one of those gracefully shaped earthen jars called by the Greeks *stamnæ* (στάμνοι), which she carries home on her shoulder. On entering the house, the bride pours some of the water over the hands of her husband, and presents him with a towel on which to dry them, receiving in return a little present. Feasting and dancing occupy the rest of the day, after which the young wife settles down quietly in her new home, relieving her mother-in-law of many of the household duties. On the following Friday, however, the bride, accompanied by her husband, returns to spend twenty-four hours under the parental roof, and pays her mother another visit on the subsequent Wednesday, when she takes with her a bottle of the native spirit called *raki*, bringing back with her an equal quantity from the family store. The nuptial observ-

---

[1] This custom of the best man taking the spoon with him may have some connection with an episode which is of frequent occurrence in Greek folk-tale. See, for instance, Von Hahn's Νεοελληνικὰ Παραμύθια ; or Geldart's translation of the Greek Cinderella story in *Folk-lore of Modern Greece*, p. 30.

ances are finally terminated three days afterwards by a feast given by the bride's father to all the relatives of the couple.

The ceremonies observed by the Greeks in connection with death and burial are almost everywhere identical, and include many archaic customs and time-honoured traditions in association with the rites of the Eastern Church.

When the end of a sick person is believed to be approaching, the priest is summoned to administer to him the last sacrament. If the death struggle appears to be prolonged, the friends of the moribund conclude that some person or persons are at enmity with him, and use their best endeavours to bring to his bedside any one whom he may have wronged. Should the injured person be dead, a small portion of his shroud must be procured. This is laid on a pan of charcoal, and the dying man is fumigated with the smoke arising therefrom, when the hostility of its owner will cease, and the soul will be able to depart in peace. The family then gather round to take their last farewell, and cheer the last moments of the departing spirit. After the first burst of natural grief is exhausted, the body is left to the ministrations of the "washers of the dead." The customary ablutions performed, it is anointed with oil and wine, and sprinkled with earth. A clean mattress and bed linen are spread on a long table, and the dead person, dressed in his holiday garments, is laid out on it, with his feet pointing towards the door and his hands crossed on his breast, on which a cup is also placed to be buried with him. The bier is decked with fresh flowers and green branches, and three large wax tapers, ranged at the foot, are kept burning the night through. A large stone is also brought into the room and left there for three days—a custom which appears to commemorate the burial and resurrection of Christ.

Greek women have in all times played a conspicuous part in funeral observances, and from the days of Antigone the fulfilment of the rites of sepulture has been observed by them as one of the most sacred duties. Homer describes how Andromáché chanted a dirge to her dead husband and her son Astyanax, how the mother and sister-in-law took up the lament, the burden of which was repeated by a chorus of other women. Such scenes as this may be witnessed at the present day in the cottage of the humblest peasant. The female relatives of the deceased, with dishevelled hair and disordered dress, now come in to perform the duty of watchers. Seated round the room on the floor, they take it in turn to chant dirges (μυριολογία) for the dead, lamenting his loss, extolling his virtues, and, in some cases, describing the cause of his death. These *myriologia* are essentially pagan in sentiment. They contain no assurance that the dead are in a state of bliss, and no hope of a happy meeting in Paradise. A dying son can comfort his sorrowing mother only by directing her to a hill on which grow "herbs of forgetfulness." The fond brother would build for his sister a mausoleum in which she could sit at ease, look forth on the green earth, and hear the birds singing. And the young wife complains that her husband has abandoned her, and wedded instead "the black earth." But, as a rule, the lost ones are mourned as carried off, by the vindictive and remorseless Charon, from home and friends and all the joys and pursuits of the upper world, to his dreary realm of Hades. This lower world is generally pictured as a tent, green or red outside, but black within, under which are held dismal banquets on the bodies of the dead. Charon goes out hunting on his black horse, and returns laden with human spoil of both sexes and all ages—

The young men he before him drives, and drags the old behind him,
While ranged upon the saddle sit with him the young and lovely.[1]

Though crudely expressed in the mixed and ill-pronounced dialects of the various localities to which they belong, these death-ballads are by no means devoid of finely imaginative and poetic ideas. Many are, no doubt, of considerable antiquity, and have been transmitted as heirlooms from mother to daughter through countless generations. Every woman knows by heart a considerable number, suited to all occasions; and if these are found insufficient to express the overwrought feelings of a bereaved mother, daughter, wife, or sister, her grief will find vent in an improvised *myriológos*, less measured and rhythmical, perhaps, than the conventional dirge, but equally marked by touching pathos and poetic imagery. The following are a few repre-

[1] *Greek Folk-songs*, p. 113.

sentative pieces in the metre and rhythm of the
originals, which may give some idea of the style of
lamentation used on these occasions.

DIRGE FOR A FATHER.

Now sit around me, children mine, and let us see who's absent:
The glory of the house has gone, the family's supporter,
Who to the house a banner was, and in the church a lantern.
The banner's staff is broke in twain, the lantern is extinguished.
Why stand ye, orphaned children, there, like wayfarers and strangers?
And from your lips comes forth no wail, like nightingale's sad singing?
Your eyes, why weep they not amain, and stream like flowing rivers?
Your tears should spread, a mere, around, should flow a cool fresh fountain,
To bathe the weary traveller, and give the thirsty water.[1]

DIRGE FOR A HOUSE-MISTRESS.

What is this noise falls on our ears, and what is this loud tumult?
Say, can it for a wedding be, or can it be a feast-day?
The good wife now is setting forth, to Hades she's departing;
She hangs her keys upon the wall, and sets her house in order,
A yellow taper in her hand. The mourners chant sad dirges;
And all the neighbours gather round, all those whom death has stricken.
Whoso would now a message send, a letter let him give her;
She who a son unarmèd mourns, now let her send his weapons;
Write, mothers, to your children dear, and ye, wives, to your husbands,
Your bitter grief, your suffering, and all your weight of sorrow.[2]

---

[1] Used in Malakassi, Epirus: *Greek Folk-songs*, p. 120.
[2] Used in Epirus: *ibid.* p. 121.

DIRGE FOR A DAUGHTER.

"O tell me, tell me, daughter mine, how long shall I await thee?
Say, six months shall I wait for thee, or in a year expect thee?
Six months—it is a weary time; a year—it is unending!"
"My mother, were it but six months, or were it but a twelve-month!
Then would the evil be but small, the time would fly full quickly.
Now will I tell thee, mother mine, when to expect my coming:
When thou shalt see the ocean dry, and in its place a garden;
When thou shalt see a dead tree sprout, and put forth leaves and branches;
When thou shalt see the raven black, white-feathered like a pigeon."[1]

The following touching lament is sung by a much bereaved father over the body of his only son. It is from the island of Mytilene.[2]

> Within a gloomy cavern I
>   Will hide me from the light,
> From cruel scourgings I'll not cease
>   Till life is put to flight.
>
> Say, O my Fate, were not enough
>   The woes of other years?
> Must thou again misfortune send,
>   To flood mine eyes with tears?
>
> I, Fate, am now a fruitless tree,
>   A honey-emptied hive;
> And all the summer of my life
>   Of joy thou dost deprive.
>
> I come, my son, to take my leave
>   Of thy two eyebrows black;
> Alas! alas! thy comely limbs
>   The worm will soon attack!

[1] *Greek Folk-songs*, p. 122.
[2] *Les Littératures Populaires*, vol. xxviii. p. 269.

A ladder will I place to reach
    Thy grave so dark and cold;
So I may come to visit thee,
    And we may converse hold.

If I a swallow were, my way
    Above thy grave I'd take;
Perhaps my tears may rouse thee still,
    And from thy deep sleep wake?

If thou thy mother dear shouldst meet,
    In thine take thou her hand,
And say, I grieve when winter chills
    Or summer cheers the land.

Couldst thou not, Charon, pity feel,
    And spare my heart's dear joy?
He was his mother's only son,
    Her musk-fed,[1] much-loved boy.

Shutters and windows would that earth
    Might make her where he lies,
That I might go and gaze upon
    His eyebrows and his eyes.

Thy childhood's haunts thou now must leave,
    And from thy village roam;
Leave all the comrades of thy youth,
    And tear thee from thy home.

My garments I will dye them black
    As raven's feathers are,
And, seeking for the child I've lost,
    I'll wander near and far.

If, when a year or two have flown,
    Thou hither com'st again,
In mourning still thou'lt find me clad,
    And thou wilt weep with pain.

---

[1] μοσκαναθρεμμένο.

O speak to me, as I to thee!
　Come, as in other years,
Let us the black earth over those
　We've lost bedew with tears.

Dost thou, O Charon, feel no ruth
　For all thou'st done to me?
Insatiate yet, my tear-dimmed eyes
　Still wouldst thou weeping see?

Two blows, two swiftly following blows,
　Thou'st dealt me with thy dart,
The one has pierced me in my head,
　The other in my heart.

LAMENT OF A WOMAN OF PLUMARI (MYTILENE) FOR THE DEATH OF HER SON.[1]

All pensively my gaze upon the hills I bend,
Why do they not for grief their snow-clad summits rend?
I pass along the road, sweet scents my senses greet,
The ground I know was pressed by Panaghióté's feet.
Put on thy rustling blue *vrakià*,[2] and thy Arabian zone,
Come from thy grave and walk abroad, thou'lt be outshone by none.
Where wast yestreen, and fore yestreen, and the long, lonesome night?
I trimmed the lamp, the tapers lit, that thou might'st see their light.
Gold coin placed on the *kólyva*, let quarter liras shine;
For 'tis his toil which all has earned, and they are his, not mine.
When first I heard that death my boy from my fond arms had caught,
Alas for me! I lost my wits, and now I'm one distraught.
Gold coins place on the *kólyva*, ten *grósia*[3] let them be,
For he Plumari's headman was, the first man here was he.

---

[1] *Greek Folk-songs*, p. 273.

[2] βρακιά. The ample baggy breeches of dark-blue cotton, worn by the Greeks of the Islands and of Asia Minor.

[3] γρόσια, piastres. Ten piastres are equal to about two shillings.

The interment usually takes place on the day after death. The invited guests assemble at the house of mourning, bringing with them flowers to lay on the occupant of the unclosed coffin. In the Balkan Peninsula the coin to pay his passage across the Styx, the ναῦλον for Charon, is placed between the lips of the corpse. In Asia Minor and in some of the contiguous islands the coin is placed in the hand. In the island of Rhodes it is customary to place in the mouth of the dead a fragment of tile on which the priest has drawn the mystic sign of the pentacle (πεντάλφα), and the words, "Christ has conquered" ('Ο Χρίστος νίκα), in order to prevent his returning to earth as a vampire. Cake and wine are handed round, and the company, as they partake of these funeral cates, murmur reverentially, "God rest him" ('Ο Θεὸς συγχωρήσει τὸν). After the preliminary prayers have been offered, the coffin is taken up by the bearers, and the procession follows it to the church. In front walk the priests, carrying crosses; behind them are the chief mourners on either side of the coffin, holding the ends of black streamers (ταινία) attached to it. As the funeral train wends slowly to the church, the clergy chant the prayers for the dead. In some inland towns the relatives continue to chant *myriologia* all the way to church, and afterwards to the burial-ground.[1] The body is placed on

---

[1] Sandys, an Englishman who travelled in the East about the middle of the seventeenth century, thus quaintly describes this custom: "Then the choice and prime women of the city, if the deceased were of note, do assist their obsequies with bosoms displaid and their haire disheveled: glad that they have the occasion to manifest their beautie, which at other times is secluded from admirers."—*Travailes, A Relation of a Journey, &c.*, ed. 1652, p. 55. Belon, a Frenchman, writing at about the same period, also says: "Le

a bier in the nave of the church, and the funeral Mass performed. The relatives are then invited to give the deceased the farewell kiss, and the procession sets out for the cemetery. Arrived here, the coffin is placed by the side of the grave, the concluding prayers are offered, and the lid is then nailed down. When the body has been lowered into the grave, the priest throws on the coffin a spadeful of earth in the form of a cross, and then hands the spade to the relatives, who do the same in turn, saying, "God rest his soul" (Ὁ Θεὸς συγχωρήσει τὴν ψυχὴν τοῦ).[1] When the grave has been filled up, the funeral party return to the house of sorrow, where, after performing a ceremonial ablution, they sit down to a repast at which fish, eggs, and vegetables only are served. The house must not be swept for three days after the dead has been carried out of it, and the broom used on this occasion is immediately afterwards burnt.

The mourning worn by Greeks of both sexes is of a most austere character. Ornaments are rigidly set aside, and all articles of dress are of the plainest black materials, cotton or woollen, and made in the most simple fashion possible. In some districts the Greeks, on the death of a near relative, send all their

coustume est que les femmes des Grecs ne se monstrent en public : et toutes fois s'il y a quelque belle femme en la ville et l'on pleure le trépassé, elle se sentira moult heureuse d'avoir trouvé l'occasion de montrer sa beauté accompaignant les autres de la ville attendu qu'elles vont en troupe toutes eschevelées et espoitrinées monstrants aumoins leurs belle charnure. En ces entrefaites les hommes s'y trouvent aussi ; ayant aumoins le plaisir de voir cette fois les femmes et les filles de leurs voisins bien à leur aise : car de les voir en autre saison, il n'y a pas grand ordre."—*Observations*, &c., fol. 6.

[1] In Rhodes a jar of water is broken over the grave at the moment of interment.

wardrobes, not excepting under-linen and pocket-handkerchiefs, to the dyers, the result, as may be supposed, being funereal in the extreme. Women, too, frequently cut off their hair at the death of their husbands, and bury it with them; men, on the other hand, allow their beards to grow as a sign of sorrow. Mourning is also worn for a considerable period. Girls, after their fathers' death, do not abandon their mourning until they marry, and widows and elderly women invariably retain it as their permanent attire. For, in many country districts, custom does not allow women to enter a second time into wedlock, and a widow who ventured thus to violate public opinion would be treated with scant respect by her neighbours for the rest of her days.

On the eves of the third, the ninth, the twentieth, and the fortieth days after burial, Masses are performed for the soul of the departed. These functions are called *kólyva* (κόλυβα); and on the fortieth *kólyva* two sacks of flour are converted into bread, a loaf of which is sent to each family of friends to invite them to the commemoration service, held in the church. One of the large circular copper trays used for baking, and which have a rim about two inches high, is filled with boiled wheat, ornamented on the top with elaborate patterns in almonds and raisins, sesame seeds, cinnamon, sugar-plums, basil, &c., and sent to the church to be blessed, accompanied by a bottle of wine for the priests. The *kólyva* is said to be symbolical of the death and re-birth of Nature, like the myth of Demeter and her daughter; and also to typify, according to the Christian doctrine, that man is "sown in corruption, and raised in incorruption." Each person present takes a handful of the *kólyva*, saying, as he does so, "God rest him." On the following day this ceremony is repeated; and after eating a frugal meal together, the mourners, with their friends, proceed to the cemetery, accompanied by the priest, to erect a tombstone over the grave. The poor of the neighbourhood are in the evening regaled with a supper, during which their wishes for the soul of the departed are repeatedly expressed. The plates and other articles of pottery used at these funeral feasts are broken and left at the grave. Such fragments are found, together with lamps and little terra cotta figures, in the old tombs in Asia Minor—so many of which were discovered during the construction of the Aidin and Cassaba railways—showing that this custom is the survival of an ancient practice.

During the forty days following, tapers are kept burning in the house, and, on the fortieth, the genealogy of the deceased is read before the assembled company, and prayers are offered for the repose of the souls of all his ancestors. These ceremonies are repeated at intervals during the space of three years, at the expiration of which the grave is opened, and the body exhumed. If it is found to be sufficiently decomposed, the bones are collected in a linen cloth, and carried in a basket, adorned with flowers, to the church, where they remain for nine days. The relatives visit the remains every evening, taking with them more *kólyva*, and, if the deceased has been a person of some standing in the neighbourhood, twelve priests and a bishop take part in the Mass performed on the ninth day. The bones are then either put in a box and replaced in the grave, or added to the other ghastly heaps in the charnel-house of the church.

If the body is not found at the end of the three years to be satisfactorily decomposed, grave fears are entertained that the spirit is not at rest, and has not entirely abandoned the body. The most terrible curse that can be pronounced against a Greek is couched in the words, "May the earth not eat you!" (Νὰ μὴ σὲ φάῃ ὁ χόμας). For, if this curse take effect, the object of it will, after death, become that most dreaded of all spectres, a vampire.[1] In order, therefore, to induce the body to "dissolve" (λυόνω),[2] the same ceremonies and prayers are repeated during another three years.

In Asia Minor a ceremony is observed, on the 5th of January (o.s.), called the *Saïa*, a sort of "Day of the Dead." Every family which has lost one of its members during the past year repairs, on the morning of this day, to weep and pray at the graves of the departed. On their return home they sit down to a table, also called *Saïa*, which is spread with Lenten fare—for this is a fast day—consisting chiefly of dishes of *jassoulákia*, or white beans, dressed with oil and vinegar, and fruit. Friends and neighbours arrive during the day, bringing with them two small tapers which they present to the hostess, receiving

---

[1] See Chap. IV.
[2] The widow of Thanasé Vaghia thus addresses her vampire-husband : ' Πὲς μου, Θανάσε, θὲν ἡλύθες ἀκόμα."—*Greek Folk-songs*, p. 129.

from her in return other two lighted ones of her own manufacture. Each guest partakes of the above-named dishes, and, before and after eating, expresses his good wishes for the soul of the deceased. The dishes are not removed until late in the evening, in order that the spirits of the dead, who are supposed to come at nightfall, may also have their share of the feast.

This same day, after sunset, the Turkish *gamins* put on a disguise, which they call *Saïa*, generally a full-sized pair of the wide, baggy breeches commonly worn in those regions, the top of which is drawn round the necks of the little rascals. With a pair of horns fixed on their heads, and as many little bells and tinkling pieces of metal as they can collect, fastened to their disguise, they go into the streets of the Greek quarter, shouting at the top of their voices:

> *Saïa* has come here;
> Tell me, hast thou heard him?
> *Saïa* has saluted thee;
> Say, didst thou salute him?
> The serpent on the rocks doth glide,
> From this *Saïa* to that he goes.
> "Had! hud!" is what he says,
> Telling me to lay me down,
> Where I find tureen of beans.[1]

The boy then throws himself at full length on the ground, and remains there until the housewife comes out and gives him either fruit or money.

[1] *Les Littératures Populaires*, vol. xxviii. p. 293.

CHAPTER IV.

GREEK WOMEN: THEIR BELIEFS AND SUPERSTITIONS.

THE essential points in which the Orthodox Greek differs from the Roman Catholic Church are: (1) The Holy Ghost being held to proceed from the Father only; (2) the administration of the Eucharist in both kinds to the laity; and (3) the substitution in the churches of pictures for images of the Virgin and Saints. The sacraments in the Eastern, as in the Western, Church are seven—Baptism, confirmation, penance, the Eucharist, marriage, administration of unction to the sick and dying, and ordination. Celibacy is required of the higher clergy, but not of the secular priests, or *papas*, though they are forbidden to contract a second marriage. The former are drawn chiefly from the better classes, and in their capacities of Bishops and Archbishops wield a temporal as well as a spiritual authority over their flocks. The Porte exercises no jurisdiction in the internal affairs of its Christian subjects, which are regulated in each diocese by a council of the chief inhabitants, presided over by the Bishop or Archbishop. The Primates also act as intermediaries between the Christians and the Turkish civil authorities when they have any disagreement with Moslems.

It is, however, impossible to conceive a clergy more ignorant than the parish priests. They belong almost exclusively to the lower ranks of the people, and are as poor and uncultured as their parishioners. Such a priesthood could naturally have very little, if any, moral influence. But the peculiar position of the Greek nation, surrounded by a dominant population, alien alike in creed and race, has caused them to look upon their Church and its ordinances as part and parcel of their national existence; and an ignorant clergy naturally attaches greater weight to outward observances and superstitious practices than to the spiritual teaching of the Church. To a people so debased as in some localities to have forgotten their mother tongue, these practical observances of religion constitute a visible catechism which has done more to keep them faithful to the Church of their fathers than could have been effected by the most eloquent sermons. For, being severely imposed and solemnly observed, they appeared to the vulgar as divinely instituted ordinances, the neglect of which would draw upon them the wrath of God and His saints as much in this world as in the next.

The natural result of such a form of Christianity is extreme free-thinking among those sufficiently educated to disbelieve all the superstitions in which they have been cradled. But whatever may be the private convictions on religious matters of the cultured classes, the Church of their fathers is respected as a time-honoured institution, which has been of the utmost service to the nation during the dark centuries of Ottoman oppression. And though many, both among the clergy and the laity, are sensible of the inconvenient length of their liturgies, and of the absurdity of the superstitious customs which have been engrafted upon, and have grown up into, their religion, yet they fear, in their present political situation, to make any reforms, as the schisms which would result would inevitably weaken the unity of the Greek nation. Even the change from the "Old" to the "New" Style of reckoning is still considered as "hazardous" as when Sir Paul Rycaut wrote, two centuries ago: "lest the people, observing their guides to vary in the least point from their ancient, and (as they imagine) their canonical profession, should begin to suspect the truth of all, and from a doubt dispute themselves into an indifference, and thence into an entire desertion of the faith."[1]

Religion, consequently, as understood by the mass of the people, consists of an agglomeration of superstitious rites concerning times and seasons, fasts and feasts. And, notwithstanding that the Greeks consider themselves Christians *par excellence*, they have remained in sentiment as essentially pagan as were their predecessors in classic times.

The life of a *papadiá*, as the wives of the lower clergy are called, differs in no way from the lives of other women of the peasant and artisan class, save, perhaps, that she has more difficulty than they have in making both ends meet on the proceeds of church fees for christenings, weddings, and funerals, which, with the few piastres paid annually

[1] *The Present State of the Greek and Armenian Churches.*

by each family, constitute the income of a *papas*. Regular attendance at the services of the Greek Church is not required of women, especially before marriage. Girls, as a rule, go to Mass only on great festivals and special occasions, when they sit—or rather stand, for seats are almost unknown in Eastern churches—apart from the men in a gallery called the *gynaikonitis*, extending to the *bema*, or chancel, and approached by an external staircase. It is recorded that St. Basil, having once detected a woman making signs to the officiating assistant-deacon during the celebration of the Liturgy, made it a rule that the easternmost part of the *gynaikonitis* should be fitted with a curtain. The elderly women are the most assiduous church-goers, as they are less occupied with household duties, and their frequent appearance out of doors is not calculated to give rise to gossip. The churches are, however, open on week-days, and the younger women may frequently be seen making their obeisances (Μετάνοια) before the "Holy Gates," or lighting a taper in honour of an *eikon* of the Virgin-Mother or a favourite saint. Greek women and girls are also the most scrupulous observers of all the formulas prescribed by the Church and by custom with respect to fasts and feasts, and the events of the ecclesiastical year. Like the Roman Catholics, they make the sign of the cross before and after meals, and before their night and morning prayers, which they repeat standing before the picture of the *Panaghia*, the Roman Catholic Madonna, which is always illuminated by a tiny lamp.

Although Greek monasteries are to be found in every part of the Empire inhabited by members of the Orthodox Church, testifying to the popularity among men of a conventual life—at least in the past—few nunneries exist at the present day, and the number of inmates in those which still survive is very small. A cloistered life naturally offers few attractions to women with whom marriage is the rule, and in whom family sentiment is so strongly developed. The nuns, called καλογρηαί ("good old women"), are generally elderly and childless widows, or plain and portionless spinsters, who, being without family ties, and without means of support, are glad of the asylum offered by the nunneries.[1] The communities are, as a rule, very small, consisting sometimes of not more than six members, and the discipline is by no means very strict. The nuns at Ioannina were very glad to let their guest-chambers, not only to the Bishop of Paramythia on his visits to the Epirote Capital, but to his friend Mr. Stuart Glennie, and his servant, during their six weeks' stay there; and welcomed him, when he cared to look in on them, either in their weaving-room, or in their divan, with the customary coffee and sweets. I have had the advantage of perusing some of the proof-sheets of Mr. Stuart Glennie's travels, and am allowed to quote the following graphic description of the architectural style of an Eastern nunnery, and the mode of life pursued therein:—

"Suppose a visitor had raised the heavy iron ring

[1] Mr. Tozer, in his *Highlands of Turkey*, inaccurately describes the Greek nuns as servants in the monasteries.

($\sigma\iota\delta\eta\rho\text{ov}$), and knocked at the outer door under my windows, it would have been opened either by my servant or by one of the black-robed nuns, my hostesses. . . . . He would have been admitted, not at once into the house, but into a gateway under my rooms, and, passing through this, he would have found himself in a little courtyard, roofed in great part by a vine, and with a draw-well on the left, from which a nun probably would have been filling a pitcher. On the left, he would also have found a staircase, outside the house, as is usual here, but covered by the far-projecting eaves. This led to the guest-chambers which I occupied. At the opposite end of the courtyard he would have observed another outside staircase, leading to the dormitory of the nuns. Into a passage under this dormitory opened two rooms—the one the workroom of the nuns, where, sitting at their looms, they wove a fine linen gauze; and the other their divan, or drawing-room, as we should say. Beyond the passage was another little courtyard, with the kitchen, other offices, and another outer staircase. And, as the front courtyard was roofed by a wide-spreading vine, the back yard was embowered by pleasantly shadowing trees, hardly yet touched by autumn, though it was now November, and we were in a highland strath 1000 feet above the level of the sea. Ascending my stair-case, a visitor would have found on the right of the landing, and projecting from the balustrade, the open-air washstand, characteristic of houses in Turkey, and on the left was the entrance to my apartments."[1]

[1] *Ancient Hellas.*

At Kallone, in the island of Mytilene, is a nunnery which is used as a penitentiary for women whose conduct has caused social scandal. They do not live in common, like the generality of nuns, but rather like the Sketé monks of Mount Athos, each having her separate little chamber and her patch of garden, which she cultivates with her own hands, and the produce of which suffices for nearly all her wants. Any further necessaries are purchased with the proceeds of their industry in spinning and knitting.

The morals of the nuns generally at the present day would seem to be fairly good, so far as I have been able to ascertain. If, however, folk-poesy is any authority, this does not appear always to have been the case, for the songs and stories belonging to the humorous class contain perhaps as many allusions to the short-comings of the "good old women" as they do to those of the "good old men."[1]

The Greek year may be said, roughly speaking, to be divided pretty equally between fast days and feast days, both being observed with equal fidelity. The fasts are kept with no less patience and sobriety than superstition, it being accounted a greater sin to eat of food forbidden by the Church than to break one of the Ten Commandments. The women and girls of the lower orders especially often incapacitate themselves for work during Lent by living exclusively on bread and vegetables; and to housewives in the Levant this period and the subsequent Easter feasting are a yearly trial, as all the native servants are

---

[1] See, for instance, in Economides' Τραγούδια του Ὀλύμπου and Aravandinos' Συλλογὴ δημωδῶν Ἠπειρωτικῶν ἀσμάτων.

more or less unfit for their duties. Even when seriously ill, no nourishing food will be taken, the patient deeming it "better to fast and die than eat and sin." For no "indulgences" are granted by the clergy in this respect, though, if applied to by the doctor, they will promise absolution to the sufferer for infringing the commands of the Church.

Besides Lent, there are three other great fasts—that of the Holy Apostles, which begins a week after Pentecost and terminates on the 29th of June; that preparatory to the Feast of the Assumption, from the 1st to the 15th of August, when women and girls abstain even from oil; and the forty days of Advent. Wednesdays and Fridays are, nearly all the year round, days of abstinence, except in the eleventh week before Easter, called in Asia Minor *Arzieburst*. A strange reason is given for this exception, which has, however, the authority of Christophoros Angelos. A dog of the name of Arzieburst belonged to certain heretics, and was in the habit of carrying letters for them. When this much-prized animal died, his owners, to show their sorrow, fasted on every anniversary of the event; and the Orthodox, in opposition to, and in order to have no conformity with, them, appointed that the Wednesday and Friday of this week should be exempt from any obligation of abstinence. All sorts of strange beliefs and odd customs are, indeed, connected with these fasts and festivals, the origin and meaning of many of which it is impossible to discover; all the reply one receives to inquiries being, "We have it so" ("Ετσι τὸν 'χωμαι ἐμεῖς), accompanied by a shrug of the shoulders, indicating the superior position and privileges of the Orthodox.

Like all the other Eastern Christians, the Greeks adhere to the Old or Gregorian Calendar, and their year begins twelve days later than ours. The 1st of January is dedicated to St. Basil (Ἄϊ-Βασίλος), who appears to have been a native of Cesaræa, or, as it is locally called, Kaisariyeh, in Cappodocia. In Asia Minor, and also in Epirus, children go from house to house on this day singing odes in honour of the Saint, which, however, generally conclude with some complimentary lines to the occupants, wishing them "A good year," and requesting *largesse*. St. Basil is always described in these songs as a schoolboy, whose touch quickens inanimate objects with new life.

> The month's first day, the year's first day, the first of January,
> The circumcision day of Christ, and likewise of St. Basil!
> St. Basil, see, is coming here, from Cappadocia coming,
> A paper in his hand he holds, and carries pen and inkhorn.
> With pen and inkhorn doth he write, and reads he from the paper.
> "Say, Basil, say, whence comest thou, and whither art thou wending?"
> "I from my home have now come forth, and I to school am going."
> "Sit down and eat, sit down and drink, sit down and sing thou for us!"
> "'Tis only letters that I learn, of singing I know nothing."
> "O, then, if you your letters know, say us your *Alpha, Beta*,"
> And as he leant upon his staff, to say his *Alpha, Beta*,
> Although the staff was dry and dead, it put forth freshest branches.

And on the topmost branch of all there perched and sang
    a partridge,
Who water took up in her claws, and oil upon her feathers,
To sprinkle on her ladyship, her nobleness to sprinkle.[1]

The Eve of Epiphany, as described in the previous chapter, is called in Cappadocia *Saïa*, and observed as a Day of the Dead. According to a local belief, a stream of gold runs in the water during a few minutes of this night. The country people accordingly hasten about midnight with their pitchers to the fountains and brooks, in order to catch, if possible, some of the precious fluid. Another superstition says that at the same time the plants bend their stems, and the trees their summits, in adoration of Jesus Christ, the following day being the Epiphany. Popular tradition relates that a certain woman witnessed this miracle several times. One night she succeeded in tying her kerchief to the top branches of a tall poplar at the moment the tree was making its obeisance. The next day the kerchief was found flying from the crest, which proof, of course, entirely convinced the hitherto incredulous.

The next Church festival is the Baptism of Christ, called the Feast of the Lights, for which there are also odes naïvely describing the accomplishment of this rite by St. John the Baptist on the person of Jesus.

The Greek observance of the Carnival varies according to locality, but it is only in Constantinople and Smyrna that it partakes of the

---

[1] Aravandinos, Συλλογή, &c., No. 152. See also *Greek Folk-songs*, p. 96, for other example.

popular character of the Roman Catholic Carnival, which precedes it. The greater importance given to this season in these cities is due no doubt to the example of the Frank population, who do not fail to

> take their fill of recreation,
> And buy repentance ere they grow devout.

It is only, however, to the Greek women of the better classes that the Carnival furnishes much amusement in the shape of fancy balls and masqued parties. The women of the lower orders must, as a rule, rest content with listening to the passing music —generally of a very primitive kind—and occasionally exchanging a little badinage through their grated windows with the young men of the quarter, who roam the streets after sunset in various disguises. In the old-fashioned houses, which have no windows looking on the street in their lower stories, even this is impossible, and the paterfamilias has to be cajoled into conducting his daughters to the more modern dwelling of a friend or neighbour, whose lighted and unshuttered windows tacitly announce the family to be "at home" to masquerading callers. On the last Sunday of the festal season this species of amusement begins in the afternoon, and is kept up till nine or ten o'clock. Then the shutters are closed, the Carnival is over, and a hard-boiled egg is handed to each person before going to bed, which "shuts the mouth to flesh" until Easter Day, when it is "opened" with another egg.

Many women and girls abstain entirely from food during the first two days of Lent, and, indeed, until they have received the communion on Ash Wednesday at noon, when they satisfy themselves with Lenten dishes. Betrothed maidens who have rigidly observed this fast, receive on the following Saturday from their *fiancé*, or his parents, a present, which is called " The gift of the three days' fast."

The Eve of Palm Sunday is sacred to Lazarus. Most of the songs sung in the streets on this occasion are a curious medley of dialogue between Christ, Martha, Mary, and Lazarus, and complimentary speeches and good wishes to the neighbours. It is almost impossible to reproduce them in rhyme, and I will attempt here only a literal translation of one belonging to Ioannina :—" Good day to you, good evening to you, we are glad to see your worships ! If you are sleeping, pray awake ; if you are sitting, pray arise ! Where wert thou, Lazarus, that thou comest forth now, and appearest in the town with thy shroud wound round thee ? "

" I was buried deep in the earth, with my poor hands crossed on my breast and my feet together, my poor eyes full of tears and my mouth of bitter poison. Then Christ came and awoke me, and raised me out of my tomb."

" Lazarus has come, and Palm Sunday, and the great and holy day. The maidens have come in flocks.[1] Maidens mine, cross yourselves, and honour the good gentleman and the good and stately lady."

On the following day, which is called *Vaia* (Βαια or Κυριακὴ τῶν Βαιῶν), similar songs are sung. It is

---

[1] Ἦρθ' ὁ μέρμυγκασ τῶν κορασίδων.
[2] Aravandinos, Συλλογή, &c., No. 155.

customary at Smyrna for the carpenters to present wooden rattles to the children of the families by whom they are employed; and all day long one's ears are assailed with the excruciating noise of these instruments of aural torture, swung round to the refrain of

> Βαίο, Βαίο, τὸ Βαιὸ,
> Τρώμε ψάρι, καὶ κολιὸ.
> Καὶ τὴν ἄλλη Κυριακὴ,
> Τρώμε κόκκινο αὐγὸ.[1]

By some extraordinary coincidence, the springs of the rattles in my neighbourhood were always found to have got out of order during the night; and as they no longer made any noise, their youthful owners speedily flung them aside for more amusing toys. On Holy Thursday every housewife boils a number of eggs with cochineal for the approaching Easter festival, and also bakes a quantity of cakes and sweet biscuits. At the hour when the Gospels are read, she takes eggs to the number of the household, including the servants, and one over, places them in a napkin, and carries them to church, where she leaves them until Sunday. The supplementary egg is laid before the Eikonostacion, or Place of the Holy Pictures, and is afterwards kept as a remedy against all kinds of ills. Many of these eggs have traced upon them in elegant characters texts of Scripture and other sacred words, with the date.

An Asia Minor superstition says that it is quite

---

[1] Palm, Palm, Palm Sunday;
Koliò fish we eat to-day
And when next Sunday comes
We eat red eggs.

impossible to make bread or cakes on Good Friday, for the water used to mix the dough would "turn into the blood of Jesus Christ!" To shave on that holy day, however, is a meritorious act, which puts to flight tooth-ache; and to wash one's head cures any malady with which it may be afflicted. But to perform either of these operations on any other Friday in the year would only augment both tooth-ache and headache. The house and every corner of the premises must be swept with scrupulous care on "the Great Friday," as any neglected spot would be sure to be found infested by worms or other insects.

During Holy Week, a kind of fortune-telling is performed by means of the hens. A day is apportioned to each member of the family, and according to the number of eggs laid on that day will be his or her prosperity during the coming year.

Late in the evening of Good Friday, a solemn service is held in the churches. I was present on one of these occasions at the Metropolitan Church at Salonica, and was much impressed by the ceremonial. On entering we were conducted to stalls facing the archiepiscopal throne, where sat the Archbishop in his resplendent sacerdotal robes and mitre, glittering with gold and gems. Near us, supported on trestles, was a full-length picture of the Christ, to which the Orthodox worshippers, as they entered the sacred building, advanced and then reverently kissed the semblance of the dead Saviour. Every class of the Orthodox community was represented in the congregation, from the polished Russian and Roumanian diplomat, and Greek Archon of name and lineage, to the ragged and barefooted *gamin*, who, unreproved by pompous verger or beadle, pushed his way through the throng to take the place to which he had an equal right, as a son of the Church, with every other worshipper. When the ritual of chant and prayer had been performed, lighted tapers were distributed, the dead Christ was taken up by the clergy, and carried outside and round the church, followed by the whole congregation. As we again approached the western entrance, the light of the many tapers disclosed what we had not observed, in the darkness, on our arrival, a dozen or so of Turkish soldiers, rifle in hand, seated on the bench inside the great gateway of the churchyard, sent by the authorities to prevent any disturbance of the rites of the Christians by the surrounding Jewish population. For at Salonica the Jews, who, made bold by their superior numbers, drove away St. Paul from this very city to Bérea, would again " stir up the people " against the Christians, and " set all the city on an uproar,"[1] were it not for the Ottoman Governors, by whom the characteristic Hebrew insolence is on occasion instantly transformed into equally characteristic cringing servility.

The Resurrection is commemorated by the Eastern Church strictly " in the end of the Sabbath, as it began to dawn towards the first day of the week "[2]—that is, about one o'clock on the morning of Easter Sunday—when a ceremony takes place of the same character as that performed in the church of the Holy Sepulchre at Jerusalem. The Archbishop, or chief officiating priest, presents to the congregation

[1] Acts xvii. 5.   [2] Matt. xxviii. 1.

a lighted taper with the words, "Δεῦτε λάβετε φῶς ἐκ τοῦ ἀνεσπέρου φωτὸς, καὶ δοξάσατε Χριστόν τὸν ἀναστάντα ἐκ νεκρῶν" (Arise, and take the flame from the Eternal Light, and praise Christ, who is risen from the dead). Those nearest to him light their tapers from his, and then pass on the flame to those behind them, until all the tapers are kindled. And then rises the triumphant Resurrecton-Song:

Χριστὸς ἀνέστη ἐκ νεκρῶν,
Θανάτῳ θάνατον πατήσας,
Καὶ τοῖς ἐν τοῖς μνήμασι ζωὴν χαρισάμενος.

Christ has risen from the dead,
By death He death hath trampled on,
To those laid in the graves Life having given.

At its conclusion, the Easter greeting, "Χρίστος ἀνέστη" (Christ is risen!), accompanied by a kiss on the cheek, is given by one friend to another, which is responded to by another kiss and the words, "Ἀληθῶς ἀνέστη" (Truly He is risen!). On emerging into the open air, shots are discharged from firearms in honour of the event, an old custom which is still adhered to, in spite of the prohibitions annually issued by the authorities in order to prevent disturbances of the public peace.

At the hour of early Mass the churches are again crowded with worshippers who have been shriven on the previous day, and now partake of the Communion. At its conclusion more salutations of "Christ is risen!" are exchanged, as they wend their way homewards to breakfast on red eggs, Easter cakes, and coffee; and then, as an old writer[1] says, "they

---

[1] Sir Paul Ricaut.

run into such excesses of mirth and riot, agreeable to the light and vain humour of that people, that they seem to be revenged of their late sobriety, and to make compensation to the devil for their late temperance and mortification towards God." The day is given up to relaxation and feasting, the most important event for the women and girls especially being the public promenade in the afternoon, for which they don their new summer dresses, the preparation of which has, it may well be supposed, much occupied their minds during the season of mortification. An equally important festival, at least at Bournabat, is the Feast of the Annunciation. On this occasion the whole of the Greek population assemble in the afternoon in the open space, called, from the adjoining great cistern which supplies the village with water, the *Havoúza*. The toilettes on this occasion are, if possible, still more wonderful than at Easter, and the sight generally attracts a large number of visitors. Manners here are, perhaps, less strict than in other localities, and a good deal of ogling and flirtation may be seen going on. In the evening, dances are held by the village people, to which the young men belonging to foreign families find no difficulty in obtaining admittance. The great dish served on this occasion is a kind of dough-nut called *Loukmas*, or "mouthfuls," eaten with a syrup made from clarified sugar.

The changes of the seasons are still celebrated by the Greeks, especially the coming of the Spring and the rebirth of Nature. In April the swallows are welcomed with songs which recall the χελιδόνισμα of the ancients:

Swallows are returning fast,
Over wide seas they have past;
'Neath the eaves they build their nest,
Sing as they from labour rest.

March, O March, thou snowest amain,
February comes with rain;
April, sweetest of the year,
Coming is, and he is near.

Twitter all the birds and sing,
All the little trees do spring;
Hens lay eggs, and O, good luck!
Already they begin to cluck.

Flocks and herds, a numerous train,
To hilly pastures mount again;
Goats that skip and leap and play,
Nibbling wayside shrubs' green spray.

Birds and beasts and men rejoice,
With one heart and with one voice;
Frosts are gone and snow wreaths deep,
Blust'ring Boreas now doth sleep.[1]

May Day is also greeted with songs, sung at the doors of houses, and wreaths of flowers and branches are twined and hung over the courtyard gateways.

An interesting custom is observed in Thessaly at the Feast of the Summer Solstice, or the "Eve of St. John," called the "Klithona."[2] It is, however, as a rule, performed only in the family circle, and many people long resident in the country are ignorant of it. At sunset, a large jar is filled with water and placed in the garden. Round it the family assemble, each

---

[1] *Greek Folk-songs*, p. 88.
[2] I have not been able to ascertain whether the name for this observance is derived from Κλείδονας, a presage, or augury, or from Κλειδόνω, to lock.

with a leaf or flower, which he or she throws in. A wild dance and chant are kept up all the time. The jar is then carefully covered with a linen cloth, and the youngest of the party goes through the ceremony of "locking" it with the house-key. It is finally set aside until the following day at noon, when the family assemble for the "unlocking." The cloth is removed, and each looks anxiously to see if his or her leaf or flower is floating on the water, as that foretells a long life, and an immersed leaf or flower an early death. A general sprinkling then ensues. The young people chase each other with glasses of water from the bowl, and consider a thorough drenching lucky. Singing is kept up all the time, and an occasional improvised couplet containing a sly personal allusion adds to the general merriment.

In Macedonia the ceremony differs a little, and is generally observed only by the girls and unmarried women, who often make up little parties for the occasion. One of the number is sent to fill a large jar of water at the well or fountain, with the injunction not to open her lips until she returns, no matter who may accost her. Into this jar each maiden drops some small object, such as a ring, bead, or glass bracelet, which is called the *Aklithona*. A cloth is then carefully tied over the mouth of the jar, which is left out all night under the stars. The youths of the neighbourhood are not unfrequently on the alert to discover the hiding-place of the jar, which, if found, they rob of its contents, which the girls have some difficulty in recovering. If all goes well, the jar is uncovered on the following evening at sunset, and one of the maidens, shutting her eyes, plunges her bared arm into the water, and, as she draws out the objects one by one, recites a distich which is received as an augury propitious or the reverse of the matrimonial prospects of its owner. After supper the bonfire is lighted before the gate, and, after taking down and casting into it the now faded garlands hung over the doors on May Day, the young people leap through the flames, fully persuaded that " the fire of St. John will not burn them."

The couplets sung or recited on this occasion, though sometimes impromptu, are generally culled from the national treasury of δίστιχα, twelve hundred of which have been collected by Aravandinos as belonging to Epirus alone. The following may serve as a specimen, though, among so large a number, it is difficult to select the most poetical:

I hear my heart a-sighing, a-weeping with its smart;
And my *nous* which calls in answer, " Have patience, O dear Heart!"

In Cappadocia, St. John's Eve is called the *Kélémené*. On the morning following the Kélémené, all able-bodied persons repair to the fields before sunrise to gather a certain herb having a most unpleasant smell, and called in Turkish *uzerlik*. With it they wreathe the doors and windows of the houses, and it is thrown on the beds of the children and aged people who have remained at home. If a person has been scorched, or otherwise suffered from the effects of the *simoon*, the wind of the desert, a bed of *uzerlik* is prepared for him, by reposing on which he is sure to recover. This superstition is common to both Christians and Turks. A similar ceremony of fire-lighting takes place in this province on the 5th of January (o.s.), and is called *Fishoti*.[1] This is also the name of a *djin*, or demon, which haunts the habitations of man after nightfall between the 27th of November and the 5th of January, when the fires of St. John scare it away. If a window is left the least bit open, or the door ajar, the Fishoti appears and calls the inmates by their names. Should any one be imprudent enough to answer, the demon tears out his tongue and runs away with it, shrieking with laughter. Infants and children of tender age must be specially guarded during this period.[2]

In Thessaly and Macedonia it is customary in times of prolonged drought to send a procession of children round to all the wells and springs of the neighbourhood. At their head walks a girl adorned with flowers, whom they drench with water at each halting-place while singing this invocation:

> Perperià, all fresh bedewed,
> Freshen all the neighbourhood;
> By the woods, on the highway,
> As thou goest, to God now pray:

[1] Messrs. Nicolaides and Roussel, the collectors of the traditions and stories of the volume of *Les Littératures Populaires*, from which I have quoted, suggest that *Kéllémené* and *Fishoti*, having no meaning in the languages of the present inhabitants of the province, Turkish, Armenian, and Greek, must be survivals of the language of the former inhabitants; and Mr. Stuart Glennie has suggested comparison with the language of the Vannic Inscriptions, as to which see Introductory Chapter I.

[2] Compare a similar Bulgarian superstition, Chap. XI.

O my God, upon the plain,
Send thou us a still, small rain;
That the fields may fruitful be,
And vines in blossom we may see;
That the grain be full and sound,
And wealthy grow the folks around;
Wheat and barley,
Ripen early,
Maize and cotton may take root,
Rice and rye and currants shoot;
Gladness in our gardens all,
For the drought may fresh dews fall;
Water, water, by the pail,
Grain in heaps beneath the flail;
Bushels grow from every ear,
Each vine-stem a burden bear.
Out with drought and poverty
Dew and blessings may we see![1]

The Greeks would seem to have assimilated, to a greater extent than any other Christian nation, the heathen festivals and observances of their ancestors; and the classical *genii loci* have only slightly changed their names. At sanctuaries, for instance, formerly dedicated to the Sun (Ἥλιος), homage is now paid to the Prophet, or rather "Saint," Elias, and almost every high hill and promontory is now, as of old, sacred to him. Power over rain is also attributed to this Saint; and, in time of drought, people flock to his churches and monasteries to supplicate the Sun-god in his other character of "The Rainy (ὄμβριος or ὕτιος) Zeus." St. Donato (Ἅγιος, or, vulgarly, Ἅϊ Δονάτος), a favourite saint with the Souliotes, is also merely the transformation of a local pagan deity, Ἀϊδονεύς,[2] the

[1] *Greek Folk-songs*, p. 108.
[2] See *Greek Folk-songs*, Introd. p. 23.

King of the Infernal Regions. And Athena, the divine Virgin (Παρθένος), is now the *Panaghia* (Παναγία), the "All Holy" Virgin Mother. The Virgin has also taken the place of Eos, the Dawn, the Mother of the Sun, who opens the gates of the East through which her son will pass.[1] The Christian celebrations of the annual festivals of these saints are, consequently, merely survivals of pagan anniversaries, held at the church or monastery of the saint who has replaced the heathen divinity. At the more celebrated of these *Paneghyria* (πανηγύρια) a kind of fair is held, which is resorted to by crowds of pilgrims from the country round and the adjacent towns. Caravans may be seen wending their way along the mountain-paths leading to the monastery, some mounted on mules or donkeys, or leading horses laden with panniers full of little ones. On arriving, the devotees at once repair to the church, and, after lighting the customary taper, their first care is to pay to the shrine of the tutelar saint any vow which they may have made during the past year, in earnest of benefits asked or received through his mediation. These offerings often take the shape of a gold or silver aureole for his *eikon*, or perhaps a hand or arm, which is fastened on that part of the painting. Gold coins, too, are often stuck on the cheek of the *Panaghia*, and napkins, embroidered with a representation in gold thread of the Queen of Heaven, are presented to her shrine in return for favours.

As the accommodation afforded by the neighbouring

---

[1] Popular Greek poetry contains many pretty allusions to the dawn. "As beautiful as the sun" is also a common expression.

villages is generally quite inadequate for the number of pilgrims, they are allowed to sleep in the church, and the votive offerings which the visitors leave behind in return for this indulgence constitute quite a little revenue for the monks or priests. Their pious duties accomplished, the pilgrims turn their attention to feasting and merry-making. For at meal-times the whole company, throwing off for the time being their ordinary exclusiveness, unite in a gigantic picnic on the greensward, on the good things they have brought with them, to say nothing of their purchases from the numerous hawkers of fruits, sweets, and cakes whom such an event is sure to attract to the neighbourhood. Dealers in other wares, too, are not lacking, who find plenty of customers among the female portion of the assembly for their gum-mastic, combs, little mirrors, rouge, antimony, and other trifles. Purchasers of the last-mentioned articles may occasionally be found hidden behind the giant bole of a plane-tree putting a few finishing touches to their eyes or cheeks. Music, singing, dancing, and story-telling are the chief amusements, which are kept up to what is considered in the East a late hour. At dawn, however, they are all astir again for early Mass, to which they are summoned by the convent bell, or the *symandrò*, a suspended board struck by a mallet.

Family *Paneghyris* are also celebrated in some parts of the country, and in the islands, on the day of the patron saint of the *paterfamilias*. In Rhodes the housewife bakes on this day five loaves, which, after having been taken to church and blessed, are cut up and distributed to the poor.

On certain feast days a large cake, called a *peta*, is prepared for the use of the family, and a similar one is made for the beggars who may call during the day. To refuse a piece to any one who may ask for it would bring all manner of misfortune to the house. Indeed, at any time, a beggar is never sent away from even the poorest cottage door without a handful of olives or an onion. And I have heard that, during a period of scarcity which occurred in Thessaly some years ago, it was no uncommon thing for a beggar to exchange the pieces of bread which he had received at the doors of the wealthy for some fruit or vegetables from a cottager. It is, however, at Smyrna, considered unlucky to give directly from one's table to the poor, " lest it becomes as empty as theirs."

The Sacred Fountains (Αγιάσματα) have also their yearly festivals, held on the day dedicated to the patron saint who has replaced the local divinity. Circumstances of various import have conferred upon many springs within the walls of Constantinople the reputation of possessing healing power, but a romantic and solitary situation in the neighbourhood of a cavern or grotto is the usual characteristic of an *Aghiasma*. On the occasion of these festivals, multitudes flock to the fountains, bringing with them their sick to drink the waters, which, however, do not as a rule possess any medicinal qualities, but owe their healing virtues solely to belief in the patronage of the tutelar saint. The shrubs and bushes in the vicinity are usually found decorated with tufts of hair and scraps of clothing, affixed as *votiva tabella* by grateful recipients of the saint's favours. The caves in which the crystal drops of water appeared to be distilled from the living rock, were no less delighted in by the nymphs of antiquity than were the perennial springs; but all such natural temples are now appropriated by the Virgin Queen of Heaven. Thus a *Panaghia Spelaiotissa*, or Virgin of the Grotto, may often be found, who receives from the Greek peasant women honours similar to those paid in classical times to the nymphs of whose temples she has usurped possession.

And yet, transformed as so many of these pagan divinities have been into Madonnas and Christian saints, a goodly number still retain their ancient forms and attributes. The "Genius" ($\sigma\tau οιχεῖον$) still haunts

"spring and vale
Edged with poplar pale,"

and is often both heard and seen by lonely shepherd, belated traveller, or maiden who has put off till sunset her daily task of fetching water from the fountain. To the first he may appear as a man-eating monster, but the last he invites in seductive language to visit the beautiful palace in which he resides beneath the water of his well or fountain. The French traveller, Villoison, met with this spirit, under the name of *Teloni* ($Τελώνιον$),[1] in Mykone, and says that there, before drawing water, it is customary to bow three times in honour of the genius of the well. Some of these *Stoicheia*, like the hamadryads of old, dwell in the trees, but have the same propensities as their brethren inhabiting the moun-

---

[1] This name, which was formerly in the plural, $Τελέσματα$, seems to be connected with the Turkish *tellestin*, and with our English "talisman."

tains, rocks, and waters, and can only be slain by that popular hero of Greek folk-song, "The Widow's Son," or by the youngest of three brothers. Many accounts of these contests occur, both in song and story, but the following differs a little from the majority, in possessing as its heroes two Widow's Sons:—

> From walnut-tree, from olive trunk, from out the roots of walnut,
> There came a dread Stoicheíon out, devouring all the heroes;
> Devouring them, destroying them, there was not one remaining.
> The King at last he heard of it, and sorely did it grieve him;
> He sends, a paper he prepares, he writes a little letter;
> He sends it to the widow's sons, to Kosta and to Yanni.
> "My sons, the King he wants you now, my sons, the King he wants you."
> "Suppose he wants to hang us now, suppose he only hangs us?"
> "He does not want to hang you, boys, he is not going to hang you,
> For the Stoicheíon he bids you go which eats up all the heroes,
> Which eats them up, destroys them all, so there's not one remaining."
> Then Yanni did at once set out, and with him too went Kosta.
> And down the mountain slopes they went, and came they to the valley;
> And all around the earth did shake, and all the mountains trembled,
> As forth to them the monster came, and swift advanced to meet them.
> To battle with him on they went, and on the plain they met him.

To Kosta's ear a cry there comes—'tis Yanni who is calling—
"Where art thou, Kosta, brother mine, my brother best
   belovèd?
O come to me, and take me out, for is not my name Yanni?"[1]
And I am Yanni the renowned, I am the famous Yanni,
Who have the fearful monster slain down here within the
   valley."
When up with him did Kosta come, dead found he the
   Stoicheíon.
Now gay and joyful Yanni was, and loudly sang a ditty—
"My Kosta, to our mother go, and go thou to our sister,
And go thou likewise to the King with my congratula-
   tions,
And say that I've the monster slain, yea, say that I have
   killed him!"[2]

A strange legend, current in Roumelia, also relates that the Stoicheíon of the sea was at war for a thousand years with the Stoicheíon of the plane-tree, and that every time a struggle took place and one was worsted, there was great mortality in that neighbourhood.

These *Stoicheía* seem to be the survivors of the beings referred to by St. Paul as "the weak and beggarly elements whereunto ye desire again to be in bondage;"[3] the "rulers of the darkness of this world;"[4] the "rudiments of the world,"[5] &c. For the translation of the word στοιχεῖα as "rudiments" or "elements," also followed in the Revised Version, completely obscures what appears to be far more

[1] Yanni would appear to have become, in the course of the combat, somewhat entangled with the Stoicheíon.

[2] Passow, *Popularia Carmina*, 514. See also *Greek Folk-songs*, "The Stoicheíon and Yanni," "The Stoicheíon and the Widow's Son"; and below, Chap. V., "The Three Wonderful Dresses."

[3] Gal. iv. 9, "Τὰ ἀσθενῆ καὶ πτωχὰ στοιχεῖα."

[4] Ephes. vi. 12, "Τοὺς κοσμοκράτορας τοῦ σκότους τούτου."

[5] Col. ii. 8, 20, "Κατὰ τὰ στοιχεῖα τοῦ κόσμου."

probably the meaning of these passages.¹ In the Apostle's use of the phrase τὰ στοιχεῖα τοῦ κόσμου, he seems to attribute to these genii, or spirits of the Universe, a distinct personality.

The *Drákos*,² though he resembles the Stoicheíon in his characteristics of haunting mountainous and lonely places, and waging war against mortals, in other respects closely resembles the *Rakchas* of Deccan tales, the Troll of Scandinavia, and the Giant of our own nursery stories. Like the generality of these creations of popular fancy, he is big and stupid, and easily outwitted by a crafty and courageous hero. These heroes are, like the slayers of Stoicheía, generally widows' sons, or the youngest of three brothers, but a Beardless Man also plays a prominent part in such adventures. The *Drakos* has also sometimes a wife, the *Drakissa*, who is endowed with propensities similar to those of her husband.³

The Nereids (Νηραίδες), Lamias (Λάμιαι), and Sirens (Τραγουδίστριαι) have also survived, and display very much the same propensities as their classical prototypes. The Nereids, though they occupy in the popular imagination of the Greeks a place similar to the Fairies of more northern countries, and like them are proverbial for their beauty, differ from them

---

¹ See Geldart, *Modern Greek*, pp. 201-5; and *The Gospel according to St. Paul*, pp. 25, &c.; and comp. Mr. Stuart Glennie's *Survival of Paganism—Greek Folk-songs*, p. 12.

² Mr. Geldart, in his translations of some folk-tales from Von Hahn's Παραμύθια renders Δράκος as "Dragon." The Greek Δράκος is, however, a Giant, rather than a Western "Dragon," or Bulgarian *Zmok*. And in the description of St. George's encounter with a "Dragon," the Greek word used is θεριό and not Δράκος.

³ See *Greek Folk-songs*, pp. 67 and 79; and Geldart, *Folk-lore of Modern Greece*, pp. 9, 47, 185, &c.

in being always of the full stature of mortals, and also in being almost universally malevolent. Like the *Stoicheía*, they haunt fountains, wells, rivers, mountains, sea caves, and other lonely places, and generally shun human society. They are, as a rule, solitary in their habits; but may occasionally be seen dressed in white, dancing in companies, in moonlit glades, or on the glistening sands of lonely isles and promontories. It is fatal to see them crossing a river, unless a priest be at hand to read passages of Scripture, and so counteract the spells of the "Devil's Daughters," as they are sometimes called. It is usual, however, to propitiate them by some complimentary epithet, such as "the Beautiful," or "the Good Ladies," in the same way as the Furies were formerly termed the Evmenídes, and as the ill-omened owl is, at the present day, euphemistically called the "Bird of Joy" ($\chi\alpha\rho o\pi o\acute{u}\lambda\iota$). They are said to have the power of banefully affecting women of whose beauty they are jealous, and to be in the habit of carrying off young children, if they are allowed to approach their haunts unprotected. Their fancy for new-born infants is, as I have already noted in the Chapter dealing with Family-ceremonies, a source of great anxiety to mothers and nurses. All kinds of maladies are attributed to the malevolence of the "Beautiful Ladies," and the women and children thus afflicted are termed "possessed" ($\nu\nu\mu\varphi o\lambda\acute{\eta}\pi\tau o\varsigma$), and can only be cured by going to reside in a church or convent, or by pilgrimage to some holy shrine. They also occasionally fall in love with men who, if they return their affection and prove faithful to them, they reward with great prosperity; but if the mortal they deign to favour with their notice ventures to slight their advances, the Nereids revenge themselves by afflicting him with some dire calamity. They possess this power chiefly at the noontide hour, when they rest under the shade of the trees, usually planes and poplars, and near springs and streams; and the wary peasant, fearful of the consequences of annoying these capricious beings, will carefully abstain from disturbing their repose.[1] Phenomena of nature, such as whirlwinds and storms, are ascribed to the agency of the Nereids, and it is customary to crouch down while they are supposed to be passing overhead. If this precaution is not taken, the Nereids seize the too irreverent individual, and carry him or her off to the mountains. Offerings of milk, honey, and cakes are made to them, and placed in certain spots which they are believed to frequent, and the country women, when they see the wind-driven cloud scudding overhead, mutter "milk and honey" (γάλα καὶ μέλι) to avert all evil from themselves. Storms are, indeed, in the East, inseparably connected with, or regarded as, demons, whose wild flights from place to place cause, or rather are, these elemental disturbances, and the church bells are rung to drive them away. Tempestuous weather is also sometimes attributed to the festivities attendant upon a wedding among the Nereids.

The little water-spouts formed of gathered wreaths

---

[1] Similarly, in ancient times it is related that shepherds refrained from playing on their pipes during the noontide hour, lest they might annoy the sylvan god.

of spray so often seen in the Ægean Sea, are looked upon with great awe by the dwellers in the islands and on the seaboard. "The Lamia of the Sea is abroad," say the peasants and fisherfolk, when they see the wind-driven spray wreaths; and having recourse to Christian aid when frightened by pagan superstitions, and *vice versa*, they cross themselves repeatedly and mutter prayers to the *Panaghia* for protection against these demons of the air and water. The Lamiæ are generally ill-favoured and evilly disposed women who haunt desert places and seashores. Sometimes, however, they take the form of beautiful women, who, like the Sirens, lure men to destruction by their sweet voices and graceful dancing, or, as recorded in the Salonica folk-song, lay wagers with them, in which the mortal is sure to be the loser.

> Then from the sea the Lamia came, the Lamia of the ocean—
> "O play to me, my Yanni, play, make with thy pipe sweet music;
> If I should weary of the dance, thou for thy wife shalt take me;
> If thou shouldst weary of thy pipe, I'll take away thy sheepcotes."
> And all day long, three days he piped, three days and nights he whistled;
> And Yanni then was wearied out, and sorely worn with piping:
> She took from his flocks of sheep, of all his goats she robbed him;
> And forth he went to work for hire, and labour for a master.[1]

Occasionally, too, they entice youths into their

Greek Folk-songs, p. 75.

abodes under the semblance of distressed damsels, who have let a ring fall into the water.[1]

There are stories of Lamiæ who have wedded mortals and borne children to them. But woe to the man who has such a helpmate! For she can neither spin, weave, knit, nor sew, and is equally incapable of sweeping, cooking, baking, or taking care of the domestic animals. So firm a hold has this belief on the popular mind, that the expression " a Lamia's sweepings " (Τὰ φροκαλιὰ τῆς Λαμίας) exists as a domestic proverb, generally applied by indignant housewives to a careless use of the broom.

The Fates (Μοῖραι) of to-day closely resemble their classical prototypes. They are represented as continually engaged in spinning the thread (νῆμα) symbolical of the life of man, and preside more especially over the three great events of his existence, birth, marriage, and death—the "Three Evils of Destiny" (τὰ τρία κακὰ τῆς Μοίρας), a very significantly pessimistic phrase. Although the Fates are perpetually roaming about in the fulfilment of their arduous labours, the peaks of Olympus constitute their special abode; and it is to this Mountain of the Gods that those who desire their assistance turn to utter the invocation:

> O! from the summit of Olympus high,
> From the three limits of the sky,
> Where dwell the dealers out of destinies,
> O! may my own Fate hear me,
> And, hearing, hover near me![2]

Perhaps the most ghastly of the Greek superstitions

---
[1] *Greek Folk-songs*, p 76.   [2] Heuzey, *Le Mont Olympe*.

is that of the Vampire, generally known in the Balkan Peninsula by the Slavonic name of *Vrykolakas*. This circumstance, and the fact of the widespread belief in this spectre among Slavonic nations, have been by some folk-lorists considered sufficient to justify their assigning it an origin purely Slavonic. This opinion, however, I venture to think, can hardly be sustained. For, not only does this ghoul bear in Crete and in in Rhodes the thoroughly Hellenic designation of *Katakhnas* (καταχνᾶς); in Cyprus, that of *Sarkoménos* (σαρκωμένος), the "Fleshy One"; and in Tinos, of *Anaikathoúmenos* (ἀναικαθούμενος), the "Restless One;" but, as Mr. Stuart Glennie has pointed out to me, there is distinct evidence that the notion of vampires has, like so many other superstitions, a Chaldean origin. In the great Chaldean epic of the third millennium B.C., Istar in Hades gives utterance to the threat, "I will cause the dead to arise and devour the living." And in Egypt also the souls were imagined to return as vampires.[1]

As has already been described, it is customary with the Greeks to exhume the body of a deceased relative at the end of three years in order to ascertain if it is properly decomposed. Should this not be the case, the dead man—the *Vrykolakas* is generally of the masculine sex—is supposed to be possessed of the power of rising from the grave, and roaming abroad, revelling in blood, and tearing out the livers of his victims. The causes of vampirism are various, and among them are the following: the fact either of having perpetrated, or of having been the

[1] Compare Lenormant, *Chaldean Magic*, pp. 37 and 100.

victim of, a crime; having wronged some person, who has died resenting the wrong; or of a curse, pronounced either in excommunicatory form by the priest,[1] or by a person to whom an injury has been done, as in the folk-song of "The Old Man's Bride":—

> Cursed may my mother be; and Earth, dissolve not in thy bosom
> The go-between whom she employed to settle my betrothal![2]

"May the earth not eat you!" (Νὰ μὴ σὲ φάη ἡ γῆς), is also a common expression in the mouth of an angry Greek. For a vampire is not, as Dr. Tylor's "Animism" requires him to contend,[3] a disembodied soul, but an undissolved body.

Vampirism is believed to be hereditary in certain families, the members of which are regarded with aversion by their neighbours and shunned as much as possible. Their services are, however, called into requisition when there is a vampire to be laid, as they have the reputation of possessing special powers in this direction. It is generally believed that the vampire retires to his grave before cockcrow, but some maintain that he visits it only once a week, on the Saturday. When it is discovered that such a *Vrykolakas* is about, the people go on a Saturday, and open his tomb, where they always find his body just as it was buried, and entirely undecomposed.

---

[1] Part of it runs thus: "Let him be separated from the Lord God Creator and lie accursed and unpardoned and indissoluble after death in this world and in that which is to come. Let wood, stones, and iron be dissolved but not he."—*Present State of the Greek and Armenian Churches*, p. 274.

[2] *Greek Folk-songs*, p. 179.

[3] *Prim. Culture*, vol. i. p. 175.

The priest who accompanies them reads certain parts of the ritual supposed to be of peculiar efficacy for putting a stop to the restless wanderings of vampires, and sometimes this course suffices to restore the neighbourhood to peace and quiet. But cases happen in which the priest is not a sufficiently powerful exorcist, and, when all his endeavours have proved inefficacious, the people of the neighbourhood go to the tomb on a Saturday, and either drive a stake through the heart of the undissolving corpse, or take out the body and consume it with fire. Nothing short of extreme necessity would, however, make Orthodox Greeks consent to perform such an act, as they have a religious horror of consuming with fire a body on which the holy chrism has been poured by the priest when performing the last rites of his religion.

I have heard and read stories innumerable of the doings of vampires, but was never favoured with a manifestation by one of those uncanny visitants. There is a touching story told in folk-song of a dead man who, though the "earth was eating" him, was called from his grave by the passionate entreaties of his mother, reminding him of his promise to bring back to her his sister who had been married to a bridegroom from Babylon.[1] The Greek poet, Valaorites, also describes, in a splendidly realistic poem, the rousing from their graves of the tyrant, Ali Pasha of Tepelen, and his Greek lieutenant, Thanâsé Vaghia, by the vampires of the massacred inhabitants of Gardiki.[2] One of the most thrilling modern vampire stories I have met with is the following, which was

[1] *Greek Folk-songs*, p. 126. [2] *Ibid.* p. 129.

related to Mr. Pashley[1] by a Cretan peasant, who had been an eye-witness of the occurrence.

"Once on a time the village of Kalikráti was haunted by a vampire (καταχανᾶς), which destroyed both children and many full-grown men, and desolated both that village and many others. They had buried him in the church of St. George at Kalikráti, and in those times he was a man of note, and they had built an arch over his grave. Now a certain shepherd, his mutual *synteknos* (σύντεκνος),[2] was tending his sheep and goats near the church, and on being caught in a shower he went to the sepulchre for shelter. Afterwards he determined to pass the night there, and after taking off his arms he placed them crosswise by the stone which served him for a pillow, and, because of the sacred symbol they formed, the vampire was unable to leave his tomb. During the night, as he wished to go out again that he might destroy men, he said to the shepherd, 'Gossip, get up hence, for I have some business to attend to.' The shepherd answered him not, either the first, the second, or the third time, for he concluded that the man had become a vampire, and that it was he who had done all these evil deeds. But when he spoke for a fourth time the shepherd replied, 'I shall not get up hence, gossip, for I fear you are no better than you should be, and may do me a mischief; but swear to me by your winding-sheet[3] that you will not hurt me, and then I will get

---

[1] *Travels in Crete*, p. 226.   [2] See above, p. 71.
[3] This oath is supposed to be the only one which binds a vampire— "μὰ τὸ διαβόλι μου."

up.' He did not, however, pronounce that oath, but said other things; but finally, when the shepherd did not suffer him to get up, the vampire swore to him as he wished. On this he rose, and on his taking up his arms the vampire came forth, and, after greeting the shepherd, said to him, 'Gossip, you must not go away, but sit down here, for I have some business which I must go after. But I shall return within the hour, for I have something to say to you.' So the shepherd waited for him.

"And the vampire went a distance of about ten miles where there was a couple recently married, and he destroyed them. On his return the shepherd saw that he was carrying some liver, his hands being wet with blood, and as he carried it he blew into it, just as the butcher does, to increase the size of the liver. And he showed his gossip that it was cooked, as if it had been done on the fire. 'Let us sit down, gossip, and eat,' said he. And the shepherd pretended to eat it, but only swallowed dry bread, and kept dropping the liver into his bosom. Therefore, when the hour of their separation arrived, the vampire said to the shepherd, 'Gossip, this which you have seen you must not mention, for, if you do, my twenty nails will be fixed in your children and yourself.' Yet the shepherd lost no time, but gave information to the priests and others, who went to the tomb and found the vampire just as he had been buried, and all were satisfied that it was he who had done all the evil deeds. So they collected a great deal of wood, and they cast him on it and burnt him. When the body was half consumed, the gossip too came forward, in order that he might enjoy the ceremony. And the vampire cast, as it were, a single spot of blood which fell on his foot, and it wasted away as if it had been burnt with fire. On this account they sifted even the ashes, and found the little finger-nail of the vampire, and burnt that too."

When a vampire-haunted community have not cared to proceed to the extremity of burning the corpse suspected of troubling them, they have occasionally, if practicable, resorted to the expedient of removing it to one of the small uninhabited islands of the Ægean, and thus secured themselves from its visitations, as a vampire cannot cross salt water.

Many vampire panics are no doubt attributable to rumours set on foot by persons who profit by such superstitions, and the following, which has been related in *The People of Turkey*, is, I think, a case in point. In 1872 the whole population of Adrianople was thrown into a state of commotion by the reported nightly appearance of a spectre in an elevated part of the town known as Kyik, inhabited both by Greeks and Turks. This spectre was represented as a *Vrykolakas* by persons who affirmed they had seen it lurking in the shadows of the houses —a long, lank object, with a cadaverous, bearded face, and clad in a winding-sheet. The Christian priests and Moslem *hodjas*, who were equally appealed to in this emergency, strove in vain during a fortnight to exorcise the wanderer by their prayers and incantations. Finally, a rumour began to be circulated that the only person possessing the power of freeing the town from this haunting spectre was a Turkish

Djinjí, or magician, famous for his power over evil spirits, who lived in another town, and who would consequently require a large fee for his services. Seven *liras* were, however, soon raised by the panic-stricken townsfolk, the *Djinjí* came, and the *Vrykolakas* was put to flight.

There are no laws in Turkey to interfere with the calling of Witches, and not only in Thessaly, where of old they were especially famous, but in every part of the Empire, they and their powers are held in great estimation by members of all creeds. To the witch repair love-sick maidens and jealous wives, childless women and mothers with ailing children, seekers of lost or stolen property, and for each of her clients the wise woman has a specific. Like the witch of Theocritus, she makes use of the magic power of moonlight to compose her spells and potions; or, crouching hag-like over her charcoal brazier, she throws on the glowing embers laurel-leaves, salt, flour, or cloves, muttering strange words meanwhile, or droning mystic incantations. Faithless lovers had need beware, and furnish themselves with counter-spells, when deserted maidens have recourse to the aid of the *máyissa*. With her aid a "wasting curse" is laid on the offending one, which is thus expressed: "May'st thou" (naming the person) "become attenuated as a thread; and pass through a needle's eye!" (Νὰ γένης . . . . λιγνός σάν χλωστί, νᾶ περνᾶς ἀπὸ βελόνι); "May'st thou become small as my finger!" (Νὰ γένης σὰν τὸ δαχτυλὸ μου). Another form of curse is—

> "Be, who will not love the maid,
> Five years on a sick-bed laid!"
>
> ("Οποιος δὲν τὴν ἀγαπᾶει
> Πέντη χρόνους ν' ἀῤῥοσταῃ.)

The anciently widespread practice of making a wax image of an obnoxious person, and sticking pins in it to injure him, still survives in Turkey, and would seem to be the reason of the reluctance generally shown by the country people in the islands and more remote regions to having their portraits taken, as they consider that the possessor of the picture has power over the original. Fortune-telling is also largely practised by the *máyissas*, and is performed by means of cards, or a tray of beans, coins, and other small objects, manipulated according to some form of calculation. I once formed one of a party of resident Europeans at a Witch's fortune-telling in the Greek quarter of Salonica. The abode of the "spay-wife" was a spacious but gloomy apartment, with a tiny barred window and cavernous chimney-place. Amid the darkness of the unceiled rafters flitted ghostly white pigeons, and when, after a little while, our eyes had become accustomed to the dimness, we descried the typical black cat, whose green eyes regarded us suspiciously from one of the smoke-blackened crossbeams overhead.

If "the oracles are dumb," dreams now serve as a very good substitute for them, and the woman who is not fortunate enough to possess a "Dream-book" ('Ονειροκρίτης) of her own has recourse to the skill of the wise woman, who interprets her dream by means of certain formulas, which have been handed down from the remotest antiquity. For magical secrets are generally hereditary in families, and the daughter, as a rule, succeeds the mother as *máyissa* of the village. In addition to her power of "spaying fortunes," the witch is also able to aid a person who has been the victim of a robbery to discover the thief. The *modus operandi* in vogue at the Dardanelles for this purpose is to procure the leg-bone of a wolf, boil it, together with a plough-share, in milk, and then burn it. The moment the bone is put in the fire the thief's leg will become paralysed. The operator takes good care, however, to let it be well known in the neighbourhood that this unfailing rite is to be had recourse to; and the guilty person, terrified at the prospect of such a punishment, generally finds an opportunity of secretly restoring the stolen property before the day appointed. The services of a *máyissa* of ill repute are often enlisted for the committal, as well as for the discovery, of crime. When brigands are desirous of possessing themselves of money or treasure which they believe to have been hidden out of their reach, they kill or mutilate the person supposed to have concealed it. A portion of his body is taken to some crafty old hag, who adds to her other professions the manufacture of tapers for religious ceremonies; the human fat is extracted, and, mixed with wax or tallow, is made into a candle. Armed with this, the brigand commences his search, in the belief that the light of his taper will be extinguished when he approaches the spot where the treasure is secreted. This superstition accounts for the fingers of captives having been cut off, even when they were not required to send to their friends to stimulate their zeal in procuring the ransom. One of the murderers of a family of seven persons was detected by his having asked a witch to make a "corpse-candle." The crime had been committed for the sake of plunder, and, as the sum found in the house was smaller than the murderers had expected, recourse was had to magic in order to discover the remainder.

A considerable branch of the witch's trade consists in providing love-spells and potions, and, occasionally, spells of a less innocent character. Persons believing themselves to be sufferers from the effects of magic —for a hint is generally conveyed to the subject of the spell—must naturally have recourse to the witch to remove it. Her skill, too, is called in request when ordinary means fail to exorcise that most dreaded of all mysterious powers, the "evil eye." For, notwithstanding the innumerable antidotes used to avert it, persons are often found to be suffering from the effects of the enviously malignant gaze of some evilly disposed neighbour. Fumigations of various kinds are often resorted to in order to dispel the baneful influence, and the wood of the olive-tree, the palm branches blessed by the priest on Palm Sunday, or, if it can be procured, a scrap of the suspected person's dress, are burnt for this purpose.

It would, however, be difficult to enumerate all the means to which recourse is had for dissipating the effects of the evil eye, as they are as numerous

K

as the preservatives against it. Among the latter I may mention the bunches of charms, consisting of gold coins, pointed bits of coral and blue glass, cloves of garlic, blood-stones, cornelians, and crosses, which are worn on the person, or fastened to the headstalls of horses, mules, and donkeys; and the horseshoes, boars' tusks, and hares' heads hung on the walls of houses and other buildings to preserve them from the baneful and mysterious power. One of the smaller charms is generally a tiny forked object of glass or ivory, the significance of which I have not been able to ascertain; but the outstretched first and second fingers appear to have the same meaning. An illustration of this was afforded me a few years ago when visiting at Smyrna an old Catholic Greek lady from the island of Tinos. Her little grandson, who had just arrived from Europe, was, during luncheon, an object of great interest to his grandmother and aunts, who overwhelmed him with laudations. To every complimentary remark, however, made to, or about him, by either this lady or her daughters, another would exclaim, "No! garlic! garlic!" ("Ὀχι! σκόρδον! σκόρδον!), at the same time pointing at the child, thus threatened with the evil eye, the first and second outstretched fingers. For the evil eye may also be cast unwittingly, and without *malice prepense*, and seems in this instance to be a survival of the notion of the "envy of the gods" (φθόνος θεῶν); and it is impossible in the Levant to speak admiringly or approvingly of any person or thing without being met with the exclamation, "*Kalé!* don't give it the evil eye!" (Καλή, μή τὸν ματιάζης!)

Blue glass bracelets are usually worn by girls and young women for the purpose of averting the evil eye, and when they get broken, which, considering the material of which they are made, is sure to happen sooner or later, the event is attributed to the *matiasma* having luckily fallen upon them instead of upon their owners.

The child of a lady whom I knew at Smyrna, having appeared to his devoted old nurse, a Greek woman from the island of Nicarià, to be ailing and out of sorts, she persuaded her mistress to allow her to send for a compatriote skilled in such matters. When the wise woman arrived, I accompanied the mother into the nursery, where we found the infant divested of its clothing, and stretched on the bed on a square of red cloth. Little piles of lighted hemp were smoking like miniature altars at each corner, and the old hag was performing a series of manipulations with the child's limbs, alternately crossing its right leg over its left shoulder, and its left leg over its right shoulder, interspersing these movements with blowings, and attentions to the little altars. The little patient appeared greatly to enjoy the operation, as he crowed and laughed all the time in the face of the witch; and when it was concluded he seemed to have recovered his wonted liveliness. But the sign of the cross made with the baby's limbs while thus "passing it through the fire" certainly represented the symbol of the pagan Sun-god, and not that of the Christian Saviour. And, strange to tell, a far less conventional passing of a sick child through the fire was recently witnessed in

Presbyterian Scotland, as recorded in a paper lately read by the Rev. Dr. Stewart, of Nether Lochaber, before the Scottish Antiquarian Society.[1]

Some people are quite notorious for their power of casting the evil eye, and, though the propensity is much dreaded, they enjoy a certain amount of consideration, as their neighbours are naturally careful not to offend them in any way. Red-haired persons are particularly suspected, and blue or grey eyes, being rare in the East, are considered especially baneful. The latter defect in my personal appearance often caused me to be accused of exercising this spell. I happened one spring day to stop in a street on the outskirts of Bournabat to watch a pair of storks who were busily employed repairing their nests in a cypress-tree, to which they had just returned from winter quarters, and was thus all unconscious that two low-class Greeks were approaching between me and the objects of my attention. A volley of vituperative language, however, in which my eyes

---

[1] "A correspondent while in a remote glen in Wigtownshire last March saw a slight smoke proceeding from a hollow. On advancing to the bank above he saw five women passing a sick child through a fire. Two of the women, standing opposite each other, held a blazing hoop vertically between them, and two others standing on either side of the hoop were engaged in passing the child backwards and forwards through the opening of the hoop. The fifth woman, who was the mother of the child, stood at a little distance earnestly looking on. After the child had been eighteen times passed and repassed through the fiery circle, it was returned to its mother, and the burning hoop was thrown into a pool of water close by. The child . . . . was a weakling, and was supposed to have come under the baleful influence of an evil eye. The hoop had been twisted round with a straw rope, in which a few drops of oil were scattered to make it burn all round at the same time. The child was passed through the hoop eighteen times, once for each month of its age. When it was taken home, a bunch of bog myrtle was suspended over its head."

were vehemently anathematised, recalled my attention to earth, and I was glad to hurry away in an opposite direction to escape the resentment of the men, who believed me to have given them the evil eye, or, in the old English phrase, to have " overlooked them."[1]

Some of the more innocent and graceful forms of divination practised by maidens have their counterparts in Western Europe. Instead, however, of consulting, like Gretchen, the daisy, in order to discover her lover's sentiments, Euphrosyne or Ianthe pull off one by one the petals of a rose, saying, " He loves me, a little, dearly, passionately," &c. To test the sincerity of a lover, one of the rose petals is placed in the palm of the left hand and struck sharply with the right. If it splits open with a report, the augury is favourable.

To ascertain the age of one's future husband three balls of different coloured cotton are placed at night under the pillow, the colour of the first drawn out in the morning indicating whether the bridegroom is to be young, middle-aged, or old.

It would prove a stupendous task to collect all the folk-beliefs and customs of Turkey, so connected are they with every detail of domestic life, and with such varied circumstances; and one generally learns them only by transgressing them. I got into terrible trouble at Smyrna by taking into my room one night a soft, fluffy, bewildered little owlet which I found between the shutter and the window, and thought of keeping as a pet. Great was the dismay, however, next morning of the old Greek nurse when I showed

[1] See Kingsley, *Westward Ho!* chap. vi., &c.

her my prize. "It was a sign of death," she cried, and some terrible calamity was sure to happen in the family. By a strange coincidence, a pet kid which was kept in the garden was on that morning found dead; and after this fatality there was no gainsaying the superstition. It was fortunate for me that the omen was thus fulfilled, or the death from diphtheria of the youngest of the family, which happened not very long afterwards, would have been laid at my door, at least by the old *paramána*. So contagious, however, is superstition, that the mother, though an intelligent and cultivated woman, declared to me that she was sure some misfortune was about to happen, as she had heard, night after night, a screech-owl crying from a cypress near her bedroom window. The sudden death of a bright young English girl was also said to have been omened by some owls having taken up their abode in the cypress-trees at the gate of the house where she lived. This evil reputation in Turkey of the owl—which is also said to precede the vampire in his nocturnal wanderings—is the more curious as, in Athens, no doubt on account of its ancient connection with Pallas-Athená, this bird is considered lucky.

The most trivial circumstances, too, connected with the birth of a child are considered good or bad omens, according to the interpretation given to them. Trifling accidents happening on a wedding-day have a gloomy signification, as have also the breaking of a looking-glass, the accidental spilling of oil (to spill wine, however, is lucky), sweeping the house after the master has departed on a journey, meeting a funeral or a priest, a hare crossing the path, and a thousand other little every-day occurrences. Things lucky and things unlucky, things to be done and things not to be done, would make a long list, but I will give a few specimens belonging both to European and Asiatic Turkey.

It is unlucky to tap a cask of vinegar after sunset, for it will be sure to turn bad.

It is also unlucky to lend a cauldron after sunset. If this is unavoidable, something dirty must be put in to counteract the certain ill effects.

If, after a shower, the rainbow appears over the cemetery, it is a bad sign, for the plague or some other terrible epidemic will certainly ensue.

After eating, do not leave crumbs or pieces of bread on the table, but eat your bread up to the very last crumb and you will be sure to be lucky.

It is unlucky to bite one's nails on Sunday. After cutting them, care must be taken to dispose of the parings so that the fowls may not find them. For if a fowl eat nail-parings it will become diseased, and every person who eats its flesh or its eggs will sicken of the same malady.

Soap must never be given directly from the hands of one person into those of another, as to do so would "wash away love."

Hearing a Greek nursemaid one day tell the children, who were making toast, that "God said bread was to be cooked once, and it was a sin to cook it twice," I asked her in what part of the Scriptures this was to be found recorded. "We believe it, but you do not," was all the reply I could obtain. Quite lately, however, I came across a Moslem tradition to that effect, which the Greeks, with the usual liberality displayed in matters of superstition, must have borrowed.

In Thessaly, Saturday is considered an unlucky day on which to begin work of any kind, and it is equally unlucky to finish work upon this day.

No money must be paid away on Monday, or "Saturday will find your purse empty."

The old proverb, "A hair of the dog that bit you," is daily illustrated in this province. Savage dogs, noted for their biting propensities, may be seen deprived of patches of hair which have been cut from their shaggy coats to cure the incisions made by their teeth, no other remedy having half the efficacy.

If mice abound in a house, and are exceedingly troublesome, it is a sign that either the children or the servants have been making free with the contents of the *kilér*, or storeroom—a not unnatural inference!

When a cat licks her paws on that part most sensitive to the stings of insects, it is a sure sign of rain.

At Seriphos, before beginning the vintage, a bunch of grapes is thrown into each house to rid it of vermin, accompanied by this exorcism: "The black grape will sicken you, the black grape will poison you! Out with you, rats! fleas! &c."

Among folk-customs, I may perhaps include the peculiar gestures which are used as a common mode of expression, dispensing with words or accompanied only by a monosyllable. The sign of the negative, the *ananeúein* (ἀνανεύειν), used also by the ancient

Greeks, consists in throwing back the head, and making at the same time a slight noise with the tongue and front teeth. To denote that a person is stingy or miserly, the tip of the thumb is placed behind the front teeth. And utter disapprobation and contempt of another is expressed by taking hold with the finger and thumb of each hand of the upper part of one's dress and shaking it with the ejaculation "Νὰ!" (There!) The climax of contumely appears to be reached when, after a dispute, one of the parties stretches out his hand towards the other's face with the words, "Νὰ σοὺ!" (There's to you!) At Smyrna the commonest form of insult is conveyed in the words, "'Στὰ παλαιὰ μ'τὰ παπούτσια!" (Get under my old shoes!); and in Thessaly an angry woman, quarrelling with her neighbour, concludes her torrent of invective with the wish, "May you burst!" (Νὰ σκάζης).

CHAPTER V.

GREEK WOMEN: THEIR FOLK-POESY.

I HAVE already in the preceding chapter described the beings who figure in the mythological class of folk songs and stories, and I have also referred to the Christian Saints who have in many instances replaced Classic Deities. Many of the stories relating to the supernatural will be found to present features and incidents similar to those which exist in the folk-lore of other nations, and especially in Keltic, Teutonic, Norse, and Eastern fairy-tales.[1] The religious legends are sufficiently numerous, and resemble in many points those told by Moslems of Dervish *Evliya*. There has no doubt been a considerable amount of mutual borrowing in this as in many other respects.

The Greeks take great delight in the histories of their Saints, and recount them with every variety of detail which their lively imaginations can suggest. Among the legends concerning those who occupy a prominent place in the Greek calendar are the wonderful adventures of St. George of Cappadocia, and

---

[1] As so many folk-songs have appeared in preceding chapters as illustrative of folk-ceremonies and folk-beliefs, and as my space here is limited, I would refer the reader interested in the subject, for further specimens of popular verse, to my translations of *Greek Folk-songs*.

the stories of St. Basil, St. Chrysostom, Kosma and Damianos, and of the head of St. John the Baptist. St. George, being the patron Saint of the Hellenes, is naturally held in special reverence, and there is scarcely a town in the Ottoman Empire, or in Greece, which has not at least one church dedicated to him. Countless and wonderful are the stories related of this holy man by his devotees, and, what is still more extraordinary, they believe them all. Ecclesiastical story says that he was of noble lineage, and that he lived in the reign of the Emperor Diocletian. On the outbreak of a fierce persecution, St. George, as the Champion of the Cross, presented himself before the pagan authorities, and boldly declared the Christian religion to be the only true and saving Faith, inveighing against idolatry and superstitious customs, and belief in pagan deities. As a punishment for his boldness, the executioner pierced his body through with a lance. But, though blood flowed profusely, the wound quickly closed again and immediately healed. He was then thrown into a lime-pit, made to walk upon the points of nails, and cast into the flames, but always came out unharmed from every ordeal. The Saint had also the power of raising the dead; and he it was who slew a huge dragon on the banks of the Euphrates. But when the time came for St. George to leave the world, the power of his persecutors prevailed against him. He was decapitated, and his soul ascended into heaven to receive the crown of martyrdom.

In folk-poesy, however, the Saint is chiefly remarkable for his exceedingly acquisitive disposition and amenability to bribery, generally giving his aid to the highest bidder for it, whether implored by human beings or animals, or for a good or a bad purpose, as indeed in the following song he assists a Moslem ravisher in his designs against a Christian maiden.

THE VOW TO ST. GEORGE.[1]

A little Turkish youth was he, one of the Sultan's pages,
Who loved, who loved a Romeot maid, but she did not desire him.
Before her does she put the hills, the mountains leaves behind her,
Within the church she gains at last, she kneels and says three prayers:
"Effendi mine, O dear St. George! now save me from the Moslem!
Of candles *litras* thee I'll bring, and *litras* bring of incense,
And oil in hides of buffalo I'll bring thee by the skinful!"
There opened then a marble slab, within it hid the maiden.
But see! see there! the Turkish youth is drawing near on horseback,
And at the church door he dismounts and there himself he crosses.
"Effendi mine, O dear St. George! now show to me the maiden;
I'll bring thee candles by the load and by the load bring incense,
And by the shipful I'll bring oil, I'll bring it by the boatload!"
Now gapes the marble slab again, and there is seen the maiden.
Then lifts she up her voice on high, cries loud as she is able:
"O list, ye mountains and ye hills, ye vilayets and townships,
The Saint for gain has me betrayed, for treasure he's betrayed me!"

In the story told in Cappadocia, however, the Saint is first made use of, and then cheated of his bribe by the cunning Reynard.

[1] Aravandinos, Συλλογή, &c., No. 159.

The Fox and St. George.[1]

Once upon a time there lived a Fox, who was in the habit of helping himself to the contents of a peasant's poultry-yard.

"I will set a trap and catch the accursed animal," thought the peasant to himself. So he set a trap at the door of the hen-house, and when Reynard came, he found himself caught.

"Here's a sorry business!" said he to himself. "Early in the morning the master will come and kill me; what shall I do? No one can save me! Yet stay, perhaps St. George will."

So Reynard lifted up his eyes to heaven, and prayed—

"Great St. George, if thou wilt deliver me, I will give thee two *okas*[2] of oil!"

The Saint heard, and hastened to deliver Mr. Fox.

"How about my two *okas* of oil?" he then asked.

"You shall have them presently. I am going to fetch them."

So Reynard trotted off to the high-road along which the traders passed with their loads of oil for market. There he lay down by the roadside, and pretended to be dead.

Soon the oil merchants passed by. The first one caught sight of the Fox, and said—

"The man who killed that fox must have been a simpleton not to take his skin!" And he picked up

---

[1] *Les Littératures Populaires*, vol. xxviii. p. 252.

[2] An *oka*, the measure used everywhere in the Ottoman Empire, is equal to about 2⅔ lbs. or 300 drachms. Liquids, as well as solids, are sold by weight.

Reynard and threw him on the back of a mule between the two jars of oil.

"I will skin him at our first halting-place," said the man to himself, "and sell the fur."

When the Fox saw that the man had returned to his post at the head of the file of mules, he began to bite the straps which supported the jars. Very soon the jars slid down to the ground, and the oil ran out in streams.

"Great St. George! great St. George!" cried Reynard, running off as fast as his legs would carry him, "I have neither scales nor weights to give you the two *okas*; come and take as much as you like!"

I cannot omit some mention of M. Clermont-Ganneau's highly interesting researches with regard to the Legend of St. George. Even an abstract, however, of his results would extend to two or three pages. And in order not to interrupt my account of Greek folk-poesy, I shall briefly summarise his conclusions on the subject in a separate note at the end of this chapter.

Kosma and Damianos, who were brothers, are also said to have been, like St. George, natives of Asia Minor. Their father was a pagan, and their mother, Theodosa, a Christian, who, while undertaking herself the religious education of her two sons, had them at the same time instructed in science and all edifying knowledge. They, however, principally applied themselves to the study of medicine, and became so skilful in its practice that no disease of man or beast ever baffled them; and this they did without fee or reward, for which cause the name of *Anaghiroi*, or "they who asked nothing," was bestowed upon them. So strict is Damianos said to have been on this point, that he broke off all relations with his brother for accepting from a widow two eggs wherewith to make an unguent or cataplasm for her sciatica; and such was his resentment that, on his death, he gave orders that his brother should not be laid in the same grave with him. On the death of Kosma this command was about to be respected, when, on the way to the place of sepulture chosen for him, the bearers were met by a camel, which, like Balaam's ass, opened his mouth and ordered them to lay both brothers in the same tomb, for that "neither was the crime of Kosma so great, nor the difference between them so lasting, but that both their bodies might be contained in the same sepulchre whose souls were already united in Paradise." Popular legend also says that adjoining a church at Athens, dedicated to the *Anaghiroi*, is a fountain, which, though dry the year round, flows with delicious water (γλικὸ νερὸ) at the first words of the Mass performed in honour of their festival, but fails at the close of the day.[1]

The head of St. John the Baptist is held to be buried beneath the church at Cesaræa dedicated to him. Concerning the removal of this holy relic from Jerusalem, and its subsequent adventures, the following remarkable story is related:—

"A certain Jew had found the head of St. John the Baptist, after he had been decapitated at the request

[1] Ricaut, *Present State*, &c.

of Herodias. This Jew made a drinking vessel of the skull, and the water placed in it acquired miraculous properties capable of curing all maladies. The fame of this wonder spread far, and soon the Christians flocked to the house of the Jew, who sold the beneficent water, and accepted in return only what was offered to him. So great, however, was the demand for it that he soon became very rich.

"A Christian of Trebizond, with whom the Jew transacted business, came from time to time to his house, and was hospitably received. And this Christian merchant saw the skull of St. John. One day he said to his friend:

"'Let me have this holy skull, which is of no use to thee. I will pay thee whatsoever thou wilt.'

"'What dost thou ask me?' cried the Jew. 'The skull is all my living, and I could not part with it.'

"'But—when thou shalt die?'

"'I shall leave it to my son as a heritage more precious than any of the Sultan's treasures.'

"The Christian still insisted, but in vain he offered large sums of money. The Jew would not consent to give up the head of St. John the Baptist.

"'I will have it by craft,' said the man of Trebizond to himself.

"He had remarked that his friend kept the head carefully locked up in an oaken chest, and, having taken the pattern and the dimensions of this coffer, he returned to his own country.

"A few years afterwards, the Christian came back to the Jew's house on the pretext of transacting some business with him. He brought with him a chest similar in every respect to that of his friend. After having settled their business, the merchant of Trebizond took leave of his host, and took away with him the chest which he had exchanged for his own. He did not, however, return to Trebizond, but went to another town on the coast, the name of which has not been preserved in the tradition. He had a prosperous voyage, and disembarked without being interfered with.

"As the Christian had taken the precaution to place an ordinary skull in the chest which he had left with the Jew, the latter was ignorant of the robbery, and continued to make use of the supposed head of St. John the Baptist. But no miracles ensued, and the pilgrims complained loudly, saying:

"'This is no longer the wonderful water which thou gavest to us formerly!'

"The Jew reflected upon this, and at last came to the conclusion that his friend had robbed him. Leaving his affairs to take care of themselves, he set out to seek the Trebizond Christian, and found him in the neighbourhood of Indjé Sou, in Cappadocia. The Christian, however, saw him coming, and he hastened to hide the chest in a ditch under a clump of brushwood. The Jew arrived soon afterwards, and overwhelmed him with reproaches.

"'Thou hast done an evil thing,' he said. 'I received thee as a friend and a brother, and thou hast stolen from me the head of St. John the Baptist.'

"'I have stolen nothing,' replied the Christian. 'Here are my clothes; search them.'

"'Thou hast robbed me, I say! Thou only hast been my guest. Who else could have taken the head?'

"'Here are my goods. Look and see if I have the head of which thou speakest.'

"The Jew searched all the boxes and chests of the merchant, but found not that which he sought.

"'Perhaps,' he reflected, 'it is not he who robbed me after all. Could he have had time to return to Trebizond, and has he hidden the head there?' Being desirous of assuring himself on this point, he accompanied the merchant into the province of Trebizond. But there, too, his search was without result.

"This Jew was persevering, so he remained one, two, three, four years in the Christian's house. But, despairing of success, he finally returned to his native country.

"When the Jew was gone, the merchant returned to Cesaræa, and searched in the spot where he believed he had hidden the head. He evidently had not made a note of the place, for he could not find the chest. After a fruitless search, he resolved to erect a church and monastery dedicated to the decapitated saint.

"Shortly after the completion of the edifice, St. John appeared in a dream to one of the monks, and showed him the exact spot where the chest with his head was hidden.

"'I desire,' said the Saint, 'that an underground chapel may be built on the place where the merchant of Trebizond buried my head.'"

The monk found the head. The original church

was enlarged in order to include the vault, and this pious structure has ever since remained a famous place of pilgrimage. No woman may, however, enter it, as the Saint dislikes the sex which caused his decapitation. St. John is the patron of all crafts and arts except that of music, the sounds of which, having accompanied the dancing of Herodias' daughter, indirectly caused his death.[1]

The profound fellow-feeling with the brute creation, and sense of the wrongs suffered by animals at the hands of their master—man—which is frequently found in folk-lore, is well illustrated by the following fable :—

The Peddler and the Serpent.[2]

A Peddler, on passing one day through a forest, came to a spot where the trees had been set on fire. A great Serpent had taken refuge in the top of a tree, and would have been burnt, had not the Peddler held out a pole to him and thus saved his life.

No sooner was the Serpent safe than he flew at the throat of his deliverer, saying, "Son of Man, thou art an ungrateful being. I will strangle thee."

"That is unjust!" cried the man; "I have just saved thy life, and thou wouldest take mine."

"It may be that I am ungrateful, but man is also ungrateful."

"Let us seek a judge," proposed the man.

---

[1] *Les Littératures Populaires*, vol. xxviii. p. 198.   [2] *Ibid.* p. 238.

The Serpent agreed, and set out with the Peddler. They came to a Tree, and made it the judge.

"The Son of Man," said the Tree, "seeks shelter under my boughs from the heat of the summer sun, but, when winter comes, he cuts off my branches to warm himself. He is ungrateful—strangle him."

The Peddler demanded another judge. This was the Ox.

"The Son of Man makes me draw his cart in summer, but in winter he forgets my services, and gives me nothing but straw to eat. He is an ungrateful being. Strangle him."

"Let us take another judge," said the Peddler.

They went a little farther, and met a Fox. The Fox scratched his ear.

"I don't understand very well. Let me see. Supposing you, Serpent, were to get into that sack which the man carries on his back?"

The Serpent, unsuspiciously, got into the sack, when the Fox made signs to the Man to tie up the mouth of the sack and kill the Serpent. The Peddler did not require to be told twice, and the Serpent died.

"In return for thy services, I will give thee a cock and a couple of hens, friend Reynard," said the Peddler.

Next day the man put a greyhound in his sack, and went to meet the Fox.

"Friend Reynard," he said, "come to the sack, and thou wilt find in it all that I promised thee yesterday."

"I am always suspicious," replied the Fox, "of

the Son of Man, for he is ungrateful. I fear that there may be some trick in that sack, and I won't go near it."

The Peddler opened the sack, and out sprang the Greyhound, which immediately went in chase of Reynard. At last it caught him by his long brush, which sweeps the footpaths. The Fox then abandoned his tail, and, trembling with pain and terror, took refuge in a dark corner of the mill.

"If the Miller sees me, he will have me torn in pieces," said Reynard to himself.

The Miller heard him, and he ran up and killed the poor Fox.

The two following folk-tales are fair examples of the Greek παραμύθια. The same incidents often recur in different stories, the chief subjects of all being heroic princes or widows' sons, enchanted or unfortunate princesses, malignant fairies or fierce monsters and wise and benevolent animals. The "Three Wonderful Dresses," which give the title to the first of these stories, occur again in the second, and are frequently met with in Greek folk-tale.[1]

The Three Wonderful Dresses.[2]

In the garden of a king's palace grew a wonderful apple-tree, which every season bore three fine golden apples. But, up to the time at which my story begins, neither the king nor his three sons had been

---

[1] See Geldart, *Folk-lore of Modern Greece*, pp. 24, 27, 38, for other examples.

[2] *Les Littératures Populaires*, vol. xxviii. p. 75.

able to taste this fruit; for no sooner were the apples ripe than a monster came and carried them off.

"Why do we never eat these golden apples?" asked one day the princes of their father.

The king explained to them that a monster came on three successive nights, and each night he took one of the apples.

"If that is the case," replied the princes, "we will watch the apple-tree, and prevent the monster taking the fruit."

"Do as you please, my children."

When evening came, the eldest brother hid himself in the garden, and awaited the arrival of the monster. Just as the palace clock struck midnight, a terrible roaring was heard, and the prince, frightened to death, ran away as fast as his legs would carry him.

The next day the second prince went, but he proved no braver than his brother.

On the third evening the youngest went, and lay down at the root of the apple-tree, and waited till midnight came. The roaring of the monster did not frighten him in the least, but, as soon as he heard him coming, up he got, took aim at him with his javelin, and wounded him severely. The monster fell on the ground, and then made off, uttering terrible cries.

Satisfied with his success, the prince went home to bed.

"Well," said his brothers to him on the following morning, "did you wound the monster?"

"Rather! I think I almost killed him. But come with me into the garden."

The brothers followed him, laughing incredulously. But when they came to the spot they were convinced that their brother had really had an encounter with the monster, for the earth was reddened with blood, a long track of which showed which way the wounded creature had gone.

"Let us follow this trail," said the youngest, "and we shall find out his lair."

The brothers assented, and they came to a deep well, where the trail stopped.

"We must descend this well," said the eldest. "Tie a cord round my waist, and let me down, while I call out, 'Cold, cold!' When I say, 'Hot, hot!' pull me up again."

They promised, and the eldest prepared to go down the well. He had hardly got half-way down when he cried, "Hot, hot!" and they pulled him up again.

"Now it is my turn," said the second.

They let him down. He went a little lower than his brother had done, but, losing courage, he cried out to be pulled up again.

"Let me down now," said the youngest, "and when I call, 'Cold, cold!' pull me up."

He went down, down, and at last came to the bottom of the pit, when, to his surprise, he found himself in a strange and beautiful country. After walking some distance, he came to a magnificent palace, and went in. When he had traversed several halls, each one more superb than the last, he came to one in which were three maidens as ravishingly beautiful as the angels of Paradise.

"Who art thou, stranger?" they ask.

"I am come in search of the monster who inhabits this country."

"Art thou, indeed? He is our tyrant. But art thou not afraid of him?"

"I am afraid of nothing."

"Listen, then. The monster is lying down in the next room. Go and find him. If his eyes are shut, he is awake, and it is all up with thee. If, on the other hand, his eyes are open, he is asleep. Throw your javelin and kill him, but beware of throwing a second javelin, for then he would come to life again, and thou wouldest be lost."

The prince hastened to the room they pointed out, and found the monster asleep with his eyes open. He threw a javelin and killed him.

"Listen, O man!" cried the creature as he was expiring. "If thou art the son of one mother—if thou art a man, throw another javelin at me."

"I was only born once," replied the prince.

"But thou wert born again in baptism," persisted the monster.

"What do I care? Die."

And the monster almost immediately breathed his last.

The prince took the good news to the captive princesses. "We are three princes," he said, "and we will marry you. Here are three rings as pledges."

He then conducted the ladies to the bottom of

the pit. Having tied the eldest, he called out, "Cold, cold!"

The princes drew the cords, and pulled up the princess. The second followed, and then the young prince said:

"Now it is your turn, my beloved, for you shall be my wife."

"Gladly, for I love you," replied the princess; "but I fear that your brothers may leave you down here. Take, then, these three walnuts, each of which contains a dress. On the first is [embroidered] the sky, with the stars; on the second, the earth, with her trees and flowers; on the third, the sea, with its fishes. These may be of service to you."

As soon as the brothers saw the betrothed of the youngest, they began to quarrel which should have her. In the meantime, the prince cried, "Cold, cold!" but the others took no notice, but hastened away, taking with them the three princesses. By-and-by the prince realised that his brothers had cruelly deserted him, and that he must work out his own deliverance. He walked about in the country down below, and at last came upon an old gardener digging one of his beds.

"Good-day, good man," said the prince.

"Good-day, Effendi."

"I am lost in this country. Can you tell me what I must do to get up to the world again?"

"I know a very easy way. You must go behind that little wood, and you will find two rams, one white as snow, the other black as ink. Then shut your eyes, and run for the animals. If you seize the white ram, he will lead you to the upper earth; if the black, he will take you to a land still further away from the sun than this."

The king's son did as the gardener had told him, and found the two animals. But alas! it was the black ram he got hold of, and he felt himself being carried still lower down into the earth. When he opened his eyes he found himself on the banks of a stream which flowed gently through the valley. Near him sat a young maiden, weeping.

"Who art thou, O lovely child?" asked the prince.

"Alas! noble stranger, mine is a sad fate. In this country a terrible dragon has made his abode, who lives on human flesh and blood. This spring is the only one in the land, and the monster will allow no one to take water unless a maiden is given to him every day. Fate has willed that to-day my turn came, and I am here waiting for the frightful dragon with seven heads to come and devour me."

"And who is thy father?"

"I am the king's daughter, his only child; and my father is sorrowing in his palace, believing me, no doubt, already dead."

"Take courage, beautiful princess. I am valiant, and perhaps I may be able to deliver you from the dragon."

As he spoke, a frightful hissing noise was heard behind a rock, and the monster with seven heads approached to devour the maiden. On catching sight of the young hero, the dragon stopped a moment as if startled, and the prince chose this opportunity for hurling a javelin straight at his heart. A torrent of flames issued from his seven mouths, together with a terrible roar, but that was all, and the monster lay dead.

The king's son cut out the dragon's seven tongues, and kept them as a souvenir of this exploit. Then, fatigued with his exertions, he lay down at the root of a tree, and slept.

He was awakened by the hiss of a serpent, which was on the point of seizing the young eagles perched on the tree overhead. With one stroke of the javelin the reptile was killed as the dragon had been, and the prince went to sleep again.

Soon afterwards the king of the eagles arrived to seek his young ones. Seeing a youth lying at the foot of the tree, the eagle swooped upon him to tear him with beak and claws. But immediately the eaglets began to cry:

"Father, father! see that you do him no harm."

"Why?"

"A serpent was going to swallow us, when this young man killed him with a javelin stroke."

The king of the eagles then spread his wide wings over the prince, and shaded him from the burning rays of the sun until he awoke.

"Young man," then said the great eagle, "thou hast saved the life of my little ones. How can I show my gratitude?"

"I deserve less gratitude than you seem to think. Anybody else in my place would have killed the serpent."

"Thou art a hero, I say. Speak! What wouldest thou?"

"Well, then, take me up to the surface of the earth."

"Alas! willingly would I do so; but the journey is so long that I should be dead of hunger and thirst before reaching it."

"Could I not get provisions for the journey?"

"Yes; but I should require forty sheep and as many pitchers of water. Where are they to be got? The king only could furnish them."

"I have just now delivered his daughter from the frightful dragon which was going to devour her. He will surely not refuse me what is necessary for the journey. I will go and ask him."

"Go; I will wait here for you."

The prince went into the city, and inquired the way to the palace. All the people were rejoicing, for the news had soon spread that a young hero had killed the dragon, and delivered the princess. Heralds had been sent out to announce that the king would give a rich reward to the man who had saved his daughter, and already knights were riding in who boasted falsely that they were the liberators of the princess. After them came charcoal-burners, who, when working in the woods near the spring, had found the dead dragon, and cut off his heads.

"We have killed the monster," they said, "and here are his heads in proof of what we say."

"No," said the knights; "we fought with and killed the monster, and left him dead near the spring. We deserve the reward."

"They are all telling lies," said the princess; "my saviour was a handsome hero—a stranger, no doubt."

At this moment the real slayer of the dragon entered the courtyard of the palace.

"Sire," said he, "I have killed the dragon, to whom you have until now paid the terrible tax of young maidens. Here are the creature's seven tongues."

The princess, who had at once thrown her arms round the neck of her deliverer, cried:

"Yes, yes, my father! It is he who killed the dragon, and all these men are impostors."

The king had the knights and charcoal-burners driven out, and embraced the young prince affectionately.

"Dost thou desire all my treasure, or the half of my kingdom? Wilt thou marry my daughter, and be king after me?"

"Sire," replied the hero, "I also am a prince, but my country is far away. I thank you for your offers, but I will ask you for forty sheep, and forty pitchers of water; I desire nothing more."

"If that is so, let it be as you desire," said the king; and he gave him all that he asked for.

The prince returned to the eagle, and loaded his back with the provisions.

"Now we will set out," said the king of the birds. "When I call 'Crak, crak,' thou must give me mutton; when I call 'Crouk, crouk,' thou must give me water to drink; if not, I shall come down to earth again. Dost thou understand?"

"I understand perfectly."

"Then get on my neck, and let us be off."

The eagle went up, up, up. "Crak, crak," he

soon cried, and the prince gave him meat; "Crouk, crouk," and he gave him to drink.

Soon, however, the provisions were exhausted. They had nearly arrived at the opening which led to the earth.

"Crak, crak! Crak, crak!" said the eagle.

The hero took out his poinard, cut off a piece of his thigh, and gave it to the eagle.

"That is human flesh," said the eagle, and he kept the meat under his tongue. At last he deposited the king's son on the earth.

"Here you are at last. Walk," said the king of the birds.

But the prince could not move, because the wound in his leg was so terribly painful.

"Walk, I say!" repeated the eagle.

And then the king's son confessed that, being short of meat, he had cut a piece from his own thigh, and given it to his guide.

"I knew it! and so I kept the piece of flesh under my tongue. Here it is;" and with this he put back the flesh in its proper place, and the wound immediately healed.

Then the eagle took leave of the prince, and flew away.

"What am I to do now?" said the young man to himself. After reflecting a little, he went towards the city, and made for the shop of the king's tailor. As he was well disguised, the man did not recognise him.

"I am a journeyman tailor, and I want a place."

"That is fortunate, for my apprentice has just died. You shall take his place," replied the tailor.

The young man applied himself to work with such diligence that his master was delighted to have met with him.

At the Court the two eldest sons of the king had been always quarrelling for the hand of the beautiful princess, but at last the king had decided that the eldest should marry her.

"I am willing," replied the princess, "if you give me three things."

"What are they?"

"Three dresses—one representing the sky with the stars; the second, the earth, with all its trees and flowers; and the third, the sea with all the fishes that live in it."

The king was rather taken aback, but he promised to fulfil the maiden's wish. The tailor was sent for, and received the order for the three dresses.

The poor man came back bewildered, wondering how in the world he would be able to accomplish such a piece of work. All day long he pondered, and all night long he dreamed of these dresses, but they were not a bit the nearer completion. The tailor finally came to the conclusion that the thing was impossible.

His workman, seeing him always pensive, at last asked the cause of his sorrow.

"Alas! the king has ordered three dresses which he is very anxious to have made; but my art is far below the requirements of my master, and the king will surely withdraw his patronage from me."

And he related to his workman what had been asked of him.

"Is that all?" cried the pretended tailor, laughing. "That is but child's play."

"Have you gone mad, young man?"

"No, I am not mad at all, and I will undertake to make these three dresses for you."

"Go along! Dost thou, who art but an apprentice, pretend to be a better workman than I, who am the master craftsman of the country, and the king's tailor to boot!"

"Once more, I repeat that I can make the three dresses."

"But when? In twenty years at least?"

"This night. To-morrow morning they shall be ready."

"But where wilt thou find the stuff?"

"I want neither stuff, nor thread, nor needles. Give me only a bottle of *raki*,[1] and a little basket of nuts; shut me up in my room, and come to me to-morrow morning."

The tailor did as the prince requested, and the young man passed the night drinking *raki* and cracking nuts, without troubling his head about the dresses. When morning came the tailor knocked at his door.

"Are the dresses ready?"

"Not yet; wait till sunrise."

As soon as the tailor had gone away, the young man opened the walnuts which the princess had given him, and took out of them three marvellous

---

[1] A kind of spirit.

dresses representing the sky, the earth, and the sea.

"Well, may I come in?" cried the tailor, presently.

"Yes, come in, for the dresses are now ready!"

The master was thunderstruck at the sight of the magnificent dresses which his apprentice showed him. The good man asked himself if he were not dreaming, or if his apprentice might not be one of those wicked and powerful *Djins* of which he had heard so many stories. He then took the dresses, and went rejoicing with them to the princess.

"Who has been able to make such beautiful stuffs?" she asked.

"I must confess that I was not able to execute such an elaborate piece of work. But my apprentice was able to complete the dresses in a single night."

"I should like to see this clever workman. Go and bring him to me."

A few minutes later the apprentice was in the presence of the lady.

"Is it indeed thou, my beloved one?"

"It is, and I have waited for thee. But thy brothers——"

"I will tell everything to my father, and thou shalt marry me."

The prince went to the king and told him of the treachery of his two eldest sons. The old king became very angry, and wished to kill them. But the princess interceded for them, and begged that they might only be exiled from the country, which was done.

The next day, they celebrated the wedding of the hero and the princess of the enchanted castle, and

M

there was great feasting and rejoicing. The happy pair lived to a great old age, and had a great many children.

The Prince and the Foal.[1]

There was once a Queen who had no children, and a Jew went to her and said, "Take this apple and eat it, and thou wilt have a child." She took the apple, pared it, and ate it; she threw away the parings, and the mare ate them. By-and-by she had a son, and the mare a foal. When the boy was twelve years old he went to school to learn the art of war; and when he returned home, he was in the habit of throwing down his satchel.

And one day the Queen—"What shall we do?" she said to the Jew (for she was very much in love with him)—"what shall we do to kill the boy that we may be free, and do what we like?"

"We will put poison in his bread," said the Jew, "now that he is coming to eat, and he will die."

But the boy, directly he came home from school, threw down his satchel and went to the Foal's stable. As he entered, he found his Foal drowned in tears, and asked him, "Why dost thou weep?"

"This and that," replied the Foal, "I heard. Thy mother loves the Jew, and they seek to kill thee, and they have put poison in the bread. Eat not of it, but say, 'I cannot, for so my teacher bid me, as I did not know my lessons.'"

"Come and eat," says the mother, "and I will

---

[1] From Von Hahn's Νεοελληνικὰ Παραμύθια.

speak to the teacher, so that he may not scold thee."

"No, I will not eat," replies the boy, and he runs off to school again.

But they, thus frustrated in their design, stoop down and put poison in the wine. The boy returns in the evening and goes straight to the Foal, which again says to him, weeping, "They have put poison in the wine; do thou drink no wine!"

The boy goes in the evening, and they say to him, "There, drink wine!"

"No, I will not drink," says he, "for he who drinks wine cannot learn his lessons."

Then the Jew says to the Queen: "Let us put poisoned needles in his mattress, and when he goes to lie down the needles will run into him, and he will die."

Again the boy comes home and goes to the Foal. And again the Foal says to him, weeping—

"They have put poison in thy mattress, thou must not sleep on it."

The boy goes in at even, and when he had eaten, his mother says, "Come, and let us lie down and sleep!"

"I," replied the boy, "am not going to sleep here; I will go and sleep outside, and learn how they sleep in the open air who go on journeys." And he went and slept outside, so that the design of the Queen and the Jew could not succeed.

Afterwards came news that the King was returning from the wars where he had been. When the Queen heard it, she feigned illness; and when the

King arrived he sent for doctors to cure her, but none of them could cure her.

Then comes the Jew and says, "I will cure her; but a certain medicine is necessary, which your Majesty will not permit."

The King asks, "What is that? Tell me, and don't be afraid."

Then the Jew says, "Do you love better your wife or your child?"

"Both," replies the King.

"No," said the Jew, "which would you rather have die, the wife or the child?"

"Rather the child," replied the King, "than the Queen, for we may have other children."

And so they decided to kill the child.

And the Jew said, "We must take out his liver, and give it to the Queen to eat."

And when the boy came from school, he went again to the Foal and found him weeping and lamenting.

The child asked him, "Why dost thou weep?"

"They will kill thee," says the Foal.

"Hush, don't be afraid; they will not kill me," said the boy.

He then went upstairs to the King, who kissed him, and said, "Thou art fair, my eyes![1] Yet they will kill thee."

"Why?" asked the child.

"For thy mother," said the King.

"Let them slay me for my mother," he said, "but first I want thee to make me a suit of clothes [like]

---

[1] Μάτια μου, a common expression of endearment among Greeks.

the sky with the stars, the spring with the flowers, and the sea with the waves; and I will put it on and go three times round the palace, and then you may slay me, and I will go contentedly to the other world."

And immediately the King gave orders, and everything was done as he desired them. Then the boy put on the sky with the stars and went round the palace, and says to the King, "Am I fair, Sire?"

"Thou art fair, my eyes! yet they will slay thee," says the King again to him.

Then he took off that and put it in a wallet, and donned the spring with the flowers, and went round the palace, and says again to the King, "Am I fair, Sire?"

"Fair thou art, my eyes! but they will slay thee," says the King again to him.

Then he put on the sea with the wave, and says, "Am I fair, Sire?"

"Fair thou art, my eyes!" he said; "yet they will kill thee."

Then said the boy to him, "May it be well with thee, and wherever thou findest me, kill me."

And he vanished thence, and went to a lonely spot, and there he took off his finery, and put it in the wallet, and put on old clothes, and took a hair from the tail of the Foal, and said to him—

"Bide thou here, and when I light the hair, be there immediately."

"Good," he says, and the boy ran away.

He was dressed in the sky with the stars, and on his head he wore a bit of tarred skin, and he went to a city, and sat down beneath the king's palace; and above, at the window, was the youngest daughter of the king. And because he was perspiring, he opened the breast of his coat, and the princess saw the sky with the stars, and she understood that he was a king's son.[1]

One day the King sent his eldest daughter to bring him a melon. She went, and brought him one so dried up as to be uneatable.

"What is this that thou bringest me?" says the King to her.

"Thus am I fading," she replied; "and I want to be married."

"Hush," says the King; "what are you saying?" and he scolded her. "Are you not ashamed of yourself?" he asks.

So he called the second, and she brought him the same as the other, and said the same to him. The King scolded her, and called the youngest; and she went and brought him a beauty.

The King said to her, "Eh, this is in its prime!"

"And I also, Sire," she said, "am in my prime."

"Eh?" said the King; "I will marry you all!"

And he gave orders that all the people were to pass under his window, and his daughters would sit above, and that each should throw a golden apple at the one she wished for. And immediately all the people passed by, and the two hit two passable men,

---

[1] The prince would appear to have put on the "old clothes" over his magnificent suit.

and the youngest one hit him she had seen with the tarred skin.

When the King saw this, "It is a mistake," he said; and ordered them to pass back again. So they passed the second and third times, and she always hit the same. Then the King went and scolded her, but she said—

"I want that one."

"Eh! If thou wantest him, take him."

And they were married, each one to the man she had hit, and she took the one with the tarred skin. And when the King saw this, he had no respect for her, neither had other people.

A few days afterwards the King fell sick, and they brought to him a physician to cure him, who said, "If you can get for him 'deathless water,' he will get well."

Then went the two bridegrooms to seek for it, and both took splendid horses. And his youngest daughter went to him, and said, "Sire, let my husband go too." And when she begged him very earnestly, "Let him go too," he said.

Then he took a lame horse, and set out, and whenever he came to a puddle he tumbled in. Then everybody mocked at and insulted him, and afterwards they left him, and went away.

Then he lighted the hair, and immediately the Foal arrived there. He put on his fine raiment, and overtook and passed them by, and went by another road and obtained the deathless water, and returned; and he met them on the road, and said—

"Good-day, handsome youths."

"You are welcome, my pallikar."

"Where are you going?" [he asked them].

"We are going to find the deathless water to bathe the eyes of our father-in-law, that he may recover."

"I have deathless water; stand and let my horse strike you on the flank, and I will give you it."

They stood still, and where the Foal struck them he left a golden impression. Then he pulled out the gourd with other water, and gave it to them. They set off joyfully, and he at once returned [by another road], mounted the lame horse, and went on. They again came up with him, abused him, and left him. They went to the King with joy, and bathed his eyes once, but—nothing! They bathed them a second and a third time—nothing!

Then comes he of the tarred skin, and his wife goes to the King, and says—

"Let him come and bathe them."

"Off with you!" he replied. "The others went and could not bring the deathless water, and will he bring it?"

"Let him bathe them. What harm can there be?" she said.

"Eh! Let him bathe them."

Then came he, and as he bathed them the first time, he saw a little; as he bathed them a second time, he saw better; and as he bathed them a third time, he saw perfectly. Then immediately the King embraced him, and said to him—

"Thou art now my son."

And he said, "If thou wouldest have me, strew

between thy palace and my hut gold pieces, and I will mount and come hither."

And immediately the King strewed the street with cloth, and upon it much gold; and all the people came out to walk. Then he [the prince] lighted a hair, and the Foal presented itself. Then he put on his best dress, the sea with the waves, and mounted his horse, and went to the King's palace, and said to the King—

"Look at the bridegrooms' flanks, and you will see the marks which they bear as my slaves."

And the King looked, and he drove them away, and lived happily ever after.

The story of "The Just One" has its counterpart in the folk-tales of many European countries. In the Venetian variant of *El Giusto*, the Lord and the Madonna, whom the peasant successively meets, hesitate to pronounce themselves just. The Breton version is, however, very similar to the Greek; and so is the German story of *Tod der Pathe*, although it ends rather differently. Hans Sachs refers in one of his poems to this legend, of which Provençal and Hungarian variants are also said to exist.

The Just One.[1]

A peasant had just welcomed his first-born.

"Who will be our son's godfather?" asked the mother.

"His godfather shall be the most just man I can

---

[1] *Les Littératures Populaires*, vol. xxviii. p. 144.

find. To-morrow I will set out to seek this infinitely just person."

The next day the peasant set out. Towards evening he met a handsome old man on the road.

"Whither art thou bound, traveller?" asked the old man.

"My father, I am seeking a godfather for my child."

"I can render you that service."

"I require a person whose justice is without equal."

"I am that person."

"What is thy name, my father?"

"God."

"Then you are not he whom I seek."

"That is strange. How? Is not God sovereign justice itself?"

"No, Lord! You are not the most just. The good things you bestow on mortals are ill distributed. To the righteous you give misery, to the wicked riches. You are all injustice. Adieu!"

The peasant continued his journey. and soon afterwards entered a cave to rest and pass the night. Next day he met a second traveller with a very benign aspect.

"Where goest thou, O peasant?" was his question.

"I seek a man supremely just as sponsor for my son."

"I am that just man. Conduct me to thy house. I will gladly be godfather to thy child."

"What is your name, worshipful sir?"

"I am the good Apostle, the beloved disciple of Jesus Christ—Saint Peter, in fact."

"Then you are not he whom I seek."

"And why so?"

"I said that I required an exceedingly just man, and you say that you are Saint Peter!"

"Well! What then?"

"Then you are not just. Every day you admit into Paradise the wicked, the misers, the dissipated, and the drunkards who have never done a good deed, under the pretext that the Pope has pardoned them. Yes, indeed! And you refuse entrance to heaven to those who deserve it, but who, unfortunately, have no money. Decidedly you are not the person I seek!"

On the third day, the peasant met another traveller, who asked him—

"Where goest thou, gaffer?"

"To seek a sponsor for my child. I have been walking for three days without finding one."

"What kind of a man dost thou want?"

"A being supremely just."

"I am just, and I will be godfather to thy child."

"I have met God, and also Saint Peter. Are you more just than they?"

"I am more just than the Lord and his Apostle."

"Who are you, then?"

"I am Death."

"Then you are right. You respect neither rich nor poor; you strike, indiscriminately, the wretch in his hut, and the king on his throne; you take the child from its mother's breast, and the old with their crown of white hair. You are supremely just. Will you be godfather to my child?"

"I will. Let us go."

And the peasant, followed by Death, returned home.

The baptism was performed with great ceremony, and Death kept his promise to hold the infant at the font. When the christening was over, Death said to the peasant, "Thou hast done me great honour, my friend, in choosing me as *Nono* to thy son. I will reward thee. Perhaps an honourable profession would please thee. Say, would it not?"

"Yes, your worship—but——"

"But what? There is nothing I cannot do. Listen. I could easily give thee riches; I have but to say the word, and that chest would be full of gold. But fortune, without credit and renown, is worthless. Thou shalt have all these things."

"I, a poor peasant?"

"Yes. From this moment thou art an eminent physician—the first physician in the world."

"I have never studied. I can hardly read and write!"

"What does that matter? The rich banker, Abraham, is ill. Go thou boldly to him, prescribe him what thou wilt, and assure him of recovery. He will not die, and will of course declare that thou hast saved his life. He will reward thee generously, and thy reputation will spread."

"But the other patients?"

"Whenever thou art called to any one, look attentively at the feet and the head of the patient.

If I am at his feet, say that he will not die; if I am at his head, know that his days are numbered. Thou wilt see that all thy drugs and remedies will make no difference."

So the peasant went to the Jew, Abraham, and cured him, after all his colleagues had asserted that nothing could save him. His reputation spread rapidly, and soon every one was talking of the wonderful doctor, who could tell in a moment whether sick persons would live or die.

In a short time, accordingly, the peasant-physician became one of the richest men in the country. The wealthy, the merchants, bishops, judges, ministers, kings, and even the Sultan himself, sent for him on the smallest indisposition, and would have kept him, if possible, always in attendance.

Years passed. The doctor grew old, but was rich and respected, and he continued to bless the lucky day on which he set out to seek a godfather for his boy.

One day he was sitting under the great olive-tree in his garden, when suddenly a stranger stood before him.

"Who are you?" he asked.

"Dost thou not, then, recognise me?"

"My eyes are growing dim."

"And yet thou knowest me when I am with thy patients?"

"Ah, is it you? Pardon me, your grace! What are your commands?"

"The number of thy days is nearly accomplished. Thou must prepare to depart."

"Depart? Die? Now?"

"Yes, now."

"Ah, mercy! mercy! Grant me a few years more, a few days only! To-morrow!"

And the doctor threw himself at the feet of Death and wept like a child.

"For the sake of your godson! I want to see him married before I leave the world! Oh, mercy! mercy!"

"Come, come, my friend, I cannot wait."

So the doctor was obliged to follow Death over plains and through forests, across rivers and seas, and over mountains and hills. They hurried on until they came to an immense plain, in the centre of which stood a wonderful palace.

"We have come to the end of our journey," said Death.

As they approached the palace, the doctor saw that the windows were as numerous as the stars of the sky; some were dark, and others brilliantly illuminated. They entered, and Death led the way into one of the lighted chambers. Many tapers were burning, and one of them was nearly burnt out.

"That taper," said Death, "represents thy existence. Dost thou not see that it will be extinguished in a moment?"

"I pray thee, O Death, to let me replace that taper by one of these!"

"They are those of thy family."

"By that one, then?"

"It is the life-taper of thy son, of my godson!"

"What matters it?"

"What matters it! Come, come, look at thy taper! See—the flame flickers—it dies, it is extinguished!"

At the same instant the doctor fell dead at the feet of the inexorable Being who shows favour unto none.

NOTE.—IDENTIFICATION OF ST. GEORGE WITH HORUS AND KHIDHR.[1]

Among the Egyptian monuments in the Louvre, says M. Clermont-Ganneau, is a piece of sculpture representing the combat of Horus with Set, or Typhon, which presents features and details of an exceptional character. Horus is here represented, as usual, as a man with the head of a sparrowhawk, but on horseback. He is dressed in a military costume, and in the act of thrusting with his right hand a lance into the neck of a crocodile which the horse is trampling under foot. The French scholar finds in this representation a striking resemblance to the most ancient representations of St. George. The slain monster, the lance, the horse, the uniform of a Roman officer worn by the victor, are identical in the Byzantine iconography, and, if the sparrowhawk head had disappeared, no one, he thinks, would have hesitated to pronounce the rude fragment a mutilated representation of the Christian Saint. There is also in the British Museum a bronze statuette of Horus Hieracocephalus, similarly in the costume of a Roman soldier.

The cult of St. George, which spread at an early period over Egypt, received a special character in Syria, where it had for its centre the town of Lydda. In the episcopal lists, Lydda bears the name of Ἁγιογιοργιούπολις, "St. George's Town," and is revered equally as the place of his birth and of his martyrdom. The inhabitants still point out "the house of Khidr," the Arab name

[1] See Clermont-Ganneau, *Horus et St. Georges*, Rev. Archéologique, nouv. sér., t. xxxii. pp. 388-397.

of the Saint. Here, too, St. George, under his Arab name, is completely identified in the beliefs common to Syrian Christians and to Moslems both orthodox and schismatic, with two other very remarkable mythical personages. These are (1) Elias the Immortal, confounded on the one hand with Ali, the son-in-law of the Prophet Mohammed, and on the other, as mentioned in Chap. IV., with Ἥλιος or Apollo; and (2) Phineas, the grandson of Aaron, who pierced with his lance Zimri the Simeonite, and who appears in the Talmudic legends as an equivalent of Elias, the worker of twelve miracles, a heroic immortal destined to be one of the Angels of the Ark, and also to play a great part at the end of the world. A Moslem *hadith* or tradition, attributed to Mohammed by the ancient commentators on the Koran, says that "Jesus will slay Antichrist at the gate of Lydda," and Antichrist is more definitely connected with the monster slain by St. George in other traditions, one of which says that "Jesus, crowned with a green turban, and girded with a sword, will pursue the *Dadjdjal* (Antichrist) to the gate of Lydda, and there slay him." This name, says M. Clermont-Ganneau, is the phonetic equivalent of that of the Philistine amphibious god, Dagon. As the gods frequently assimilated to themselves the qualities and characteristics of the beings over which they triumphed, so, says M. Clermont-Ganneau, we find among the Egyptians Set-Typhon completely replacing Horus in certain localities, and at certain epochs. And it has occurred to me that similarly the St. George-Horus, triumphing over the amphibious monster, took upon himself the attributes of Genius of both Sea and Land which characterise him in his Moslem form of Khidr. For the maritime Khidr is plainly indicated in his numerous Moslem shrines found all along the Syrian coast, and which are specially resorted to by native sailors and childless women.

In the Moslem mythical story of Alexander the Great, it was Khidr who led the hero to the Stream of Life, situated in a Land of Darkness, in an isle of the Isles of the Sea. And in Oriental folk-belief he is held to be continually travelling about on the earth, suddenly appearing for the succour or reproval of men, and disappearing with equal suddenness. His help is also frequently invoked either under that name or the connected one of *Hasreti* (Prophet) *Elias*.

This myth of St. George is also connected with that of Perseus and the Dragon; and the name of Khidr with Ὕδωρ—water being divinised as one of the " Eight Powers" which govern the world. On the other hand, the word Γεώργιος is derived from γεωργὸς, and thus connected with agriculture. According to Mogaddesy,[1] the signal for sowing the corn was given by the Great Feast of St. George held at Lydda on the 23rd April. Khidr also signifies "verdant" according to some authorities; according to others its meaning is the same as that of the Greek γλαυκὸς; while M. Lenormant is of opinion that it is a mere contraction of Hasis-Adra, the hero of the Chaldean deluge tradition, or of Xisuthros, the Greek form of the same name.[2] The ramifications and transformations of this curious and interesting myth appear, however, to be endless, and I must not attempt here to follow them any further.

According to M. Amélinau, however, "the legend of St. George slaying the dragon is unknown to the Copts, and it is incorrect to say that the Copts have identified Horus and St. George: it is St. Michael who is identified with Horus": *Contes et Romans de l'Égypte Chrétienne*, p. liv. And Gutschmid identifies St. George with Mithra: *Ueber die Sage vom hl. Georg*, &c. (in *Berichte ü. d. Verhandlungen der Koniglich Sachsischen Gesellsch. d. Wissensch. zu Leipzig*, 1861, pp. 185-202). Compare the Coptic legends translated by Mr. Budge.

[1] Or Mukaddasi of Jerusalem, an Arab geographer who wrote about 985. See L'Estrange, *Palestine under the Moslems*.
[2] *Origines de l'Histoire*, tom. ii. p. 13.

CHAPTER VI.

ARMENIAN WOMEN: THEIR SOCIAL STATUS AND ACTIVITIES.

THE Armenians, as stated in the Introduction, hardly appear in history till the sixth century B.C., when Dikran, or Tigranes, king of Armenia, is said to have maintained his independence against Cyrus the Great. In 328 B.C., however, Vahé, the successor of Dikran, fell in battle with Alexander the Great, the conqueror of Darius, the successor of Cyrus. Only from this date does authentic Armenian history begin. But the Armenians,[1] a few years later (317 B.C.), threw off the Macedonian yoke, chose a king of their own, and, some seventy years later (250 B.C.) established an Arsacid dynasty, related to that then reigning in Persia. After a century or two of national prosperity, Armenia was, at the beginning of the Christian era, added to the Roman Empire, and its king, Artavasdes, was carried prisoner to Alexandria by Antony, and beheaded by Cleopatra (30 A.D.). Armenia, however, though conquered, was not wholly crushed, and again recovered its independence, which it retained until the eleventh century, when the Byzantine emperors "succeeded

---

[1] I summarise the epitome of Armenian history given by Mr. Stuart Glennie in *Europe and Asia*, pp. 47-54.

in subjugating Armenia, but not the Armenians." Their national development continued, and to their elementary consolidation—begun at the separation of the Armenian from the Greek Church at the end of the fifth century—was soon added a new monarchical consolidation. Rhupen (Reuben), a relative of the last king of the Pagratid dynasty, which had succeeded the Arsacid, retired to the north of Cilicia, and founded, in 1080, in the shelter of the Taurus, a small principality, which, gradually extending its boundaries, became known as the kingdom of Lesser Armenia. This Eastern Christian State maintained its independence until the end of the fourteenth century, when its last king, Leo VI., a prince of the house of Lusignan, defeated by the growing Moslem power, sought refuge in Europe. After living for some years on a pension from the English and French monarchs, Leo VI. died in Paris in 1393, and was buried with royal honours. The Armenians of this city still honour the last king of their country by performing a pilgrimage to his tomb at St. Denis on the anniversary of his death, when Mass is performed by a priest of the Gregorian Church, who comes for the purpose from Marseilles.

But I ought not, perhaps, to pass over the legend of the Armenians concerning their eponymous ancestor, Haik, from whom they derive their native name of *Haikians*, and the name of their country, *Haiasdan*. This Haik was, according to the story—which, however, evidently received its present form after the conversion of the Armenians to Christianity —the great-grandson of Japhet, or, according to some, of Noah. He had first settled in Mesopotamia, but, finding the rule of Bel, the king of that country, irksome, had removed with his tribe of 300 persons to Armenia. As he refused to return when summoned to do so by Bel, the latter marched an army against the emigrants. But in the battle which ensued Bel was slain by an arrow from the bow of Haik; and the patriarch succeeded in consolidating his new kingdom, which, at his death, he transmitted to his descendants.

The Armenians, besides constituting the bulk of the population in Armenia proper, form large communities in Constantinople and Adrianople, at Broussa and Smyrna, and are also found in several of the smaller towns of European Turkey, such as Gallipoli. In Constantinople and Smyrna, the wealthier members of the Armenian communities are much more advanced in every respect than elsewhere in Turkey; and at Smyrna their adoption of Western manners and education dates farther back than at the Capital. At Smyrna, as elsewhere, the Armenians occupy a separate quarter of the town; and this compares favourably, both as to the width and cleanliness of its streets and as to the architecture of the houses which border them, with the *mahallás* of any of the other races in the city, not excepting even the so-called "Frank," or European, quarter.

It would be impossible to find a more striking illustration of the freedom from Moslem molestation now enjoyed by the subject races, as compared with their position at the beginning of the century, than that which is afforded by the difference in the style of houses built about that period and of those built during the past twenty or thirty years. The older houses are gloomy and prison-like in outward appearance, having on the lower floor no windows overlooking the street—save perhaps one or two small grated ones, ten or twelve feet from the ground—and the great arched folding door is faced with iron, and defended inside with heavy bars and bolts. This door gives access to a large hall or court, on which, and on the garden beyond, all the ground-floor rooms open. The upper stories far overhang the street, and in the narrower thoroughfares, as in the streets of old London, one might almost shake hands across. This style of architecture presented many advantages when the dwellings of the Christians were exposed to the attacks of the insolent and lawless Janisseries, though it did not always protect the occupants from violence.

The modern houses are much more cheerful in appearance, though not less solidly constructed than those just described. A great number, however, owing to the frequency of earthquake shocks at Smyrna, are only of one story. The wide doorways being above, instead of below, the level of the street, as in the older houses, are approached by handsome steps of white marble, and the spacious hall within is paved with large slabs of the same material. In the smaller one-storied houses the drawing-room windows alone overlook the street, all the other rooms receiving their light and air from the hall. The far end of this apartment, which is used as a general sitting-room, often contains a fountain, and is converted into a species of conservatory, with creepers and choice shrubs in vases. The rest of it is furnished with a Turkish sofa, a few common chairs, and, in winter, a carpet.

This is, however, but a middle-class dwelling. The abode of a wealthy Armenian is a palatial edifice replete with European luxuries, and even comforts, though many comforts might be dispensed with in such a glorious climate. Orange, lemon, and pomegranate trees blossom and bear fruit in their gardens, which are also fragrant with flowers all the year round. On the broad raised footpaths, tesselated into graceful patterns with black and white pebbles —for garden-walks are in the East always higher than the beds, on account of the prevailing system of irrigation—saunter the Serpuis and Tarquis, in loose Oriental garments, and with slipshod feet, or in the latest fashions from Paris, according to circumstances and the time of day. The beautifully situated village of Buyukdéré,[1] on the Bosphorus, is a favourite resort of the wealthy Armenians of the capital, many of whom pass the summer months in the elegant marine villas which, rising behind each other up the steep hill, command a magnificent view of the wonderful waterway and its picturesque banks.

The dwellings of the poorest class of Armenians— the *hammals*, or porters, and the boatmen and fishermen—though small, are not as a rule without a certain amount of decent comfort, suited to their mode of life. There is very little, if any, overcrowding among any of the Christian or Moslem poor of Turkey, each family having its own separate

---

[1] So called from the picturesque "Great Valley" at the entrance to which it stands.

cottage, generally approached by a little courtyard. And the exclusiveness of Oriental family life renders any sub-letting to lodgers extremely rare.

The houses in Armenia proper present a striking contrast to those above described, owing to the more rigorous climate, and to the primitive mode of life pursued by their inmates. Even in the large towns of the province the better sort of houses lack the comfort and cheerfulness generally found at Smyrna and Constantinople. At Erzeroum, for instance, they have a most gloomy appearance, being built of dark-coloured stone, with tiny double glazed windows like port-holes, sometimes in two rows, one above the other. This town is situated at the foot of a mountain, up the lower slopes of which the houses climb, each room being built like a separate house with a flat roof, which communicates with those above and below it by means of steps. One may walk along these terraces from house to house over a great part of the town, and, when stopped by a street, a moderate leap will easily clear the chasm, so narrow are the thoroughfares. The space of ground occupied by a rich man's house is prodigious; and the top, being covered with grass, resembles a small field. Here, in the summer time, the women and children come out, bringing their mattresses and cushions, to bask in the balmy air, and here the lambs are left to graze when the wind is not strong enough to blow them into the street. The floors of all these houses are below the level of the roadway. A low door gives access to a dark central passage, on one side of which is the ox stable, or byre; and, on the other, the kitchen, storeroom, and private apartments of the family. Each room has a rude stone fireplace, in which is burnt *tezek*, the common fuel of the country, made of compressed cow-dung mixed with straw. Some of the wealthier houses may boast chairs and tables, and perhaps a gilt-framed mirror; but, as a rule, the furniture consists of a divan running round three sides of the room, covered with beautiful stuff of native manufacture, and some valuable Persian or Kūrdish rugs spread over the thick carpet of grey felt (*tekké*), which covers the floor. The walls are whitewashed, and the wooden ceilings are curiously carved and painted. The meals are served on a *sofra*, or tray and stand, similar to that used by Moslems, and this substitute for a table is also used by the poorer class of Armenians at Smyrna and in the capital. In fact, many of the Armenian domestic arrangements are identical with those of the Osmanlis, for there is a certain amount of truth in M. de Moltke's saying that "the Armenian is but a baptised Turk."[1]

The ox-stable is the most curious part of the building. It contains sometimes scores of cattle, whose animal heat, during the winter months, contributes considerably towards the warmth of the house. One end of this room has a raised floor, or daïs, railed off from the rest, and used by the men of the family as a selamlik, or reception-room. It is furnished in very much the same style as the rest of the house, with rugs and carpets, and a low divan running round three sides, while on the walls above are

[1] *Lettres d'Orient.*

suspended saddles, guns, pistols, and other weapons. Under the platform the dogs have their abode ; and on the divans, safely out of their reach, repose the beautiful so-called "Persian" or "Angora" cats, which, however, come from the Armenian town of Van.

Mr. Curzon, who visited Erzeroum in winter, gives the following graphic description of the town and neighbourhood at this season:

" The whole view, whichever way one looked, was wrapped in interminable snow. . . . . The tops of the houses being flat, the snow-covered city did not resemble any other town, but appeared more like a great rabbit warren. Many of the houses being wholly or partly subterranean, the doors looked like burrows. In the neighbourhood of the Consulate there were several large heaps and mounds of earth, and it was difficult to the uninitiated to discriminate correctly as to which was a house and which was a heap of soil or stones. . . . . Very few people were about, the bulk of the population hybernating at this time of the year in their strange holes and burrows. The bright colours of the Oriental dresses looked to my eyes strangely out of place in the cold, dirty snow."[1]

The dwellings of the peasantry are, in many parts of the Armenian highlands, like some of the Erzeroum houses just described—mere burrows in a hillside. The front is formed by cutting away the surface of a slope perpendicularly for the space of a few yards, the room or rooms are partly excavated in the hill, and all the soil dug out is

[1] *Armenia*, p. 34.

thrown against the side walls and on the roof, which is supported by strong wooden beams. A thick crop of grass soon covers all, on which in summer the lambs graze and the children play, and during the short hot season the whole family may occasionally sleep here "at the moon's inn," without disturbing the storks, who build on the broad mushroom-shaped chimneys, returning with every succeeding spring. In fact, most of the dwellings of the peasantry are still precisely like those described in Xenophon's *Retreat of the Ten Thousand*.[1]

The absolute indissolubility of marriage imposed by the Armenian religious law, together with special social and political conditions, combined, in the past, to make expedient the seclusion, if not subjection, of women. The modification of these conditions by external circumstances, which I have already referred to in the case of the Greeks, has also, at Constantinople and Smyrna, greatly changed the social position of Armenian women. And the contrast between the manners and social life of the inhabitants of the chilly highlands of Armenia and those of the dwellers on the sunny coasts of the Ægean and the Bosphorus is now as great as is the difference in their physical surroundings.

Patriarchal customs are still rigidly adhered to in the former remote regions, and also, to a great extent, in the Turkish towns of the interior, such as Broussa and Kaisariyeh. The "house-father" gathers beneath his own roof-tree his sons and their descendants to the third or fourth generation,

[1] Ἀνάβασις, iv. 5, 24.

one household often consisting of some thirty or forty persons, all of whom must necessarily be subject to his supreme authority. In former times girls were married very young, often when only twelve years of age; but this is no longer the case in the large towns. In order to ensure harmony among the numerous women brought into the house as wives for these successive generations, a practice, which may be termed "the subjection of the daughter-in-law," is resorted to, the wisdom of which, under the circumstances, cannot but be recognised. On the Saturday after a bride has been brought to her new home she performs the ceremony of kissing the hands of all her husband's relatives who are older than herself. Preparatory to this formality she dons a veil of crimson wool, which partly obscures her features, and which she does not thenceforward lay aside until she has the house-father's permission to do so. The young wife must now not venture to address her husband's parents or any of his relatives save those who are her juniors, neither must she speak to her husband in the presence of his parents until such time as the patriarch of the family may see fit to give her permission, which he does by removing her red veil. This, however, seldom happens until she has borne a son—for, as the native proverb says, "a wife shows her character at the cradle"—and the restriction may not be removed for many years. Her period of probation passed, the young wife assumes a higher position in the household. When the head of a house dies, his eldest son succeeds as house-master, but the widowed mother retains her former position and authority, and is associated with him in the management of the family.

An amusing example of the consequences of too rashly removing the prohibition of silence is to be found in the *Memoirs* of Artemi of Wagarshapat. The author and his mother, a widow, finding it inconvenient not to hold converse save by signs with the wife of his younger brother, the fourth member of their small household, and considering the national custom somewhat absurd, agreed to free her a few months after marriage from its observance. The neighbours were naturally scandalised, but Artemi's mother cared little for the opinion of neighbours who had always been jealous of the superior education which, by her self-denying efforts, she had succeeded in obtaining for her elder son, and the crimson veil of silence was removed. They had, however, reason to repent this hasty resolution, for the new inmate of their home soon proved herself to be a woman of ungovernable temper and bad disposition, and the quarrels which ensued effectually drove peace from the home, and convinced Artemi—but too late—of the unwisdom of lightly setting aside time-honoured customs.

The Armenian proverb, "I speak to thee, my daughter, that thou, my daughter-in-law, mayest hear," well illustrates the attitude of a mother towards her son's wife, and suggests that, though the new-comer is not spoken to, she is none the less "talked at." "A house will not be found convenient if two wives command in it," also shows the wisdom, under the patriarchal system, of assigning the daughter-in-law a subordinate position. National etiquette also forbids a young wife to go abroad during the first year of her married life, even to church, save at Easter, and at the Feast of the Assumption. This restriction, perhaps wisely, prevents her carrying every little trouble to her mother, who during this period pays her only an occasional formal visit.

All these patriarchal customs are, however, in the cities of the Ægean, and in the towns of European Turkey, things of the past. Western education and ideas are, with every succeeding generation, more and more permeating every class, and though a good many of these apparent changes are merely superficial, and present strange and sometimes ridiculous anomalies, unavoidable in a period of transition from Eastern to Western habits and modes of thought, real progress is no doubt being made by this section of the nation. A young wife becomes the mistress of her husband's house, his parents merely receiving her on her arrival according to the ancient etiquette in matters of marriage, which I shall presently describe, and which is still to a great extent adhered to. She now enjoys the same freedom of action and social status as the European ladies with whom she may be acquainted. All the usual facilities for social intercourse are at her disposal, and she may, if philanthropically disposed, spend some of her leisure time in endeavouring to ameliorate the condition of those of her countrywomen less favoured by fortune.

She has her box at the theatre, and attends the balls given at the casinos of the different nationalities as well as those more exclusively Armenian. I was once, when at Smyrna, invited to a fancy dress ball, given during the Carnival by the members of the Armenian *Cercle* or Club, where I found myself the only European present. The arrangement of the rooms left nothing to be desired, and the stewards were perfect in their duties. The costumes of the ladies especially were extremely rich, varied, and picturesque, and set off to great advantage the beauty of many of the wearers. Many of them were ancient Oriental dresses of a style no longer worn, and composed of rare silk damask decorated with exquisite old embroidery. Others were of the more conventional type of Floras, "Nights," and Shepherdesses. Though none of the company had probably ever had a dancing lesson, there was little fault to be found with their performance, and some of the younger ladies, indeed, waltzed most gracefully. Many of the company spoke English, nearly all expressed themselves fluently in French, and I was indebted to them for a very enjoyable evening.

The travelled Armenian lady often returns to her native town imbued with a sense of her own superiority, and sometimes, I must admit, inclined to treat with contempt her less favoured sisters. I was some years ago slightly acquainted with a lady of this description, who posed as a complete *Parisienne* and *femme du monde*. One day among the numerous callers, both native and foreign, whom we met in her drawing-room, was an Armenian lady whose resplendent toilette was completed by a pair of bright blue kid gloves. After some conversation with this lady and her party, the hostess crossed over to where I sat with my friends, saying, as she joined us, " Je viens m'asseoir du côté de la civilisation ; ces gants bleus là m'ont donné mal au cœur." On another occasion this very " civilised " lady, after deploring the want of literary taste at Smyrna and Bournabat, said, referring to the English Levantine ladies who constitute the principal element of "society" in that suburb, " Really they have no topics of conversation beyond the success of the last *boughádha*[1] and the price of soap!"

The domestic virtues of the average Armenian woman are, however, many. Her house is a model of neatness and cleanliness, and, even if she is sufficiently wealthy to employ several servants, she will often assist in making the many choice delicacies for which the Armenian *cuisine* is famous, but which I fear that I have not here space to describe. She is a fond and devoted, if not always a judicious, mother, and an affectionate wife ; and, as a rule, the greatest harmony prevails in Armenian households. When, however, family dissensions occur, they are often aggravated by the fact of the absolute indissolubility of the marriage bond, for, though a separation may be effected, neither party is free to contract a fresh union.

As has been already pointed out in the Intro-

[1] The "great wash" performed every three or four weeks, when the clothes are bleached with the ley of wood ashes.

duction, two entirely distinct types are to be found among the Armenians—the fair and the dark, or, as the Turks designate them, the "Pure" (*Indjé*) and the "Coarse" (*Kalun*). It is, no doubt, to this fact that we may attribute the very contradictory estimates formed by different authors of the personal attractions of Armenian women. Dora d'Istria, writing some forty years ago, describes their beauty in glowing terms;[1] while Sir Paul Ricaut, though speaking favourably of the appearance of the men, can find nothing to say in favour of that of the other sex.[2] At the period, however, when this quaintly interesting author recorded his impressions (1679) it was customary for Armenian ladies, even at Smyrna, to live in great seclusion, and when abroad to be veiled and cloaked like Moslem women;[3] and consequently the female specimens of the race with whom he would, under these circumstances, come into contact, would be only women of the lowest class and of the most mixed blood.

The Armenian ladies of Constantinople enjoy a great reputation for beauty, and those of Smyrna may, I think, be said to be not far behind them in this respect. One of their greatest charms consists

---

[1] "La beauté des Arméniennes quand elle n'est pas défigurée par une embonpoint précoce est véritablement remarquable. ..... Leur fraicheur est merveilleuse, leur taille svelte et élancée, leurs sourcils quoiqu' épais, parfaitement dessinés, &c."—*Les Femmes en Orient*.

[2] "Their women are commonly ill-shaped, long-nosed, and not one of a thousand so much as tolerably handsome."—*The Present State of the Greek and Armenian Churches*, p. 386.

[3] The Armenian were distinguishable from the Turkish women by the dark colour of their *feridgés* or cloaks, and by the red shoes which the sumptuary laws of the time obliged them to wear when abroad.

in the languorous expression of their dark, almond-shaped eyes. These beauties naturally belong to the "pure" type, and have, as a rule, black hair and eyes; though brown hair and blue eyes are not unfrequently met with, and are distinctive of some families. The complexion of this type is also good, the figure and carriage graceful, and the hands and feet are frequently small and well shaped. A Viennese painter was so struck with the exquisite proportions of the hand and arm of an Armenian lady of my acquaintance that he begged her to sit to him as a model for that part of a picture upon which he was then engaged. This lady belonged to a family famous for the beauty of its female members, among two generations of whom quite half a score of handsome women might be counted, mostly of the brown-haired and blue-eyed type, though of pure Armenian blood, and belonging to the Gregorian Church. And the window of a house in the Armenian quarter of Smyrna, where several of these belles were often visible, was named by their admirers "The Seventh Heaven of Mohammed." A comely specimen of the "coarse" type may occasionally be met with, but, as a rule, there is not among them, as Sir Paul Ricaut says, "one in a thousand so much as tolerably handsome."

But, whether "coarse" or "pure," Armenian women resort more or less to the use of cosmetics, either to enhance their charms, or to conceal their defects. Nor is this practice a result of the emancipation from ancient customs of the daughters of Smyrna and Constantinople. For earlier in the century, when Armenian women still went abroad veiled and cloaked like Moslems, as above described, and were, in their homes, equally secluded from the gaze of strangers, the passion for "getting up," which appears to be as inherent in the plain little hired drudge as in the elegant *kokona*, was perhaps more largely indulged in than at the present day, when the practice is being abandoned by educated women. I was greatly amused during some idle summer weeks at Bournabat by witnessing the open-air preparation and subsequent application of the mysterious compound used for the purpose by the gardener's wife, who lived in an adjoining cottage. The result of her many hours' pounding, mixing, shaking, and straining was generally made use of on a Sunday or Feast-day, and the effect was truly dazzling. On the opposite side of the lane lived two girls of a rather higher grade, whose daily occupation might be summed up in the words—they "painted their faces, and tired their heads, and looked out of a window;" and the attempts of the gardener's wife to rival these "young ladies" were highly amusing. The concoction and sale of these "washes" constitute, in the cities of the East, one of the minor domestic industries. It is generally carried on by elderly women, who are also skilled in the manufacture of rose- and orange-flower-water and of the delicious preserves met with only in the East. On one occasion, when I had expressed a wish for some rose-water, one of these persons was sent for, who brought with her a handkerchief full of fresh roses (the *Rosa moscata*), and a small still. Setting up the latter in the garden, over an impromptu fireplace of stones, she in a few hours produced, for the modest charge of six piastres, or one shilling, two large bottles of exquisite rose-water.

The native Armenian costume is now, in the cities of the seaboard and the towns of European Turkey, a thing of the past. A few of the elderly women still retain, it is true, as among the Greeks, the old-fashioned head-dress of the *taktikios*, which consists of a red fez, the full tassel of which is combed and spread all over it, surrounded by a kerchief of dark-coloured muslin, with a painted border and an edge of coloured needle-point lace. The hair, plaited into one tress, is twisted round the *taktikios*, and secured with a gold or silver pin.[1] A long plain skirt of stuff or silk, and a loose jacket lined with fur in winter, complete the costume, both for outdoor and indoor wear, though a shawl is sometimes added. In adopting Parisian fashions, Armenian women have retained their partiality for the vivid dyes which accorded so well with their ancient style of dress, but which now often asserts itself in combinations of colour most unpleasing to a Western eye; and the outdoor display they make of their superabundant jewellery says more for the security of property than for the taste of the wearer. But this tendency generally, if not always, disappears after a visit to Paris, or some other European capital.

There are, however, very few of the Europeanised Armenians who, in the privacy of their homes, are

[1] Twenty years ago, all the elderly women of Smyrna of every class, whether Armenian, Greek, or Frank, wore this head-dress, and also many middle-aged matrons belonging to the two former races.

neat in their attire. All those I have known were in the habit, immediately on their return from a walk or a visit, of exchanging their Parisian finery for a loose skirt and jacket, their high-heeled and many-buttoned boots for slippers (generally down at heel), and their elaborate coiffure for two plaits, hanging loosely over their shoulders. In this guise, too, they sit at their windows, their fair elbows resting on the cushioned sill, chewing gum-mastic, a practice which, though common to all women of the Levant, is more especially characteristic of the Armenians, and in the motions it gives to their jaws, unpleasantly recalls ruminating animals. This bad habit, however, is said to be good for the teeth.

The native costumes still worn in Armenia and in the far interior of Asia Minor vary in form, but the garments, worn one over another, of which they consist are all equally brilliant in colour and durable in material. At Van, the women allow their luxuriant black hair to fall loosely over their shoulders, and on their heads they wear a fez of red cloth, round which is folded, turban-fashion, a many-coloured kerchief. The remainder of the costume closely resembles that formerly worn by all Osmanli women, and still retained by them in many parts of the Empire. It consists of the *intarie*—a long gown of striped cotton, fitting tightly to the figure; the *shalvar*—full trousers of raspberry-coloured silk, drawn in at the ankles; the *shápo*—a long sleeveless jacket reaching to the feet, and open at the sides up to the waist; and, over all, the *jupbé*—an ample pelisse leaving exposed to view only the front of the *shápo* and the cuffs of the *intarie*, which are shaped *en sabot* and edged with "needle-lace." The pattern always found on the *shápo* deserves a word as illustrating a survival of the cone-fruit so frequently found on Chaldean monuments. This garment is made of a kind of cashmere of mixed silk and cotton in wide stripes of contrasting colour. On these stripes are printed various running patterns, of which the leading motive is always the cone. This favourite design of Oriental artists is, however, also said to be merely a modification of the figure of a cypress with its crest bent by the wind, that tree being, both in the folk- and culture-lore of most of the nations of Eastern Europe, the type of grace and beauty.

The costume of the women of Kaisariyeh, in Cappadocia, where the Armenians number some 16,000, is composed of very beautiful stuffs, and decorated with embroidery of remarkable delicacy. The headdress is particularly rich. Strings of gold sequins cover the front of the fez and hang over the forehead. From behind the ears are also suspended strings of seed pearls, and the neck and wrists are similarly decorated with ornaments of gold and pearls. The dress now worn at Sivas is said to be identical with that of the women of ancient Persia. Out of doors, however, all the women of the interior conceal the luxury of their costumes under a cloak of plain stuff, similar to that worn by Moslem women, and shroud their heads and faces with a thick veil.

Armenian girls of the poorer classes manifest an even greater repugnance than Greek girls to employment outside the sphere of their own homes, and the latter are often employed as servants in Armenian houses, owing to the difficulty of obtaining Armenian domestics. To see the Armenian girls lounging about their doorways one might indeed say that their leading characteristics are apathy and listlessness. Yet, though so much less energetic than their sisters inhabiting the less enervating climate of Armenia, they can hardly, as a class, be stigmatised as indolent. Many little home-industries are pursued, such as the making of the coloured lace called *vya* or *bibil*, formerly so much in demand for trimming the native costumes both of Armenian and Turkish ladies, and also embroidery in gold and silks. The taste and aptitude displayed by Armenian girls for the latter pursuit led to the formation of a class of "art needlework" in connection with the Industrial Institution for Girls, founded at Constantinople in 1887 by Mr. Ohannes Nourian, a philanthropic Armenian resident of that city. To the pupils of this establishment, who now number one hundred and twenty, and are presided over by thirty teachers, was entrusted the task of decorating with their needles the State apartments occupied by the Emperor and Empress of Germany during their recent visit to the Sultan's capital. The Empress's satisfaction with their handiwork was, it is said, expressed to the Sultan in such glowing terms that His Majesty conferred decorations on the lady directresses of the institution.[1] The silk factories of

---

[1] It is a rather curious fact that the conferment of Orders on Women should have been initiated in Turkey.

Broussa, as before mentioned, afford employment to a considerable number of women, of whom a certain proportion are Armenians, who are, I am told, greatly valued for their powers of steady work.

In Armenia Proper it would appear that the women are not less industrious than their Christian peasant sisters in other parts of Turkey, and, in this respect at least, they rival the men of their nation, who are indefatigable workers. Besides her household work, and the care of the family and domestic animals, the manufacture of clothing for the family and furniture for the house also devolves upon the Armenian woman. The spindle is to her what knitting is to a German housewife, and, with the help of her daughters, many beautiful tissues are produced on the loom, the surplus of which find their way to the bazaars of the capital. Among these are fine linen and silk gauzes; so-called Turkish towels, and *havlús*, or bathing gowns of the same material, with fringed and embroidered borders, made chiefly at Trebizond, Erzeroum, and Van; cloth of fine camel's-hair, and handsome stuffs for covering the seats and cushions of divans. The process of making the felt or *tekké* carpets so much used in the country is very simple. On a mat, larger than the carpet and strengthened at the back with stout linen, the dyed wool is arranged according to the pattern intended. On this another layer of more finely carded wool is placed to the depth of about a foot. Several persons then carefully roll up the mat, and the cylinder thus formed is rolled about and pressed with the feet until the wool is reduced to the thickness of half an inch.

The upper surface is then carefully clipped in order to accentuate the outline of the pattern.

A distinguishing trait of the Armenian character is their fondness for, and consequent kindness to, animals, which contrasts very favourably with the cruelty displayed by their Greek, and more especially by their Jewish, neighbours towards their dumb fellow-creatures. To kill a cat, a rat, or a bird was formerly considered so grave a crime as to deserve ecclesiastical punishment, and M. Fleurian[1] records a case in which a fast of twenty years' duration was imposed by the priest upon a woman for killing her cat. And though much leniency is not, I believe, shown at the present day to the larger vermin, I well remember the horror and indignation of some Armenian ladies at Smyrna on witnessing the inhuman treatment by a Greek baker of a rat which had been caught in a trap in his shop. In Armenia, as before mentioned, the dogs are housed under the platform of the *selamlik*, and the beautiful white cats with long silky fur, and tails oddly dyed of a reddish hue with henna, sit on the knees of their masters or purr by their sides on the cushions of the divan. Besides these more common animals there are the tame, or half tame, lemmings, jerboas, and *kara guez*, or "black-eyes." The last are pretty little creatures, with soft grey fur. Like the pink-eyed lemmings, they hybernate every year, and are easily domesticated. As for birds, the popular reverence for them is so great that it, to some extent, accounts for the immense numbers to be found in Armenia. Some

[1] *Etat présent de l'Arménie*, p. 25.

travellers describe them as literally "covering the ground;" and their variety appears no less great, for Mr. Calvert, when Consul at Erzeroum, collected as many as one hundred and seventy different species.[1]

Armenian salutations and greetings partake of a decidedly religious character. The reply to good-morning and good-evening is invariably, "The blessing of God to you." On separating in the evening the reply to good-night, "And a good dawning," extends the salutation to the next day. At Easter, and for forty days afterwards, the greeting is, "Christ is risen from the dead!" and the response, "Blessed be the Resurrection of Christ." The ordinary form of felicitation on the marriage of a son or daughter, the birth of a child, or any other happy domestic event, is "Light to your eyes!" and the acknowledgment, "May you also enjoy the light."

From the above described contrast between the social life and manners of the two sections of the Armenian nation in Turkey, naturally follows a wide difference in the degree of education to which they have respectively attained. While in point of culture the Armenians of the Ægean would compare not unfavourably with Europeans, the dwellers in the remote Fatherland have advanced but slowly, and female education especially is in a very backward state. Great efforts are, however, being made to remedy this defect, and various educational associations have been organised, which number among

[1] Curzon's *Armenia*, p. 154.

their most active members many ladies belonging to the communities at Smyrna and Constantinople. The "Philomathic Society of Armenian Ladies" have founded at Koum-Kapou, Constantinople, a Training College for native schoolmistresses to be sent to Armenia, Cilicia, and elsewhere; and in this establishment seventy-five have already been trained, and appointed to schools in those districts. The "National Society of Armenian Women" also maintains five girls' schools in the towns of Moush, Hadjin, Keghi, Seghert, and Alashguerd, at which some six hundred pupils are now being educated. The "United Societies for the Promotion of Education in Armenian Centres" have also in their list ten girls' schools, scattered over four different provinces, in which instruction is, according to the returns for 1889, afforded to more than seven hundred girls. All these institutions are maintained by voluntary contributions; for, though the Porte imposes an "Education Tax" on its Christian subjects, Moslem schools alone are benefited thereby. The proportion of girls' to boys' schools, however, notwithstanding all the praiseworthy efforts of these various societies, is as yet, as with the Greeks of Turkey, only as one to four.

The American missions to the Armenians, which have been established for more than half a century at Kharput, Kaisariyeh, Sivas, Van, Erzeroum, Aintàb, and some other places, have already done much for the education of the female portion of the nation in these towns. The schools attached to these establishments, and presided over by devoted ladies from the

Far West, are attended not only by the daughters of Protestant converts, but of orthodox Gregorians, some, who come from a considerable distance, being received as boarders. Many parents who would gladly follow their example are, unfortunately, too poor to be able to pay even the very low fees required for board and education. The course of instruction comprises the English, Turkish, and Armenian languages, Scripture lessons, arithmetic, and more advanced subjects for those who wish to be trained as teachers.

Among the Armenians, as formerly among the Greeks, the Turkish language has, in some districts, and notably at Broussa and Kaisariyeh, entirely replaced the mother-tongue, which is there used only in the church liturgies. This fact forcibly illustrates the state of denationalisation into which this nation has in many places sunk during the Ottoman domination. With the re-birth of national sentiment and aspiration, a reaction has, however, naturally set in, and the rising generation now everywhere learns in the national schools the mother-tongue, which will, it is hoped, soon entirely supersede the use of Turkish, save as a foreign language. Good schools both for boys and girls have long been established in the capital and in Smyrna, and for very many years past the teaching of French has in the latter city been obligatory. Some of the wealthier families at Smyrna send their daughters to the establishment of the German Deaconesses, where, besides receiving a sound general education, they add a good knowledge of English, French, and German to the three native languages of Armenian, Turkish, and Greek, which they have orally acquired in childhood. Many girls are also educated at home by European governesses, who find their pupils, as a rule, extremely intelligent and painstaking. While Armenian men have been engaged on translations of such works as Milton's *Paradise Lost* and Homer's *Iliad* and *Odyssey*, some of the Armenian women of the Capital and of Smyrna have occupied themselves with rendering into their native language, for the benefit of their less cultured sisters, the more popular works of Victor Hugo, Dumas, Ohnet, and other French authors. A literary *Salon*, too, has been formed at Constantinople, though whether the "culture" of its members is, or is not, of the kind satirised by Molière in *Les Précieuses Ridicules* and *Les Femmes Savantes*, I am not in a position to say. Armenian women are also in considerable demand as actresses in Turkish theatres. The plays most in vogue in this country are French operettas, the librettos of which are translated into Turkish, though original comedies are also often placed on the boards. The Sultan employs a company of these women, and himself writes, or rather furnishes, the plots for some of the comedies and burlesques. Armenian literature, the most brilliant period of which was from the fifth to the seventh centuries, long neglected, is at present in a transitional stage, and there is now, I am informed, "more imitation than creation." The recent revival of education and national sentiment, however, will no doubt be followed by a revival of letters, and of this there are, indeed, already various unmistakable signs. Old traditions are being collected and published; periodicals started, devoted to the national cause; and, as before mentioned, great efforts are being made in the schools to restore the use of the ancient language of Armenia.

I ought not, perhaps, to close this chapter without some remark on the patriotism of the Armenians. For however far from the land of his ancestors a son of Haik may roam, he never forgets its former greatness, nor ceases to long for its deliverance from a foreign yoke. And this sentiment seems to be as strongly developed in the communities which have lived so long in exile that they still retain forms of speech which are obsolete in the Fatherland, as in the emigrant of yesterday. Indeed, the couplet from the ancient folk-song,

> Thy native land still bear in mind,
> To it be ever true and kind,[1]

attributed to an old nurse when taking leave of an Armenian princess about to be married to a foreign monarch, seems always to find an echo in the Armenian breast. And from the women no less than from the men of such far-off colonies as those of Batavia and Sourabayia, in Java, as well as from those inhabiting the Turkish cities, come messages of sympathy, accompanied by more substantial assistance, to the Armenian Patriotic Associations lately established in Europe.

[1] Alishanian, *Armenian Popular Songs*.

CHAPTER VII.

ARMENIAN WOMEN: THEIR FAMILY CEREMONIES.

The customs observed by the Armenian women in connection with the birth of a child resemble in many particulars those of their Turkish neighbours under similar circumstances, and the ceremonies attending such an event are of an equally superstitious character. As with the Greeks, the mother and child should not be left alone until the latter has been baptised. If, however, this is unavoidable, either a picture of the Virgin or a text from the New Testament is hung over the bed, or a prayer-book is placed under the pillow, to keep away the demons; and, in order to guard against the evil eye, holy water is sprinkled every night over the susceptible persons, who are also fumigated with the smoke of the Palm Sunday branches. The mother holds a reception on the third day, to which her friends and neighbours flock, in order to satisfy their curiosity concerning the new arrival. The baby is rolled up and bandaged in innumerable wraps, with its toes turned in, until it can move neither hand nor foot, and, among the poorer classes especially, these garments are frequently not removed or changed for days together. The baby is washed every day in warm water until it has been baptised, but afterwards only once a week. For few people in the East give their children the benefit of a daily bath, an idea being generally prevalent that it is an injurious custom, causing all manner of ailments. Kept neither clean nor neat, and indulged with every variety of food, they struggle through infancy in a very irregular manner, but—owing, perhaps, to their being so much in the open air—they grow up, as a rule, strong and healthy.

An Armenian baby is baptised when eight days old, and the rite is administered with great pomp and solemnity. The child is carried to church by the midwife, accompanied by the godfather (*gnkabib*) and relatives, male and female. Arrived at the porch, they are met by the officiating priest, a deacon, and acolytes, and the service commences with the words, " Blessed be the Holy Ghost, the true God." The priest then recites, alternately with the deacon, the 51st and the 131st Psalms, while a string of red and white threads is being twisted, which, when finished, is blessed, prayed over, and reserved for the subsequent ceremony of confirmation. The party advance into the porch, where the midwife kneels as many times as the infant numbers days. The baby is then laid on the threshold of the church, where it remains while the godfather makes his sacramental confession in order to undertake the office of sponsor while in a state of grace. The godfather absolved, the priest takes up the child and gives it into his arms with a Scripture text. The sponsor kneels with it three times, and the priest, placing his hand upon the infant's head, makes the exorcisms by pronouncing some devout invocations, and then recites more psalms. The godfather then turns to the west, and the priest to the east, when the former renounces, in the child's name, all the pomps and vanities of this wicked world in these words: "We renounce thee, Satan, and all thy frauds, thy deceptions, and thy worship, thine inspiration, thy ways, thy wicked will, thy wicked angels, thy wicked ministers, thy wicked agents, and all thy wicked power."

The priest, addressing the child, then asks, "Dost thou renounce? Dost thou renounce? Dost thou truly renounce?" For whom the sponsor replies, "I do," to each repetition of the question. Giving to the godfather a lighted taper, the priest says: "Turn to the light of the knowledge of God." He then questions the child concerning his belief in the Creed, which is in substance the same as the Apostles' Creed of the English Church, and for the child the godfather again replies, "I do believe;" as also to the following questions, "Dost thou believe in the Father, true God? Dost thou believe in the Son, true God? Dost thou believe in the Holy Ghost, true God?" The priest then reads part of the 28th chapter of St. Matthew's Gospel, and then the Nicene Creed, in which the godfather joins.

While these preliminary ceremonies are being performed, the doors of the church are closed, and remain so until the 20th verse of the 118th Psalm is reached, when, at the words, "This gate of the Lord, into which the righteous shall enter," they are thrown open, and the men of the party enter, and advance to the font, singing a psalm. The warm water for the baptism which has been brought by the *gnkabib* from the baby's home, being ready, the priest proceeds to consecrate it by the recital of special prayers, and by invoking upon it the virtue of the Holy Ghost, and then pours it into the font in the form of a cross, the deacons chanting all the while. After reading several passages of Scripture from the Old and New Testaments, the deacon exhorts those present to "pray for the peace of all the world, for the prosperity of the Church, for the life and eternal salvation of the Patriarch, for the worthy administration of the present rite, for the spiritual regeneration of the child, and for all the faithful."

This finished, the priest recites over the font the following prayer:

"Thou, Lord, through Thy great power didst create the sea and the earth, and all the creatures that are in them. Thou didst divide and establish the waters in heaven, the abode of Thy celestial hosts, who glorify Thee incessantly. Thou didst send Thy holy Apostles, commanding them to preach to and baptise all infidels in the name of the Father, the Son, and the Holy Ghost. Thou didst decree, also, by Thy unerring word, that those who are not regenerated through the water shall not enter into Paradise. Of which thing being afraid, this Thy servant, desiring Thee, who art the eternal life, came willingly to be baptised, spiritually, with this water. We pray Thee, Lord, send Thy Holy Spirit into this water, and bless [making here the sign of the cross] and purify it, in the same manner that Thou didst purify Jordan by descending into it, Thou, our Lord Jesus Christ, who wast all pure from sin, typifying thereby in this fountain of baptism the regeneration of all men. Grant unto him, through this water, by which he is now baptised, that he may obtain pardon for his sins, receive Thy Holy Spirit, be numbered with those who are affiliated with Thee, heavenly Father, and be worthy of an inheritance in Thy celestial kingdom, in order that, purified from sin, he may live in this world according to the pleasure of Thy will, and in the future life may receive, with all Thy saints, the infinite good blessings, and gladly glorify the Father, the Son, and the Holy Ghost, now, and throughout all ages."

After the repetition of other prayers, the "holy chrism" is, with much reverential ceremony, added to the water in the font. Before opening the box in which it is preserved, candles are lighted, and the priest takes successively in his hand the cross, the gospels, and the chrism, makes three times the sign of the cross over the water, and pours into it three drops of the sacred oil, chanting, "Hallelujah, hallelujah, hallelujah! May this water be blessed and purified through the sign of the holy Cross, of the holy Gospel, and of the holy Chrism; in the name of the Father, and of the Son, and of the Holy Ghost;" to which the deacon responds thrice, "Hallelujah!" The infant is undressed by the godfather and given into the hands of the priest, who, after the recital of a short prayer, asks the child: "What dost thou demand?" The godfather responds: "I demand to be baptised." " Dost thou truly demand it?" again questions the priest. To which the sponsor replies: "I demand with faith to be baptised and purified from sin, to be released from the demons, and to serve God;" whereupon the priest says: "Be it unto thee according to thy faith."

The child's name is given to the priest, who, with his left hand under its neck, and, with his right, holding its feet, dips it into the font in such a way that its head is towards the west, its feet are towards the east, and its eyes toward heaven. Then, placing the infant in an upright position in the water, he says: "N——, servant of God, coming by his own will to the state of a catechumen, and thence to that of baptism, is now baptised by me in the name of the Father, and of the Son, and of the Holy Ghost," pouring a handful of water over the child's head at each name. He then dips the baby three times into the water, saying at each immersion: "Redeemed by the blood of Christ from the servitude of sin; receiving the liberty which arises from affiliation with Thee, heavenly Father; he becomes co-heir with Christ, and a temple of the Holy Spirit." These three immersions are held to be commemorative of the three days during which Christ remained in the grave. The priest then washes the whole of the child's body, saying, as he does so: "Ye that were baptised in Christ, have been clothed in Christ, hallelujah! And ye that were illuminated in God the Father, may the Holy Ghost rejoice in you, hallelujah!" Some verses of the 34th Psalm are then read, followed by a passage from St. Matthew

(iii. 13-17); and at the words—" And Jesus being baptised, forthwith came out of the water "—the priest takes out the child and delivers him to the godfather. The ceremony is concluded with prayers adapted to the occasion.

In the Armenian, as in the Orthodox Greek Church, a baby is confirmed immediately after baptism, and receives at the same time his first communion. While the " Hymn of the Holy Chrism " is being chanted, the priest takes the infant from the godfather, and, dipping his thumb in the consecrated oil, he makes with it the sign of the cross on nine different parts of its body, as follows. First on the forehead, saying: " May this sweet oil, which is poured upon thee in the name of Christ, be a seal of the celestial gifts "; on the eyes, saying: " May this seal, which is offered to thee in the name of Jesus Christ, illuminate thine eyes, lest thou sleep the sleep of death "; on the ears, saying: " May this anointment of sanctification make thee obedient to the commandments of God "; on the nose, saying: " May this seal, in the name of Jesus Christ, be to thee as a sweet savour of life unto life "; on the mouth, saying: " May this seal, &c., be to thee as a watch, and as a solid door to thy lips "; on the palms, saying: " May this seal, &c., be to thee the cause of good works, of virtuous deeds, and of life "; on the heart, saying: " May this divine seal, in the name of Jesus Christ, create in thee a clean heart, and renew a right spirit within thee "; on the spine, saying: " May this seal, &c., be to thee a shield of safety, wherewith thou mayest be able to quench all the fiery darts of the wicked"; and, lastly, on the feet, saying: "May this divine seal, &c., direct thy steps to eternal life, and keep thy feet from erring."

The priest then blesses the garments of the child, and clothes him, after which, with the red and white thread twisted at his baptism, he binds on his forehead, or on his little finger, according to locality, a small gold cross. When he has covered the baby with a white cloak, he places in its hand a taper, coloured red and green, saying: "Receive the lamp of faith and of good works, so that, when the Bridegroom shall come, thou mayest be worthy to enter in unto the wedding of light, and enjoy eternal life." The child is now carried to the altar, with the three sides of which his lips are brought into contact, and also with the cross. As baptism is usually administered during the performance of Mass, the baby is brought to the altar at the moment the celebrant communicates; and he, after dipping his finger into the chalice, puts it into the infant's mouth, saying: "Plenitude of the Holy Ghost."

About the ninth day the mother goes with great ceremony to the bath, attended by her friends, who partake with her in the "cooling-room" of a substantial luncheon, in which the favourite national dish of *yahlantchi dolmas* plays a prominent part.

Eight days after the christening the priest repairs to the baby's home, and removes the string from its head, or its finger, accompanying this ceremony with suitable prayers. When the child is forty days old, he is carried to the door of the church, accompanied by his mother, and the priest there reads over them special prayers. They are then led into the church, and the priest, taking the child in his arms, places him upon the steps of the altar as if in the act of adoration. A hymn in honour of the Virgin is chanted, the priest blesses the mother and child, and the ceremony is concluded.

If, before the baby is forty days old, any animal belonging to the household has young, the child must be passed three times over the newly born creature. If this rule is not observed, the child will grow up melancholy and a prey to malaria. It is said that young brute animals, over which this ceremony has been performed, have often been known to die of the ailments from which these traditional prescriptions have preserved the human animal.

Should a sack of flour be brought into the house before the expiration of the forty days, the baby must be placed at the door on a seat higher than the sack; and, when the latter has been placed in the storeroom, the child must be passed three times over the sack, or it will be afflicted with melancholy and malaria. Also, if a funeral pass within this period, the mother must take her infant up to the terrace till the procession has gone by. If she fails to do this, "the dead will take the child with him." When the bread is put in the oven, the baby must be covered with a quilt, or he will pine and die.

If the baby is attacked with malarious fever, he must be bathed in tepid water which has dripped from a mill-wheel. If this is not procurable, a woman is sent at break of day, on a Friday, to collect water from all the wells and fountains of the village. If she meets any person while on this errand, she must neither accost him nor answer any questions he may put to her.

If the mother is obliged to go out before the forty days, and meets in the village street another woman similarly circumstanced, they must exchange needles. If they have none on their persons, they must borrow from neighbours.

The baby must not be taken out before it is forty days old, nor must it be left alone for fear of the demon. One evening, however, a woman of Indjé Sou, near Cesarœa, found it necessary to go to a neighbour's house. What to do with her baby she knew not—to take it with her was as dangerous as to leave it alone. The latter at last seemed the only alternative. So she put the baby in the cradle, and placed on its breast as preservatives against the demon a piece of bread, a pair of scissors, and a picture of Christ, and went out. But great was her surprise and horror to find the cradle empty when she returned. She searched everywhere, ransacked the house, shrieked and wept, but all in vain. At last, after having turned the house upside down all night, she found the child standing upright behind the flour-sack. A moment afterwards the cock crowed. At sunrise the woman hastened to the village priest, and told him what had happened.

"You could not have taken the proper precautions," said the priest, "and so the *djin* was able to take your child. If you had not found him before cockcrow, you would never have seen him again."

The priest then accompanied his parishioner to

her house, whence he drove away the *djin* with a prayer, which prevented his ever returning. An ill-conditioned, unmanageable child is often reputed to be the changeling of a *djin*.

Contact with Europeans has, in the cities of the Levant, modified to a slight extent the observances of the Armenians with regard to the affairs of marriage, but in their leading features the national customs connected with the ceremony itself have suffered very little change. Second nuptials are permitted to both sexes, but a third marriage, if not precisely forbidden by religious law, is considered highly reprehensible. The clergy, or friends of the family, fulfil the office of matrimonial go-betweens, thus giving from the outset a religious character to the proceedings. If the parties are found not to be related within the forbidden degrees, which, as with the Greeks, extend to the seventh, and include conventional relationships, and the match is deemed suitable, the betrothal may at once take place. This ceremony consists merely in sending to the bride, by the hands of one or two priests, according to the means of the parties, a gold or silver ring accompanied by presents of jewellery. The priest places the ring on the finger of the maiden with some Scriptural words suited to the occasion, and receives from her mother a similar ring which he conveys to the bridegroom. But, though so simple in form, this betrothal is considered binding, and can only be set aside for very serious reasons.

towns of Armenia, Cappadocia, and Cilicia almost as much secluded from inter- other sex as are their Moslem sisters, and the betrothed couple are consequently, as a rule, comparative strangers to each other. This is, however, not the case in Smyrna or Constantinople, where European manners are more or less cultivated by the better class of Armenians, and where marriages of affection are not uncommon, nor in all the villages, where a certain amount of courtship often takes place. But national prejudice, in the towns of Armenia, forbids any but the most formal intercourse between the betrothed couple, and all the arrangements for the auspicious event are made by the respective parents. If the bridegroom is wealthy, he may send with the cross a present of jewels or a purse of money to his future bride, who, unless she happens to be an heiress, brings only linen for the nuptial chamber, though, if her parents are wealthy, a certain amount of jewellery and silver plate may be added to her trousseau. The patriarchal custom of bringing home a bride to the paternal roof, though almost entirely abandoned in Constantinople and Smyrna, is still practised in Armenia and other inland places.

When all is ready for the bridal, the *dandigin* (the mistress of the ceremonies, who superintends all the arrangements connected with the wedding feast) is commissioned to notify the fact to the bridegroom and his parents, and also to inform them of the day appointed for the *Hars'nik*.[1] Matrimony is never celebrated on fast days, on dominical feasts, or during seven weeks after Easter. Monday is considered a propitious day for the religious ceremony,

---

[1] An abbreviation of *Harsanik*, an Armenian word signifying the period of festivity attendant upon a wedding ceremony.

and the preceding festivities commence on a Friday. The bride is on this day taken by her friends with great ceremony to the bath, and invitations are issued to all who are to assist at the wedding. On Saturday, musicians are called in, and the bride and her maiden friends pass the time in dancing, feasting, and ministering to the poor, for whom a table is spread and open house kept.

The Sunday of the *Har'snik* is a red-letter day among the Armenian youth, for on this day the young men are allowed to wait upon the girls at the feast given in the afternoon. When the girls leave the table, the married couples sit down, wife and husband side by side, in patriarchal fashion. When the youths have also supped they are again admitted to the society of the maidens, under the pretext of handing round refreshments.

The religious ceremony at the church takes place on Monday evening. The priest, accompanied by his deacon, arrives before the guests assemble to bless the nuptial pledge, or ring, and the wedding garments, over which he offers prayers, imploring God to "make the betrothal happy, and bless the dowry, so that the outer ornaments of the body may be a continual excitement to her to adorn her soul with such angelic virtues as are proper to the condition of matrimony into which she is about to enter." After the arrival of the company, the bride retires with her near relatives and girl companions to be dressed in the national wedding array. The indoor bridal robe is a loose flowing garment of brocaded silk, trimmed round the edges with the silk lace called *oya*, described in the preceding chapter. But, like the generality of Orientals, the Armenians consider it necessary to disguise their brides. A silver plate is accordingly fastened on the girl's head, and over it is thrown a large piece of crimson silk, which reaches to her feet and covers her whole person. This is secured under the plate and at the side with ribbons; and in some localities a large pair of cardboard wings (*sorgoosh*), covered with feathers, are attached to her head. In this extraordinary disguise she is led back to the reception-room, where she opens the dance with her father, or nearest of kin, during the performance of which small coins[1] are showered over her. This concluded, she takes her seat on a pile of cushions placed in the corner of the wide divan which runs round three sides of the room. If the company is very large, the ladies will dispose themselves on this divan in three rows, sitting on the back cushions, the centre, and the extreme edge, the old *kokonas* taking the most comfortable positions, and the young *doudous* finding places where they best can.

The bridegroom has, in the meantime, been occupied with his toilet, surrounded by a group of lively friends, including the best man, the *Gnkahair*, who has been escorted to the house by a band of musicians.

---

[1] This ancient Armenian custom is referred to by Moses of Khor'ni, when describing the wedding of the great Artaxés—

"At Artaxé's wedding gold-strewn was the ground;
At Sathanig's bridal fine pearls rained around."

Similar munificence was, until quite recently, observed at Turkish royal weddings, and is frequently referred to in folk-tales.

The barber, an important functionary at all these ceremonies, commences his operations, razor in hand, a towel over one shoulder and leather strop over the other. With story and joke he prolongs and repeats the details of his calling on the face of the happy man, whose friends reward the gossip's efforts for their entertainment with presents in the shape of towels, handkerchiefs, scarves, &c., which they suspend on a line stretched across the room. When he deems the generosity of the company exhausted, the barber gives the signal for the production of the wedding garments, which, like those of the bride, have been previously blessed by the priest. Arrayed in these gorgeous robes, and with a scimitar[1] in his girdle, the bridegroom proceeds to the house of rejoicing, a torch borne on each side of him, and attended by a numerous company, some of whom, carrying his presents to the bride, precede him with a band of music.

On arriving, he is conducted with much ceremony to the reception-room. His future mother-in-law greets him with a gift, in return for which he respectfully kisses her hand, and she then presents him to the bride, who rises from her cushions, and, descending to the floor, makes him a lowly reverence. A second betrothal now takes place. The priest repeats the 89th Psalm, after which he gives

---

[1] Owing to the frequent carrying off of Armenian brides by Moslems on the wedding day, an Imperial Firman was granted to the nation, allowing a bridegroom to wear a sword, and permitting him also to use it against any person attempting to molest the bridal party. Although such abductions are now of rare occurrence, the right to guard against them is still exercised.

the right hand of the girl into that of the man, saying, "When God presented Eve's hand to Adam, Adam said: This is now bone of my bone, and flesh of my flesh; she shall be called woman, because she was taken out of man; therefore shall a man leave his father and his mother, and shall cleave unto his wife, and they shall be one flesh. What therefore God hath joined together, let not man put asunder." Then, approaching their foreheads until they touch, he ties upon each with a crimson silk thread a small cross, reciting meanwhile a prayer composed of Scripture texts.[1]

Still holding each other's hands, the betrothed pair proceed to the house-door, where the bridegroom hands over the maiden to the bridesmaids, and, accompanied by his own party, leads the way to church, the poor blindfolded bride following with her friends. No person is allowed to cross the road between the two parts of the procession, as this would be a bad augury for the future happiness of the couple. On entering the porch of the sacred edifice, the principals, while making three times the sign of the cross, give mental utterance to the dearest wish of their hearts, in the belief that whatever they ask at that moment will be granted them. The first part of the service takes place in the porch. The couple kneel three times during the reading of the 122nd Psalm, after which they confess and receive absolution. Two garlands are then twisted,

[1] According to a folk-belief which has its counterpart in the West, if the bride succeeds either during this ceremony, or during the marriage service in the church, in placing her foot above that of the bridegroom, the future supremacy will be hers.

to be used in the ceremony, psalms being read meanwhile. The priest then takes the cross, and, holding it aloft, pronounces an exhortation, reminding the couple that the bond upon which they are about to enter is indissoluble, and concludes by asking them if they are prepared to "bear all the burdens and fulfil all the duties connected with matrimony." He then asks separately of the pair: "And if thy husband [or wife] become blind, sick, crippled, deaf, or poor [omitted when addressing the husband], wilt thou remain faithful to him [or her] unto death?" When they have replied in the affirmative, the priest joins their hands, saying to the man: "According to the divine order which God gave to our ancestors, I [name], a priest, give thee now this wife in subjection. Wilt thou be her master?" To which he replies: "With the help of God, I will." Then, turning to the woman, he asks: "Wilt thou be obedient to him?" She answers: "I am obedient according to the order of God." These interrogatories are repeated three times. Various exhortations, prayers, and passages of Scripture relating to matrimony follow, after which the doors are opened, and the wedding train, led by the priest, and chanting the hundredth Psalm, advances to the altar. The nuptial Mass follows. When the crowns have been blessed, they are placed on the heads of the company with more prayers, exhortations, and passages of Scripture,[1] after which the holy communion is ad-

---

[1] I am told that, a few years ago, the Armenian priests were ordered in their marriage service to add after "I wed you in the name of the Lord," the words "and of the Sultan"!

ministered. The religious ceremony concluded, the wedded pair walk hand in hand to the church-door, where the bridesmaids again take charge of the bride, and lead her to her new home. As they go, hymeneal songs and psalms are chanted, and corn and small coins are showered over the heads of the couple. At the moment of their arrival a sheep is sacrificed on the threshold, over the blood of which the wedding party step to enter the house. The bridegroom seats himself on a sofa, specially prepared for the occasion, and places the bride at his right hand. A costly cup is filled with wine and blessed by the priest, who presents it to the couple in turn. The guests meanwhile chant a hymn, in which, in the name of the Church, they augur all kinds of felicity, temporal as well as spiritual, for the happy pair. The repetition of the Lord's Prayer terminates the ecclesiastical ceremony, when all come up in turn and felicitate the couple by kissing their garlands or the crosses on their foreheads, and drop coins into a plate for the benefit of the officiating priests. The bride, refreshed with a cup of coffee, is again consigned, in the loneliness of her veil, to a corner. A baby boy is placed on her knees, with the wish: "May you be a happy mother!" When the baby has been removed, all the children present rush to take off the bride's stockings, and scramble for the money which has previously been hidden in them. After formally opening the dance with her husband, the bride again retires to her corner, where she sits for the rest of the evening a mute and veiled image, taking no part in the festivities going on around her. The bridesmaids remain, during the period of "wearing the crowns," in attendance upon the companion who is leaving their ranks. This may be from three to eight days, both bride and bridegroom retaining their wedding finery all the time, even at night, and living separately until the crowns are removed by the priest. This ceremony is, however, nowadays generally performed on the Wednesday evening following the religious ceremony. A little before supper-time the priest arrives, accompanied by his deacon. Placing the pair with their foreheads in contact, he rests on their united heads a sword and a cross, invoking for them every marital blessing, and reminding them that unfaithfulness will be followed by the Divine wrath, of which the sword is a type. The bride and bridegroom again partake of consecrated wine from the same cup, after which the party all sit down to supper.

When the couple are at last left alone, the husband offers his bride a present, generally a piece of jewellery. If the recipient deems the gift of smaller value than she considers herself entitled to, or than the giver's means permit, she may refuse to receive him as her husband until he shows himself more generous. The priest's wife, who has also been present at the family supper, spends the night in the house, and on the following morning is sent to announce to the bride's parents that their daughter has honourably entered upon her married life. At noon relatives and friends flock to the house to offer their congratulations, and are entertained at the expense of the bridegroom's father. National etiquette does not, however, allow the bride's parents to visit her until at least a week has elapsed.

On the Saturday after the wedding the bride goes through the ceremony of formally kissing the hands of her father- and mother-in-law in the presence of the rest of the family. On this occasion she dons the veil of crimson crêpe, which she will continue to wear until her father-in-law, when granting her permission to address her husband's relatives, allows her to lay it aside. When a young wife kneads bread for the first time in the house it is customary for the husband to throw into the trough some pieces of money, which she must pick up with her teeth without touching the dough even with her lips. On the fortieth day after the wedding the bride is taken to the fountain or well for the first time. As she goes she must kiss the hand of the first person she may meet, whether man or woman. Arrived at the well, she anoints the stones with butter, evidently in propitiation of the water spirits, and throws handfuls of corn to the birds. This rite performed, she is entitled to fill her pitcher with the limpid water.

During these forty days the wedded pair are supposed to be more than usually subject to the power of evil spirits (*djins*), who are perpetually on the watch to do them a mischief. It is only, however, between sunset and sunrise that their malice is to be feared, and the persons thus menaced are careful not to open their doors, or to go abroad after nightfall. If this is unavoidable, they must be accompanied by some responsible member of the family, when the *djins* cannot touch them, though they may frighten them with the noises by which they make their presence known.

The custom of having the wedding garments blessed by the priest is also a precaution taken against the supposed practices of the above-mentioned supernatural beings. It is a popular belief, common to both Armenians and Moslems, that if a new article of dress is added to a person's wardrobe without having been previously blessed in the name of either Christ, or the Virgin, or Mohammed, the *djins* will be able to borrow it to wear at their festivities. A story is told of a Turkish woman who, some thirty years ago, was carried off by these spirits to their underground palace, and kept there for three days. On her return home she related her adventures to her gossips, and described the spirits as dressed in clothes evidently borrowed for the occasion from mortals. One of these garments she had recognised as belonging to the daughter of the headman of Indjé Sou.[1] The matrons were disinclined to believe this explanation of the woman's absence. But this privileged individual triumphantly produced a scrap of the dress in question, which she had surreptitiously cut off the skirt, and desired them to ascertain the state in which it had been returned to its irreligious owner.

With the Armenians, as with all other Orientals, there are lucky and unlucky days for marriages, and on those considered most propitious for this event a number of couples often present themselves at church on the same day and at the same hour, and great

---

[1] Indjé Sou, a name signifying "clear water," is a small town in Cappadocia to the south of Cesarea.

confusion ensues. Mrs. Blunt describes an amusing incident which happened on one of these occasions in the church at Broussa. The brides, all dressed alike and equally blindfolded by their enveloping crimson veils, were pushed forward by the dense crowd of relatives, friends, and spectators towards the altar, and in the confusion two of them alike in stature changed places. One of them was a pretty peasant girl, the promised bride of a blacksmith; the other the plain daughter of a wealthy burgher, whose bridegroom was a man of her own station. The mistake was not discovered until the conclusion of the ceremony, when, as there was no remedy, all the parties concerned wisely decided to make the best ot it, and accepted the partners whom Fate had unexpectedly assigned them.

It is customary among the Armenians, as among the Greeks, to administer the Eucharist to sick and dying persons, but the character attributed by members of the Roman Catholic Church to "extreme unction" does not appear to be attached to this sacrament by the Eastern Churches. The rite administered, the priest departs, leaving the dying person to spend his last moments in undisturbed intercourse with those to whom he is most closely attached by the ties of family. When the last breath has been drawn, the corpse is carefully and reverently washed, and a consecrated wafer (*nishkarc*) is placed on the lips, and secured there with a strip of linen. The ears, nostrils, and hollows of the eyes are filled with cotton-wool and incense; the two hands are tied together, and crossed on the breast over a taper brought from Jerusalem; and the legs are fastened together by the great toes. The body is then, after being enveloped in a linen sheet, bandaged from head to feet, dressed in its holiday costume, and laid on a bed of state surrounded with flowers and fragrant herbs. Friends come in, singly or in little groups, to take their last farewell, and add their floral tribute to the bier. Finally, the priest, accompanied by his deacon and acolyte, proceeds to the house of mourning to perform a service of prayer and song, and to fumigate the corpse with incense. At the hour fixed for the funeral the relatives assemble to accompany the body to its last resting-place; and as the solemn procession nears the church it is augmented by friends and neighbours, who show their regard for the departed with sighs, groans, and tears. At the church-door the body is met by the clergy, whose number varies according to the rank and means of the deceased. The funeral service is exceedingly solemn and impressive, and at the same time of so touching a character as to excite in the highest degree the emotional feelings of the congregation. Chants and hymns, sung in dialogue form, poetically simulate a leave-taking between the soul and body of the departed, who also makes his last adieux to the church and sanctuary which he has so often visited, to the priest who has taught him the holy Gospel, and finally to his relatives and friends. This pathetic recital concludes with an expression of regret for their lost friend on the part of the living, and of their persuasion of the fleeting and uncertain nature of all earthly joys and pursuits.

The service in the church concluded, the procession takes its way to the burial-ground, which is generally outside the town or village, funeral psalms and hymns being sung by the clergy all the way and for some little time after arrival at the grave. These concluded, the priest takes up a handful of earth, and, having blessed it, strews it in the grave in the form of a cross, saying: "May this earth fall with the divine blessing into the grave of this servant of God. In the name of the Father, Son, and Holy Ghost." When this has been done three times, the body is lowered into the grave, and the priest again sprinkles earth on the coffin in the same manner, saying: "Remember, O Lord, Thy servant, and bless, in Thy mercy, his grave. For dust he was, and, according to Thy will, to dust has he returned." Then, making three times the sign of the cross, he prays: "May the divine blessing descend upon the ashes of this our departed one, and raise him up at the last day. In the name, &c." After some concluding prayers the grave is filled up, when all kneel, and in hymns and prayers supplicate Heaven for the eternal peace of the departed. Holding the Gospels over the grave, the priest again blesses it and the assembly present, and recites the Lord's Prayer. The people approach in turn to kiss the sacred book, and then disperse.

For eight successive evenings the priest visits the

house of mourning to offer prayers for the departed soul, and to console the afflicted family.

On the Saturday of the week after the funeral, the family of the deceased make, and distribute to relatives and friends funeral, cakes, to remind them that their prayers are desired for him. On the following day, and for forty subsequent days, alms and food are distributed to the poor, and Masses performed in the church. The clergy visit the graves on the second, seventh, and fifteenth days after burial, and also on the anniversary, in order to repeat part of the funeral ceremony, and so ensure the repose of the dead.

When a child under the age of nine dies, the parents engage a priest to pray constantly for the space of eight days, during which time he is entertained at their expense; and on the ninth day a solemn ceremony is performed in the church.

Ancient Armenian tombstones often took the form of rude representations of quadrupeds, such as horses, cows, or even elephants, some of which may still be seen in their cemeteries. This is, however, characteristic only of Armenia Proper, the dwellers in the Turkish cities appearing to have always conformed in this respect to the customs of their Christian neighbours.

At the death of a person of means, the priest is commissioned to announce in church that a funeral feast will be given on a certain day, to which all the inhabitants of the village are invited. If the deceased is advanced in years, the feast usually takes place on the day of death; but if he is young, it is held a week afterwards.

Another Armenian funeral custom, observed in Cappadocia, seems to be a curious mixture of ancient Greek and modern Turkish usage. Every person dedicates, according to his or her means, a sum of money or some household goods to be distributed at death to the poor in order to ensure their prayers for the souls' repose. This bequest is called "toll money," or "passage money," and the recipients engage to perform every day, for three days, three prayers, accompanied by genuflexions, for the free passage to Paradise of the deceased, and that he may not be hindered on the way by the toll-takers who guard the roads of heaven. If this custom is disregarded, the soul will be harassed by these celestial officials, and will not find the road to the celestial regions. When a person is lying *in extremis*, great care must be taken that a cat does not pass either over his head or on the roof above it. As the roofs are in Armenia mostly flat, and are consequently a favourite resort of that harmless, necessary animal, such a calamity can only be guarded against by all the neighbours shutting up their pussies for the time being, and, indeed, until the funeral is over, lest one should leap across the narrow street and over the bier. If, notwithstanding all these precautions, a cat should succeed in leaping over the corpse, it is a sign that the deceased has been excommunicated by one of the clergy, and great is the distress of his relatives until a priest is discovered who will admit the excommunication in order to obtain the ransom required for removing the ban.

According to vulgar belief, the psalms and hymns which are chanted by the side of the grave are prolonged in order to give the soul of the departed time to go to Jerusalem and prostrate itself before the tomb of Jesus Christ. This act of devotion performed, it returns to the body, embraces it, and then wings its way to heaven. The Armenians seem to have borrowed this notion of the soul accompanying the body on its way to the grave from their Mohammedan neighbours, with whom it is a fixed belief.

On the eighth day after the funeral, the relatives visit the grave, from which they take small portions of earth, and drop them down each other's backs between the clothes and the flesh, in the strange belief that the parents, children, brothers, or sisters of the deceased may thus obtain for themselves the remainder of the life which he has not been permitted to enjoy.

Easter Monday is the day ordained by custom for visiting the graves of deceased relatives. After weeping and lamenting a while over the remains of their lost ones, the mourners dry their tears, and, retiring to the shade of some spreading plane-tree, forget their sorrow under the influence of the good things which they have provided for their annual picnic.

CHAPTER VIII.

ARMENIAN WOMEN: THEIR BELIEFS AND SUPERSTITIONS.

ALTHOUGH the great majority of the Armenians are members of the ancient Gregorian Church, the Pope has, since the sixteenth century, had a considerable number of adherents belonging to this nation; and the labours of the American missionaries in Armenia have resulted in the formation of numerous Protestant communities.

The history of the Gregorian Church may be divided into three periods. The first, however, from 34 to 302. is mainly legendary; the second, from 302 to 491, begins with the establishment of Christianity in Armenia by St. Gregory, and terminates with the rupture with the Greek Church of which the Armenian had until that time formed a branch; and the third period extends from that event to the present day. To the first period belongs the legendary correspondence between Jesus and Abgar, king of Edessa and of the surrounding countries, an account of which is given both by Eusebius and Moses of Khor'ni. This king, having heard of the miracles performed by Christ, and desiring to see and be cured by him of a disease with which he was afflicted, sent to him a letter which, in the version of Eusebius, runs thus:

"Abgarus, king of Edessa, to Jesus the good Saviour, who appeareth at Jerusalem, greeting :

"I have been informed concerning thee and thy cures, which are performed without the use of medicines or herbs.

"For it is reported that thou dost cause the blind to see and the lame to walk, that thou dost cleanse the lepers, and dost cast out unclean spirits and devils, and dost restore to health those who have been long diseased, and also that thou dost raise the dead.

"All which when I heard I was persuaded of these two things :

"Either that thou art God himself descended from heaven, or that thou art the Son of God.

"On this account, therefore, I have written unto thee, earnestly desiring that thou wouldst trouble thyself to take a journey hither, and that thou wouldest also cure me of the disease from which I suffer.

"For I hear that the Jews hold thee in derision, and intend to do thee harm.

"My city is indeed small, but it is sufficient to contain us both."

The reply to this epistle Moses of Khor'ni attributes to St. Thomas, who was deputed by his Master to write the answer. It is as follows :

"Happy art thou, O Abgarus, forasmuch as thou hast believed in me whom thou hast not seen.

"For it is written concerning me, that those who have seen me have not believed in me, that those who have not seen might believe and live.

"As to that part of thy epistle which relates to my visiting thee, I must inform thee that I must fulfil the ends of my mission in this land, and after that be received up again unto him that sent me; but after my ascension I will send one of my disciples, who will cure thy disease, and give life unto thee and all that are with thee."[1]

The seeds of the Christian faith are said to have been sown in Armenia by St. Thomas and St. Bartholomew: and, according to Tertullian, a Christian church flourished in this country so early as the second century.

St. Gregory, called "The Illuminator," the inaugurator of the second period, was a prince of the reigning family of the Arsacidæ, who, having been converted to Christianity, was eager for the conversion of his countrymen. In his missionary work he endured many persecutions, the accounts of which were embellished by the early Christians with marvellous details. According to the popular story, as Tiridates the king was sacrificing to the heathen goddess Anahid,[2] he remarked a young man among the surrounding crowd who appeared to take no part in the solemnity. The king ordered him to be brought up to the altar, and commanded him to complete the sacrifice. Gregory refused, and was in consequence subjected to the most cruel tortures, which he bore

[1] Curzon, *Armenia*, p. 213.
[2] I am told that a fragment of the statue of this Goddess was discovered about four years ago by a peasant of Erisa (Erzinginan), who sold it for £10. The head proved to be of massive gold, and the purchasers re-disposed of it for £10,000.

with superhuman patience and fortitude,[1] and was finally cast into a dungeon so damp, dark, and loathsome as to be a fit habitation only for bats or serpents. But here, for thirteen years, St. Gregory survived, forgotten and neglected, save by a poor widow—according to other authorities, an angel—who brought him a daily supply of bread and water.

Another manifestation, however, of the king's ruthless cruelty resulted in the release of St. Gregory. There lived at that time at Rome a noble and beautiful maiden, named Ripsimeh (Rosina), who, with her nurse and seventy other virgins, had taken a religious vow. Her beauty had attracted the attention of the Emperor Diocletian, who wished to marry her. In order to escape the Imperial solicitations, Ripsimeh, with her nurse, Gaianeh, and her seventy companions, fled from Rome, and finally, after many wanderings, arrived at the capital of Armenia, Vagharshabad. Having succeeded in discovering her retreat, Diocletian gave Tiridates the option of sending her back to Rome or marrying her himself; and when the king beheld the beauty of Ripsimeh, he was minded to avail himself of the Emperor's permission. The fair Roman, however, remained faithful to her vow, and the king, infuriated by repeated refusals, commanded that not only she, but all those who had come in her train, should be first tortured and then executed. The wrath of Heaven towards the perpetrator of this crime was

---

[1] An account of the tortures inflicted upon St. Gregory was subsequently given by Agathange, secretary to Tiridates, in a work which has, I believe, survived both in Armenian and Greek.

shown by the infliction on Tiridates and his courtiers of the punishment of Nebuchadnezzar—for they lost their reason and became as the beasts of the field. The king's sister, Khosrovitouhd, having, after this terrible event, been repeatedly visited in a dream by an angel who told her that St. Gregory only could restore her brother to reason, finally sent men to the dungeon, with orders to release the Christian if, perchance, he were still alive. The Saint was found not only alive, but strong and healthy, and his prayers on behalf of the afflicted king and his nobles were speedily answered. The first use Tiridates made of his newly recovered reason was to kneel to St. Gregory and beg his forgiveness. After assuring the penitent monarch not only of his own forgiveness, but of that of Heaven, the Saint solemnly asked him, "Where are the Lambs of God?" The dismembered bones of the martyrs, which had been scattered in the fields, were reverently collected and accorded honourable burial, and over the place of their sepulture St. Gregory watched and prayed all that night. During his vigil a wonderful and glorious vision appeared to the holy man, and was at the same time explained by an angel, who also commanded him to build a church over the sacred relics. The spot is now occupied by the monastery and cathedral church of Etchmiadzin, the seat of the Catholicos, or Patriarch, of the Armenian Church. St. Gregory was consecrated Bishop of Etchmiadzin by Leontius, the Bishop of Cesaræa, and, owing to this circumstance, it long remained customary for the Primates of the Armenian

Church to receive investiture at the hands of succeeding Bishops of the capital of Cappadocia.

In point of doctrine, there is very little difference between the Greek and the Armenian Churches. The Gregorians accept the articles of faith as promulgated by the seven Œcumenical Councils, but reject the Western addition of the *filioque* to the Nicene Creed and deny the distinctive doctrines of the Romish Church.[1] The Liturgy used is said to date from the first century, and to have been adapted from that originally used by the early Church of Jerusalem. St. Gregory remodelled it, and introduced into it the Nicene Creed with the comminatory clause, and a conclusion of his own. As regards the future life, although the doctrine of purgatory is not explicitly taught by the Church, the long and numerous prayers appointed for the dead, the Masses performed for the souls of the departed, and the almsgiving practised with the same object, all testify to a practical belief in an intermediate state. Popular belief is, however, very vague on this point, for, while it is denied that any save the Virgin and Elias have yet seen the face of God, the aid of saints and martyrs is invoked as in the Latin and Greek Churches.

The fasts and feasts of the Armenians coincide with those of their Greek neighbours, save for the addition of ten national saints to the already large number included in the calendar of the Orthodox

---

[1] A priest at his ordination makes this profession of faith: "I believe in Jesus Christ, one person and two natures, and in conformity with the Holy Fathers we reject and detest the decisions of the Council of Chalcedon and the letter of St. Leon to Flavian; and we say anathema to every sect which denies the two natures of Christ."

Greek Church. The fasts are, however, observed by the Armenians with much greater severity, neither shell-fish nor olive oil being partaken of in Lent, and the first meal of the day during that period being deferred until late in the afternoon. The three degrees of self-mortification are called respectively, *bakh, dzom,* and *navayatik*. In the first, meat, fish, eggs, cheese, and other dairy produce is abstained from; in the second, nothing is eaten before sunset; and the third signifies total abstinence from food. As in the Greek Church, no indulgences are granted by the clergy for disregarding these ordinances, excepting in cases of severe illness.

It is less easy than in the case of the Greeks to ascertain to what extent the Church feasts of the Armenians are survivals of Pagan festivals. That some of them had their origin in the Nature-worship of their Aryan ancestors there can, however, be no question. The ancient festival of Vartevar— the "Feast of the Blossoming Roses"—is, for instance, now replaced by the three days' feast commemorative of the Transfiguration of Christ. The advent of May, too, is greeted with various observances, many of them identical with those of the Greeks. The streets of the Armenian quarter at Smyrna are, early on May-day morning, alive with promenaders on their way to greet the dawn of the merry month. Their destination is a *kaféné*, or coffee-house, in appearance like a small classic temple, standing in a large garden on the banks of the Meles, close by the Bridge of Caravans. It is too early yet for the long files of not always patient camels, laden with huge bales of raw cotton and other produce from the interior, and conducted by a little nigger boy on donkey-back, from which the bridge and the road leading to it derive their names. But the storks are astir in the cypress-trees on either hand, which, over the graves of departed Moslems, "uplift," as the great mystic poet[1] says, "their silent hands to Heaven."

Around little tables dispersed among the flower-beds of the *kaféné* garden they all presently gather to breakfast on lettuces and *kattyméria*—a kind of pastry much in vogue at Smyrna, supplemented by tiny cups of Turkish coffee. And having thus greeted the flowery month, the company disperse, the women and children returning to their homes, and the men proceeding to the day's business.

The Armenian women of Symrna and the capital, like the Greek, usually have an *eikon*, or, as they call it, a *badguer*, of the Virgin in their sleeping apartments, before which they repeat their morning and evening prayers. These holy pictures are also often decorated with an aureole, a hand, or an arm of silver, presented to *Surp Mariam*, or Saint Mary, in gratitude for benefits supposed to have been accorded through her intercession. An incident which occurred while I was on a visit to an Armenian family living at Bournabat afforded an interesting illustration of the reverence paid to these representations of the patron Saint *par excellence* of women. A fire had broken out at night in a neighbouring house, and, on the alarm being raised, the two daughters of my host, who slept in the only up-

---

[1] Jelalû-'d-Dîn er Rûmi, *The Harper*, Redhouse's translation, p. 147.

stairs room, hurried down, leaving all their treasures behind them, but bearing in their arms the two *ikons*, which, frightened as they were, they had stopped to take down from the walls of their chamber. The danger past, we were again dispersing to our several apartments, when my dear old hostess, Kokona Mariem,[1] took up the pictures from the table, and, kissing them with affectionate reverence, ascribed to their sacred protection our escape from the calamity which had overtaken her neighbour.

The Armenian women of the interior are not required to attend the public services of the church more regularly than are the Greek women. In Armenia during the first year of her married life a young wife goes to church only twice—at Easter and at the Feast of the Annunciation. At Smyrna and Constantinople, however, in this as in every other respect, the women enjoy much greater freedom, and follow the example of the Catholic and Protestant women among whom they live.

The wives of the *Derders*, or inferior clergy, like those of the Greek *Papades*, enjoy no social rank, but live, in the country, like the rest of the peasant women, and, in the towns, like the wives of artisans. The Derders are allowed to marry once only, and the higher clergy, though they may have married before entering the Church, must, when ordained, be either bachelors or widowers. The office of Derder is usually hereditary, and though a son of one of these parish priests may, before he is called upon to succeed

---

[1] The common pronunciation at Smyrna of Mariam—*i.e.*, Mary.

his father, be engaged in a lucrative calling, he is obliged to relinquish it in order to take upon himself the sacred office, for which he is often unfitted both by education—or, rather, want of education—and by inclination. Very poor indeed are the generality of the inferior clergy, their incomes being drawn solely from the small annual contributions of their parishioners, the fees paid for special services, and such small gains as may be derived from the manufacture and sale of tapers and other religious commodities. A few pence are also paid to the priest by each family at his periodical " Blessing of the House," which takes place at Easter, and consists of the repetition of a prayer, accompanied by the burning of incense and the aspersion with holy water in the *sala,* or central room of the house. Wealthy families have this ceremony performed also at the New Year, and sometimes they have every room in the house thus blessed,[1] though, as my informant added, " *ils paient de ce luxe.*" One New Year's Day, when I came in for my share of the benediction, the Derder having sat down after the ceremony to chat with the ladies and partake of a cup of coffee, the youngest daughter went off to the larder, whence she emerged with a quantity of the sweet biscuits always prepared for seasons of festivity, with which she proceeded to fill the pockets of his rusty black *jupbé,* saying to me in English as she did so : " These are for his wife and children ; he is so dreadfully poor that I am sure they have none at home."

[1] On the completion of a new house every room is blessed by the priest before the family take up their abode in it.

Besides the ordinary pilgrimages which the Armenian, like the Greek, women make to the shrines and churches of saints and martyrs, a few undertake the longer pilgrimage to Jerusalem. Among the Christian, as among the Moslem, nationalities of Turkey, the accomplishment of this act of religious duty entitles the person who has performed it to the Turkish title of *Hadji*, which is prefixed to his, or her, name. An Armenian lady of my acquaintance had a servant, the daughter of a priest, whom she never addressed without this title, although it lengthened her name of "Antaram" to five syllables; and by her fellow-servants she was naturally treated with even greater respect.

The internal arrangements of the Armenian churches differ from those of the Greeks and Latins. The floor of the chancel, or sanctuary, is raised several feet higher than that of the rest of the building, and the altar is again raised above the floor of the sanctuary. A large curtain conceals from the congregation, at certain periods of the service, both chancel and altar. During the whole of Lent this curtain is kept drawn, and the services are performed behind it. This custom is said to typify the expulsion of Adam and Eve from Paradise. A second and smaller curtain screens the altar only, and is drawn during the celebration of the Eucharist, and at the conclusion of the services. On the altar stand a crucifix, with candlesticks on either side, the Gospels, in gorgeous binding, covered with an embroidered napkin, and a copy of the Prayer-book. The sacramental bread and wine also remain perpetually in a tabernacle upon the altar, and tapers are kept continually burning before them. There are no stalls in the choir; the inferior clergy sit cross-legged on mats or rugs spread on the floor, the bishops and other dignitaries only being honoured with chairs. In some churches a gallery is provided for the women, approached, as in the Greek churches, by an outer staircase; in others, the women occupy one side of the nave, as in Catholic churches. Except in the town churches there are no seats for the congregation, who sit either on the matted floor, or on cushions they bring with them.

The ancient metropolitan church and monastery of Etchmiadzin, before mentioned, have been restored again and again, and have recently, I am told, been considerably enlarged. The monastery was formerly celebrated for its extensive library, which contains, however, at the present day, only some seventeen or eighteen hundred volumes, consisting chiefly of Armenian manuscripts. Among the relics treasured in the monastery are the lance which pierced the side of Jesus, brought to Armenia by the Apostle Thaddeus; a piece of the True Cross, presented to Tiridates by Constantine the Great; the head of St. Ripsimeh; and the hands of St. Thaddeus, St. Gregory, and St. James of Nisibis. St. James was the finder of the remains of Noah's Ark, which he presented to the Fathers of Etchmiadzin. Climbing one day the steep sides of Ararat, the saint, overcome with fatigue, laid himself down to rest, when in a vision an angel appeared to him, and pointed out the spot where the fragments of the Patriarch's vessel were concealed.

Many strange legends are current among the people concerning this centre of Armenian worship. One of these relates that on the spot where the church and monastery now stand rose three rocks in a triangular form, under each of which was a cavern, whence the voices of spirits issued, giving answers to questions after the mode of the Oracles of Delphi. But Jesus Christ, intending to have his name worshipped in that place, descended in person from heaven, and, taking the Cross on which he suffered, struck a blow on each rock, upon which they sank into the ground, and the diabolical spirits were displaced. Another version states that Jesus permitted these spirits of the earth to keep their abodes in the cavities of the rocks on which the convent is built, in order that they might serve the holy monks, its inmates, as slaves and drudges; and that they still invisibly perform their allotted tasks, washing the dishes, sweeping the floors, and fulfilling all the offices of good servants.

The Armenians, in common with the rest of the Christian world, have adopted Nicholas of Damascus' identification of their Mount Massis, "the Mother of the World," with the Ararat of the Deluge. According to Lenormant,[1] however, the word *Ararat,* or *Ararad,* originally signified, not the mountain-peak of Massis, but the whole country watered by the Araxes, whence came the name of Alarodians, given by Herodotos to its inhabitants. St. Jerome, too, applied the name of

---

[1] *Origines de l'Histoire,* tom. ii., 1re partie, p. 2, &c.

Ararat exclusively to the plain at the foot of the mountain. The story told by Berossos of the stranding of the ship of Xisouthros, the Koranic story of Noah and the Deluge,[1] and other traditions, agree in localising the mountain-peak on which the vessel rested in Kurdistan, to the south-west of Lake Van; and the Chaldean epic poem of Ourouk describes the vessel as resting on the mountain of Nizir in this region. The inhabitants of Cappadocia also claim for their Mount Argæus the honour of having been the resting-place of the Ark.

The mountain of Massis, or Ararat, which is also called by the people of Erivan *Mouthen Aschkark*, the "World of Darkness," appears to have been from the remotest antiquity invested by the inhabitants of the surrounding country with a supernatural character, easily accounted for by the frequent volcanic disturbances which have from time to time changed its aspect. As the Greek gods were located on Olympus, so the summit of Massis was regarded as the abode of supernatural beings whose mysterious proceedings produced the awe-inspiring convulsions which seemed to shake the mountain's very foundations.[2] On the introduction of Christianity, the

---

[1] Mohammed makes Noah disembark on El Djoudi, which he calls "the Kurd mountain," situated to the south-west of Lake Van.—Lenormant, *Origines*, &c., tom. ii. p. 5.

[2] In an ancient Armenian poem, the hero-king, Artaxés, in his anger, thus addresses his son Artabazes:

"If, when thou followest the chase, thou approachest the mountain, great Massis,
Then shall the Famous Ones seize thee and bear thee away upon Massis.
There shalt thou bide, and for ever be hid from the gladdening sunshine."

location of the resting-place of the Ark on this already sacred mountain endowed its supposed inaccessible peak with new mystery; and the traditional first footsteps of the second father of the human race constituted the adjacent country a holy land. A ravine which penetrates deeply into the heart of the mountain formerly held the village of Arghouri, destroyed by an earthquake in 1846, above which, at an altitude of 6000 feet above sea-level, stands the monastery of St. James. Here, says the legend, Noah planted his vineyard, and the monks still show the withered roots of a vine rendered sterile by the divine malediction, the juice of its fruit having caused "the Just One" to fall into the sin of drunkenness. The monastery is said to occupy the spot on which "Noah builded an altar unto the Lord," and the Lord made a covenant with him "and every living creature." Just above the site of the ruined village, a bent and stunted willow is accredited with having grown from a fragment of the Ark which had there taken root! Not far off is the "grave of Noah's wife;" Erivan, which signifies "First Seen," lies to the north; and Naktchivan was the city first founded by the patriarch on his descent from the mountain. It is also related that the three Magi, one of whom, Gaspar, was an Armenian, were on Mount Massis when they perceived the Star in the East, and started thence for "the place where the young child lay."

According to the story, this prince actually disappeared in a hole at the base of Massis.—Dulaurier. *Chants Populaires de l'Arménie: Rev. des Deux Mondes*, Av. 1852.

The Armenian Paradise-tradition places the Garden of Eden on the present site of Erzeroum. This fact is the more curious and noteworthy seeing that Mr. Stuart Glennie appears to have shown that the Paradise-stories are all derived from actual traditions of early settlements of the White Founders of the Civilisations of Egypt, and particularly of Chaldea; and that among the Chaldean Paradise-legends was one pointing distinctly to the north.[1] Reland and Brugsch[2] have pointed out that in South-western Armenia and in the neighbourhood of Erzeroum, four great rivers have their sources—the Phasis or Araxes, the Kyros, the Euphrates, and the Tigris. Mr. Curzon has remarked that from one spot on a rocky mountain-top, 10,000 feet above sea-level, and only three hours' distance from Erzeroum, may be seen "the sources of the Euphrates, of the Araxes, and of another river which falls into the Black Sea near Batoum."[3] And Delitzsch has shown that the Euphrates and Tigris are certainly identical with the Euphrates and Hiddequel of the Hebrew variant of the Chaldean tradition.[4]

A local Moslem tradition says that the flowers of Paradise bloomed in luxuriant splendour in this now barren region until the time of Khosref Purveez. This mighty Persian monarch was one day encamped with his army on the banks of the Euphrates, in the plain of Erzeroum, when a messenger arrived from the

[1] *Traditions of the Archaian White Races: Trans. Roy. Historical Soc.* 1889.
[2] *Persischen Reise*, Bd. i. s. 145 *et seq.*
[3] *Armenia.* The river thus vaguely indicated is evidently the Tchorouk, the ancient Acampsis.
[4] *Wo lag das Paradies?* p. 171.

Prophet Mohammed, then an insignificant pretender, offering this magnificent Sovereign his protection if he would give up the faith of his fathers and embrace that of Islam. Khosref Purveez threw, in derision, the Prophet's letter into the river, when, in dismay, the bounteous stream, which formerly bestowed wealth and abundance upon the country, shrank into its bed, refusing any longer to fertilise the earth, and all the trees and flowers on its banks withered. Cold, frost, and barrenness have since been the consequence of the Persian king's impiety; and not only this, but the days of his kingdom were from that moment numbered, and a few years afterwards the blacksmith's apron, the standard of the Persians, fell into the hands of the Prophet's general at the battle of Kudseah.

"Some flowers of Eden" Erzeroum may, however, still claim to inherit, for on the mountain sides in the vicinity of the town flourish several species almost, if not quite, unknown elsewhere. Among these the *Ravanea coccinea*, the Armenian *Jotn Yegpaïr*, or "Seven Brothers' Blood," is, perhaps, the most curious and beautiful. The plant is a parasite of the wormwood; it is from eight to twelve inches in height, and its lily-like blossom and stem, for it has no leaves, appear to be covered with crimson velvet. The *Morena Orientalis*, locally named *Aravelian Draghik*, "Flower of the Sun," has something of the appearance of a thistle with flowers growing closely all up the stalk, and its scent resembles that of the honeysuckle. Another of these rare flowers, called in Armenian *Vaïrihagogh*, "Wild grapes," or *Tschahagogh*, "The grape-like," has a tough, carrot-like root, about two feet long, with leaves like bunches of tussock grass, and, under them, drooping bunches of grape-like globes, each containing a seed. This plant is, however, poisonous.

Although missionaries of the Dominican Order had found their way to Armenia as early as the fourteenth century, it was not until the sixteenth that Roman Catholicism obtained a secure footing in the country. Its successful establishment at the latter period was due to the efforts of the Jesuits, who, after the triumph of the Reformation in the West, were sent by the Pope to "carry into the birthland of Protestantism the revenge of Catholicism."[1] There are, however, at the present day but few adherents of the Papacy in Armenia, except in Erzeroum, Naktchivan, and the other large towns. The greater number are to be found in Constantinople and Smyrna, where they form the higher and wealthier class of the Armenian community. The "United Armenians," as they are called, have retained in their ritual the use of the mother tongue, and also certain forms of worship used in the National Church. Identity of creed being, in the East, considered a closer bond of union than identity of race, marriages between United Armenians and Catholic Franks are not uncommon, the Armenian element being, in one or two generations, completely lost sight of.

It must, however, in justice be admitted that the

---

[1] Stuart Glennie, *Europe and Asia*, Introd. 51. It was from Armenia that the so-called Paulician heretics, the early Church Reformers, came, about the sixth century, to Europe.

perversion of this section of the Armenians has in no way lessened its patriotism, but has, on the contrary, enabled it to confer immense benefit on the nation. Under "Uniate" auspices a literary and educational propaganda was set on foot in the seventeenth century which has had great results, and which still continues at the present day. The pioneer of this movement was Mekhitar, a native of Sivas, the ancient Sebaste, or Ancyra, in Galatia. His zeal having exposed him to persecution in his own country, he removed to the Morea, then in the hands of the Venetians, where he established a small brotherhood of fellow-workers. Taken prisoner and enslaved by the Turks, he escaped with a few followers to Venice, where he obtained the grant of two small islands in the lagoons. On one of these he established the monastic institution of St. Lazarus, in which he set up a printing-press for the production of religious works in the Armenian tongue. An immense number of books on historical, educational, and religious subjects have, during the past two centuries, been printed in the monastery, and disseminated among the Armenian nation. The demand for native literature has increased with every year, and the Mekhitarist Brothers have now at work five printing presses. At St. Lazarus and at Vienna Armenian journals are also published, which find their way to the various communities of Armenians scattered throughout Turkey, Persia, India, and the West. This Armenian "Society for the Propagation of Christian Knowledge" also maintains a college for literary missionaries, who, in the course of their travels as colporteurs through the mountains of Haiasdan, collect valuable manuscripts relating to the past of the country, which are made the bases of national histories. Patriotic ideas have, indeed, always been inculcated by this society in their educational work, and the National Armenian hymn, composed, I believe, by Mekhitar, commemorating Vartan's heroic defence of his country against the Persians in 451, continued to be sung in all the public schools until a few years ago, when its use was forbidden by the Turkish authorities. The Armenian Bible, books of which had been from time to time printed, was first issued entire by the Lazarist press in 1805; and the thoroughness of the work bestowed upon this translation has, I am informed, obtained for it the title of "Queen of Versions." The Old Testament contains three apocryphal books—namely, the *Testament of the Twelve Patriarchs*, the *Book of Jesus the Son of Sirach*, and the *History of Joseph and his wife Asenath*. The last named is extremely rare, and has never, I believe, been printed in any European language.[1] The New Testament includes a *Third Epistle of St. Paul to the Corinthians*, and an *Epistle of the Corinthians to St. Paul*.

I have already referred to the educational work in Armenia of the American missionaries, whose converts have now existed as an independent Church for nearly half a century. This separation from the

---

[1] Curzon's *Armenia*, p. 225. Mr. Curzon believes himself to be the sole possessor of an English translation of an Italian translation of this curious legend.

National Church was not, however, originally desired by the missionaries, whose object seems rather to have been that of exposing the absurdity of the popular superstitions, and of teaching a purely evangelical doctrine to individuals. The immediate cause of the separation was the persecutions to which the converts were subjected by the Catholicos and his clergy. These finally became so vexatious that recourse was had to the intervention of the Porte, which, in 1846, officially recognised the Armenian Evangelical Church, and forbade any further interference with its members. The enmity of the Patriarchate has now, however, almost, if not completely, died away, and the native Protestant pastors not unfrequently exchange pulpits with their Gregorian colleagues. These pastors have all been trained by the missionaries in their colleges at Kharpūt and Aintab, and at the other centres of mission work, and are established wherever there seemed an opening or a demand for Protestant teaching. The community, which is now estimated at some sixty thousand souls, is to be found chiefly in the districts surrounding Kharpūt, Kaisariyeh, Aintab, Sivas, Van, and Erzeroum; and some thousands of Protestant Armenians have, with their families, emigrated to America, under the auspices of the missionaries.

CHAPTER IX.

ARMENIAN WOMEN: THEIR FOLK-POESY.

ARMENIAN literature is sufficiently rich in poetry celebrating the exploits of national heroes, both mythical and historical, and which, though epic in intention, is lyric in style and rhythm. The legends contained in these ancient national records cannot, however, justly be termed folk-poesy, as they are no longer traditionally current among the people, and are found only in works written before the eleventh century.[1] But, apart from these now forgotten national legends, Armenia offers a rich and hitherto almost untouched field to the folk-lorist, the difficulty of grappling with the language—the alphabet even of which was described by Byron as a "very Waterloo of an alphabet"—having hitherto baffled European collectors. The subject is now occupying the attention of cultured Armenians, but few of the results of their researches are, unfortunately, as yet available, and I cannot therefore claim that the few specimens with which I have been furnished are at all representative.

[1] The specimens of Armenian folk-poetry given by the Countess Martinengo Cesaresco in her *Essays on Folk-lore* have, with the exception of one or two of the songs from M. Alishanian's collection, been translated from old Armenian MSS. by that author and by M. Dulaurier, on whose article in the *Revue des Deux Mondes* this author chiefly bases her essay.

The following curious folk-ideas concerning the Creation of Man and the Fall are current among the Armenian labouring population of Constantinople and its suburbs.[1]

The Story of the Fall.

God took earth from seven mountains and water from seven rivers to make the clay with which to fashion the body of Adam. As soon as the Creator had put the finishing touches to his work, the horse approached the new being and examined it. Knowing by instinct that this creature would desire to mount him, he aimed at Adam a kick, and galloped off. His hoof struck Adam between his feet, and caused the cleft there which man retains to the present day.

When God the Father had formed the body of Adam, God the Son took charge of his maintenance, and God the Holy Ghost breathed into him the breath of life.

God loved Adam, but the chief of the angels was jealous of this preference. "What," said he, fuming with rage, "is it possible that this plaything of yesterday is preferred to me?" And so wrathful was he that he refused to present himself before God one day when it was his turn to adore and serve him. This rebel and his sympathisers were in consequence precipitated from the highest heaven and transformed into devils. Those of them who stopped midway in air,

---

[1] I am indebted for these legends to M. Minasse Schérax, who has published them in French in his journal *L'Arménie* for Nov. 1889.

as the good angels began to sing the old Armenian hymn of the *Guétzo* (Stabat), received the name of "suspended devils."

Satan then swore to compass Adam's fall. Under the form of a serpent he approached him and persuaded him to eat of the forbidden fruit. The apple proved difficult to swallow, and stuck in the middle of the throat of Adam, who made fruitless efforts to dislodge it. And this is the origin of the protrusion seen in the throats of many men, and hence called "Adam's apple."

The sun set for the first time on the day which saw Adam driven out from Paradise. He who had never known darkness groped about in the gloom for some time, beside himself with terror. At last he fell asleep, and saw in a dream Christ on the Cross. Awaking with a start he cried, " O Cross! come to my aid!"[1] He was weeping in the darkness, when Satan came to him and offered to recover the light for him on condition that he placed his hand on a stone and pronounced these words: "Let those who may be born of me be thine!" As soon as Adam had accepted this condition the darkness became deeper, and to this day the Armenians call the darkest period of the night, *Atama mouth*, "the darkness of Adam." But Satan encouraged Adam by assuring him that the night was drawing to an end, raised him by his arm, and before long pointed out to him the shimmering edge of the rising sun on the threshold of the east. Since that day a star has

---

[1] These words are, at the present day, inscribed at the head of every Armenian primer.

shone towards morning, and is called Lucifer. Satan hid in the Jordan the stone on which Adam had sworn, but Christ was baptised on this very stone, and it shivered to pieces under his feet.

Adam, driven from Paradise, was devoured with rage. He wished to revenge himself on the serpent, on his wife, and on God. But being powerless to reach the other two, he approached, under cover of the darkness, Eve, who sat leaning against a wild fig-tree, weeping. Adam threw her on the ground, bruised her with his knees, and embraced her while foaming with rage. This kiss gave birth to Cain.

Eve, terrified, fled away and hid herself in a deep forest, where she lived among the apes.[1] Adam, wearying of his solitude, went to seek his wife, and promised not to ill-treat her again. Eve melted into tears, and Adam consoled her by pressing her tenderly to his heart. This kiss gave birth to Abel.

On the following day Adam said to his wife, "Thou didst love me when I could lay at thy feet Eden and all its delights. What are thy thoughts towards me now that, from a king, I have become a beggar?" Eve replied, "I love thee still." And Adam rejoined, "Thy love makes me forget Paradise." But the serpent, hidden behind a bush, hissed out: "She loves thee, because there is none other." Eve blushed, and Adam stroked his forehead sadly.

One day Eve called to her Cain and Abel, who, still little children, were playing on the grass. She held

---

[1] The Flight of Eve is a prominent feature in the Moslem story of the Fall, as told, for instance, in the *Travels* of Evliza Effendi.

out to her firstborn her right arm, and to her second son her left, and said, "Bite them, I command you." The elder boy bit till he drew blood, but Abel merely imprinted a long lingering kiss on his mother's arm. Then said Eve to her husband, "Our Cain will be a wicked man."

Adam and Eve loved Abel dearly. Cain was jealous of their partiality. He wished to kill his brother, but knew not how. Satan took the form of a raven, picked a quarrel with another raven, and in Cain's presence cut his opponent's throat with a pointed black pebble. Cain picked up the stone, hid it in his girdle, proposed to his brother a walk on the mountain, and there cut his throat with the pebble. The peasants of Armenia to this day call flints "Satan's nails," and conscientiously break every pointed black one they may find.

Cain, after his crime, dared not return to his parents; the blood of his brother still adhered to his hands. In vain did he hold them all day long immersed in a neighbouring spring; the stain was still there. Night came on, and, not being able to sleep, he wandered long and far, seeking a waterfall. Guided at last to one by the noise of its waters in the still night, he lay down on the bank and held his reddened hands under the cascade. There he held them, day and night, summer and winter, during a whole year, without sleep and without food, but at the end of that time they were still as crimson as on the day of the crime. And so long as Cain lived, he was never able to get rid of the proof of his fratricide.

Some story-tellers give additional details, and other

versions of parts of this legend. According to one, when God had finished making the body of Adam, there remained still a little earth in his hand. This he threw at the feet of Adam, and it turned into gold; so that man beheld gold on the first day of his existence, and has clung to it ever since.

If Adam had not succumbed to temptation, man would have lived without food, and would never have known death. His whole body was covered with nails overlapping each other like the scales of a fish—the nail being indestructible, and consequently immortal—for such was the body of Adam, to whom God left, after his Fall, only the nails on his extremities to remind him of the past. Adam manifested no repentance, and hence the horny scales with which his body was originally covered were changed into flesh, in order that this might in its turn be resolved into dust.

Adam was not tempted by the fruit of the apple-tree, but by that of the fig-banana called "Adam's fig" by the Armenians and Persians—or, as others say, by the fruit of the Indian or Egyptian fig-tree.

Christ[1] created Adam in a form as beautiful as his own. One day they were sitting side by side; and the archangel Gabriel presented himself before them. For Gabriel commands a host of angels, and has for his colleague the archangel Michael, the leader of the second and last host of angels, the other five having been transformed into cohorts of demons.

[1] Christ, as God the Son, has, in the popular mind, usurped the place of Yahveh, or God the Father, as among the Egyptians about the sixth century B.C., Horus and his mother Isis were worshipped rather than "Our Father," Osiris.

And, mistaking Adam for the Creator, Gabriel prostrated himself to him, saying, "Bless me, O Lord!" But Adam refused his homage, and said to him, "May the Lord bless thee!"

Many of the stories told by the Armenians are, no doubt, borrowed or adopted from the folk-lore of their Turkish and Greek neighbours, though the occurrence of words belonging to the former language cannot be taken as a direct proof of this, seeing that, as before mentioned, the Armenians in many places have substituted it for their own. The piety, not only of animals, but even of inanimate objects, is certainly a frequent theme with Moslem poets and story-tellers;[1] but we find human faculties and sentiments attributed to our "elder brethren" in the folk-lores of all nations. And the following is one of these Armenian stories:—

How the Tame Goose lost the Use of its Wings.

Once upon a time, two geese agreed to take a long journey together. On the eve of their departure, one said to the other, "Mind you are ready, my friend, for, *Inshallah* [if God will], I shall set out at sunrise to-morrow." "And so will I," replied the other, "*Inshallah* or no." Next morning the pious goose, having eaten his breakfast and quenched his thirst in the waters of the stream, rose lightly on the wing,

---

[1] I may instance the legend of the wooden pillar against which the Prophet was accustomed to lean when preaching, and which, when deserted for a more convenient situation, sobbed and sighed till it attracted Mohammed's attention. It is related in a poetical form by Jelalû-'d-Dîn in his *Mesnevi*.

and flew away to a distant land. The impious bird, however, could not spread his wings, and, after many vain attempts to fly, was caught by a fowler who had observed his movements. And ever since then the tame goose has been unable to fly because he would not say *Inshallah*, while the pious wild goose still enjoys his original freedom.[1]

The moral of the following story is, I think, sufficiently evident. But no doubt the conduct of some of the animals must have been very trying to the temper and patience even of "the Just One." Gratitude, however, is a rather novel feature in the Satanic character. And evidently the Devil "believed" in the coming of the Flood, "and trembled."

How the Devil invented the Rudder.[2]

Shortly before the beginning of the Deluge, the Devil presented himself before the Ark, and said to Noah:

"I pray thee, O Noah, let me come into the Ark."

"No," replied the Just Man. "Off with thee!"

Soon afterwards Noah wanted to drive an ass into the vessel. The obstinate animal, however, refused to advance. Noah coaxed, shouted, swore at, and struck him, all to no purpose, and finally cried—

"Wilt thou go in?—go in, go in, Devil from Hell!"

[1] Curzon, *Armenia*, p. 149.
[2] *Les Littératures Populaires*, vol. xxviii. p. 250.

The real Devil, who was lurking not far off, gave a great leap and entered the Ark.

"What is this?" said Noah. "How darest thou enter my place without my permission?"

"Thou hast just given me permission."

"When?"

"When thou wast driving in thy ass, thou saidst: 'Go in, Devil from Hell!'—and so, I came in."

Noah said no more, but left the Devil on board the Ark. In reward for the good man's hospitality, his Satanic majesty steered the Ark with his feet, and so suggested the invention of the rudder, the use of which had been previously unknown to man.

In the following fairy-tale are many elements found in other Aryan folk-stories. The simile of the three melons occurs in an almost precisely identical form in the Greek story of "The Prince and the Foal." The three Péris who endow the child with magical gifts resemble in some respects the Greek Moirai and Bulgarian Samovidas, and, in others, the Fairy Godmothers of the West; while the Oriental element is present in the incident of the erection of the palace, which recalls *The Tales of the Thousand and One Nights*.

The King's Daughter and the Bath Boy.

Once upon a time, in a certain country, there reigned a powerful king, who had three daughters. They were all old enough to be wedded, but their father had always refused to give them to the princes who had asked them in marriage. The princesses were anything but pleased at the prospect of becoming old maids; but what could they do when the king was so determined? They finally decided to consult the royal tutor on the matter.

"I will tell your Royal Highnesses what to do," said he. "Buy three water-melons, and present them to his Majesty."

The sisters followed his counsel, and procured the fruit. The king was much surprised at their present; but told his servants to cut them up, and found that the one offered by his eldest daughter was rotten; that brought by his second daughter was over-ripe; and the third was in fine condition.

"What does this signify?" he asked of the royal tutor.

"Prince," replied the learned man, "these watermelons represent your three daughters. The rotten melon is your eldest born, for whom the age of marriage is passed; the over-ripe one, your second child, for whom it has almost passed; and the good melon, your youngest, who is at a marriageable age."

"Thou art right," said the king. "Send for the heralds!"

When the heralds arrived in the presence, the king said to them:

"Go into all the highways and bye-ways of the capital, and announce that the king will give his daughters in marriage to those whom they may choose, be they rich, poor, or even beggars."

The heralds departed. A few days afterwards, a

crowd of suitors filled the palace square. The three princesses came forward, each with a golden ball in her hand. The first threw hers at the son of the Grand Vizier, and so chose him for her husband; the second chose the son of the Lord Chamberlain, a handsome youth, whom she had long loved; and the third, looking around, saw, sitting at the door of the baths, a poor young man, dressed in rags, who was busy ridding his clothes of vermin, and to him she threw the ball.

"This is madness!" cried the king. "Let her throw again."

Another ball was given to the maiden, who once more threw it to the bath boy.

"I will never accept such an one for my son-in-law," protested her father. "Come, my daughter, make a better choice!"

The princess threw the third ball in another direction, but again it struck the bath boy. Her father, furious, refused to allow her to marry such a miserable wretch.

"Very well, then I will marry him without your permission," replied his daughter.

The wedding of the two eldest daughters was celebrated with great pomp, and the rejoicings attending it lasted forty days.[1] At the end of this period, the youngest princess helped herself to a quantity of precious stones from her father's treasury, and went at night to seek the bath boy.

Rat-tat-tat. "Open the door!"

---

[1] The usual duration of royal wedding festivities in the East at the present day.

"Who is there?"

"Open the door!"

"What do you want?"

"To bathe."

"People don't bathe at this time o' night."

Rat-tat-tat. "Open the door!"

"Who is there?"

"The king's daughter, thy betrothed."

The door was opened, and the prnicess found herself face to face with the bath boy as miserably dressed and dirty as before.

"Wilt thou marry me?" she asked him.

"Willingly, princess, for I love thee to distraction."

"Come, then; let us go to a distant country and be married."

The two lovers quitted the country, and were married. When some months had passed, they returned to the royal city. After consulting as to what they should do, they decided to buy the baths, and took possession of them.

In course of time the young wife found herself on the point of becoming a mother. The king was aware of it, and published an edict forbidding any of the nurses in the country to attend her until her child was born. Her husband sought far and wide for a wise woman, but all feared to disobey the orders of the king. Much distressed at being left alone in her trouble, the princess went into the large apartment of the bath, and laid herself down on the large round stone in the centre, and there she fell asleep.

All at once the wall opened, and three young Péris, as beautiful as the Dawn, came to the aid of the king's daughter, who, soon after, gave birth to a sweet little girl.

"Now that you are the mother of a pretty child," said the Péris, "we will bestow upon her our most precious gifts."

The first hung round the baby's neck a powerful talisman, capable of preserving her from every ailment.

"This shall be my gift," said the second,—"every time she smiles, an unfading rose shall blossom on her cheek."

"And mine," added the third,—"that all her tears will become fine pearls."

"That is not enough," said the second,—"the grass on which she will tread shall become beds of sweet flowers."

"And the water which touches her head shall become pure gold," added the third.

And as the mother and child had no further need of their services, the three Péris left them, and flew back to their sylvan haunts.

When the father returned he was enraptured to find his wife well, and her baby born. He kissed his daughter again and again, and could not take his eyes off her.

"My dear husband," said the princess, "I should dearly like some white bean soup."

"I will go to the market, and buy some vegetables," he replied.

But when he arrived there, no beans were to be had; all were sold. He returned home.

"Go to my sisters, and ask them for some of their soup," said the young mother.

The bath-master (*hammamdji*) went to the palace, and spoke to his sisters-in-law. But the wicked women only took some dirty water from the kitchens, and boiled in it one bean. When her husband brought the soup to her, the princess perceived the malice of her sisters. She, however, partook of the soup.

The little girl grew strong and tall, and her beauty and sweet temper increased. And now the wife of the former bath boy was richer than her royal father, thanks to the magical gifts which the Péris had bestowed upon her daughter. She became discontented with the *hammam*, and begged these nymphs to build for her in a single night the most superb palace imaginable. By means of their magical powers, the Péris were able to fulfil the princess's desire.

When the king got up in the morning, he was much astonished at seeing this new palace so suddenly built opposite his own. He sent for its master, and asked him, "Who art thou, who art so rich and powerful?"

"Do you not know, sire? I am your son-in-law, formerly the bath boy."

"How didst thou build such a palace?"

"The Péris who were present at the birth of thy daughter's child were the architects and masons of my new abode."

"If it is so, I was wrong to refuse you the hand of my youngest daughter. From this day thou art my favourite son-in-law, and at my death thou shalt reign in my stead."

But the other two sons-in-law were far from being satisfied with this sudden revulsion of affairs.

One of the princesses, being also about to become a mother, resolved to do as her youngest sister had done. So she went to the baths and lay down on the circular stone. The wall opened as before, and three Péris entered. But they were black, ugly, and of forbidding appearance.

"Who art thou?" asked the three nymphs, sternly.

"I am the king's daughter."

"And what seekest thou?"

"I wish you to preside at the birth of my child."

"Darest thou, then, ask our help, who wast hard and cruel to thy good little sister? Art thou not ashamed?"

But the princess begged so earnestly, that they finally consented, and there came into the world a frightful little creature in the shape of a girl.

"Shall we go away without giving her a dowry?" asked the Péris of each other.

"As for me," said the first, "I will that the earth she treads become barren."

"And I, that her tears change into pus."

"And I, that every time she smiles the * * *[1] shall appear on her forehead."

So the dusky goddesses departed, leaving the princess choked with anger and disappointment.

Some years afterwards the king died, and, as he

[1] A coarse expression.

had willed it, the former bath boy succeeded him on the throne. The young princess so richly dowered by the Péris was now fifteen years old, and was more beautiful than ever. The son of a neighbouring king, having heard of the surpassing charms of the princess, asked his father's permission to go and offer her his hand.

"You may go," replied the king, "on condition that you bring to me one of the unfading roses which blossom on her cheek when she smiles."

The prince put on the dress of a dervish, and set out for the city where the former bath boy reigned. After a long journey he came to the capital, and began to seek an opportunity of speaking to the lovely maiden.

One morning he met her in the carriage, accompanied by her maid, on her way to the *mekteb* (parish school). The pretended dervish took off his *kulah*,[1] threw it up in the air, kicked it as it fell, and then caught it on his head, which made the princess laugh. Immediately a rose of extraordinary beauty appeared on the cheek of the Péris' favourite. The youth approached the carriage, and timidly begged the maid to give him the rose.

"No," she replied; "I have only this one, and I will not give it away."

The dervish then performed another trick, which made the princess laugh, when he asked for the second rose.

"Take it. I give it to you," replied the princess.

[1] High, conical felt cap worn by the so-called "Dancing Dervishes."

The prince departed full of joy, and in a month's time arrived at his father's palace.

"Well, hast thou brought the wonderful rose?"

"Yes, my father; look at it, and say if there is anything in the world to equal it."

"No, indeed! Never have I seen anything like it. Now I have but to send my ambassadors to ask for the hand of this princess."

This was done. The neighbouring king accepted the proposal, and it was arranged that the maiden should set out immediately for the country of her betrothed. The princess's mother went to her eldest sister, and begged her to accompany her daughter to her new home. She willingly consented, for reasons which will soon appear. The king loaded forty camels with valuable presents, and the party set out for the neighbouring kingdom.

When they had gone a little distance, the young princess's aunt began to ill-treat her, and would not even give her food to eat. One day, when the girl was hungry, she asked her aunt for some bread.

"If I give you bread, will you give me the talisman you wear round your neck?"

"Willingly. Take it."

The woman took the charm, and hung it round the neck of her own daughter, but gave to her niece in return only a piece of bread which was full of salt.

The following day the bride again asked for bread.

"Let me take out thy right eye, and I will give thee some."

"I consent," said the poor girl.

The next day, again, the unfortunate princess was obliged to allow her other eye to be taken out, in order to satisfy her hunger. The cruel aunt put both of them carefully away in a box which she hid in a chest. At the next halting-place she led the blind girl to a desolate mountain, and left her there. By-and-by the caravan arrived at its destination. The eldest princess said to her daughter:

"My child, above all things beware that thou laugh not, weep not, and walk not in the gardens of the palace."

"I will be careful, mother."

When the king's son met his betrothed he did not recognise her, and at first refused to marry her. But his father compelled him to consent, for fear of a war with his neighbour. Great feasts were also prepared for the occasion, and the rejoicings lasted forty days.

A shepherd who kept his flocks in the valley was seeking a wolf which had carried off several of his sheep. Hearing sounds proceed from behind a bush, he thought it was the beast he sought. and, raising his gun, he was in the act of firing, when he perceived that it was no animal.

"Art thou an evil *djin*, or a demon?" he cried.

"I am neither," was the reply.

"Then what art thou?"

"An unhappy, deserted creature."

The shepherd went up, and saw the blind girl. Touched with pity for her, he took her by the hand and led her to his hut among the rocks.

The following day the princess said to her benefactor:

"My kind friend, take a sack, and hasten to the spot on which you found me. There you will find the pearls formed by my tears."

The shepherd did as he was directed, and found the pearls in thousands. He filled the sack with them, and returned, bent under his precious burden. From this day the poor peasant found himself the richest man of the country, but he was distressed at not being able to do more for the unhappy maiden whom he had received under his roof. One morning, however, the princess smiled for the first time since her arrival in the shepherd's hut. She took the wonderful rose which grew on her cheek, and gave it to her host, saying:

"Go to the king's palace, and offer to the prince's mother-in-law this unfading rose. She will offer you a fortune for it, but give it only for an eye which she keeps in a box at the bottom of a chest."

The worthy man set out. How it happened he knew not, but he travelled as swiftly as the birds, so that in twenty hours he traversed a distance which would have taken any one else twenty days.

As soon as he arrived in the city, he began to cry in the street:

"Who wants to buy an unfading rose?"

The cruel princess hastened to him to buy the wonderful flower. She offered thousands of gold sequins for it, but the man would only exchange it for an eye taken from a certain box. The woman agreed, and gave him the eye. Soon afterwards the shepherd again came to the palace, and sold another rose for the second eye.

When the maiden had recovered possession of her two eyes, she replaced them in the sockets, and regained her sight. She did not, however, perceive that she had put the right eye in the place of the left. But what mattered it? She was more beautiful than ever!

"My friend," said she to her benefactor, "bring me a large cauldron full of water."

The man obeyed. The princess washed her head in the water, which at once turned to pure gold.

"This is a reward for your kindness to me," said she, "for I am about to start for the capital."

The shepherd shed tears at parting with her, and accompanied her to the end of the valley. Soon afterwards the princess arrived in the city, and went and stood before the king's palace.

"Péris, my godmothers!" she cried, "change me into a cypress!"

And, behold, a tall and slender cypress shot up at the palace gate, to the great astonishment of the city.

The false princess had offered the two roses to her husband; but still he would not believe that they grew on her cheeks. In the meantime his father died, and he ascended the throne. He sent for the Patriarch, and said to him:

"This woman has been forced upon me by my father, but I cannot believe that it is she whom I wished to marry. If she and her mother have deceived me, what ought I to do?"

"The marriage is null, and thou mayest, my son, destroy these deceitful women."

"That is well. Thou art just. I will follow thy advice."

But the king could obtain no proofs against the two princesses, although he himself had no doubt on the subject. When the cruel aunt saw the cypress, she concluded that it must be her niece who had been thus transformed by the Péris.

"This is what thou must do," said she to her daughter. "Pretend to be ill, and go to bed. I will send for the doctor, and will come to an understanding with him."

The ugly princess went to bed, and the Court physician was sent for. The mother gave him in secret a large purse of gold, and told him what to prescribe.

"Well," said the king, "what must we do to cure my wife?"

"Order the cypress to be cut down, and make from it a tisane for the queen."

The tree was cut down, and boiled in a huge cauldron, and the tisane given to the princess to drink. A little bit of the tree, however, was left in the court, and a poor woman picked it up, and took it home to burn. The next day the old woman went out. On her return she found the house clean and neat, the table spread, and an excellent repast ready in the kitchen.

"It must be the neighbours' daughters who have done this," said the good woman to herself.

But the next and the following days the same

thing happened. So she resolved that on the morrow she would hide behind the door, and discover the mysterious servant. She did so, and saw a maiden, more beautiful than the angels, busy putting the house in order.

"Ah! my beautiful child," cried the poor woman; "don't run away. Stay with me; be my daughter, and I will love thee as well as a mother!"

The princess consented, and from that day there was plenty in the house. One day she said to her adopted mother:

"Good mother, go to the king, and ask him for the lame and lean mule which is in his stable; say that you want it to carry your grain to the mill."

The woman went to the palace, and borrowed the poor old beast. The princess led the animal into the garden, and allowed it to feed on the flowery herbage which sprang up under her footsteps. In a few days the mule got quite fat, and in a very short time became stronger and more spirited than any that were in the royal stables.

"Now," said the princess to her hostess, "go to the king, and ask him to send for the mule."

When the old woman arrived, the grooms laughed, and said:

"Never mind, old lady; keep the mule; we are only too glad to be rid of her."

"What is the matter?" asked the king.

"Oh! your majesty, it is about the old mule which was lent to this poor woman."

The king, thinking that the animal was dead, ordered his soldiers to fetch it away and bury it.

But when they saw the mule they cried, "What a beauty!" and tried to catch it, but in vain. So they went to tell the king, who came himself to the old woman's house.

"Ah, what a magnificent creature," he cried. "Tell me, good woman, by what miracle has this animal become so spirited and strong?"

The woman invited the king to be seated, and related to him the story of the maiden as the maiden had told it to her.

"Then it must be my betrothed! Quick! good woman, bring the princess here!"

The princess hastened in, and threw herself into the arms of her beloved prince.

"Come with me to the palace, my beautiful betrothed; I will set about punishing your aunt and cousin as they deserve, and afterwards we will celebrate our wedding."

The princess accompanied the king to the palace, and the two deceitful princesses were sent for. In the meantime, the maiden hung round her neck the talisman, which her lover had found in a box.

The wicked women, finding their trick discovered, would have fallen upon the goddaughter of the Péris had not the talisman prevented them.

"Guards, bind these women!" commanded the king.

Then, turning to the prisoners, he said:

"Choose! forty swords, or forty mules?"

They chose the forty mules.

"So be it. Now, my guards, take forty wild young mules, fasten them together with a long rope, tie these women by their feet to the rope, and let the animals loose on the mountain."

The guards immediately obeyed, and the princesses, dragged over hill and dale, were dashed into as many pieces as there were rocks on the mountains and stones in the valleys.

The wedding was then celebrated, and the whole city held a wedding feast of forty days' duration. The sky rained honey and the streams ran wine. And didn't they enjoy themselves, my children!

The folk-songs of a people would seem to be influenced in a much greater degree than their folk-stories by climatic and political conditions. And while the tales told in the long winter evenings, by the hearth on which the *tezek* peats are glowing, deal with love, adventure, and enchantment, the subjects which inspire the Armenian rustic muse are the snow-bound hills, the late returning spring, with the birds which herald it or follow in its train; or, it may be, a souvenir of past national glory and a passionate longing for liberty. The inhabitants of Van and its neighbourhood, who are said to possess remarkable poetic powers, and also to have preserved to a great extent the old folk-lore, have an additional subject for song in the ever varying aspects of their mountain-girt lake. The versification of many of these folk-songs is very regular, and, as will be seen from the two following translated specimens, in which the original form has been strictly followed, consists in many instances of double rhymes :—

THE STORK'S WELCOME.[1]

(Arakil, paror egir.)

Welcome, Stork, O welcome here!
Welcome, O Stork, O welcome here!
Thou com'st to tell us Spring is near,
And with thy news our hearts to cheer!

Stork, fly down, fly down and rest,
On our poor roof descend and rest;
Upon our ash-tree build thy nest;
Of all the birds we love thee best.

Stork, I'd tell to thee my tale;
Stork, I'd tell my mournful tale;
My thousand griefs to thee bewail,
My thousand griefs to thee bewail.

Stork, when thou away didst hie,
From our ash-tree far didst fly,
The with'ring winds did moan and sigh,
And caused our smiling flowers to die.

The brilliant sky was overcast,
Dark clouds across it drifted fast;
They broke the snow above amassed,[2]
Came winter's flower-destroying blast.

Beginning on Varaca's[3] height,
Beginning on Varaca's height,
Soon all the earth with snow was dight,
And our green field was glist'ning white.

---

[1] This and the two following songs are from Dr. Issaverden's collection of *Armenian Popular Songs*, which are accompanied by an English prose translation. Though, as before mentioned, many of the pieces in this little book were obtained from old MSS., those I have selected are, I am assured, current at the present day among the people. For the exact rhyme and rhythm of the originals I am indebted to the kind assistance of Mr. M. Sevasly, editor of the *Haiasdan*.

[2] Literally, "from above they were breaking the snow in pieces."

[3] A rocky mountain to the east of the lake and town of Van.

Stork, our little garden here,
Wrapped in snow, lay cold and drear;
And all the roses of the year
Lay withered on their icy bier.

The partridge, it would appear from the next poem, is to the Armenians, as to the Greeks, an ideal of grace, both in form and movement :—

THE PARTRIDGE.

The sun beats from the mountain's brow;
    Pretty thing, pretty thing!
The partridge from his nest comes now,
To welcome him the flow'rets bow,
As flies he from the mountain's brow;
    Pretty thing, pretty thing!
Partridge with brown-spotted wing.

Thy nest's bedecked with many a flower;
Narcissus, basil sweet, embower;
And lily, with her fragrant dower,
Breathes perfume at dawn's dewy hour;
    Pretty thing, pretty thing!
Partridge with brown-spotted wing.

All glossy soft thy feathers shine;
Long-necked, thy beak is small and fine
Thy wing is marked with many a line;
Than dove thou'rt sweeter, birdie mine;
    Pretty thing, pretty thing!
Partridge with brown-spotted wing.

When down thou fliest from tree-top tall,
And softly to thy mate dost call,
The world around thou cheerest all,
And joys the heart whate'er befall;
    Pretty thing, pretty thing!
Partridge with brown-spotted wing.

And bless thee all the birds of air,
Flocking round thee everywhere;
Chirping, they proclaim thee fair;
None can, in sooth, with thee compare;
  Pretty thing, pretty thing!
Partridge with brown-spotted wing.

The following children's song is the Armenian counterpart of Dr. Watts's "How doth the little busy bee." Popular reverence for St. Gregory, "the Illuminator," here assigns to him the place of the Recording Angel :—

CHILDREN'S SONG.

Light appears! Light appears!
O Light most blessèd!
To tree flies sparrow,
To perch the chicken,
Twelve months would the sluggard sleep!
Workman, rise; to labour haste;
Open are the gates of Heaven;
There appears the golden throne,
Seated on it Christ behold,
The Illuminator near.
Pen of gold he takes in hand,
Writes he down both great and small;
Sadly weep the sinners now,
But the just are filled with joy.

CHAPTER X.

BULGARIAN WOMEN: THEIR SOCIAL STATUS AND ACTIVITIES.

It must not be supposed that the autonomy granted to Bulgaria, and the subsequent incorporation with the Principality of Eastern Roumelia, has released all Bulgarians from Ottoman rule, any more than the creation of the Kingdom of Hellas released all Greeks from subjection to the Sultan. Bulgarian communities are scattered over the whole of Macedonia and Thrace, occupying in some places isolated villages, in others forming the majority of the population of a district, and constituting an important element in many of the towns of the interior. As has been already pointed out in the Introduction, the Bulgarians are of two distinct types, the Tatar and the Slavo-Greek. The former is distinguished by the high cheek-bones, broad flat faces, small sunken eyes, nose flat at the top and inclined to be globular at the end, eyebrows thick and prominent, and dark complexion usually found in members of this race. The other type resembles in its general characteristics the rest of the mixed Christian population of these provinces, and some of the women are extremely pretty.

The habitations and mode of life of the townspeople differ in no way from those of the Greeks;

and, as the religious marriage law and surrounding circumstances are identical, the social status of women in the towns is the same. Foreign influence has, as yet, affected the towns of the interior in a very small degree, and the lives of the Bulgarian women of the well-to-do class are still very simple and monotonous. They take an active part in all domestic matters, do all their own needlework, and amuse themselves by promenading and paying and receiving calls on feast-days, and now and then attending a christening or a wedding. On rare occasions an evening party, or even a ball, may be given, if one may dignify with such a name the meeting of a number of people of both sexes who display on their persons every gradation of garment from *bonâ fide* evening dress down to native costume, and including every style that has been "the fashion" for some twenty years past. The deportment and manners of the company at these gatherings are as amusingly unsophisticated as their attire, and their terpsichorean performances are diverting in the highest degree. Such parties are generally given on the "name-day" of some member of the family, that is to say, the day of the saint whose name he or she bears, and on which it is *de rigueur* for all friends to call and offer their felicitations. If dancing is not to form part of the evening's entertainment, native games of cards, vocal music, and similar diversions are substituted. Light refreshments, such as native wine or lemonade and fruit sherbets, fruit and cakes, are handed round from time to time, as well as the inevitable coffee and preserves (*slatko*), which are offered to every guest on arrival. Such entertainments even among the working classes usually conclude in an orderly manner, for though some of the younger men may drink to excess on the occasion of a great feast or fair, it is the exception and not the rule, and the women of all classes and creeds are most abstemious. Among the educated classes, many of whose members have either travelled abroad or visited the capital, the amusements are directly copied from those of Europeans, and music, conversation, and theatricals occupy the evenings, though deficiencies in dress, etiquette, and other details are often noticeable. There is very little social intercourse with Greek or other neighbours, each nationality keeping exclusively to its own circle, a practice which naturally confines the ideas of the women especially within a very narrow horizon.

The Bulgarian women of the peasant class, however, having no opportunities for copying the manners of more "civilised" neighbours, adhere rigidly to their own national customs, and circumstances combine to give them a much more independent position and freer life, not only than that led by the Bulgarian townswomen, but by the generality of Greek peasant women. For the Bulgarian peasant women, taking, as they do, an equal share with the men of the family in field and farm work, are naturally accorded a co-equality with their husbands and brothers. Added to this, the women marry comparatively much later in life than the generality of Orientals, and, subject to the approval of their fathers, themselves select their husbands.

For a Bulgarian peasant is in no hurry to get rid of the daughters who take such an active part in all that concerns the welfare of the home, and requires from the youth who would transfer the services of any one of them to himself, a certain equivalent in money according to the position of the parties. But though the young husband does not always take his wife home to his father's roof, but sometimes builds a cottage for himself, he yet remains associated with his father in the farm, and is consequently more or less subject to the parental rule; and his wife will in future work for her father-in-law instead of, as formerly, for her father.

In Bulgarian folk-song we find incidents faithfully recorded which illustrate every phase of social life, tragic and comic, to which the above-noted circumstances would naturally give rise. But though one sister-in-law may tyrannise over another, and a virago of a stepmother make the life of her son's too submissive wife a burden to her, an *esprit de corps* is occasionally manifested, and the authority of the paterfamilias made light of by the women of a household, as, for instance, in the song of "The Three Reapers," the eldest of whom addresses her husband's father as "You worn-out donkey!"[1] And we have also here depicted the better side of feminine nature, the brother's sister full of helpful counsel to the maiden whose lover has been beguiled away from her;[1] and the matron who teaches her daughter-in-law how she may regain her husband's wandering affections.[1] For though, as before mentioned in the case of the

[1] See next chapter.

Greeks, divorce is permitted by the Eastern Church, its practice gives rise to social scandal; and when a mother has already a daughter-in-law whose character pleases her, she is naturally unwilling to exchange her for another of whose disposition she has not made proof.

The houses of the better class of peasant farmers are solidly constructed of stone, and sufficiently comfortable. The cottages of the poorer class, however, are of the most primitive style of architecture. A number of poles mark out the extent to be given to the edifice, the spaces between them being filled up with wattles of osier, plastered thickly within and without with clay and cow-dung mixed with straw. When dry, the walls are whitewashed within and without, and the dome-shaped roof is covered with tiles or thatch. The interior of an average cottage is divided into three rooms—the common living-room, the family bedroom, and the storeroom. The floor is of earth, beaten hard, and is covered with coarse matting and thick home-made rugs. The furniture consists chiefly of cushions covered with thick woven tissues, which also serve the family as beds. On the walls are a few of the engravings in very odd perspective, which, though produced in Russia, are distributed to pilgrims by the monks of Mount Athos, and there is also, perhaps, a picture of some saint with a tiny oil lamp suspended before it. The shelves contain some articles of crockery, the brightly burnished copper cooking-pans found in the poorest house in the East, and various odd articles. The bedding, rolled up, is tidily piled in one corner, in another is the *bulka's* spinning-wheel, and in the inner apartment is the loom on which she manufactures the tissues used for the furniture of the house and the clothing of the family. Outside are sheds for the cattle, pig and sheep pens, poultry-house, the oven, and perhaps a well, all enclosed by a wall or fence, and guarded by dogs.

Like all the peasants of Turkey, the Bulgarians are most economical and even frugal in their habits. They are content with very little, and live generally on rye bread and maize porridge, or beans seasoned with vinegar and pepper, supplemented by the produce of the dairy. On great festivals a young pig or a lamb is added to the usual fare, with home-made wine and a heavy kind of cake called a *banitza*.

The clothing of the peasant women is warm and comfortable for winter wear, but must be found intolerably hot and heavy in summer. Only the sturdy frame of a Bulgarian could, I believe, easily support the weight of the full gala costume, with all the ponderous silver ornaments worn on head, neck, waist, and wrists. Indeed, I have never found it possible to wear for more than half an hour at a time the costume I obtained at Salonica, with the object of using it as a fancy ball dress. All the materials of the various garments which compose the dress are home-made, and are of the most durable character. The costume varies a little according to district; that worn in the neighbourhood of Salonica is, I think, one of the most picturesque in style, and pleasing in colour. It consists of a gown of unbleached linen or cotton, reaching from the neck to the ankles, and decorated round the borders, and especially on the wide sleeves, with elaborate embroidery and drawnwork in fine coloured wools. Another gown without sleeves, similarly decorated, and open at the sides, is sometimes worn over this, and, over all, a sleeveless coat of white felt, finely braided in artistic patterns and colours round the borders and seams. A sash several yards long and about two inches in width, curiously woven by hand, is twisted round the waist, and the costume is completed by an apron which is sometimes entirely covered with elaborate needle-work. On the head is worn a tiny cap covered with gold and silk braid, from which hangs over the shoulders and below the waist an ample fringe of braided scarlet wool, or gold and black silk; and over all is thrown a square of white cotton, embroidered round the borders with silk, and fastened to the cap with innumerable silver ornaments and strings of coins. The working dress is of the same pattern, but of plainer make and more sober colour, and two or three such costumes last a woman from her wedding-day to the day of her death. The women usually go barefooted when about their daily avocations, and put on their shoes and embroidered socks only on great occasions.

The frequent holidays observed by the Bulgarians as members of the Orthodox Church make it necessary for them to work doubly hard on other days in order to accomplish the year's work in twelve months. Consequently, during the spring, summer, and winter the whole family are at work from sunrise to sunset, the women and girls, as soon as their household duties are finished, going out to assist the men and boys in the fields. The spinning, weaving, and other home manufactures are carried on chiefly in the winter, when the female portion of the family is less called upon for outdoor work than in other seasons.

The work of cutting the grain in autumn is accompanied by these simple people with observances and rejoicings quite Arcadian, enlivened by the sound of the bagpipe, and perhaps also by song. The whole family, from the old grandparents down to the babies, picnic in the fields from morning till night, and the women work as hard as—or, according to some travellers, harder than—the men till all the corn is bound in golden sheaves. Not even the old women past field work are idle, for, while "minding the babies," they are still busy with distaff and spindle. When the tax-collector has taken his tithe, and the rest of the grain has been carried, the work of threshing begins. The earth of the hurdle-fenced enclosure before each cottage is beaten and stamped until it acquires the necessary solidity for the purpose, when the process is carried on in much the same manner as described in a previous chapter. The winnowing and sifting of the grain is done entirely by the girls, who then house it in the queer wooden granaries constructed for the purpose.

After the corn harvest comes the vintage, when the grapes are gathered in the same light-hearted fashion. Besides wine and the spirit called *raki*, or *mastica*, a kind of treacle, called in Greek *petmaiz*, is made from the juice of the grape, and stored up for winter use with the oil, grain, and other provisions.

Large quantities of plums are also dried and exported, a considerable proportion of which, after passing through some mysterious process in France, find their way into the European market as "French plums."

In some districts the culture of the rose-trees, from the blossoms of which the famous attar and water of roses are made, forms an important branch of industry. The flowers, which are of the species *Rosa moscata*, and have very few petals, are grown in plots or gardens of considerable extent, immense quantities being required to yield one ounce of the precious oil.

The picturesque scene presented in such a fragrant harvest-field has been graphically described by Mrs. Blunt in *The People of Turkey*,[1] and, as I have not myself been fortunate enough to witness it, I cannot do better than quote her description:

"At dawn, a tap at my door announced that it was time to rise and witness the rose-gathering, which I had expressed a wish to see. The roses begin to be collected before sunrise, in order to keep in them all the richness of their perfume. The work requires expedition and many hands; so large bands of young men and maidens, adding pleasure to toil, while gathering the roses, amuse themselves by carrying on flirtations and love-makings. The large garden to which I was conducted belonged to the wealthy *Tchorbadji*,[2] in whose house I was staying. It was at some distance from the town, and by the time we reached it the bright rays of a lovely spring morning were fast spreading over the horizon. The

[1] Vol. i. p. 197.
[2] Literally, "the soupmaker," the headman of a small town or village.

field was thickly planted with rose-bushes, bearing a rich harvest of half-open dew-laden buds. The nightingales, in flights, hovered over them, as if disputing their possession with the light-hearted harvesters, and chorused with their rich notes the gay songs of the scattered company, who, dressed in their *Prasnik* (feast-day) clothes—the youths in snow-white shirts and gaudy sleeveless vests, the girls in their picturesque costume, the coloured kerchiefs on their heads floating in the breeze—had the appearance of a host of butterflies flitting over the flowers. The girls were actively employed in stripping off the buds and throwing them into the baskets slung on their left arms. The youths helped them in the task, and each was rewarded with a bud from his sweetheart, which he placed in his cap. The children ran to and fro, emptying the baskets into larger receptacles, presided over by the matrons, who sat under the shade of the trees and sorted the roses. The whole picture was so bright and happy, and in such perfect harmony with the luxuriant beauty surrounding it, that it completely fascinated me, and I felt almost envious of those happy beings—the careless, simple children of nature."[1]

Bulgarian women are also employed to a considerable extent in silkworm rearing, and in tending and gathering the tobacco crops; and, when they have no land of their own to till, will hire themselves out for field and other outdoor work. Half a dozen of these women labourers were employed at the

---

[1] Kezanlik, the neighbourhood of which is here described, suffered most severely during what are called the "Bulgarian atrocities" of 1876.

Consulate at Salonica when part of the garden was being transformed into a lawn tennis court. They were all of the Tatar type, their faces tanned by sun and wind to a rich brown, and, though not one of them exceeded five feet in height, their broad and sturdy frames seemed incapable of fatigue. Great was their amusement when an officer of H.M.S. *Condor*, anxious for a little healthy exercise, took the spade from one of them and worked with a will for half an hour—that any one should work for amusement was past their comprehension. And the drawing-rooms, especially, of the Consulate, which they were shown one evening by the Abyssinian maid, Milly, were to these simple peasant women as the apartments of an enchanted palace. They did not attempt to enter them, but stood, as if spell-bound, in the corridor outside.

A small number of Bulgarian women belonging to the poorer class in the towns become domestic servants, and, when once they attach themselves to a family, prove most devoted and faithful to their employers. Mr. and Mrs. Blunt had the misfortune a year or two ago to lose an old servant of this description, who had lived for some thirty years in their family. *Kyrà*, or Dame, Maria, as she was called, after being superannuated as cook, had been retained in the capacity of housekeeper. She was short, stout, and Tatar-faced, with a "wooden" countenance, and a capacity for wearing several stones'-weight of clothes on the hottest summer day, though, being a townswoman, her costume consisted chiefly of skirts and jackets one over the other, and for outdoor wear a long fur-lined pelisse of dark-coloured cloth. Truly dragon-like was her watchfulness over her employers' interests, and the zeal of "the Circumference," as we irreverently dubbed her, led her sometimes almost the length of refusing her mistress the key of the storeroom, for fear that she would be too generous with its contents. It was indeed her firm conviction—which she occasionally expressed—that, were it not for her stewardship, the *Madama* would, by her generosity, long ago have ruined herself. Like the generality of Eastern servants, she was clothed by her mistress, and she allowed her wages, during all these long years of service, to accumulate, and at her death bequeathed her little fortune to the only son of her employers, to whom she was passionately attached. Kyrà Maria was exceedingly pious, and religiously made herself ill every Lent; and her death was, I understand, due to sunstroke when on her way from the Metropolitan Church in the heat of the day. Though she could, I believe, neither read nor write, she spoke Bulgarian and Turkish equally well, but her broken Greek was chiefly exercised for my benefit. Some of her expressions in this language became quite proverbial with us, as, besides being always very much to the point, they were often most laconically put. On one occasion, when I was busy in my room with the manuscript of *The People of Turkey*, she had brought me a cup of tea and some cakes, and, returning to fetch the cup some quarter of an hour afterwards, found that I had forgotten all about it. With a grunt expressive of extreme disapproval of such neglect of creature comforts, she ejaculated, "Γράπση, γράπση, τσαὶ ὅλο κρεόνη," which may be translated, "Writey, writey, tea all coldy!" and, after fetching me another cup, she waited to see that it was emptied before it again became "all coldy." Any slight indisposition of mine she always attributed to my disregard of her continual injunction to βάλε σάλη, or put on a shawl. "Eh," she would grunt in her curious Greek, as she came into my room, "not well, Mam'zell? Why would you not put on a shawl?"

The Bulgarian, like the Greek women, have no amusement but the song and the dance. Unlike the Greeks, however, who dance only at appointed times and seasons, the Bulgarians are always ready for this national pastime. At the first discordant sound of the *Gaida*, the Eastern bagpipe, the young men and girls form a circle, holding each other by the girdle, and enter enthusiastically and untiringly into the dance, which is called by the Greek name of *hora* (χόρος), and is of a similar character. The married women do not, as a rule, take part in the village dances, though occasionally one of more independent spirit will insist upon continuing this favourite pastime of her maiden days. On unimportant festivals, the girls form themselves into small parties in the immediate neighbourhood of their homes, but on great feast-days, such as Easter, St. George's Day, &c., they assemble on the village common, or in some communal orchard or vineyard. The youths join them with the piper, and the dancers form a long chain with the *horovodka*, or "dance-leader," at one extremity. This damsel commences the song, in which she is accompanied by half the performers, the other half repeating the verses after them. The song finished, the next in the line becomes *horovodka,* and so on in turn until all have officiated. In some places, however, the maiden endowed by nature with the best voice and the most retentive memory retains the position of conductress; and each village and parish is generally found to possess one or two thus specially gifted. Dancing also plays a great part in wedding rejoicings, when nuptial songs are substituted for those used on other occasions.

Another amusement in which the Bulgarians occasionally indulge is the " bear-dance." This dance, which is chiefly pantomimic, is performed by a man dressed in a bear-skin, and led by a girl who makes him perform all kinds of pranks and buffooneries for the entertainment of the spectators. Sometimes the company join in the dance, and the performance concludes with a general chase of the bear.

The brigands of the Balkans played almost as great a *rôle* in the recent history of the Bulgarians as did the brigands of Olympus and Pindus in the struggle for Greek independence. The wives of the *haidouts,* as the brigands of Bulgaria are called, often accompanied their husbands to the mountains in men's attire, fared like the rest of the outlaws, and often shared their fate. Love of adventure, however, seems to have led numerous young women to adopt this calling, which is by no means in more disrepute among the Bulgarian, than among the Greek peasants. After a few years, if they escaped capture or death, in their encounters with the Turkish troops, the *haidout* women often returned home, married, and settled down to domestic life, like Penka in the folk-song.¹ M. Miladinov, the Bulgarian folk-lorist, met in his wanderings a *ci-devant* brigandess, Sirma, then a woman of eighty, who is the heroine of a song beginning,

> Say, who has ever seen a maid
> Of seventy-seven the captain ?²

The morals of Bulgarian women would seem to be, on the whole, very good. In the towns, manners are very much the same as among the Greeks; but the peasant women, as has been already described, enjoy much greater freedom, and few restrictions are placed upon intercourse between the sexes. Even Messrs. St. Clair and Brophy, whose rabid Turcophilism would not allow them to see any good in the male Bulgar, admit that their "morality is tolerably good for a people with whom religion has no real force," but ascribe the superiority of morals found among this nation, as compared with the Servians and Roumanians, to the fact of their having Turkish neighbours, whose example "shames" the Bulgars "into morality." Turkish peasants are, no doubt, most virtuous people; but Oriental Christians do not, as a rule, copy the manners of their Moslem neighbours in other respects. And I venture to

---

¹ See Chap. XIII.
² Compare the Greek song on Haidée the Klepht beginning:
> Who fishes on the hills has seen,
> Or deer upon the waters?
> Who an unwedded girl has seen
> Among the *pallikária*?

think that the reason of this comparatively higher morality is to be found rather in national temperament, and in social conditions. As among the Greeks, considerable facilities for divorce exist, but they are naturally seldom abused by people whose leading characteristics are industry, thrift, and solid good sense.

The educational progress already made by this people in so short a time appears the more remarkable when we consider the immense difficulties with which they have had to contend. The greatest of these was presented by the language itself. The language brought by the Bulgarians from their original home on the Volga has been almost lost sight of in the successive admixture of Slav, Greek, and Turkish, and the result is a curious dialect difficult to reduce to grammatical form. The first book in Bulgarian was published in 1806; but the more polished style which writers attempted to give the language rendered it almost unintelligible to the vulgar. Numerous grammars have been written, but they all differ widely from each other, not only in their general principles but in their details. Some entirely disregard the popular idiom, and impose the rules of the Russian or Servian language; others attempt to reduce to rules the vernacular, which, being of so very composite a character, is no easy matter. How these difficulties have been got over, I am not in a position to say, as, unfortunately, some official information which I was promised on the subject has not reached me in time for insertion. The first Bulgarian school worthy of the name was opened at Gabrova in 1835, but after that date schools increased so rapidly that before the last Turco-Russian war they numbered 347. Only twenty-seven, however, of these were girls' schools. For with the Bulgarians, as with other nations, education is deemed of importance only so far as it is of commercial value.

In point of education the Bulgarian women of Macedonia and Thrace are now, in the towns, much on a par with their Greek neighbours. Formerly, in districts where Bulgarian national schools did not exist, the girls attended the schools belonging to the Greek communities. But since the Principality acquired its autonomy, the anti-Hellenic movement which had previously been set on foot, has succeeded, to a great extent, in substituting Bulgarian for Greek education in the Turkish provinces. Teachers are supplied from the training Colleges of Bulgaria Proper, where education has already been made compulsory, and where the schools are organised on the newest and most approved European systems. There is at Philipopolis a girls' Lyceum, established some eight years ago, at which a hundred and fifty girls receive a "High School" education, many of whom eventually become mistresses of Bulgarian schools in the Turkish provinces. Mr. Samuelson, who visited this college not long ago, describes the pupils as "remarkably bright and intelligent, fully equal to girls of any other country, drawn from every class of society."[1] The daughters of wealthy Bulgarians are frequently sent to Constantinople to

[1] *Bulgaria, Past and Present*, p. 148.

be educated, and, it would appear, with very satisfactory results. For I have just been reading over a letter written a dozen years ago to Mrs. Blunt by the daughter of the *Tchorbadji* before mentioned,[1] and which is not only couched in perfect French, but contains a most interesting and ably written description of the rise and progress of the educational movement among her countrymen.[2]

[1] Above, p. 305.   [2] *The People of Turkey*, vol. ii. p. 208.

CHAPTER XI.

BULGARIAN WOMEN: THEIR FAMILY CEREMONIES.

Ancient customs connected with domestic events are fast dying out in the towns of Free Bulgaria, where the people are with every succeeding year coming more and more into contact with Western civilisation. But in the country districts of Macedonia and Thrace especially, they still generally survive, and will, no doubt, long continue to be observed. The hardy peasant woman makes very light of the troubles of maternity, but the baby at first has a very hard time of it. The Bulgarian wise-woman, who unites the professions of Mrs. Gamp and village witch, or the matron who may replace her, brings into the room, as soon as the baby is born, a reaping-hook, which she places in a corner in order to keep off all malevolent spirits, Youdas, Strougas, or Samovilas,[1] who may be lurking about. She then proceeds to bathe and salt the baby all over, and, after dressing it, lays it by the side of the mother, while she makes a kind of omelette with eggs, oil, and pepper, as a poultice for the infant's head. It appears to be a popular belief that if a child is not thus salted, its feet or some other part of the body will become malodorous,

[1] See next chapter.

and the poultice is intended to solidify the skull and render it proof against sunstroke. While the baby is screaming its loudest in protest against this treatment, its nurse proceeds to fumigate the room for fear that the presence of the reaping-hook should not have all the effect desired, and the Powers of the Air be attracted by the child's cries. A clove of garlic and some of the charms before mentioned as used by the Greeks for that purpose, are fastened to the baby's cap against the Evil Eye. The mother, though she may be up and about her numerous household duties in a day or so, is not supposed to leave the precincts of her house until forty days after the birth of the child, and, consequently, like the Greek mother, is not present at its baptism, which takes place on the eighth day, and is conducted in a fashion precisely similar to that of the Greeks. On the occasion of her first going abroad, namely, when she goes to be "churched," she uses as a walking-stick the shovel with which the bread is put into, and withdrawn from, the oven.

The upper classes of the Bulgarians follow the customs of their Greek neighbours in matrimonial affairs, the first advance being made by the girl's parents, who commission a professional match-maker—called, in Upper Macedonia, *stroinikote*, or, if a woman, *stroinikitza*; and, in Bulgaria, *swaty*—to procure a suitable husband. Of late years, too, the custom of receiving a dowry with the wife has been gaining ground. The betrothal is a formal religious ceremony, which takes place before witnesses, when the documents containing the wedding contract are exchanged.

Among this class, however, native observances are being gradually laid aside, and an attempt is made to conform to European usages. The bride's *trousseau* is ordered from Vienna; as are the wedding-dress, wreath, and veil which the bridegroom presents to her. The fond mother, too, generally adds to her daughter's "tocher" a number of articles for household use of home or native manufacture, such as embroidered towels, and bed- and table-linen, and charming fabrics made of rich raw and floss silk, or silk and linen.

But with the Bulgarians as with the Greeks, old customs must be sought for among the peasantry, and the observances connected with marriage are not the least curious and interesting. A young peasant cannot marry until his parents, for whom he has hitherto laboured, can afford to give him a sum of money sufficient to buy him a wife. The price ranges from £50 to £300, according to the position of the contracting parties, and is settled by the *svatobi*, or proxies, as well as another and smaller sum, called the *bash parasi*, or "head-money," which is paid to the mother. The *godu*, or betrothal, then takes place, a Wednesday or Thursday evening being considered the most auspicious time for the ceremony. It consists of the exchange of documents certifying, on the one hand, the sum of money to be paid by the bridegroom, and, on the other, the quantity and quality of the *trousseau*, or rather "plenishing," promised by the maiden's parents. Rings are also interchanged by the couple after being blessed by the priest, who acts the part of notary on such occasions. A short blessing follows, the *fiancée* kisses the hands of the assembled company, and then retires with her friends to feast apart, unawed by the presence of the elders, for whom a table is spread in the principal room. The word table is, however, a misnomer, for such articles of furniture are found only in the dwellings of the wealthier farmers, and the cloth is generally spread on the floor, or perhaps for the elder and more distinguished guests on the low, broad stools called by the Turks *sofra*. The young people afterwards dance outside the house, and sing songs at intervals. The *fiancé* then produces his presents, which consist of various articles of feminine apparel, including several pairs of native shoes, a head-dress and necklace of gold and silver coins, a silver belt, bracelets, earrings, and other ornaments. The value of these gifts is freely discussed by the girl's father, and a bargain generally ensues, the suitor adding to the necklace or head-dress coin after coin until the goodman is content. These treasures are bestowed in the *tekneh*, the wooden trough which serves equally for kneading the bread and cradling the little ones, and the festivities are resumed. On the following day the young woman proudly dons all this finery, and parades herself in the village as " engaged."

Many Bulgarian marriages are no doubt love matches, though more practical considerations often influence Petko and Yanko in the choice of their helpmates. And a helpmate in every sense of the word a Bulgarian wife must be; for, as already described, a very large share of the labour of the farm devolves upon her, until the children grow up to take a part in it. Petko, therefore, will probably choose his wife, as he would a team of oxen, for her muscular strength and probable working powers, the more so as, like his oxen and buffaloes, he must purchase her with a considerable sum of money; and, consequently, the most physically powerful wife is considered the best investment.

The marriage does not take place until at least six months after the *gody*, and is sometimes deferred for years by selfish parents who wish to retain the services of their daughter as long as possible. Sometimes the couple find it necessary to take matters into their own hands, and elope to the *papas* of some neighbouring village, who unites them in holy matrimony. The girl has generally some sympathetic friend who hides her in her own house until the wrath of her father is somewhat appeased, and he consents to receive her back and give the indispensable wedding feast.

The bridegroom in the meantime must build himself a house, and furnish it according to Bulgarian ideas of what is fitting. Certain domestic animals must also be purchased—a pair of oxen or buffaloes for ploughing and draught work are considered indispensable, and a cow and some poultry should be installed in the farmyard. When all is in readiness, the young man sends his parents or the *swaty* to announce to his future father-in-law that he wishes the wedding to take place in the course of a few weeks. The *swadba* decided upon, the domestic preparations begin. Weddings are generally celebrated in the season when little work is going on in the fields, in order that more time may be devoted to the festivities, for feast-days, on which idleness is imperative, are so numerous that the peasants can ill afford to make holiday on working-days.

During the week preceding the marriage, the parents of the couple complete the furnishing of the new home, and, this accomplished, the girl's mother turns her attention to preparing her house for the auspicious event. The walls, ceiling, and floor are cleaned and lime-washed, the copper pots, pans, and dishes, and all the articles of German china and glass that adorn the shelves of the better cottages, are taken down, thoroughly washed, scrubbed, and polished, and returned to their places. A store of carpets and rugs is then produced from the walnut-wood chests, and spread on the mattress-sofas, and on the floors of the rooms and verandah; and lastly, the cakes are made, the fatted calf is killed, and the wine jars are brought up from the cellar. These cakes are sent round to friends, in lieu of invitation cards, requesting the pleasure of the recipients' company on the wedding-day, Sunday, and also, in the case of the women and girls, to view the *trousseau*. All the articles composing it are on Friday hung up on a cord stretched across the room for the inspection of the matrons, who freely criticise the quality of the materials and the handiwork bestowed upon the various garments in the way of embroidery, braiding, and other decorations. The maidens meanwhile assist the bride to add any finishing touches which may be necessary, or dance and sing before the door.

Two of the girls, who act as bridesmaids, come again on the following day to help the bride with her toilette. After washing her from head to foot, they proceed to plait her hair into a multitude of minute tresses, which will not be again undone for several days at least. While this task, which takes some time, is proceeding, the village maidens arrive with offerings of sweetmeats and flowers, and at its conclusion they all sit down together—on the floor—to a vegetarian meal, after which singing and dancing are the order of the day.

On the morrow, in the early forenoon, the wedding guests arrive, the matrons with their daughters dressed in their gayest, decked with silver ornaments, and garlanded with flowers. The bride is seated in state, her face dotted with spangles, and perhaps concealed by a scarlet veil. The upper part of her elaborately embroidered costume is almost equally hidden by the quantity of ornaments and coins, made of alloyed silver, which hang over it. When picnicking one day at the large Bulgarian village of Neokhori, a few miles from Salonica, we had the privilege of seeing a peasant bride "on view." It was a holiday, and all the village was *en fête*, the women and girls standing in their picturesque red and white costumes at their doorways. Most of the men were away, the chief industry of the village being one which necessitates their being frequently absent. As we passed up the street, we came to a cottage, a mere hovel, round which a number of persons were gathered, and we, being strangers and "Franks," were courteously invited in "to see the bride." It was, however, some minutes before our eyes became sufficiently accustomed to the gloom of the interior to be able to distinguish this much bedizened damsel. And as soon as we had in turn saluted and sufficiently admired her, we gladly escaped from the crowded, stuffy, and windowless apartment to the fresh and sunny outer air.

The religious ceremony, which is the same as with the Greeks, may take place in the church, or in the house of the bridegroom's father. In any case, if both parties belong to the same village, the wedding party return after the service to the house of the bride's parents. Corn, the emblem of plenty, is showered over the happy pair on their arrival, and as soon as the guests are seated the bride makes the round of the room, kissing the hands of all the matrons, from each of whom she receives in return a dried fig.

The wedding feast is then held, and the male portion of the company endeavour to rival their ancestral heroes in their gastronomic feats. Singing and dancing also occupy the younger members of the party until it is time to escort the bride to her new home.

Taking home the bride is, however, performed in much more picturesque fashion by the Bulgarian communities in some parts of Macedonia, especially when the home of the husband is at some distance; and the ceremony has something in common with that attending the Vlach weddings already described. The bride is conducted to the gate of the homestead by her father, who assists her to mount the horse prepared for her. The rest of the guests, also mounted, form a procession led by one of their number, who carries a flag surmounted by an apple. With their garlands of flowers and vine leaves, their songs and strains of wild music, their gleeful shouts and gay laughter, this wedding procession presents the appearance of an ancient chorus of Bacchanals wending its way by mountain-path and ravine to some old shrine of the vinous god. On entering the village for which they are bound, the company are met by the *Nunco*, or "best man," with other functionaries called respectively *Maldever* and *Stardever*, who, like the Kanephoroi in the Dionysiaka, carry baskets of fruit and cakes, and flasks of wine, all provided by the *Nunco*, who himself carries the bridal crowns and leads a goat with gilded horns.

On arriving at the gate of the bridegroom's dwelling, the standard-bearer enters, followed by the bride, who reins up her steed in front of the flag, which he plants in the centre of the courtyard. A verse is now sung which may be thus translated:

O Maldever, O Stardever, why linger ye outside!
Dismount, dismount, and enter now thy husband's house, O Bride!

The song concluded, the bride bows three times to the company, and is assisted by the bridegroom's father to dismount. After kissing her horse on the forehead, she takes hold of one corner of a handkerchief extended to her by her future father-in-law, and is thus led into the lower story of the house, used generally as granary and storeroom, and lighted only by narrow slits in the walls. The centre of this apartment is occupied by a wine barrel crowned with the wedding-cake, on which stands a glass of wine. The priests, in their gorgeous sacerdotal robes and tall black hats, range themselves around, holding crosses, and over this Bacchanalian altar the Christian marriage rite is performed. After having tasted the wine, the principals walk three times round the barrel, while cakes, fruits, and comfits are showered over them.

The newly married couple are, in Bulgaria, required to observe a week of seclusion in their home, during which time they may neither go out nor receive visits. At the termination of this *solitude à deux*, the married women arrive to conduct the bride, who carries two water-pails slung, yoke fashion, on her shoulders, to the well, round which she walks three times after throwing in her offering to the *genii loci*. She then draws water and fills her pails, the contents of which are immediately emptied over her by her companions. In return for this service she kisses hands all round, receiving from each person, as she does so, a fig. On the same day the young wife also visits her mother, escorted by the matrons of the village. In Macedonia, however, the Bulgarian brides for the most part follow the Greek custom of making their peace with the water nymphs on the day after the wedding.

The funeral customs of the Bulgarians differ much more from those of the Greeks than do those connected with birth and marriage, although the religious ceremony is the same in both cases. The Bulgarian views the approach of death with a fatalistic indifference almost equal to that displayed by the Ottoman.

Doctors are few and far between in the country districts, and if the simples prescribed by the wise-woman do not cure the patient, it is evident that he, or she, has no longer "life to live." When the end is deemed near, the priest administers the last sacrament, and the moribund, if conscious, sets his affairs in order. The room is meanwhile crowded with female relatives, who give expression to their grief in the most demonstrative fashion. As soon as the spirit has departed from the body, all the pots, pans, kettles, and vessels of every kind are turned upside down in order to prevent its taking refuge in one of them, and subsequently troubling the family. The corpse is laid upon a double mattress between sheets, and completely dressed in its holiday costume, including shoes and stockings. A pillow of homespun linen or cotton is filled with handfuls of earth by all the persons present, and placed under the head. The head is decked with fresh flowers, an *eikon* is laid on the breast, and also a plate with flowers and candles, placed there by persons who wish the dead by these means to carry messages to other lost friends.

When all the preparations are complete, the priest arrives to read part of the burial service, after which the women, watching round the body, chant dirges through the night, and until the clergy arrive on the following morning to conduct the dead to his last resting-place. An ox or buffalo cart is brought to the door, and in this primitive hearse the corpse is conveyed to the church where the funeral Mass is to be performed. At the grave a barrel of wine is broached, and boiled wheat and small loaves are distributed to all present, who, as they receive these funeral cates, ejaculate *Bogda prosti* ("God have mercy"). The gala costume is taken off, oil and wine are sprinkled on the body, which, wrapped in a shroud, is finally replaced in the coffin, and lowered into the grave.

Returning to the house of mourning, the company wash their hands over the fire, and three days afterwards every article in the house is washed, or sprinkled with water, and exposed to the air for three days. Any household goods which cannot be so purified are sold or given away. On the evening following the funeral, the relatives and friends of the deceased assemble at a great Death Feast, a similar ceremony being repeated ten days later. A widow visits the grave of her husband every day for forty days after burial, and throws water on it in order that he may not die of thirst. And so ineradicable are old pagan beliefs, notwithstanding centuries of professed Christianity, that after feasting on Palm Sunday at the grave, the relatives leave there some of the food and wine, in the belief that the dead will partake of them during the night; and on Easter Monday a red egg is placed on every grave. Ceremonies similar to the *kólyva* of the Greeks, and called by the Bulgarians *Pominki*, or Commemorations, are held at the grave at intervals for three years, at the end of which time the body, if found to be sufficiently decomposed, is disinterred, with the same formalities observed by the Greeks.

CHAPTER XII.

BULGARIAN WOMEN: THEIR BELIEFS AND SUPERSTITIONS.

THE Bulgarian Church, originally a branch of the Orthodox Greek Church, had, in the thirteenth century, thrown off the supremacy of the Patriarch of Constantinople, and continued to exist independently until 1767, when it was once more brought under the jurisdiction of that See. The Bulgarian bishops were immediately replaced by Greeks, their monks sent adrift, and the revenues of the monasteries appropriated by the new clergy. The Greek was also substituted for the Bulgarian language in the services of the Church and in the schools, with the view of extinguishing the Panslavist spirit and substituting for it Pan-Hellenism. Such tyrannical action, though perforce submitted to for a time, was none the less resented by the Bulgarian nation. In 1858, a struggle for a free Church was commenced, which, after being maintained for fourteen years, finally resulted in the issue of an Imperial Firman, releasing the Bulgarians from the spiritual supremacy of the Greeks, and empowering them to elect a religious chief of their own. The dogmas of the Bulgarian Church are consequently precisely similar to those of the Greek, and its fast and feast days are also identical.

The dogmas and precepts of Christianity are, however, things not dreamed of in the philosophy of the lower classes; and to the Bulgarians, as to the members of the sister Church, religion is not a spiritual, but a practical matter, and consists in the superstitious observances connected with periods of penance and festivals of saints, and the other outward forms ordained by the Church and by custom. All these various events of the ecclesiastical year are so inextricably mixed up with fragments and relics of old pagan beliefs and customs, that the lower clergy, being as ignorant as their parishioners, cannot distinguish between *adets*, as these customary observances are called, and the religious beliefs actually professed by the National Church. The vaguest possible notions exist as to the immortality of the soul, and the life beyond the grave. Heaven, Hell, and Gehenna—the purgatory of the Greek Church—present no very distinct notions to their minds, and though a peasant woman may describe the first as the place where the saints and angels are, and the second as the abode of the demons, she will deny all practical belief that the souls of her departed relatives are either in bliss or torture, by following the pagan custom of leaving food and drink for them upon their tombs.

The long connection of the Bulgarian with the Greek Church naturally led to the assimilation of many of its superstitious beliefs and customs, but the paganism of the Bulgarians has remained, in its leading features, distinct from that of the Greeks. It is, in fact, a survival of the pantheistic worship of the ancient Slavs, which the invading Bulgarians adopted together with the language of the conquered people among whom they settled, and it teems with wild cosmogonic myths.

The festivals of the Bulgarians are, consequently, a curious fusion of old heathen rites with superstitious Christian observances. Owing to the great number of holidays enforced by the Eastern Church, the Anniversaries of the Saints, which have replaced the heathen Gods and the Feasts of Nature, often coincide in date, and are simultaneously celebrated with a strange admixture of Christian and heathen ceremonies.

The year opens during the feast of the winter solstice, called by the Bulgarians *Kulada*. Like the Hallowe'en of Scotland, it is a great time among the girls for all kinds of divinatory rites respecting their future spouses, and to every line or verse of songs sung during this festive period is added the refrain of *Hey Kulada moy Kulada*. The elementary spirits or demons are, at this season, supposed to be especially alert and powerful against mankind, and the Bulgarians, like the inhabitants of Asia Minor during the similar observance of the *Fishoti*,[1] consider it necessary to take every precaution against their malevolence. A log of wood is carefully left in every cart, and some water in every pitcher, in order to prevent any demon's taking possession of them, and by his presence rendering them too heavy to draw, or lift.[2]

[1] See Chap. III.
[2] Mr. Stuart Glennie informs me that, at Braemar, in the Scottish Highlands, one of the "pliskies" or rather "ploys" of the young men on Hallowe'en, of which he has been himself a witness, is secretly to make off

On the feast of St. Demetrios, these supernatural beings threaten the domestic animals, and are exorcised by the placing of lighted tapers in the stables and cattle-sheds, and in the place where firewood is chopped.

The 13th of January is called the *Baboudien*, or "Matron's Day," when the married women celebrate a kind of saturnalia, and, according to some accounts, indulge pretty freely in wine on the occasion.[1]

Lent is most rigorously observed by the Bulgarians, who pursue their usual avocations on a meagre diet of bread, onions, garlic, and vegetable soup. The first day of the second week of this period of penance is observed as the Day of the Dead (*Dusz Nitza*), or All Souls' Day, when the women go from house to house carrying lighted candles.

The month of March is called by the Bulgarians *Baba Mart*, or "Mother March," and is the only female month of the year. During this period the women are allowed to assert a kind of temporary supremacy over their husbands, and to be as idle as they choose. They accordingly, in order to propitiate Baba Mart, abstain from washing, weaving, and spinning, and even from "pipe-claying" the floors of their houses, a task usually performed once a week;

with and hide as many as possible of the carts and other vehicles of the farmers; and he suggests that the "spunkies" may thus be keeping up a practice formerly attributed to unpropitiated spirits.

[1] Mrs. Blunt, whose long residence in various districts inhabited by Bulgarians enabled her to form a correct judgment on the manners of the natives, says that Uskup was the only place where she observed a tendency on the part of the women to make use of wine or spirits; and even here it was only in the privacy of their own homes, for, in the East, women do not frequent the *cafés*, or wine-shops.

for, were they to perform any of these domestic duties, the goddess would give no rain during the rest of the year, but send instead lightning to destroy the house. The 25th day of March, on which the "Mother" is specially honoured, is called the Blagostina, and its observance and that of St. Constantine's day, with which it coincides, are curiously mixed up. It is most probably a survival of the feast of the Vernal Equinox.

Though this festival occurs during Lent, when both fish and oil are forbidden by the Greek Church, the Bulgarians partake of both; and they explain the exception in favour of the former by the following well-known legend, in which the titular saint seems to be curiously confounded with Constantine Palæológos. According to the Bulgarian version of the story, the Byzantine Emperor was, on the last day of the siege of Constantinople, frying fish in his palace, in front of which was a pond, when terrified messengers came to announce that the Turks were mounting the breach, and that the city would soon be taken. The Emperor refused to admit the possibility of such an event. "The Turks," said he, "will no more take the city than these fried fish will jump into the pond!" As he spoke, the fish leapt from the pan into the water, all cooked as they were, and have swum in the pond ever since. Why this should entitle the Bulgarians to an "indulgence" on the day of the Blagostina is, however, not very clear. According to the peasants, this day is a great feast for all creation, and on it even the swallows and bees abstain from labour, in celebration of the re-birth of Nature. It is also the Feast of Serpents, which now come out of their holes, and are sure to bite during the coming year any who profane their Sabbath day with manual toil. In the evening three large bonfires are lighted, round one of which dance the young people; the matrons form a circle round the second; while round the third the men gather for their potations; and all three parties enliven their proceedings with song.

On St. George's Day, the Bulgarians make a sacrifice of lambs, and relate as their reason for this practice the following curious legend, which seems to be of Moslem origin, and is evidently a compound of the story of Abraham's sacrifice and a legend concerning a Dervish Saint named Sari Saltik.[1]

One day the Almighty entered the house of a very poor man, and asked for some food. The man had neither lamb nor kid to set before him, but, in order to fulfil the sacred duty of hospitality, he took his little son, cut his throat, and put him into the oven. Presently the Lord, being hungry, asked if the food was cooked.

"It will soon be ready," replied the host.

"Open the door of the oven, and see if it be not ready."

The father opened the oven, and saw with astonishment that his son, instead of being roasted, was comfortably seated, and engaged in writing upon his knee in the Turkish fashion. The Almighty then

---

[1] This Moslem story, as told by Evlya Effendi, "The Traveller," bears also in some of its features a striking resemblance to the Greek legend of St. George.

commanded him in future to sacrifice a lamb on the anniversary of that day.

A Bulgarian folk-song, however, sung on St. George's Day, refers to Abraham by name. Unfortunately, I have not yet been able to procure this song, save in a fragmentary form.

St. John's Eve is observed in Bulgaria with the customary bonfires and other nocturnal commemorations of that universal solar festival.

On the Feast of the Assumption of the Virgin, sacrifices of lambs and kids are made, accompanied with offerings of wine, honey, cakes, &c., to one of the Saints. The Saint who is to be thus honoured is chosen by lot. Candles are lighted, in front of three *eikons*, and the candle first touched by a little child brought in for the purpose, decides which Saint is to preside. Each person present then drinks a cup of wine with the words, "Sphete [Saint] So-and-so, to thee is the offering!" The lambs or kids are now killed, and, if honey forms part of the offering, the bees are smothered. In the evening all the inhabitants of the village assemble to partake of the various sacrificial meats.

As will have been evident from the foregoing, Bulgarian mythology presents a considerable survival of the Nature-worship which was no doubt the primitive religion of this, as of the Greek and other races. The powers of Nature, however, as has been pointed out in the Introduction, are regarded in two ways. In what Mr. Stuart Glennie calls "the Zoönist folk-conception of Nature," animals, plants, mountains, and rivers are regarded as actuated by sentiments of sympathy with mankind. In what he distinguishes as the "Spiritist conception," or the conception of natural objects as but the abodes of supernatural beings, these beings are regarded for the most part as malevolently disposed, and they must either be propitiated or guarded against. These supernatural beings are believed to haunt not only the mountains, valleys, rivers, and springs, but even the habitations of human kind, and are endowed by popular imagination with powers and forms equally varied. Nereids, Lamias, Stoicheia, have been borrowed by the Bulgarians from their Greek neighbours and confounded with the Slav nymphs of antiquity; the Vilas, Samovilas, Samodivas, and Youdas; and the Drakos and Drakissa of the Greeks with the firebreathing *Zmok* and *Oyenik*, or Dragon. The Fates, whose duty it originally was to carry out the decrees of Destiny, have now come to represent in the popular mind that power itself, and are even sometimes confused with the Samodivas and Youdas.[1]

The relative degrees, however, of expression given to the Zoönist and the Spiritist conceptions of Nature probably vary greatly with different races. And the direct personification of natural objects appears to occupy but a small place in Bulgarian folk-poesy, and chiefly occurs with reference to the exploits of the Sun, who occasionally falls in love with a mortal maiden, and seeks to wed her. Though he is, in the Greek poems, represented as the ideal of manly beauty, he is by no means considered a desirable spouse. Indeed, it would appear, from popular expressions among all the

[1] See Chap. XIII.

Christian peoples of the East, that his glance is considered particularly pernicious to the beauty of maidens, and precautions are taken, especially about the time of the vernal equinox, that the "sun may not blacken us" (Νὰ μὴ μας μαύροσε ὁ Ἥλιος). In Roumania a tiny gold coin is worn for this purpose, tied round the wrist with parti-colored silk thread, apparently in order to attract the attention of his solar majesty from the wearer, as other charms are used to divert the Evil Eye to themselves. The expression, "a maiden whom the sun has never seen" (που δὲν τὴν βλέπει ὁ Ἥλιος), also occurs frequently in Greek folk-song. But besides the many supernatural creatures which the Bulgarians borrowed long ago from Slavs and Greeks, there exists a host of others to terrify timid folk. Most curious among these are the demons to whose touch such maladies as ague, paralysis, or even the nightmare, are attributed; and to exorcise them recourse is had to all kinds of spells and charms. Ghosts, however, as we understand the term, are, so far as I have been able to ascertain, non-existent, though, here and there, local apparitions may be met with which partake more or less of their shadowy character.

Among the superstitions adopted by the Bulgarians from their Turkish neighbours is the belief in buried treasure guarded by gigantic negroes or statuesque women, called *tellestim*, or "talismans." The tellestim is also a spirit created by the act of building or making. According to an Oriental belief, every object or building is possessed by such a spirit, which dies when its habitation is destroyed. The dispositions of the tellestims vary, it is said, according to the character of the beings whose shadows fall upon the foundation stone. Sometimes a lamb is sacrificed, in order that the tellestim may be mild and gentle in disposition; and a story is told of a stingy Bulgar who, having sacrificed a kid instead of a lamb, produced a jumping tellestim, whose antics made the house uninhabitable, and it had to be abandoned. The *ajins*, which haunt ancient ruins, are also, no doubt, analogous to the tellestims which came into existence at the time of their erection.

Although the Vampire is as much a Bulgarian as a Greek superstition, the propensities attributed to the *obour* by the Bulgarians differ from those attributed to the *katakhnas* by the Greeks. The favourite food of the *obour* is carrion, and his beverage the blood of sickly cattle; but, though he does not usually seize on human victims when coarser food is available, he is regarded with no less horror and dread than is the *katakhnas*, and the Bulgarian has fewer scruples than the Greek about the means he makes use of to put a stop to his wanderings.

A Bulgarian, like a Greek, may have inherited this post-mortem tendency to annoy his former neighbours as an *obour*, or may have otherwise acquired it, as, for instance, by having been strangled by another *obour*. This tendency can be detected by the person having only one nostril and also a sharp-pointed tooth. The vampire, however, according to the Bulgarian superstition, does not in the first instance leave his grave in bodily shape, but nine days after death assumes an aërial form. His presence in this condition is ascertained at night by the appearance of a number of sparks, and in the daytime by a shadow, the density of which varies according to his age as a vampire. In this stage he is comparatively harmless, and is able to cause annoyance only by various impish tricks, such as those attributed to the Teutonic Kobolds, the Irish Phooka, or the English Puck. He also "roars in a terrible voice," or amuses himself by calling persons out by name from their cottages, and then beating them black and blue. When the *obour* has passed forty days without being "laid," he becomes a full-fledged vampire, and may not only revisit the "glimpses of the moon" in his bodily shape, but also pass himself off as a human being, living honestly and naturally, going out at night only on his hideous errand.

The prayers of Christian priests and Moslem *hodjas* are equally resorted to against all these powers of darkness, and the village witch has also her special means of rendering them harmless to human beings. For in every Bulgarian, as in every Greek village and town, there is some old woman learned in all ancient customs and ceremonies of divination, and in the worship of all supernatural powers—whether anathematised, or winked at, by the parish clergy. She is also the possessor of an unlimited number of *marifets*, or charms, for all kinds of purposes, from that which will bring rain when the *papas'* prayers have failed to do so, to that which will drive away the demon of fever. This sorceress is able to cast spells which will cause the person against whom they are aimed to die the lingering death of the bewitched, or to cure him of the bite he has received from a Spirit of the Fountain, under the form of a cat. The witch is, indeed, the most important person in the village. She assists the Bulgarian at his entrance into and exit from the world; is not only the doctress and sorceress, but the high priestess at all the pagan festivals above described; and, while forming the complement of the *papas*, occasionally poaches even on his preserves.[1] When a witch is called in in her capacity of doctress, she first proceeds to ascertain the gravity of the disease, its nature being apparently of little importance. She produces a scarf or girdle several yards long, in which a knot has been tied, and, after some preliminary words of incantation, proceeds to measure it on the patient's arm, from the elbow to the finger tip. If the knot falls on the hand, the malady is but slight, or merely imaginary; if midway, it is serious; but if on, or near the elbow, it will prove fatal. As the wise-woman has acquired, from long experience, a certain practical knowledge of diseases, she no doubt occasionally succeeds in correctly diagnosing the case, and her wide acquaintance with the use of simples also enables her to prescribe an effectual remedy, the real efficacy of which is disguised under some accompanying incantation or other form of deception. For the witch is naturally not disposed to be communicative on the subject of her pharmacopœia; and, as she and her patients invariably attribute the malady to spells, or demons, she attri-

---

[1] St. Clair and Brophy, *The Eastern Question in Bulgaria*, p. 43.

butes their cure to the magical practices to which she has had recourse in their behalf.

Many of the antidotes used by the Bulgarians against the Evil Eye are similar to those used by their Christian and Moslem neighbours. The following are, however, I believe, peculiar to this nation:—Take six grains of salt, place them on the eyes of the afflicted person, and then cast them into the fire with a malediction against the person suspected of having caused the evil. Take three pieces of red-hot charcoal, place them in a green dish, and pour water over them with one hand while making over them with the other the sign of the Cross. Drink some of the water, wash your hands with the rest, and then throw it on the ground outside the house. On the last day of February (o.s.) take the heads of forty small fish, thread them on a string, and hang them up to dry. If a child has been affected by the Evil Eye, soak the heads in water and let him drink the decoction. The dried stomach of a stork is also esteemed a sovereign cure for this most prevalent of all maladies.

Among the other folk observances and beliefs affecting every-day life are the numerous *adets*, or customs, non-compliance with which is considered unlucky, or even sinful. These would form a very long list, but the following may serve as specimens:—It is unlucky to give a child a spoon to play with; to give away or sell a loaf without breaking off a piece; to bathe a child under seven years of age; to sell a sack of flour without first making a loaf from it; to clean a stable, sell milk, or fetch water after dusk, &c. &c. The flour must be fumigated with incense when it is brought from the mill —more especially if the miller be a Turk—in order to drive away any demon which may have entered into it; and before bringing into the house water from the fountain a small quantity from each jar or pail must be spilt on the ground, as some elementary spirit might otherwise be floating on the surface, and, not being thus thrown out, take up his abode in the house, or enter into the body of a person drinking the water. It is also a sin to give alms to a gipsy, Jew, or other "infidel,"[1] or to allow a dog to sleep on the roof of a house, as this disturbs the repose of deceased members of the family. On the first day of Lent, all the dogs of the village are caught, and receive a careful beating, to prevent their going mad during the year. This custom, as before mentioned, is observed by the Vlachs in all parts of Turkey. In order to rid the house of vermin, venomous insects, and snakes, the Bulgarian women, on the last day of February, beat copper pans all over the house, and call out at the same time, "Out with you, snakes, scorpions, flies, bugs, and fleas!" One of these pans is then taken up with a pair of tongs and carried into the courtyard, as if to induce the creatures mentioned to follow it. An attempt is also made to get rid of the two last-named insects, which are the domestic pests *par excellence* of Turkey, by enclosing a few in a reed and handing it to the butcher, with the words, "Here is flesh and blood for you. Take it, and give

[1] A similar superstition exists among Moslems.

us something better in exchange!" As all natives unfortunately rest content with some such feeble attempts to clear their houses of this "small game," it is not surprising that it constitutes, in every part of the country alike, one of the greatest drawbacks to travel or residence.

CHAPTER XIII.

BULGARIAN WOMEN: THEIR FOLK-POESY.

THE Bulgarian language, as spoken and sung by the people, is as far from being identical with that used in books and journals as is the language of Greek folk song and story with the polished literary tongue of Athens. The Slavonic of the popular tongue contains a large admixture of Turkish and Persian, and also of Italian, Greek, and other European words. One of the peculiarities which it presents is, that not only Turkish adjectives and substantives, but also Turkish verbs, are largely made use of, and verbs of purely Slavonic origin are declined with Turkish inflexions of mood and tense. The old Bulgarian language was merely a spoken vernacular, and, as before mentioned, it is only within the present century that efforts have been made to give it a literary form in printed books, which are not, however, much "understanded of the people."

Bulgarian historical traditions, except in the form of songs, are not numerous, and strangely confound comparatively modern Bulgarian or Servian heroes with those belonging to more mythical periods. Kral (King), or Deli,[1] Marko is the favourite hero,

---

[1] A Turkish word, meaning literally "mad," but used in a complimentary sense, signifying excess of bravery.

and he figures in no fewer than twenty-one of the popular songs collected by the brothers Miladinov. The following tale of his encounter with, and discomfiture by, the Devil, at once recalls, if we substitute Loki for this Christian genius of evil, one of the best known of the Norse stories of the heroes of Asgard:—

"Once upon a time the world was peopled only by Heroes and *Zméï*,[1] and of all the heroes Kral Marko was by far the strongest and most famous. One day the Devil was amusing himself with his great mace of wood, bound with iron, which weighed a hundred *okas*,[2] throwing it up in the air and catching it again in one hand. Deli Marko found him thus employed, and wished him 'good morning' (*Dobra déni*) very politely.

"'You are welcome!' (*Hosh geldin*), replied his majesty.

"'Well found!' (*Hosh boldouk*), responded the hero.

"When these usual compliments and greetings had been interchanged, Deli Marko asked the Devil what he was doing there.

"'Don't you see?' was the reply; 'I am practising for the championship' (*Pehlivanlik*).

"'Let us have a bout together,' suggested Deli Marko.

"'With all my heart,' responded the Devil. 'Go and take your place.'

"Satan hurled his mace a hundred yards, but the hero caught it in the air like a ball.

[1] Dragons, plural of *Zmok*.
[2] An *oka*, the standard measure for both liquids and solids, used throughout Turkey, consists of 300 drachmas, or two pounds and three-quarters English.

"'Bravo!' exclaimed his opponent. 'Now it's your turn—throw the mace for me to catch.'

"But Marko let the Devil's mace lie on the ground, and took up his own, which was also of wood and iron, and weighed three hundred *okas*.[1] This he pitched with a good swing, and the poor Devil, trying to catch it, was knocked down, and a good deal bruised. Deli Marko then took up the mace of his unlucky rival and threw it up to the sky, where it stuck, and he walked away whistling.

"The Devil went back to his own dominions, very sore both in body and mind, and set about forging an iron tube, which he loaded with a little dust from the infernal smithy, and a leaden bullet. When these were ready, he appeared on earth again, and called upon Deli Marko.

"'Dobra deni, Deli Marko.'

"'Hosh geldin!'"

"'Hosh boldouk! Come, Deli Marko; you beat me the other day, and you caught my mace, which weighed a hundred *okas*. Do you think that you can catch this little ball, which weighs only two *drachmas*?'

"'There's my hand,' said Deli Marko, laughing disdainfully. 'Throw your little ball, and let's see whether I can't catch it.'

"Then the Devil took his tube, lit the powder, and the bullet struck Deli Marko in the palm, and passed completely through it. The Kral looked sadly at the wound, and sighed out, 'Now that guns are invented, the earth is no longer a place for heroes!'"

[1] 825 lbs.

And as there happened to be a *Zmok* passing, he called him up, got on his back, and flew away for ever. The same day all the other Heroes followed his example, and that is the reason there are no longer either Heroes or Dragons to be found in the country."[1]

The story of Yanko, Johnny the Wrestler,[2] which exists in ballad form, would appear to be much older, and his gastronomic exploits certainly equal those of the heroes of Scandinavian mythology. As I have not been able to meet with the words or ascertain the metre of the original, I will not attempt to give it in verse form.

Yanko Krym Pehlivanko.

Yanko the Wrestler said to his mother, " O my mother, my reputation is declining! So tell the furrier to make me a *kalpak* [fur cap] of nine wolf-skins, and let the tenth be the skin of a bear."

And she goes, the mother of Johnny, to the furrier, that he may make the kalpak of the nine wolf-skins, and the tenth the skin of a bear.

Yanko the Wrestler again to his mother says : " I am going to the furrier that he may make me a pair of breeches for wrestling. For a firman from the Czar[3] is come to me, and commands me to wrestle

---

[1] St. Clair and Brophy, *The Eastern Question,* &c., p. 56.

[2] Wrestling was formerly the great diversion in Turkey among all races, and is still a favourite manly exercise in the East generally. A wrestler is called *Pehlivan,* and the above is merely a diminutive for this word. Yanko is evidently, though not described as such, that popular Oriental hero, a " widow's son."

[3] Probably some Byzantine Cæsar.

with his Pehlivans, and I am going to wrestle with the Pehlivans of the Czar, who are blood-thirsty bears."

And his mother says to Yanko: "Ah! go not, my son! Nine Pehlivans have gone to the Czar, and all the nine were eaten by the bears!"

But Yanko answers his mother: "Open the Hungarian chest, and find me a handsome suit of clothes that I may set out to go to the Czar, and fight his bears, so that his bears kill me not, and I be not ashamed before the Czar." And to his mother Yanko also says: "Bake me nine ovenfuls of bread, and kill me nine fat cows, and broach for me nine barrels of wine." And Yanko eats the nine ovenfuls of bread, and eats the nine fat cows, and drinks the nine barrels of wine, and now he will set out for the Czar's to wrestle.

When Yanko arrives at the Czar's, the Czar sends his black *Chenguin* (gipsy) to announce the combat by sound of trumpet. And he cries and proclaims for three days and nights: "Let great and small assemble in the fields or on the tumuli,[1] for a great wrestling-match will take place between Yanko Krym Pehlivanko and the blood-thirsty bear of the Czar!"

And, great and small, they assemble in the fields and on the tumuli, and the regiment of black gipsies too is there. And nine black men guard with the curved steel, and nine conduct with chains of steel, the terrible bear. And the chains are loosed, and the bear utters a cry. At this cry the earth trembles and the sky thunders.

Yanko the Wrestler was afraid when he saw this

[1] Tumuli or barrows exist in great numbers in European Turkey.

bear. But he hid his fears from the Czar, that the Czar might not laugh at him.

So they catch hold of one another—the bear of blood and Yanko Krym Pehlivanko. Three days and nights they wrestle, but neither the bear nor Yanko falls. Where Yanko grips, the black blood flows; where the bear grips, the white flesh flies. Three days and nights they wrestle, but neither Yanko is thrown nor is the bear thrown.

The Czar says to Yanko: "I see how it will be, Yanko Krym Pehlivanko! Thou wilt die of thy wounds, but my bear will live!"

At this Yanko the Wrestler is very angry. He takes a good grip of the bear, lifts him up to the blue sky, and dashes him against the earth, and in four he breaks him, and the four pieces bury themselves in four holes in the ground. Then the Czar was afraid of Yanko Krym Pehlivanko, and said: "In future, Yanko, if you kill a man, you are absolved beforehand from the guilt of murder." And he commands his black regiment: "Bring hither to Yanko Krym Pehlivanko nine heavy mule-loads of gold as a *bakshish* for Yanko."

And directly the nine heavy mule-loads were brought as a *bakshish* to Yanko, and were given to Yanko Krym Pehlivanko. And he goes off and arrives at his dearly loved mother's, and he calls to her, "Come down, mother, and take these nine heavy mule-loads of gold!" and the mother of Yanko comes down, and she sees the nine loads of gold. "*Brĕ!*"[1] she exclaims. "Yanko, thou hast not been to the

---

[1] A Turkish word, here indicating astonishment.

Czar to wrestle, but thou hast been at some *hăĭdout-lĭk* [plundering exploit], and thou hast robbed the Czar of these nine heavy mule-loads of gold!"

"The Czar gave them to me, mother," he replies; "and, more than that, he has allowed me to kill any man I choose; such is the permission that he has given to Yanko Krym Pehlivanko—that is to say, to me!"

Rhyme is absolutely non-existent in Bulgarian poetry, versification being founded on the number of syllables and on the accent, which is the same as in the spoken language. The number of syllables contained in a line range in number from four to fourteen, but the metre most commonly used contains either eight or ten syllables, divided either after the fourth or after the fifth syllable. The latter, divided into two equal hemistyches, is most generally used in Macedonia, and presents the fewest irregularities. The versification of Bulgarian folk-songs, unlike the Greek and the Servian, is, however, extremely irregular, and offers, in Macedonia especially, a strange mixture of metres. M. Dozon suggests that this may be accounted for by the fact that the women, who are to a great extent the composers and transmitters of the songs, know little of, and care less for, metrical regularity. This might, however, be said with equal truth of the composers and transmitters of Greek folk-songs.

But, whatever the literary quality of Bulgarian popular songs, there is certainly no lack of quantity, and in their infinite variety they illustrate every phase of domestic life and mythological belief.

Many of them serve as an accompaniment to the dance.

With us Dancing songs have completely disappeared, save as an accompaniment to children's games. But among the peoples of the East, who live under a different social system, they have remained the national diversion *par excellence*, and the national poetry is taught in the school of the dance. The wealth of Bulgarian folk-poesy is proved by the voluminous collections made by native folk-lorists, who have naturally found the women to be its chief depositaries. The brothers Miladinov have included in their volume no fewer than 674 pieces; and that of M. Verkovich contains 335, though this is but a small portion of what he collected. Two hundred and seventy-five of these were from the lips of one woman, Dafina of Serres; and the brothers Miladinov obtained 150 from a young girl of Strouga. "When one has written down so many songs," they say, "one supposes the supply exhausted; and yet it is only necessary to pass to a neighbouring quarter to find a mine equally fruitful."[1]

National talent in the direction of original composition seems, however, to have almost died out, for modern efforts take chiefly the form of satirical couplets and burlesques founded on incidents of every-day life. Although some of the love-songs breathe sentiments of a pure and tender character, there is an element of brutality in those—and especially the more ancient ones—treating of married life. The woman, for example, whose misfortune it is to be childless, or to

[1] Dozon, *Chansons Populaires Bulgares*, Preface.

be the mother only of girls, is despised and ill-treated, or even, like the wife of Momir, threatened with mutilation. The ballad in which this is described also illustrates so many curious phases of folk-belief that it cannot, I think, but be found interesting even in the very abridged form in which it is given by M. Dozon.[1]

The young wife of Momir had nine girls, one after the other. When she was expecting the advent of her tenth child, the Voïvode, Momir Bey, said to her: "Little wife, little wife of Momir, if thou givest me another girl, I will cut off thy legs by the knee and thy arms by the shoulder; I will put out thine eyes, and thou wilt remain a young prisoner; thou wilt remain a cripple." When the time drew near for the birth of her baby, the mother took with her Todora, her youngest daughter, and went out into the greenwood, where she sat down under a leafy sycamore-tree. There the baby was born. But it was not a tenth girl, but a lusty boy. So bitterly does he cry that the leaves fall from the tree. The young Momiritza looks around her, and, perceiving a fire on the mountain side, she sends her little Todora for a light from it. Lambent flames envelop the new-born infant, and warm it. The young Momiritza sleeps. The three Fates appear. But Todora does not sleep; she watches, and hearkens to the words of the Fates. The first says, "Let us take the child." The second says, "Let us not take him till he is older, till he is seven years old." The third says, "Let him grow up; let him become a young man fit to marry; they

[1] *Chansons Populaires Bulgares*, p. 331.

will affiance him to a beautiful girl, and let him take her; when they are going to church, we will carry off the young man." Upon this they disappeared.

Everything happened as had been predicted. The boy grew to a youth, and the youth to a man. When his marriage day was near, Todora related to her mother the words of the *Youdas*, and informed her of her resolution to cheat them of her brother. Her ruse, which, strange to say, succeeded, was to personate her brother at the wedding, dressed in his clothes. The bridal party repaired to church, when there arose tempestuous winds, clouds, and thick dust, followed by a blinding snow-storm. On the wings of the hurricane came the Youdas; they seized the supposed bridegroom, and carried him off to the clouds. *What has happened is irrevocable.*

In the conclusion of this song is illustrated a peculiarity of sentiment found among the Slavs and other Eastern nationalities, and also in the Teutonic mythology. This is the extreme solicitude evinced by women for the welfare of their brothers, who appear to occupy in their affections a much higher place than their husbands.

The meteorological disturbances above referred to are often represented as the *Youdas*, or Fates, themselves; for, in another song, the *Samodiva*, struggling with a mortal youth, thus calls them to her aid:

> Tempests, elements, my sisters!
> Stoïan now prevails against me!
> And the elements came lowering,
> And the whirlwinds wildly whistled;

> From the earth they carried Stoïan
> High upon a branch they hung him.

In the following folk-song the Samodiva closely resembles the Greek Lamia in allowing herself to be married to a mortal, and also in her professed inability to perform any housewifely function. The incident of stealing the magic dresses I have, I think, met with in Keltic stories, but the introduction of St. John as best man and godfather is, so far as I know, peculiar to the Bulgarian variant.

THE SAMODIVA MARRIED AGAINST HER WILL.[1]

> Stoïan led his flocks to pasture
> In the haunts of Samodivas,
> Where they dance, and play the reed-flute.
> There had met three Samodivas,
> And in merry round were dancing;
> Danced they gaily, and, when wearied,
> Upward soared, and lightly floated
> Far above the dark-green fir-trees,
> Where the forest fountains bubble;
> Far above the flowering meadows.
> Down on the green plain they 'lighted,
> They would bathe them in the river.
> So they doff their dainty dresses,
> And their golden-bordered kerchiefs.
> Doff, too, their green virgin-girdles,
> And their Samodivas' bodice.
> Stoïan drove his flock before him
> Down the hill-slopes to the valley;
> He surprised the Samodivas,
> And he stole away their dresses.
> Came the fair ones from the water,
> Not a thread of clothes among them;
> And all three did pray of Stoïan:

[1] *Chansons Populaires Bulgares*, No. 4.

"Stoïan, O thou youthful shepherd,
Give us back our clothes, O Stoïan!
Give us back our magic dresses!"
Not a thing would Stoïan give them.
Then the eldest thus conjured him:
"Give me back my dress, O Stoïan,
For I have but a step-mother,
A step-mother who would kill me."
Stoïan made to her no answer;
Back to her her clothes he rendered.
Then the second said to Stoïan:
"Give me back my raiment, Stoïan,
For I have at home nine brothers
Who would kill thee, who would kill me."
Not a word to her said Stoïan,
But he gave her back her garments.
Spake the third one then, Marika;
Thus and thus she said to Stoïan:
"Give me back, Stoïan, my garments,
Give me back my magic raiment;
I'm my mother's only darling,
I'm to her both son and daughter.
Hear my words, O Stoïan; seek not
For thy wife a Samodiva—
Samodivas are not thrifty,
Know not how to tend the children."
Gently then to her says Stoïan:
"Such an one have I been seeking,
Who's her mother's only daughter."
To his own abode he took her,
Dressed her in the garb of mortals;
Wedded too the Samodiva,
With St. John to be the best man.
Full three years they'd lived together,
When was born a son to Stoïan,
Who St. John had for his sponsor.[1]

---

[1] With the Bulgarians, as with the Greeks, the "best man" at a wedding becomes the godfather of the children of the marriage.

When the christening was ended,
Every one sat down and feasted.
Good St. John then took a fancy,
And he turned and said to Stoïan:
"Stoïánë, *kymtche*,[1] Stoïánë,
Play for me upon thy *gaida*;[2]
Dance thou, dance thou, my *kymítza*,[3]
The gay dance of Samodivas."
Stoïan played upon his *gaida*,
And began to dance Marika,
But she danced the mortals' *hora*.
Said St. John: "My dear *kymítza*,
Why dost thou not dance, Marika,
In the Samodiva fashion?"
"Good St. John, my worthy *kymtche*,
Ask, I beg of thee, my husband
That he give me back my raiment,
My own Samodiva garments,
Else I cannot dance their measure."
Stoïan let St. John persuade him,
For he deemed not she would leave him,—
Was she not his young son's mother?—
So he gave her back her garments.
Then Marika pirouetted,
Up the chimney swift ascended,
On the roof she poised a moment,
Whistled, Samodiva fashion,
Turned, and thus addressed poor Stoïan:
"Said I not to thee, O Stoïan,
Samodivas are not housewives?"
And she clapped her hands together,
Sprang aloft, and far she sailed
To the deep, green forests lonely,
To the haunts of Samodivas.

---

[1] The relationship between a sponsor and his godchild's father, for which we have, I believe, no equivalent in English: see p. 71, σύντεχνος.

[2] The Bulgarian bagpipes

[3] Diminutive of *kyma*, feminine of *kymtche*.

> Bathed she in the virgins' fountain,
> And, become once more a virgin,[1]
> Wended homeward to her mother.

In the following song a class of spell aimed at the powers of Nature is evidently indicated. A similar power of commanding the elements was formerly, and is indeed at the present day, attributed to the Lapp magicians, both male and female, and possibly indicates such a partial community of race as is suggested for them in the Introduction. Shakespeare's witches, too, laid claim to power over the elements.

RADA CARRIED OFF BY A DRAGON.[2]

> Rada went to fetch some water
> From the Fountain of the Dragons.
> As she homeward was returning,
> On the way she met two Dragons,
> Two fierce Dragons, flaming creatures.[3]
> One goes by and harms not Rada,
> But the younger stops fair Rada,
> Slakes his thirst from out her pitcher.
> Then he Rada thus addresses:
> "Rada, Rada mine, my dearest,
> Every eve you've come to see me
> You have brought a brighter posy
> Than the one you bring this evening."[4]

---

[1] The Greek Nereids possess also this privilege: "ἀναλαμβάνουσι λουόμεναι τὴν παρθενίαν τῶν."—POLITES, Μελέτη ἐπὶ τον βίου τῶν νεώτερων ἑλλήνων, 1871.

[2] Dozon, *Chansons Populaires Bulgares*, No. 8.

[3] *Ognenik*, a word derived from *ogœn*, fire, and consequently not identical with the monster called Δράκος in the Greek folk songs and stories, and rendered by some translators "dragon." See Dozon, as above.

[4] Referring probably to the offerings it is customary to make to the genius of the fountain before taking water from it.

Rada answered thus the Dragon:
" Dragon, Dragon, flaming creature,
Let me go my way, O Dragon!
Sick in bed my mother's lying,
Sorely does she pine for water."
Said the Dragon unto Rada:
" Rada, beautiful and youthful,
You may lie to any other,
But you'll not deceive a Dragon,
Soaring in aërial regions,
With keen eye the ether piercing.
I've just passed above your cottage.
There I saw thy mother sitting,
Thy wise mother, the enchantress.
She for thee did sew a garment,
To it divers herbs she fastened,
All the herbs which love do hinder,
Souls divide, and hatred kindle.
So that I may hate thee, Rada,
She has witched the woods and waters;
She has ta'en a living serpent,
In a cauldron new she's placed it,
Fire of thistles white she's lighted.
In the cauldron writhed the serpent,
Writhed and hissed he in his fury
While her spells thy mother chanted:
' As this serpent writhes in torture,
For the love they bear to Rada
Thus may writhe both Turks and Bulgars,
And the fiery Dragon hate thee,
So the Dragon, hating, leave thee.'
Since her spell has not availed,
Hence with me I now will bear you."
Hardly had the Dragon spoken
Than he seized upon the maiden,
Bore her up unto the welkin,
Bore her to the mountain summits,
Hid her in the darksome caverns.

The next song appears to open with a spell pronounced by the maiden's mother on the Sun before sending her to the fountain.

THE SUN BEWITCHED.[1]

"My two sorrows, griefs accursed,
Change yourselves to two dark storm-clouds,
Wing your way to highest heaven,
Bear with you the dust in whirlwinds,
Veil the moon's rays, veil the sunshine!"
Radka goes to fill her pitcher,
And the bright Sun comes to meet her.
Says the Sun, the Sun to Radka:
"Radka, thou bewitching maiden,
Would that God would slay thy mother,
Slay thy mother, the enchantress!
On the Sun has she cast magic.
Sun and Moon has she enchanted,
Forest wide, and fresh green herbage,
Witched the earth, and witched the water.
She has taken writhing serpents,
And with a white thorn transpierced them,
While she sang this incantation:
'As I pierce these writhing serpents,
So may youths transpierce their bosoms
For the sake of lovely Radka!'"

The idea contained in the following quaint little song would seem to be a reversal of the usual practices of the Samodivas in the presence of the infant Christ. As before mentioned, the visits of these nymphs to infants are considered particularly baneful, and are specially guarded against. In this case, however, not only are they powerless to do Jesus

[1] Dozon, *Chansons Populaires Bulgares*, No. 12.

harm, but for his service they perform acts utterly foreign to their nature. On the other hand, it may be that the *Naretchnítzas*, or Fates, are indicated under the name of Samodivas.

CHRIST AND THE SAMODIVAS.[1]

Shine, O Sun, thou little Moon, shine,
Light ye up the woods and mountains;
In the woods there is a convent,
Dedicate to St. Elias.
There's a cell within the convent,
And within the cell is Mary,
She who is of Christ the mother.
After that her Son was cradled,
Three days only she awaited
Ere she went forth from her dwelling,
On a golden shovel leant her,[2]
Silken swaddling bands to bring him.
To her babe when she returned,
Who beside him found she sitting?
In a row there sat three women,
Women who were Samodivas.
One for him a shirt was sewing,
One was knitting him a bandage,
One with coins did deck his bonnet.[3]

In the domestic songs we find not only step-mothers and step-daughters on the best terms with each other, but also daughters, mothers, and sisters-in-law giving mutual sympathy and counsel. Penka, the ex-brigandess, is an illustration of the *haidout*

---

[1] Dozon, *Chansons Populaires Bulgares*, No. 6.
[2] Referring to the Bulgarian custom described above.
[3] Against the evil eye?

women mentioned in a previous chapter as having accompanied their husbands or brothers to the mountain; though love of adventure, rather than necessity, seems to have been this heroine's incentive to don "manly garments."

PENKA'S ADIEU TO HER BRIGAND LIFE.[1]

Thus to Penka spoke her mother:
"Penka, treasure of thy mother,
Though but thy step-mother am I,
Yet I'd give to thee good counsel.
When the day comes for thy wedding,
When thou leadest the procession,
Bow thyself before thy sponsors,
And salute thy husband's parents,
Bow before his youngest sister,
Bow before his youngest brother.
See that thou thine eyelids raise not,
See thou look not to the mountains,
Lest the *svátobi*[2] imagine
Thou hast walked the hills a brigand."
To her mother answered Penka:
"I of thee would ask a favour—
Ask it also of my father,
That he give to me a tocher,
Give me back my manly garments,
Give me, too, my pair of pistols,
My own sabre bright Frank-fashioned,
And my good, long-barreled rifle.
Once again as man I'd wander,
Were't but two or three days, mother,
Were it but a few hours only.
Once more to the hills I'd hie me,

---

[1] *Chansons Populaires Bulgares*, No. 18.
[2] Plural of *sváti*, a matchmaker or go-between.

> To the balkan [1] with the brigands.
> There the gallant ones await me.
> 'Neath each tree there stands a hero,
> And a standard in each valley."[2]
> Scarce had Penka finished speaking,
> When she donned her manly garments;
> Pistols two she girded round her,
> And her bright, sharp sword, Frank-fashioned.
> To the stable dark she hastened,
> Straight let out the well-fed courser,
> On his back she girthed the saddle;
> Penka to the hills betook her,
> To the mountain of the brigands,
> Bearing presents to the heroes.
> To each one she gives a kerchief,
> Folded round a golden sequin,
> To remind her ancient comrades
> Of the day when Penka wedded.

The method of winning back a faithless lover advised by Nedka's sister-in-law, in another song, is also recommended to a deserted wife by her mother-in-law. The latter tells her son's wife, who has been too much occupied with household duties to be able to pay attention to her personal appearance, to put on her gala dress, and to ornament her head, neck, and waist with a few pounds weight of silver jewellery, and so to regain her faithless husband's affections.

[1] *Balkan* signifies literally "mountain."
[2] These two lines recall the Greek klephtic song:
  "For I have forty-two high peaks, and sixty-two fresh fountains,
  And every peak a standard bears, and every branch a klephtë."
  PASSOW, *Carmina*, &c., 131.

THERE'S BUT NÍKO IN THE WORLD.[1]

"Sister Neda, husband's sister,
Mother has convened a 'bee';[2]
She has also bidden thee;
Twice to thy home has she gone,
So that thou may'st surely come,
And thy people with thee bring—
Bring thy parents to the bee."
To her sister Neda said :
" Brother's wife, dear brother's wife,
I before thee am ashamed ;
I am shamed, yet will I tell
Unto thee my sore distress.
For Nikólas is betrothed—
Yea, Nikólas, my first love—
Unto Stancha, down below.
It is not that she is fair,
Nor that she industrious is ;
But that she is blithe and gay.
Heartily she greets the youths,
And a table for them spreads,
Where she bids them eat and drink.
Dear is Níko still to me—
Five years we've each other loved ;
Dear is Níko still to me ;
To the bee how can I go ?
All the girls will laugh and say,
' They who love are not betrothed ! ' "
" Husband's sister, sister dear,
Do not be distressed at this.
Bathe thyself—I'll comb thy hair ;
Put thou on thy gayest dress,
Tie thy kerchief 'neath thy chin,

---

[1] *Chansons Populaires Bulgares*, No. 69.

[2] This Americanism perhaps expresses better than any other word a practice resorted to in Bulgaria and in some of the United States, when a number of hands are required to accomplish quickly some necessary household, or field work.

> On thy head wreathe brightest flowers.
> Take thy coloured distaff, too,
> Bind around it whitest flax.
> Come, and I will with thee go!
> When unto the bee we come,
> Pass, my sister, 'fore the girls,
> Like a wether 'fore the flock;
> Sit thou, sister, 'mid the girls,
> Like the moon amid the stars.
> Call and sing, yea, loudly sing,
> Like two voices from one throat;
> For, as you have lovers been,
> There's but Níko in the world."

The next piece, which may serve as a specimen of Bulgarian comic song, shows the independent spirit often displayed by the Bulgarian women, but at the same time illustrates the former insecure state of the country.

THE IDLE REAPERS.[1]

> They are going, going, gone,
> Five young wives, five brothers' wives:
> Going to cut the millet yellow.
> When unto the field they came,
> Said the eldest to the others:
> "Sisters, let us rest and sleep
> Till the sun's great heat be past,
> Till the cooling dew shall fall."
> Down they lay them, and they slept
> Till their father-in-law appeared
> With a waggon for the grain.
> Now they looked at one another,—
> What a scrape they all were in!
> Said the eldest of the sisters:
> "Open none of you your mouths;

---

[1] *Chansons Populaires Bulgares*, No. 81.

Leave the talking all to me."
When up comes the old papa,
Banteringly she him addresses:
" Hé! papa, you worn-out donkey,
Sowing fields so near the highway,
All day long have we been running,
Turks and Janissaries shunning,
Who have passed along the road!"

A warning to young wives not to neglect their personal appearance for the sake of household duties, would seem to be conveyed in the following song. The second bride had apparently no objection to replace a first wife who had lost her good looks, but declined to marry a man who had repudiated his former wife without what she deemed just cause.

THE TOILETTE; OR, THE HELPFUL STEP-MOTHER.

Marko thus said to Dafína:
" I, my dear, will now divorce thee,
For thou art not now so comely
As the day on which we wedded,
Nor when two years we'd been married."
Then to Marko said Dafína:
" My dear Marko, my dear Marko,
Do not cast me off, I pray thee;
Ever 'twas to me unpleasant
On the road to meet a widow,
Widowed, cast off by her husband.
But, my dear, bring hither rather
To our house the fair Todóra,
That she help me in my labour;
For 'tis more than I can manage.
Every day I heat five ovens,
Bread unleavened bake within them.
It is more than I can manage,

By myself to wash the linen.
If the washing I accomplish,
Then I leave undone the mending;
If, my dear, I do the mending,
Then I have not time to wash me;
If, my dear, I wait to wash me,
I can't plait my hair in tresses."
Marko yet would leave Dafína,
And he goes to take Todóra.
To the garden went Dafína,
There gave vent to bitter weeping.
"O, my flow'rets! O, my treasures!
Who did plant you where you're growing?
Who will, tell me, now transplant you?"
To Dafína said the mother:
"Daughter-in-law, my young Dafína,
Do not waste thy time in weeping.
Wash thyself, and I will comb thee;
I will plait thy hair in tresses,
On thy tresses I'll hang ducats.
Put thou on thy widest fringes,[1]
Cover thou thine arms with bracelets,
Dress thee, busk thee, in thy brightest,
Deck thyself in silk and woollen,
Deck thyself in gold and silver;
Then descend thou to the cellar,
Bring forth thence wine bright and ruddy,
Fill with it a yellow bottle;
Then go forth and meet the wedding."
As the mother bade, Dafína
Went to the *hammam* and bathed her;
Wove her hair in braids the mother,
On the tresses hung gold ducats.
Thus bedecked, in silk and woollen,
Forth she went to meet the wedding.
With his bride then came up Marko.
When Todóra saw Dafína,

---

[1] Part of the head-dress already described in Chap. X.

Thus she cried to her attendants:
"O ye bridesmaids, and ye bridesmen!
Ere I make the salutations,
And the numberless hand-kissings,[1]
I of you would ask a question:
Is that one the wife of Marko?—
She who's so exceeding handsome?—
Is she the divorced of Marko?
How, then, should he wish to wed me?—
Take me home again, I beg you."

---

[1] Referring to the custom already described (Chap. XI.) of the bride's kissing the hands of all the company on arriving at her husband's house.

CHAPTER XIV.

FRANK WOMEN; THEIR SOCIAL STATUS AND ACTIVITIES—FAMILY CEREMONIES—BELIEFS AND SUPERSTITIONS—AND FOLK-POESY.

As already mentioned in the Introduction, the women generally included under the designation of Franks, though descended chiefly from the Venetian and Genoese who settled in the country at different periods, have also in their veins the blood of nearly every European nation. Now, as at the time of the Turkish conquest, they chiefly occupy at Constantinople the quarter of Pera, and the so-called *Franko-mahallas*, or Frank quarters, of the principal cities and towns of the Empire. The Franks belong almost exclusively to the Roman Catholic Church, and their communities are generally clustered round the religious establishments—church, schools, orphanage, and hospital—of the Brothers of St. Benoît or the Lazarists, and the Sisters of the Order of St. Vincent de Paul. All live under the protection of the Consuls of one or other of the Great Powers, but belong to no country in particular, and in their utter want of national traditions, and consequently of national sentiment, form a striking contrast to the other native Christians. This community puzzled me greatly on first arriving in the country, as it no doubt has puzzled other strangers, for, on inquiring the nationality of many of the people I met at Smyrna, I was informed that they were Catholics. "Are they French, or Italian?" I would further ask. "Oh, neither," would be the reply; "they are not Europeans; they are only Catholics." So I gave it up, thinking that perhaps time and experience might solve the mystery of Frank nationality.

As might be expected of people who are "only Catholics," neither the social morality nor the intellectual culture of the Franks is of a very high order. Being strict Papists, marriage is, of course, with them indissoluble, but, at the same time, considerable laxity of manners may be, and often is, indulged in without loss of social position. Though the majority of the Franks belong to the mercantile and professional classes, the want of refinement in their conversation is very striking; indeed, the coarseness of expression indulged in by the Franks of Salonica in the presence of children and young people could hardly be outdone by the Turks, who make no pretension to calling a spade anything but a spade. The girls' schools and orphanages are conducted by the Sisters of St. Vincent de Paul; and though these excellent and devoted women are above all praise in their care of the sick and the poor, they are naturally, from the peculiarity of their position and training, little fitted to raise the tone and enlarge the ideas of the girls committed to their charge. Though instructed fairly well in modern languages and needlework, a Frank girl leaves the school in which she has passed the most important years of her youth imbued with the most illiberal and bigoted notions, and with interests and ideas restricted to the narrow limits of the conventual horizon. The female orphans, too, who are trained in these establishments mainly with the view of their obtaining employment in families as sewing-maids, though they are expert with their needles, do not, as a rule, prove satisfactory in other respects. For, as the punctilious performance of religious observances is generally substituted for a sound moral training, these girls, having no family ties, often become, when freed from conventual restrictions, very unsteady in their conduct, and consequently very troublesome in a household. On the other hand, they are encouraged by the Sisters to insist upon being allowed to attend the church services at all kinds of inconvenient hours. Under these circumstances, both Catholic and Protestant ladies are often unwilling to receive such servants into their houses. Indeed, one Frank-English lady, who had had considerable experience with servants of all nationalities, informed me that she had never known one of these convent-trained orphans to turn out well.

The foreign governesses, French, English, German, and Swiss, by whom the daughters of the wealthier members of this community are educated, can do little or nothing to counteract the effects of this early training and surrounding example, although they may impart a certain amount of outward polish to the manners of their pupils. The consequence of such a training is that the Frank women, though assiduous observers of all the outward forms of religion, good housewives, most devoted mothers, and charitable to the poor of their community, are, as a class—though, of course, there are exceptions—devoid of honourable feeling and true refinement, and have, for the most part, no ideas or interests beyond their immediate surroundings, while the staple of their conversation is mere personal gossip in its most contemptible form. Like most Orientals, they are polyglots, and are usually acquainted, more or less imperfectly, with French, Italian, and colloquial Greek and Turkish, according to locality. Their conversation, however, is generally carried on in a strange compound of the three first-named languages, in which the verbs, pronouns, and prepositions are chiefly Greek, the substantives French or Italian, and the adjectives from all three languages in turn. On asking a Frank lady one day how her daughter was getting on with her music, she replied, " Ο ἔκαμει *progrès*" (she has made progress). And one may, for instance, hear such exclamations from them as " Κύτταξε τή *verdura* τῆς *montagnas*, τί *magnifique* πού εναι!" (Look at the verdure of the mountain, how magnificent it is!)

In personal appearance, however, the Franks do not compare unfavourably with the other races of Turkey. They are usually elegant of figure, dark haired and dark eyed, with good complexions, and much vivacity of expression. Though many of the better class dress neatly and becomingly, an exaggeration of Parisian fashions is characteristic of Frank women generally; and it is said that, in order to meet native taste, a special style is designed every season by the French houses which supply the shops of Smyrna and Constantinople. The modest black dress and lace mantilla are, however, still worn to some extent by the Frank matrons as a church-going costume.

The Protestant section of the Frank community are chiefly of English and Scottish extraction, though Swiss and Dutch names are to be found among them. Some few families are descendants of members of the various Companies of "Merchants trading to the Levant," who established themselves in Turkey in the seventeenth and eighteenth centuries The remainder, though later arrivals, have been settled in the country for many generations. They number some hundreds in Constantinople and Smyrna, where they inhabit the Frank quarter and the suburban villages. The so-called English have, however, intermarried with other Protestant residents, and also to some extent with the Catholics, and with Greek and Armenian natives; and, their descendants having again intermarried, it would be difficult to determine what proportion of British blood flows in the veins of many of those who bear English or Scottish names. A few are entirely ignorant of English, while the majority of those who retain the use of this language speak it with a curious twang, in which the accent is laid chiefly on the prepositions: and they frequently interlard their conversation with idioms translated literally from other languages, and also with words and expressions of corrupt Modern Greek. Every sentence, too, especially at Smyrna, is prefaced by them with the word Καλή, which, though meaning literally "fine," or "good," is used as equivalent only to the English "I say."[1]

The Protestant girls at Smyrna are chiefly educated at the establishment of the German Deaconesses in the *Rue des Roses*, and by visiting masters and governesses. Some few are sent to school in England, but even these are seldom able to get rid of the habits contracted in their earlier girlhood, and, in spite of every educational advantage, the manners, conversation, and style of dress of the generality of these "English" ladies, especially at Smyrna, strike a stranger very oddly. Indeed, they struck me more particularly, I think, when, after an absence of a few years, I spent a day at Smyrna on my way back to Salonica. At Bournabat, where there is quite a little colony of these families, the ladies were—and, I suppose, are still—in the habit of going out walking without either hat or gloves, and, on their return, usually congregated outside the garden gates of the principal houses, which are all furnished for that purpose with seats of masonry covered with wood. Often, when going to pay a call, one would thus find the whole family in the road, and fulfil the social duty there. All the families are related and interrelated by marriage to a most complicated degree, and to this may perhaps be attributed the *sans géne* of manners and dress into which they have fallen. To such an extent is this occasionally carried, that I

---

[1] It has occurred to me that this ejaculation may be a local survival of the invocation of Artemis under her designation of 'Η Καλή—Ephesus, the ancient centre of the cult of this goddess, being only some thirty miles distant.

have known ladies belonging to the best families to present themselves at evening parties in cotton morning gowns and dressing jackets; and a wealthy lady of my acquaintance, who herself always went to church in a pair of native heelless slippers such as the Greek servants wear, sent her daughter to a ball in a printed muslin skirt and white "Garibaldi" jacket.

In winter the Smyrniote ladies pass a great deal of their time sitting at the *tandour,* an old-fashioned Turkish warming apparatus, which, though superseded elsewhere by American stoves, is still in great favour in this city. It consists of a four-legged, square deal table, with a shelf of the same size as the top, covered with tin, a few inches from the floor, on which stands a charcoal brazier. Over all is thrown a large quilt, which the ladies, sitting in the angle of the divan—found in every room in Turkey—draw over their knees and sometimes up to their shoulders. An amusing story is told at Bournabat *à propos* of this custom. An English traveller, arriving with introductions to one of the principal families there, was ushered into the marble-paved corridor, which, covered with a thick Turkey carpet in winter, is at all times a favourite sitting-room. Seeing his future hostess, with one of her daughters, reclining on the divan, and nearly hidden by the quilt, he fled precipitately, exclaiming to the son of the house, who had accompanied him from town, "Why, the ladies are in bed!"

The wives of many of our Consuls in the Levant belong to the above-described community, and when, as not unfrequently happens, these ladies add to their knowledge of native languages and manners a large amount of tact and intelligence, they are able to exert a very beneficial influence in the localities where their husbands are stationed. In Turkey, legal and other matters are usually settled by the method known as *hatir*—favour, or interest; and, though there may not be "one law for the rich and another for the poor," as in more "advanced" countries, there is no law at all for those who cannot afford to pay for it. Accordingly, the poor and oppressed who are unable to plead their own cause before the authorities, Moslem or Christian, have recourse to the good offices of the *Consulesa* in all kinds of emergencies.

Sometimes it is a poor woman whose husband has been shut up for months without trial in a Turkish prison, pleading for intercession with the Pasha, or a widow who has been defrauded of her property, seeking justice. On another occasion it will be a Greek woman, who wants to be divorced from a drunken husband, and begs the Consul's lady to represent her case to the Archbishop. No *Consulesa*, perhaps, is more resorted to by persons of all creeds and nationalities in trouble than the wife of H.M. representative at Salonica, where the long unsettled state of the surrounding country gives rise to all kinds of abuses and acts of tyranny. Sometimes, however, the cases referred to her are of a somewhat comic character, and one I remember in particular afforded great amusement both to us and to the officers of the British man-of-war then lying in the bay. On this occasion, as on many others, the *hatir* began with one of the servants, the faithful old Bulgarian housekeeper, Kyrà Maria, who came upstairs to inform her mistress that a young couple were below in the courtyard who had eloped from the village of which the butler was a native. On inquiry, it appeared that the parents of the girl had affianced her, against her will, to an elderly and wealthy suitor, and, to avoid being forced into marriage with him, she had run away with the youth of her own choice. There would probably be, in a few hours, a hue and cry after the runaways—would the Madama not do something to prevent the poor girl's being carried back by her parents and condemned to a life of misery? Every one's sympathies were naturally at once aroused, the girl was safely bestowed, and the Archbishop communicated with. Presently the angry parents arrived in quest of the fugitives, and, proceeding to the "Metropolis," as the archiepiscopal palace is termed, requested the aid of the Greek Primate in their search for their daughter, and the punishment of her abductor. Much to their surprise, his Holiness in reply read them a severe lecture on the wickedness and tyranny of their conduct in forcing the girl to marry for merely pecuniary advantages, when her affections were elsewhere placed; and he declared her absolved from her plighted troth. The good Primate then informed the parents that their daughter had obtained powerful protectors, and refused to inform them of her whereabouts until they promised to wed her to the youth of her choice, when he would himself officiate at the ceremony. The father and mother could not but obey the spiritual chief of their community; and, a few days later, the happy couple again arrived at the Consulate, accompanied by the bride's parents, to take a grateful leave of their kind protectress before returning to their home. The bride, a pretty little creature, all smiles and blushes, dressed in the Macedonian peasant costume, was greatly admired by the English officers present, who all insisted upon shaking hands with, and congratulating, her and her husband, but were quite horrified when she attempted, native fashion, to kiss their hands in return.

The amusements of the Frank ladies differ little from those of the other native races. Chief among them is the promenade on Sundays and holidays, when the Franks of the capital flock in crowds either to the Petits Champs—an open space with an extended view over the Bosphorus—or to some favourite suburban resort on the banks of those wonderfully picturesque and historically interesting Straits. At Smyrna, the popular resort on these occasions is the broad new quay, which presents a most picturesque and lively, but at the same time most incongruous, scene. The festivals and holy-days of Jews, Moslems, and Christians—or even those of Greek and Latin Christians—rarely coincide. And while the dusty roadway and the gardens of the *cafés* in the background are thronged with Frank ladies in dainty silks and laces, and the Frank *jeunesse dorée*, in smart suits and wonderful collars and cuffs which would astonish a London " masher," the rest of the population of this "Petit Paris de l'Orient"—as I once heard a Frank term it—are pursuing their wonted avocations. The horn of the tramcar conductor mingles discordantly with the notes of the band which is discoursing airs from the last French comic opera to the holiday-makers, who, seated on rush-bottomed chairs in the *café* garden, are alternately discussing ices, *rahat loukoum*, and their neighbours' toilettes. Every now and again a string of camels, laden with great bales of cotton, file past with their leisurely swinging gait, jostled by sturdy *hamals* (porters) bent under the weight of some quarter ton of merchandise for one of the ships in the harbour. At the various *scalas*, or boat-steps, stand groups of Greek watermen, vociferously placing at the disposal of the Asiatic and European crowd their *péramas*, which are dancing below on the glittering blue waters of the beautiful landlocked bay.

Sitting at their open doorways in summer, and at their windows in winter, is a no less favourite pastime with the Franks than with the other Christian women of Turkey. This practice is perhaps seen to greatest advantage at Smyrna, and forms a rather striking contrast to the usual rigidity of manners with regard to intercourse with strangers. For, though custom does not allow young women to receive in the house the visits of the other sex, they may, in the afternoons, hold *levées* at the windows. And the presence of the duenna is often a mere formality; for not only is she usually seated, cross-legged, with her knitting, in a comfortable corner of the divan in the background, but the conversation at the window is frequently carried on in some European language of which she is completely ignorant—so far in advance of their parents are the younger generation of to-day.

During the Carnival, these window *levées* are also held in the evenings after dark, when gay parties composed of young men belonging to every nationality of this Asiatic capital roam the streets in disguise, giving notice of their approach by music, or merely by beating the primitive *doubana*, an earthen jar with a piece of parchment stretched tightly over the opening. The windows of the modern houses are about six feet above the street, and, below those which they find unshuttered and lighted, the masquers station themselves with offerings of flowers or bonbons for the fair ones, who, with elbows supported on the cushioned window-ledges, lean out above them, eager to discover their identity. This, however, is no easy matter, unless the disguised ones choose to give some clue. For these polyglot Orientals are generally able to speak the languages which accord with their costumes; and I was on one occasion puzzled for nearly half an hour by an "English" neighbour who had assumed the nasal dialect with the dress of a Greek Islander. Soon the party pass on to mystify others, and make room for fresh groups, perhaps still more fantastically attired—demons from the lower regions, Arabs from Mekka, Dervishes of all orders, and a hundred other disguises. Watching these wild figures in the dark, narrow Oriental streets, with their mysterious retreating gateways and overhanging upper stories, seen in the dim, uncertain light of the Chinese lanterns carried by the revellers, always transported me in fancy to the scenes of the stories of the *Thousand and One Nights*. Nor was the illusion dispelled when the old Turkish watchman, in ample white turban and pelisse, and armed only with an iron-tipped staff and an old-fashioned lantern, passed on his round, regarding with calm contempt the incomprehensible pranks of the *Giaours*.

On the last Sunday of the Carnival this custom is also observed during the afternoon, when, however, daylight certainly deprives it of much of its interest and charm. One of the thoroughfares in which it is seen to the best advantage is the extension of the Rue Franque called "The Point." The street is thronged with a lively crowd on foot and in carriages, and open house is kept by the inhabitants for their friends from other parts of the town and from the suburban villages. The gaily dressed women and girls who occupy the open windows are besieged by a succession of visitors, and the very atmosphere seems sparkling with fun.

Women do not often take part in these masquerading excursions, and when they do so their destination is, as a rule, the house of a friend to whom an anonymous notification of the proposed call has been sent. These self-invited guests often find on arrival that not only have hospitable preparations been made for their reception, but that others have been asked to meet them, and the party generally terminates with an impromptu dance. At Salonica a Carnival project of this kind once afforded us considerable amusement. The house of a wealthy, but more than usually inhospitable, Greek resident was decided upon by a band of some twenty conspirators, native and foreign, who were all sworn to secrecy. The victim was, of course, not informed of our intention, but a hint was conveyed to the local *restaurateur* that a supper might be required on a certain evening at very short notice. A secret, however, divided among a score of people did not naturally long remain one, and we soon heard, to our consternation and regret, that Mr. —— had taken to his bed and declared himself very ill! Instead, however, of relinquishing our project, we decided to make one of the chief conspirators, the Russian Consul-General, our host instead. On our arrival at the residence of this gentleman—all of us, both men and women, disguised in calico bags drawn over our heads and concealing our evening dress—we were most hospitably welcomed. The noisy barrel-organ which had accompanied us was dismissed; a band of Roumanian musicians, who had just arrived in the town, were sent for, as was also the supper; and we did not separate until past midnight.

The Franks, being, as we have seen, of such very mixed origin, have naturally neither national traditions nor folk-lore of their own. They, however, make up for the latter deficiency by borrowing largely from the superstitions of the lower orders of the people among whom they dwell, and particularly from the Greeks. For, as a general rule, the nurses of all the Christian children of the East are Greek women; and, whatever the mother-tongue of their parents, the first language the children speak is that of their *dádi*. These often devoted, but seldom judicious, guardians early instil into the minds of their nurslings a respect for all the folk beliefs and observances in which they have themselves been nurtured; croon to them their quaint, ancient *nanárisma,* or lullabies; or delight their waking hours with tales of enchanted princesses, adventurous youths, and supernatural beings.

Franks, however, both male and female, figure in Greek folk-poesy. We have from Ioannina the song beginning as follows, and entitled—

YANNEOTOPOULA.[1]

O, thou Frank, thou Frankopoúla,[2]
Beautiful Yannotopoúla!
Who has said I do not love thee,
That in worn-out clothes thou'st dressed thee,
And in soiled garb thou sittest?
Busk thee, busk thee, in thy gayest.
Come with me when evening cometh.[3]

And from Parga we have the following colloquy between a Greek mother and daughter concerning a Frank suitor:—

A FRANK I'LL NOT MARRY.

Over in Roïdo, in Roïdopoula,
A Frank fell in love with a Romeopoúla.[4]
To love him the Romeot girl could not bring her,
Though still in her ears thus her mother would ding her:
"Take him, my daughter: now be thou his dear,
And thou narrow trousers henceforward shalt wear."

---

[1] Daughter of Ioannina.   [2] Daughter of the Frank.
[3] Aravandinos, Συλλογή, &c., No. 392; *Greek Folk-songs,* p. 150.
[4] A Daughter of the Romeots, the name by which the Greeks formerly designated themselves; see p. 31.

"*Mána*, I never will marry a Franko,
To hear his '*Per Dio*,' and his '*Ali mango*."[1]
"Take him, my daughter, he wears a tall hat!"
"I a Frank husband won't marry for that."
"Take him, my daughter, he's plenty of cash!"
"I don't want a husband who has no moustache!"
"Take him, my daughter, and wed now the swain;
You may, in three months' time, divorce him again!"[2]

The Franks have also found their way into the Greek mythological folk-lore, where they figure both in song and story, and, ignorant of, or neglecting, the precautions taken by Odysseús of old,[3] are said to be, with their ship, bewitched by the song of the Siren, as thus narrated :—

THE SIREN AND THE SEAMEN.

('Η Τραγουδίστρια.)

A maid was singing as she sat within a splendid window;
Her song was on the breezes borne away upon the ocean.
As many ships as heard her lay, moored, and made fast their anchors.
And one *tartána* of the Franks, that was of Love the frigate,
Furled not her sails upon the yards, nor yet along was sailing.
Then to his men the captain called astern, where he was standing :
"Ho, sailors! furl the sails at once, and climb into the rigging,
That to this charmer we may list, who sings so passing sweetly.
Hear what's the melody to which this rare song she is singing."

---

[1] "Περντίο καὶ ἀλὶ μάγκο," the Greek form of two common Italian expletives. A Jew broker at Salonica, who hawked about curios for sale, made such frequent use of the former oath that it was finally given to him as a nickname, and I never heard him called by any other name. The derivation of the second is unknown to me. At Smyrna it is pronounced as one word, *alimanos*, and is generally used as an expression of dismay.

[2] Aravandinos, Συλλογὴ, &c., No. 404. Compare also Passow, Nos. 574 and 575.   [3] *Od.* xii. 39.

So sweetly on their ears then fell the warbling of the maiden,
The skipper turned his ship once more, and to the shore he steered it;
And on the masts the mariners were hanging in the rigging.[1]

Perhaps this song may not be an inappropriate conclusion to my account of the Christian Women of Turkey, symbolising, as it may, the fascination which folk-lore exercises on all those who have once fallen under its spell. And in another volume I hope to give some account of the Semitic and Moslem Women of Turkey and their Folk-lore.

[1] Aravandinos, Συλλογὴ, &c., No. 457.

FORTHCOMING WORKS by Miss GARNETT and Mr. STUART GLENNIE.

GREEK FOLK-SONGS:

LITERAL AND METRICAL TRANSLATIONS;
WITH INTRODUCTION ON THE SURVIVAL OF PAGANISM,
AND CONCLUSION ON THE SCIENCE OF FOLK-LORE.

Third Edition, Revised and Enlarged.

DERVISH MYSTICS:

THEIR PRINCIPLES, ORGANISATION, AND POWERS;
WITH ESSAYS ON THE HISTORY OF MYSTICISM, AND
THE PSYCHOLOGY OF ECSTASY.

FORTHCOMING WORKS by Mr. STUART GLENNIE.

THE NEW PHILOSOPHY OF HISTORY:

OUTLINES OF A NEW THEORY
FOUNDED ON THE ULTIMATE LAWS
OF EXISTENCE AND OF THOUGHT.

A New Edition, Revised and Enlarged.

THE ARCHAIAN WHITE RACES:

THE TRADITIONS, MYTHS, AND MIGRATIONS
OF THE EGYPTIAN, CHALDEAN, AND RELATED
FOUNDERS OF CIVILISATION.

ANCIENT HELLAS:

A JOURNEY THROUGH THE IONIAN ISLANDS,
ALBANIA, THESSALY, MACEDONIA, AND
THE THRAKIAN ISLANDS.

By Miss GARNETT and Mr. STUART GLENNIE.

GREEK FOLK-SONGS.

LITERAL AND METRICAL TRANSLATIONS;
WITH INTRODUCTION ON THE SURVIVAL OF PAGANISM,
AND CONCLUSION ON THE SCIENCE OF FOLK-LORE.

OPINIONS OF THE PRESS
ON THE FIRST EDITION.

ATHENÆUM.

"This book is an honest piece of work. Both authors have resolved to do their best, and the result is likely to add to the number of those persons who take a lively interest in Greece. . . . . Great judgment and taste are shown in the selection of the poems, and a very good idea can be formed from them of the varied themes, spirit, and character of Greek popular poetry. Many of them have never been translated before. . . . . Mr. Glennie . . . . shows wide research, and great earnestness and power of thought. He sketches the history of modern Greek, and explains the nature of the dialects in which the poems are written. He also furnishes a vivid picture of the scenes in which they were composed, and, in urging that the sentiments are to a large extent pagan, he draws attention to many marked characteristics of the ballads. . . . . We recommend the book heartily to all who wish to form some idea of the popular poetry of Greece."

ACADEMY.

"Miss Garnett's translations are spirited, rhythmical, and well sustained."

SATURDAY REVIEW.

"Mr. Glennie points out with truth that the animistic attitude of mind (as we may call it 'for short') endures, and in the ballads all things are equally conceived of as animated and personal. . . . . A full and typical set of selections, of great interest to all students of popular ballads. . . . . The choice of pieces which he directed is deserving of praise."

LITERARY WORLD.

"It is hard to realise that this poem ('Thanasé Vaghia'), at once so vivid and so dignified, is a translation."

ST. JAMES'S GAZETTE.

"Mr. Glennie's elaborate introductory essay on the 'Survival of Paganism' is learned and acute, with much useful and picturesque information on Greek topography, and fully conclusive as to the writer's main proposition. . . . . Miss Garnett's translations are in general excellent, terse, simple, and energetic."

MORNING POST.

"Preceded by an able preface, with literal and metrical translations by Lucy M. J. Garnett, this book of 'Folk-Songs,' edited by John S. Stuart Glennie, M A, and to which he has added a comprehensive Historical Introduction, offers unusual interest."

ILLUSTRATED LONDON NEWS.

"To a perfect acquaintance with the uncouth and difficult dialect of the original, derived from a long residence in the country, the translator adds a happy literary instinct which has enabled her to seize upon the appropriate tone for dealing with the various classes of compositions comprehended in her volume, and a command of pure idiomatic English reflecting the artless simplicity of the original. . . . . Miss Garnett's translation reflects every mood in turn with equal felicity, and skilfully combines literary form with perfect fidelity to the original."

SD - #0013 - 180723 - C0 - 229/152/25 - PB - 9781333867942 - Gloss Lamination